BUILDING THE CITY OF GOD

BUILDING THE CITY OF GOD

Community & Cooperation Among the Mormons

Leonard J. Arrington
Feramorz Y. Fox
Dean L. May

Deseret Book Company
Salt Lake City, Utah
1976

To the memories
of Feramorz Y.
and Anna Wilcken Fox

Contents

Illustrations

Preface

During the Great Depression of the 1930s, Feramorz Young Fox, grandson of noted Utah pioneers and president of LDS Business College in Salt Lake City, made a comprehensive study of Mormon efforts to solve the problems of want and inequality. Beginning with Joseph Smith's Law of Consecration and Stewardship, introduced in 1831, the Latter-day Saints had experimented through much of their history with idealistic economic arrangements. Some scholars had studied the Law of Consecration and Stewardship; others, the group-sharing proposals by which the Saints migrated to the West. Still others had investigated Brigham Young's United Order of the 1870s and John Taylor's Board of Trade movement of the 1880s. But no one had traced in depth the entire span of Mormon economic idealism when economist-historian-educator Feramorz Fox wrote his treatise in the 1930s.

"Experiments in Cooperation and Social Security Among the Mormons: A Study of Joseph Smith's Order of Stewardships, Cooperation, and Brigham Young's United Order," a 426-page typescript that President Fox completed in 1937, was, for unknown reasons, never published. It is known that the manuscript was submitted for publication. Perhaps publishers felt the market in those depressed years was not sufficient to justify the expense of publication.

When I began my own studies of Mormon economic activities in the summer of 1946, I found a bound copy of Dr. Fox's typescript in the Mormon Church Library-Archives and was immediately impressed with its soundness and thoroughness. I made a point of meeting President Fox and discussed the various research projects in which he had been engaged relating to Mormon history. Always generous and helpful, he was kind enough to lend me a copy of his manuscript to microfilm for the library at Utah State University, where I was at that time a professor of economics. He also furnished me with a bibliography of his personal works, which included articles in the *Deseret News*,

Improvement Era, and other journals and periodicals.

Having unsuccessfully encouraged President Fox to publish part or all of his monumental study on cooperation prior to his death, I was offered an opportunity to edit his chapter on the Richfield United Order for publication in the *Utah Historical Quarterly* in its Fall 1964 issue. Five years later, Dr. Karl A. Fox, son of President Fox and at the time head of the Department of Economics at Iowa State University, after consultation with Richard Thurman, director of the University of Utah Press, asked me to prepare President Fox's typescript for publication under a collaborative arrangement. I was happy to respond, although my responsibilities at Utah State University prevented me from completing the task immediately. I was fortunate to have the help of my former secretary, Mrs. JoAnn W. Bair, on the rewriting project; and my research assistant, Richard Daines, an honors graduate of Utah State University, wrote a preliminary draft of the chapter on the Church Welfare Plan. Dr. Dean May, now senior historical associate at the Historical Department of The Church of Jesus Christ of Latter-day Saints in Salt Lake City, Utah, helped me through the past few months of revision and enrichment. I acknowledge his thorough research and insightful writing. Indeed, his contributions to this volume, which include original drafts of chapter 1, 10, 11, 13, 16, and Appendix 1, have been so extensive that I have asked the publisher to list him as a co-author.

Readers who have a prior acquaintance with the Fox manuscript will discover that Dr. May and I have relied heavily on Fox for the information presented in chapters 3, 4, 5, 7, 8, and 9, and that we have written the remaining chapters as the result of our own research, although we have felt free to incorporate material—in some cases substantial material—from the Fox manuscript. Dr. May and I have made substantive contributions to all the chapters, and the entire manuscript, including that borrowed from President Fox, has been run through our own typewriters at least twice, and in some instances, three times. Thus, we hope to have achieved a book with stylistic and organizational unity—a work that represents a real merger of ideas, expressions, research, and writing. In this respect we are grateful for the stylistic improvements suggested by Maureen Ursenbach Beecher, editor of the Historical Department of The Church of Jesus Christ of Latter-day Saints, Salt Lake City. With the consent of the

University of Utah Press we have submitted the resulting manuscript to Deseret Book Company, and we are grateful for their willingness to publish a book that was designed for non-Mormon scholars as well as for Latter-day Saints. We trust that members of The Church of Jesus Christ of Latter-day Saints will appreciate that we have followed the style of secular scholars and will bear in mind that we are active and believing Latter-day Saints.

Dr. May and I are particularly proud to acknowledge the inspiration, insight, and careful scholarship of President Fox; we have dedicated this volume to him and to his wife, Anna, who spent many hours in searching through unindexed source materials and in editing preliminary drafts of his chapters for the 1938 typescript.

Born September 28, 1881, in Salt Lake City, Feramorz Young Fox was a son of Jesse W. and Ruth May Fox. His mother, at 104, was still alive at the time of her son's death. President Fox married Anna Wilcken in 1906; they later became parents of three children. Graduated from the University of Utah the year of his marriage, Dr. Fox devoted his career to a series of teaching and administrative positions at the LDS University in Salt Lake City, becoming its president in 1926. At the University of Utah he had been a gifted and versatile student with interests in chemistry, geology, and English literature. In 1910 he was awarded a Willard D. Thompson scholarship at the University of California, Berkeley, where he completed a masters degree in economics in 1912 with a thesis on "Cooperation in the Raisin Industry of California." He was offered a temporary instructorship at Berkeley and urged to complete his Ph.D. with additional research on the economics of cooperation, but illness in his family compelled his return to Salt Lake City. In the 1920s his research interests shifted to land economics, and he completed his doctorate at Northwestern University in 1932 with a dissertation on "The Mormon Land System."

Thus, President Fox brought a unique set of qualifications to the study of experiments in cooperation among the Mormons, which he began in 1932 at the depths of the Great Depression. He was well versed in the economics and history of cooperatives in England and the United States and was also thoroughly familiar with the economic problems of Utah agriculture and the rural communities based upon it. His grandfather had surveyed the streets of Salt Lake City; President Fox, like his father before him, had grown up in the Salt Lake City milieu. Finally, President Fox combined the skills of a trained economist with a mature understanding of the behavior of people in organizations.

When he became its president in 1926, the school then known as the LDS University consisted of a high school, junior college, and business college. The junior college was discontinued in the late 1920s and the high school in 1931; President Fox guided the LDS Business College successfully through the depression, war, and postwar years until his retirement in 1948. He was an active member of The Church of Jesus Christ of Latter-day Saints, serving as a high councilor in Emigration Stake and member of the Sunday School board of the Ensign Stake. He was past president of the Salt Lake Kiwanis Club, the Executive Club, and the Emeritus Club of the University of Utah. He died on November 29, 1957, at the age of 76. The editor of the *Deseret News* wrote at the time of his death: "Blessed with a capacity to go the extra mile for every student, endowed with a subtle sense of humor, a devoted educator, and a capable scholar, quiet Dr. Fox was a power for good."

Leonard J. Arrington

Acknowledgments

The writers are grateful to Joseph Fielding Smith, Alvin Smith, and A. William Lund, who assisted President Fox with his use of the materials in the Church Library-Archives in the 1930s. Others who assisted President Fox at that time included LeRoi C. Snow, who assisted with the chapter on Brigham City; Harold Bennett of ZCMI, who gave access to the early records of that institution; LeGrande C. Heaton, Henry Esplin, and Mr. and Mrs. Charles W. Carroll, of Orderville, Utah; R. T. Thurber and James B. Ramsay, Richfield, Utah; Herbert H. Bell and John E. Heppler, Glenwood, Utah; Severin N. Lee, David Reese, and Mrs. J. H. Forsgren, Brigham City, Utah; Ernest Munk, Mrs. Joseph Munk, and Peter Munk, Manti, Utah; John R. Young, Kanab, Utah; and James T. Hammond and Archie B. Kesler, Salt Lake City. Clerical help was provided by students and staff members of the LDS Business College, particularly Ruth Snow, Ruby Tatton, and Miriam Parker. President Fox's wife, Anna W. Fox, spent many hours in searching through unindexed material, read preliminary drafts of his chapters, and helped to clarify the text and improve the style.

Leonard Arrington is particularly grateful to Evan B. Murray, his friend and long-time department head at Utah State University, for his encouragement and sound advice. Others presently or formerly at Utah State University who were helpful on this project include Robert P. Collier, D. Wynne Thorne, Joseph Geddes, S. George Ellsworth, Everett E. Thorpe, and Charles Peterson. Also helpful were Dr. Wendell O. Rich and Dr. Eugene E. Campbell, formerly at the LDS Institute of Religion in Logan, Utah.

Leonard Arrington and Dean May are grateful for the editorial help of JoAnn W. Bair, now living in Vancouver, Washington; Maureen Ursenbach Beecher; and Christine Croft Waters, secretary to Leonard Arrington. We are also grateful for the suggestions of our colleagues, James B. Allen, Davis Bitton, Earl E. Olson, and Donald R. Schmidt, and for the comments of Dwight

Israelsen of the Department of Economics at Brigham Young University, Jonathan R.T. Hughes, professor of economic history at Northwestern University, and Christine Meaders Durham, a practicing attorney in Salt Lake City. Lloyd L. Young of Monticello, Utah, grandson of John R. Young, offered helpful suggestions on Chapter 11. Jill Mulvay and Christine Waters were kind enough to prepare the index.

Finally, we are grateful for the opportunity of incorporating portions of articles and chapters that we have prepared that have appeared previously in other publications and that the publishers have generously allowed us to use. These include the following, listing them chronologically:

Feramorz Y. Fox, "The Consecration Movement of the Middle Fifties," *The Improvement Era*, 47 (1944): 80 ff., 146 ff.

_____, "United Order: Discrimination in the Use of Terms," ibid., 47:432 ff.

_____, "Consecration: Some Distinguishing Features," ibid., 49 (1946): 368 ff.

Leonard J. Arrington, "Zion's Board of Trade: A Third United Order," *The Western Humanities Review*, 5 (1950-51): 1-20.

_____, "Property Among the Mormons," *Rural Sociology*, 16 (1951): 339-52.

_____, "Early Mormon Communitarianism: The Law of Consecration and Stewardship," *The Western Humanities Review*, 7 (1953): 341-69.

_____, *Orderville, Utah: A Pioneer Mormon Experiment in Economic Organization* (Logan, Utah: Utah State University Monograph Series, 2 (1954): 1-44.

_____, "Railroad Building and Cooperatives 1869-1879" in *The History of a Valley: Cache Valley, Utah-Idaho*, Joel E. Ricks, ed., Everett E. Cooley, assoc, ed. (Logan: Cache Valley Centennial Commission, 1956), 170-204.

_____, ed., "Experiment in Utopia: The United Order of Richfield, 1874-1877 by Feramorz Y. Fox," *Utah Historical Quarterly*, 32 (1964): 355-80.

_____, "Cooperative Community in the North: Brigham City, Utah," ibid., 33 (1965): 198-217.

Dean L. May, "Mormon Cooperatives in Paris, Idaho, 1869-1896," *Idaho Yesterdays*, 19 (1975): 20-30.

CHAPTER 1

*Mormonism
and the
American dream*

HEN SIR HUMPHREY GILBERT'S SHIP was swept by a sudden storm from her companion vessels in 1853 and lost with all on board, it would have been appropriate, as historian Felix Gilbert observed, if he had been clutching a copy of Thomas More's *Utopia*.[1] The Elizabethan adventurer had just completed the initial step in his design to found the first English colony in North America. After exploring and claiming Newfoundland for England's Queen Elizabeth, he was beginning his return voyage to further prepare for the colonization effort when the storm overtook his fleet.

The possibility that a pristine New World might offer Europe a chance for better beginnings gave hope to those troubled by the incertitude that accompanied the rending of the medieval world. The unexplored hulk of the American continents loomed persistently in the European mind of the seventeenth century, suggesting to visionaries, as Frank E. Manuel has noted, that "if there were new lands and new inventions, there could be new societies molded by man's accumulated knowledge."[2] It was in this spirit that John Winthrop counseled the Puritan colonists aboard the *Arabella* before their landing in New England. "Wee must be knitt together in this worke as one man," he told the saints.

Wee must entertaine each other in brotherly affeccion, wee must be willing to abridge our selues of our superfluities, for the supply of others necessities . . . alwayes haueing before our eyes our Commission and Community in the worke, our Community as members of the same body, . . . that men shall say of succeeding plantacions: the lord make it like that of New England.[3]

A vastly altered New England nurtured Joseph Smith and Brigham Young two centuries after Winthrop had voiced his pious hope for a regeneration of society in the New World. The Puritan Fathers' nagging fear that the wilderness which protected and preserved their own experiment might as easily harbor heretics and dissidents had proved well founded. Shortly after the initial settling, a procession of otherminded began to go out from Massachusetts Bay to the Narragansett and into Connecticut, filling the voids of the continent with a cacophony of strange doctrines and practices. Order, the value Puritans prized above all others, could not be maintained in the immensities of America. The very geography induced diversity in cultures and ways of life.

The visions leading Joseph Smith to found a new religion were a consequence of the young man's concern over religious pluralism in the upstate New York community where he spent his youth. In every surviving written account of the circumstances leading to his calling as prophet, he emphasized the anxiety caused him by the spectacle of competing religions, an anxiety no doubt exacerbated by division within his own family on religious questions.[4] The central messages he took from his first and subsequent visions were that all churches were in error and that if he prepared himself, God would make him an instrument in restoring the one true church. A major aspect of his subsequent life's work was the effort to organize and unify for himself and his followers a structured haven in a society that seemed about to disintegrate from the excesses of individualism and pluralism. "Behold, mine house is a house of order, . . . and not of confusion," God declared to Joseph Smith in an important revelation recorded in 1843.[5] The statement became one of the most oft-quoted maxims of church organization and government among Mormons.

The Law of Consecration and Stewardship, which Joseph Smith announced in February 1831, known variously as "the Lord's law," the "Order of Enoch," the "First United Order," or the "Order of Stewardship," was intended to be a major instrument in reorganizing the social and economic patterns of life among his followers.[6] Moreover, it was to provide the model upon which all human society would be organized when the Savior returned to the latter-day Zion in Missouri. It would build unity among a people fragmented by their individualistic search for economic well-being. It would impose order upon the chaos of a society suffering from an excess of liberty. An ideal community of the Saints would be prepared to administer Christ's millennial reign—a people divested of selfishness and greed, living in square-surveyed towns and villages, surrounded by productive farmlands. Order, unity, and community were the supreme values of the Prophet's ideal society—values strikingly at odds with those characteristic of antebellum America.

More Puritan than Yankee, Joseph Smith consciously sought to stay the forces which threatened to disrupt the ordered rural village life of the early nineteenth century. His was not, however, just a rearguard holding action. In some respects it could be said that his aim was to realize the Christian commonwealth which had been the ideal of John Winthrop. Pushing himself in this direction, the Prophet's designs became positive more than negative, forward-looking rather than backward-looking. He passed well beyond mere admonitions that more "brotherly affeccion" was needed. He designed specific programs whereby the wealthy would be asked on a continuing basis "to abridge" themselves of their surplus "for the supply of others' necessities." There is a hard practicality about Joseph Smith that seems somehow alien to John Winthrop. Mere piety alone will not assure perfection in the pioneer community. Specific programs must be worked out and applied. Christian ideals must be made flesh through positive action. Not the avoidance of sin only, but active pursuit of societal perfection would lead men into the Millennium. With supreme confidence, Joseph Smith took men into his hands and sought to reshape them. His self-assured but benevolent manipulation of the lives and fortunes of thousands of followers was certainly one of the marvels of his age.

The derivation of his more distinctive doctrines has been a matter of considerable comment and speculation. It is well-known that many of his early converts were recruited from the underground of Protestant sectarianism—Shakers, Campbellites, and others—groups that bore certain affinities to the Anabaptists of the sixteenth century.[7] Found among these groups were beliefs in an eventual restoration of an unsullied primitive church, a conviction that the Lord's return was imminent, a desire to adjust prevailing social and economic patterns to conform more closely to some form of Christian communalism, a fondness for spiritual manifestations, and a literalistic interpretation of the Bible, all of which became in some form a part of the revealed religion. It is tempting to see Joseph Smith as a direct heir to the tradition of

Jan Mathijs and John Bueckelson, whose communal, polygamous theocracy, set up in Münster in 1534, tainted the whole of what George Huntston Williams has aptly called the Radical Reformation. Several groups of Anabaptist descent fled to the New World in the seventeenth and eighteenth centuries. Their ideas there had become diffused among a broad spectrum of dissenting groups, ranging from Quakers to Unitarians, by the time the Mormon prophet began to formulate his own system of belief. A large number of the religious communitarian experiments in antebellum America derived from this tradition, a tradition with which several of Joseph Smith's early followers had clear ties.

Joseph Smith might also have been influenced by the widespread enthusiasm for the ideas of British industrialist and reformer Robert Owen, who established his own experimental community at New Harmony, Pennsylvania, in 1825. Owen favored the union of the human race into "family commonwealths," cooperative industrial and agrarian communities designed to eliminate self-interest as the primary engine of wealth-producing activities. Several communities based upon his ideas were founded in America in the decade of the 1820s. More important, perhaps, his ideas enjoyed widespread circulation and were more influential than has been generally recognized in encouraging the spirit of reform in early nineteenth-century America. Though insisting stoutly that elimination of the pernicious effects of religion must be a first step toward a total reformation of society, Owen propounded a value system derived almost entirely from the Christianity which he so adamantly rejected, and his reform proposals could, for the most part, be readily adapted to the purposes of religious reformers. Certainly he encouraged many Americans in the optimistic hope that the traditions of the past need impose no limits upon their ability to build a better society.[8] His lesson was powerful, because, as Martin Buber has noted, it was practical and experimental, taking reform out of the speculative world of French social theorists Saint Simon and Fourier and offering "the empirical solution of the problem as opposed to the speculative one."[9]

Joseph Smith's methods of reform were, if anything, practical and experimental. Not the least practical aspect of his endeavor was that before he announced plans for his ideal society, he had begun to build a community of believers held together by commitment to a common set of distinctive religious beliefs and

already facing out against a world that seemed bent upon destroy-
ing them. The spiritual community existed before the physical
community. The early Latter-day Saints were possessed of an
exultant sense that they were the vanguard of history-shaking
events, expressed perfectly in Parley P. Pratt's 1840 hymn:

> The morning breaks; the shadows flee;
> Lo, Zion's standard is unfurled!
> The dawning of a brighter day
> Majestic rises on the world.
>
> Jehovah speaks! let earth give ear,
> And Gentile nations turn and live.
> His mighty arm is making bare,
> His covenant people to receive.
>
> Angels from heaven and truth from earth
> Have met, and both have record borne;
> Thus Zion's light is bursting forth
> To bring her ransomed children home.[10]

These were already, in a sense, a reformed people, and the building of a reformed society was but a natural expression of the spirit
that they already possessed.

It would be foolhardy to suggest that Joseph Smith's communitarian ideals derived more from the Shakers than from the
Owenites—that Rappites contributed more to his thinking than
Campbellites. Biblical accounts of primitive Christianity undoubtedly influenced him as much as did the living experiments
he saw about him. A detailed genealogy of possible influences
upon the Prophet would not explain his successes or his failures.
The combination of ideas that he took into his system became, by
his joining them together, logically and appropriately his. Perhaps
the most distinctive aspect of his designs was one that he shared
more with sixteenth-century Anabaptists or seventeenth-century
Pansophists than with the Disciples of Christ. No pietistic recluse,
he was planning a system that he and his followers confidently
expected would take over the reins of world government. His was
no patent-office model of reform.[11] He consciously pursued
power in earthly political realms as a preliminary to eventual
world dominion. His design for the city of Zion included a plan
for the proliferation of satellite cities in indefinite numbers,
destined to fill up the inland stretches of the North American
continent from the Missouri to the Pacific.[12]

A New England town. The social ideals of Joseph Smith and his
immediate ancestors, with stress upon unity and order, were shaped in
communities such as this. (Photo by George Edward Anderson, Church
Archives)

Joseph Smith's efforts to build an ideal society under a communitarian Law of Consecration and Stewardship failed before they had fully begun. The Latter-day Saints first attempted to live the new order in 1831 at their early gathering place in Kirtland, near Cleveland, Ohio. This attempt was almost immediately abandoned, however, and the participants were sent to help populate the "City of Zion," designated through revelation to be in Jackson County, Missouri, on the westernmost borders of the advancing line of white settlement. Earlier settlers resented the Mormon presence, however, and the Saints fled hostile Missouri in the late 1830s to build a city-state in Illinois, which evidenced little of the social and economic experimentation of the earlier period. But it would be wrong to conclude from this that Joseph Smith had given up all hope of realizing his dream. It was generally assumed that tithing, instituted in place of the new economic order, was to help prepare the people for a day when they would be asked again to live the higher law.

Brigham Young, who succeeded Joseph Smith in 1844, was consistently faithful to the memory of his predecessor. Forced to leave Illinois in 1846, he led the people to a new gathering place in the Great Basin. His attempts to invoke the Law of Consecration in Utah in the 1850s, his launching of the cooperative movement in the late 1860s, and his final institution of what he called the United Order in 1874 can all be seen as deliberate progressive steps toward the realization of Joseph's dream. Certainly external events entered into President Young's plans. The lure of California, the approach of the Utah Expedition in 1857, the advent of the railroad in 1869, all can be seen to have had specific effects upon his economic and social policies. But there seems to be a direction and momentum in the character of the responses he devised, all culminating in a heroic but premature, or perhaps too-long-delayed, attempt to place an entire regional population under a communitarian order at a stroke. His effort was hardly more successful than Joseph Smith's had been. Most of the United Orders founded in Utah in 1874 failed within the year. A few stretched on for a decade or more as isolated instances of extreme devotion to the vision of Joseph Smith as articulated by his successor. None survived into the twentieth century. The living of the United Order was again deferred until some future day when the Latter-day Saints would be better prepared to live the "higher law."

It would seem paradoxical that the Latter-day Saints were so strikingly unsuccessful in their attempts to institutionalize the communitarian ideals of their founder. Suggesting possible factors that favor the success of communal experiments, Martin Buber observed that

it is precisely where a Settlement comes into being as the expression of real religious exaltation, and not merely as a precarious substitute for religion, and where it views its existence as the beginning of God's kingdom—that it usually proves its powers of endurance.[13]

Certainly the Mormons met the conditions Buber suggested. But for various reasons their experiments did not endure, at least in institutional forms corresponding to those Joseph Smith suggested. The reasons for their early failure in Missouri seem at least partly to have been a consequence of being too successful. The older settlers in Missouri sensed early how great a threat the self-sufficient Mormons presented to their own vision of what the economic and social shape of the growing community should be. They resorted to mob action to bring the Mormon experiment to a close before it had really begun. There is evidence that in Utah the anti-polygamy crusade of the federal government worked in a similar manner to sap United Orders of badly needed leadership and expertise before they were fully established. In both instances there were internal difficulties as well, but it is conceivable that these might have been resolved had the Mormons been free to work them out under more favorable circumstances.

It is interesting, however, that Latter-day Saints rarely blamed their persecutors for the failure of communal experiments under Joseph Smith and Brigham Young. More often, they blamed themselves. Moral imperfection in the form of selfishness and greed kept them from living the high law of God. There is implicit in this self-condemnation an interpretation of the role of institutions in reform that sets Mormons apart from modern reform traditions. Living under ideal institutions is not, in the Mormon view, an experience that perfects man. Rather, it is an evidence that man has achieved perfection. A Mormon did not enter a commune to *become* good, but because he *was* good. The idea of limited progress under beneficent institutions was not ruled out entirely. A people failing to live a higher law would be given a lesser law that presumably might prepare them for an eventual restoration of the more perfect order. The fundamental idea remained, however, that institutions are unworkable as reform instruments if they are too far above the moral plane of the society to which they are given. There was in Joseph Smith's system no Owenite dream of gathering the flotsam of humanity together where they would be perfected under the influence of enlightened institutions. Men must first organize their own lives; then they might be united into a more perfect social and economic order. Faith was the instrument of change—not institutions.

The discontinuance of the formalized United Order structure during the late 1870s and early 1880s did not signal an end to Mormon economic idealism. Anticipating the harsh federal legislation that dealt a death blow to many of the Orders, John Taylor, successor to Brigham Young as leader of the Latter-day Saints, formed Zion's Central Board of Trade. This provided some central church planning and assistance to new industries and enterprises and maintained a unified approach to social and economic affairs—as much as confining federal legislation would permit. Boards of trade functioned until 1885, when the enforcement of the antipolygamy Edmunds Act drove most Mormon leaders into hiding and made the system unworkable. Thereafter, the principles of the United Order were manifested primarily in the maintenance of various kinds of cooperatives—agricultural, mercantile, and industrial—and church assistance to such enterprises as canals, beet sugar companies, and public utilities.

In 1936 a modern attempt was made to institute a system that would incorporate the basic principles of the Law of Consecration and Stewardship, or at least those principles consistent with prevailing United States statutes. This was the Church welfare program, which provided for the operation of farms and factories by local congregations of volunteers, the production of commodities that were placed in bishops storehouses, and the distribution of the commodities to individuals, families, and communities in need. This system is still in existence today (1976). By means of their donations toward building funds, missionary work, welfare, tithes, and other donations, and a heavy contribution of leisure time and of expertise to church activities, Latter-day Saints in the 1970s give a generous portion of their surplus to support church programs.[14] In their holdings of property they are (or are urged to be) mindful of the needs and interests of the communities in which they live. Some Latter-day Saints are going farther than this and are establishing communally supported enterprises in many parts of the world. These include schools, medical clinics, and agricultural cooperatives in Latin America and family-like student living quarters adjacent to many university campuses. Though collectivism among Mormons in the twentieth century could more accurately be termed cooperative rather than communitarian, church leaders continue to draw heavily upon the communitarian ideals set by Joseph Smith and Brigham Young in urging present-day members to support and participate in collective enterprises.

If we were to search for the underlying causes of the oft-noticed Mormon habit of cooperation, we would be forced to conclude that ultimately it is historical experience more than a conscious response to exhortations of church leaders that accounts for their successes in such undertakings. If the Saints failed to live the "more perfect law of the Lord" in Missouri, the exigencies of their forced removal from the state in 1838 made practice of that law a condition of survival. The exodus from Illinois in 1846 had a similar effect, as did the early settling process in the Salt Lake Valley and the commencement of irrigated agriculture.

It is a curious fact that experiences Mormons would have gladly avoided—forced migration and repeated pioneering of new settlements—would seem to have been more powerful agents in teaching the habit of cooperation than conscious initiation of cooperative experiments. Nevertheless, the attempted establishment of ideal communities was an experience long reminding faithful Mormons of a promise unfulfilled that they might be called upon at any moment to bring to fruition.[15] A frequently used measure against which Mormons still test their faith is to ask themselves rhetorically if they could live the United Order if called upon to do so. The ideal thereby becomes a concrete reference point in time and group experience that gives it far more significance than if it were not rooted in the historical past. Ultimately, however, one must conclude that it was religious faith—a force ill understood by twentieth-century academicians—that sustained early Mormons while their communitarian spirit was being built. Quite simply, nineteenth-century Mormons believed that God's commands to all the modern world were channeled through the mouths of Joseph Smith and his successors. To cut oneself off from that source of divine guidance was to jeopardize a chance for eternal exaltation.

Were it not for that belief, the Mormons would almost certainly have failed to sustain themselves through the trials that forced upon them the necessity and ultimately the habit of cooperation. Neither institutions nor sermons alone, but a common experience endured because of faith, established the cooperative spirit for which Latter-day Saints are known.

Significantly, in both the Missouri and Utah communal efforts, there existed a tension between spirit and law. In both cases, only the broad outlines of the proposed Orders were given by church leaders. Details had to be worked out by the members through experience. In the Utah experiment there was characteristically a short period of optimism during which good will prevailed and generous concessions of property and time were made to the Order. This was followed by a movement toward legalization—a demand that accurate records of work credits be kept, that wage-labor scales be established. Resentment appeared against those whose possessions outside the Order took time that they could have been devoting to Order affairs. In essence there was apparent fear that others might shoulder less than their share of the cooperative responsibilities. Legalization represented an effort to insure that rewards would be given only in amounts commensurate with labor expended. At the same time it became necessary to protect the experiment against dissidents whose withdrawal of property they had consecrated might destroy the whole enterprise. In such situations appeal to civil law would almost always work to the advantage of the dissident and against the Order. Brigham Young himself, in his desire to protect the Orders from a hostile federal court system, recommended the formulation of detailed rules and credit systems, the careful keeping of records, and the assumption of legal corporate form by the Orders. Not surprisingly, many of those who later recalled their experience with the United Order felt that much of the spirit was lost in the assumption of legal forms and that the high point of their communal endeavor had been during the period when good will had to compensate for the absence of prescribed rules. There was at least one instance where stalwarts of the communal principle formed their own United Order under the original "gospel plan" after the Order in corporate form had been dissolved.

There is something awesome in the spectacle of Brigham Young attempting to organize a regional economy of more than 80,000 inhabitants into a communal commonwealth. The sheer scale of the undertaking imposed problems of a magnitude that makes it hardly comparable to the small self-selected communes characteristic of nineteenth-century American communitarianism. There is, in addition, a marked poignancy in the vision of President Young, aging and in ill health, putting all his resources to the task of realizing in his lifetime the vision of Joseph Smith—and failing. Surely he and other Mormons who knew the founding prophet could not without remorse have admitted the failure of their effort to make of Joseph's dream a reality.

In many respects the United Order experiment in Brigham Young's Utah may be seen as an afterclap of the social idealism of Joseph Smith. The Prophet's experiments took place during the heyday of communal experimentation in America. Though singularly far-reaching in design, they fit appropriately into a society where social ferment was proliferating communes in unprecedented numbers. Brigham Young's reprise of Mormon communitarianism was by contrast out of time and place—an unusual manifestation of anticapitalist economic idealism at a time when Andrew Carnegie and John D. Rockefeller were becoming national heroes. A federal government that earlier, in the name of states' rights, had stood by while local officials destroyed Mormon experimentation now aggressively pursued the same end in its own drive to stamp out Utah's "un-American" cultural and economic values. The hundred-year period from the Civil War to the Vietnamese War was not an auspicious time for the launching of communal experiments in America.

Communalism in America experienced a remarkable rebirth between 1965 and 1970, however, with more than 2,000 new secular communes being founded in many parts of the United States. The formation of these communes represented, according to one student of the movement, "an intense reaction against a fragmented, commercialized society whose institutions—from the family on up to the community—had, they were convinced, lost vital, unifying vision."[16] Mormonism itself, a century before, had represented in many respects a reaction against increasing fragmentation in society. Nineteenth-century Mormons shared with modern utopians a consuming desire to effect harmony and order in their respective Americas. Mormons, like the moderns, were not afraid to làunch radical experiments in family and community relationships, departing deliberately and dramatically from the norms and values of the main society in their effort to counter the excesses of individualism and pluralism that they saw about them.

The precise character of the Mormon response, however, was markedly different from that of recent communitarians. There is in contemporary communes a strongly egocentric flavor that places individual needs and values above those of the group— paradoxically running directly counter to the traditional communitarian ideal. A pronounced concern with self-definition and personal liberty seems to militate against the possibility of sustained communal relationships. Strong anti-authoritarianism inhibits the development of leadership that might evolve systematic and orderly solutions to social and economic problems naturally arising in the course of such experiments. The dictum that individuals be free "to do their own thing" serves to keep communes small, transient in population, and ideologically ill-defined. In effect, the modern utopian movement seems to celebrate the excesses of pluralism and individualism that the Mormon communal experiments were attempting to curb.[17]

This implicit faith in the creative potential of anarchy is alien to the system Joseph Smith established. "Organize yourselves," Latter-day Saints were commanded in an important early revelation, "and establish a house, even a house of prayer, . . . a house of glory, a house of order, a house of God."[18] The name Brigham Young chose for his communal experiment, the United Order, expressed in both its terms the essence of what Mormonism subsequently tried to accomplish for its people: to create unity out of diversity and to maintain order in the face of threatening chaos. Mormons have become instinctively more Tory than Whig, more Federalist than Republican. Deference to high church authority and obedience within a clearcut hierarchy of church offices and responsibilities have become prominent aspects of Mormon group character. These qualities caused the well-known economist Richard T. Ely to comment in 1903 that "the organization of the Mormons is the most nearly perfect piece of social mechanism with which I have ever, in any way, come in contact, excepting alone the German army."[19] Values have changed dramatically in America since 1903, and what Ely meant as a compliment would today be taken in many circles as condemnation. Nevertheless, a corollary of his observation, as he pointed out, is that Mormonism has been remarkably successful in teaching individuals to sacrifice their own interests for those of the group.

A powerful demonstration of Mormon selflessness occurred in the early summer of 1976 when the Teton Dam in the Snake River Valley of southeastern Idaho burst, flooding the communities and farms of approximately 40,000 persons, over 90 percent of them Latter-day Saints. Less than three hours after reports from the flood area reached Salt Lake City, trucks were dispatched from Welfare Square to supplement supplies of commodities already available in nearby bishops' storehouses.

The Church organizational structure was employed in subsequent weeks to account for missing persons, to provide temporary food and housing for the more than 15,000 homeless, and, after the waters receded, to clean and repair hundreds of damaged homes. Well into the summer of 1976, crews of Latter-day Saint volunteers from areas in other parts of Idaho and in Utah were bussed regularly to assist in the massive reconstruction effort. For several weeks an average of 2,000 volunteers rode daily from Cache Valley, Utah-Idaho (200 miles away); Star Valley, Wyoming; Davis County, Utah, and elsewhere to help in the cleaning and rebuilding process. Church leaders from the flooded areas, requesting electricians, were supplied with more than 400 trained men in one week, including 263 of them from the Kaysville Utah Stake, 300 miles away.

It seems likely that when the story of this disaster is fully told, the combination of Mormon priesthood structure and the instinct for cooperative endeavor among the members will be seen as the most powerful agent combatting the effects of the Teton flood. The group character displayed during the aftermath of this disaster would be essential to the successful functioning of a society that seriously attempted to distribute goods and services according to need and exact contributions according to ability. It may be that in the degree of their social achievement as well as in the scope of their design, the Mormons remain the most accomplished of all the communitarians America has produced.

CHAPTER 2

Communitarianism under Joseph Smith: The Law of Consecration and Stewardship

HE BEGINNING of Mormon communitarianism, the Law of Consecration and Stewardship, was first outlined in a revelation to Joseph Smith dated February 9, 1831.[1] Briefly, the law was a prescription for transforming the highly individualistic economic order of Jacksonian America into a system characterized by economic equality, socialization of surplus incomes, freedom of enterprise, and group economic self-sufficiency. Upon the basic principle that the earth and everything on it belongs to the Lord, every person who was a member of the church at the time the system was introduced or became a member thereafter was asked to "consecrate" or deed all his property, both real and personal, to the bishop of the church. The bishop would then grant an "inheritance" or "stewardship" to every family out of the properties so received,[2] the amount depending on the wants and needs of the family, as determined jointly by the bishop and the prospective steward. The stewardship might be a farm, building lot, store, workshop, or mill. It was expected that in some cases the consecrations would considerably exceed the stewardships. Out of the surplus thus made possible the bishop would grant stewardships to the poorer and younger members of the church who had no property to consecrate. The words of the basic revelation were as follows:

Behold, thou shalt consecrate all thy properties, that which thou hast unto me, with a covenant and a deed which cannot be broken; and they shall be laid before the bishop of my church, and two of the elders, such as he shall appoint and set apart for that purpose. . . . The bishop of my church, after that he has received the properties of my church, that it cannot be taken from the church, he shall appoint every man a steward over his own property, or that which he has received, inasmuch as shall be sufficient for himself and family.[3]

This redistribution of wealth was designed to place all family heads on an equal economic footing, considering their respective family obligations, circumstances, needs, and "just wants." The Law of Consecration and Stewardship was thus a leveler, designed to bring about a condition of relative temporal equality among the early converts to the church, for according to another 1831 doctrine, "it is not given that one man should possess that which is above another, wherefore the world lieth in sin."[4] The system aimed at equality in consumption but not in the capital controlled or managed by individuals. Men were to be given responsibilities proportionate to their needs, circumstances, and capacities. The system was intended to dispose, once and for all, of the problem of charity by giving the poor a stewardship over sufficient property to provide for their own wants.

Once the Saints had been placed on an equitable economic footing, the equality was to be maintained by requiring family heads to consecrate annually all their surplus production to the storehouse provided by the bishop for this purpose. This surplus (or residue, as it was called) was to be used primarily to distribute to those who for one reason or another—perhaps unseasonal arrival, illness, improvidence, or misfortune—failed to produce sufficiently to provide for the needs and just wants of their families. The surplus was also to be used to provide for special church expenditures, such as for publications, temples, and education, and to finance the stewards who needed funds for improvement and expansion. The wording of the revelation was as follows:

> The residue shall be kept to administer to him who has not, that every man may receive according as he stands in need; and the residue shall be kept in my storehouse, to administer to the poor and needy, as shall be appointed by the elders of the church and the bishop; and for the purpose of purchasing lands, and the building up of the New Jerusalem, which is hereafter to be revealed; that my covenant people may be gathered in one. . . .[5]

This annual consecration of the social surplus to the church for redistribution to the poor was a device to insure continued (relative) temporal equality; it was also a means by which the church would control investment and insure that the social surplus was used for purposes that the church felt were necessary and desirable. It mitigated against luxurious living and against competitive expansion. If the surplus was adequate, it also insured primacy to those investment projects in which the church was most interested.[6]

While the collection, administration, and investment of the initial and annual consecrations were to be under the supervision of the presiding bishop and his advisers, there was to be freedom of enterprise in production and in the management of properties held as stewardships. That is, the properties placed at the disposal of each family head were to be used in producing whatever goods and services he desired, with whatever combinations of factors of production he selected, from among the limited opportunities open. Church leaders might give advice on these matters, but the Law of Consecration and Stewardship did not provide for minute and intimate regulation of economic activity. Each member was free to work as he pleased within the limitations of his steward-ship. The profit system, the forces of supply and demand, and the price system presumably would continue to allocate resources, influence production decisions, and distribute primary or earned income. Some of the institutions of capitalism were thus retained and a considerable amount of economic freedom was permitted. Above all, there was to be no communism of goods. While "God's chosen" were counseled to "live together in love," they were also admonished to "pay for that which thou shalt receive of thy brother."[7]

Despite a considerable measure of freedom of enterprise, however, the system was distinctly communitarian in conception and in application. An 1831 revelation that paralleled the Law of Consecration and Stewardship commanded the members of the infant church to "be one."[8] Common suffering, persecution, and group migration strengthened the forces making for unity. Social union, in turn, was indispensable to the establishment and opera-tion of an exemplary Mormon community whose convert-citizens would have the disposition and means to prepare the earth for the return of the Savior and the institution of the kingdom of God. John Corrill, an apostate Mormon bishop, in one of the first published histories of the Latter-day Saints, emphasized the role of the Law of Consecration and Stewardship as follows:

It is believed by them [the Latter-day Saints] that the Church ought to act in concert, and feel one general interest in building up the "great cause"; and that every man ought to consider his property as consecrated to the Lord for that purpose. . . .[9]

Orson Pratt, also a participant in church affairs in the 1830s, drew a distinction between dividing property, which he characterized as a "gentile" doctrine, and uniting property, which was "God's plan of making His Saints equal in property,"[10] "as joint heirs with Him, or as His stewards."[11]

The Latter-day Saint community was to be established as the result of a "gathering" of "the faithful in heart" from "out of the bosom of Babylon" to a place designated as "Zion." Thus, the Saints would be organized "in close bodies." Once gathered, the Saints were then to devote themselves assiduously to the task of building up Zion: "Thou shalt not be idle; for he that is idle shall not eat the bread, nor wear the garments of the laborer." Plainness in living and financial self-sufficiency were to characterize this New Jerusalem: "let all thy garments be plain, and their beauty the beauty of the work of thine own hands; . . . contract no debts with the world." Thus, an industrious, frugal, independent society was to be established under the direction of the priesthood. Nevertheless, in contrast with many contemporary communitarian societies, each family was to live separately, possessed of its own stewardship, and communal living was eschewed.[12]

One crucial point in regard to the system has never been made clear, namely, the relationship of the Law of Consecration and Stewardship to the common-stock systems of the Shakers, Harmonists, Ephratists, and other contemporary communitarian societies. The Mormons disclaimed any resemblances between their law and the many types of communal orders prevalent in early nineteenth-century America, holding that the incorporation of the stewardship principle permitted a large area of individual initiative and enterprise. The surviving evidence indicates that Latter-day Saint leaders did not originally intend that the stewardship be held in fee simple, with all the legal privileges that that form of property right might accord to the "owner." Indeed, the title to all property was apparently vested in the bishop. The original revelation read: "he that sinneth and repenteth not shall be cast out, and shall not receive again that which he has consecrated unto me."[13] This implies that a stewardship was a life-lease subject to revocation by the bishop. Both theory and practice of stewardship as it was first established in Missouri disallowed unilateral conveyance of consecrated property by a steward to other persons with whom sales and exchange might be contemplated, including wife, children, and heirs.

There seem to have been three specific reasons, historically speaking, for the initial revelation establishing the Law of Consecration and Stewardship. The first was the desire of Joseph Smith to establish an alternative to a specific communal society with which several of his early converts had close ties. One of the earliest converts to Mormonism was Sidney Rigdon, a leading Protestant minister in the Western Reserve. Rigdon had been a follower of the noted leader of the Disciples of Christ, Alexander Campbell, but had broken away from Campbell, partly over a dispute as to the wisdom of attempting to duplicate the communism of the early Christians, as described in the Acts of the Apostles: "And all that believed were together, and had all things common; and sold their possessions and goods and parted them to all men, as every man had need."

Rigdon, a person of considerable intellectual stature in his earlier years, was familiar with the experiments of Robert Owen, the Rappists, and the German Separatists at Zoar, Ohio. Rigdon's followers at Mentor and Kirtland, Ohio, two communities on Lake Erie, east of Cleveland, attempted to establish communal societies called "The Family." He and most of his Kirtland congregation were converted to Mormonism late in 1830. So important was this group that Joseph Smith moved immediately, with some of his followers, from New York to Kirtland. When the twenty-six-year-old prophet arrived at the new headquarters on or about February 1, 1831, one of his first acts was to request "The Family" to abandon the common-stock principle in favor of what he called "the more perfect law of the Lord."[14] Some positive explanation of the "law of the Lord" was necessarily forthcoming. A week later the Law of Consecration and Stewardship was revealed, thus serving to replace common stock with stewardship, and "The Family" with a considerable measure of individualism.[15]

The need to suggest something positive to replace the impractical common-stock principle was one purpose of the revelation. A second function of the Law of Consecration and Stewardship was to provide a religious incentive whereby the Kirtland Mormons would agree to divide their farming lands, building lots, and other property with poor families who had come, upon Joseph Smith's recommendation, from New York and elsewhere to Ohio (and later to Missouri). The law was also a device by which a surplus could be accumulated to purchase additional lands, care for the temporal needs of those called into church service, finance the publication of books and periodicals, make possible the construction of meetinghouses, and supply means for carrying out other worthwhile spiritual and temporal projects. Insofar as converts were convinced of its practical efficacy or divine origin, the Law of Consecration and Stewardship would assure the use of the social surplus for charitable and religious purposes.[16] It is quite possible that the law would have been announced for this immediate and compelling financial reason even if the Kirtland Family situation had not confronted Joseph Smith and his associates.

There was undoubtedly a third and more far-reaching objective in the revelations on consecration and stewardship. As the founder of "restored Christianity," Joseph Smith saw it as his responsibility to establish the social and economic basis for a Christian society. The passage in Acts previously quoted was doubtless a challenge to the youthful prophet, as it was to Bible-reading Christians generally. In addition, scriptures already brought forth by Joseph Smith portrayed Book of Mormon peoples and the citizens of the ancient city of Enoch living an ideal, communal economic order. The prophecy of Enoch was particularly powerful, holding up to the Prophet's small group of followers a perfect society "of one heart and one mind, . . . and there was no poor among them."[17]

Joseph Smith was also exposed to several contemporary communitarian reform efforts. In a period of unusual social ferment, religious enthusiasm, and economic reform, scores of communistic and/or communitarian societies and experiments sprang into existence.[18] In 1840 Emerson wrote to Carlyle: "We are all a little wild here with numberless projects of social reform. Not a reading man but has a draft of a New Community in his waistcoat pocket."[19] Within a few miles of the Vermont community in which Joseph Smith was born were the Groveland Society of the Shakers, in which all property was held in trust by the community, and the organized followers of Jemima Wilkinson. Furthermore, his associate, Sidney Rigdon, as mentioned before, was well acquainted with the systems of the Rappites and the Owenite Socialists. Thus, it was logical, and perfectly within the order of events, that the new prophet should have announced the Latter-day Saint version of "the more perfect law of the Lord." Sprinkled through his revelations on the subject are phrases that indicate the lofty ideal to be held up before his followers: "be alike . . . and receive alike, that ye may be one"; "let every man esteem his brother as himself"; "my people [must be] united according to the union required by the law of the celestial kingdom"; and "thou shalt live together in love."

Thus, the Law of Consecration and Stewardship could be seen as a consequence of practical need and Christian idealism. It is not surprising that the plan should have been intensely practical in certain respects, and that it should have overestimated the possibilities of human altruism in other respects. It was equalitarian, communitarian, and a potentially good revenue-producer. It was to a degree individualistic, though with strong elements of group control and influence.[20]

During the first few months after the enunciation of the Law of Consecration and Stewardship, an attempt was made by some of the Latter-day Saints in Ohio to comply with its provisions. A group of Saints from Colesville, New York, established themselves at Thompson, near Kirtland, Ohio, in May 1831, and consecrations were importuned to apply on the purchase of their farming lands. Before this group was completely organized, however, one or two of the wealthier members backed out and successfully sued in the civil courts for the return of their consecrations. This introduced such confusion in their affairs that the Thompson Saints and others were called to settle Jackson County, Missouri (or "Zion," as it was called, the New Jerusalem whose building up was anticipated in a February 1831 revelation), arriving there in July 1831. Nevertheless, the introduction of the system, even for that brief period, did facilitate the removal of the poor from New York to Ohio, and from Ohio to Missouri.[21]

In Jackson County, Missouri, the second attempt was made to institute the Law of Consecration and Stewardship. The form of the settlement was directed by Joseph Smith two years after Mormons began to arrive in Missouri. In accordance with his "Plat of the City of Zion," every family was to receive a building lot in the city.[22] In addition, the farmers were to receive an allotment of land outside the city. The mechanic was to receive the necessary tools and materials for his trade, and teachers, writers, and musicians were to have a home site and a license or appointment to serve the community according to their respective abilities. The town residents, of course, would participate in the produce of the farmers through regular commercial channels or through the redistribution of a central storehouse.

To purchase lands for the new community, missionaries and

agents were asked to canvass congregations throughout the East and Midwest for donations. The principal source of funds, however, was expected to be the consecrations of those going to Independence, the Jackson County "City of Zion," to live. The bishop was instructed to receive these consecrations, to allot inheritances to properly certified family heads, and to notify the church-at-large from time to time as to "the privileges of the land," so that the gathering would not take place faster than lands were purchased.[23] The bishop was further directed to establish a storehouse for the reception and distribution of consecrations. This enterprise, operated under his management, was operating by the end of 1831.[24] A printing concern was also established, the first such firm west of the Missouri River to publish weekly and monthly periodicals.[25]

By July 1832, roughly a year after the call to settle Jackson County, between 300 and 400 converts had arrived at Independence, almost all of whom were located upon their inheritances. By the following July, almost 1,200 had gathered in Missouri, of whom 700 were converted Latter-day Saints.[26] While the group was officially reported to be "in good health and spirits" and "doing well," the burden of migrating, of purchasing land, of establishing the printing office and store, and, above all, of transforming a "wilderness and desert" into a "garden of the Lord" was greater than most had anticipated.[27] Evidently, the consecrations were insufficient to provide inheritances for all who were entitled to them.[28] From the frequent exhortations in *The Evening and the Morning Star* and in revelations of Joseph Smith, one would also gather that idleness was a problem.[29] Perhaps some of the immigrants, filled with the millenarian spirit of the times, did not understand the necessity of laboring to build up Zion.[30] Officials found it necessary to caution prospective immigrants not to give away their property before leaving for Zion.[31] Despite these hindrances, however, some participants later wrote of the Jackson County experiment with pronounced nostalgia.

> There was a spirit of peace and union, and love and good will manifested in this little Church in the wilderness, the memory of which will be ever dear to my heart. . . . Peace and plenty crowned their labors, and the wilderness became a fruitful field, and the solitary place began to bud and blossom as the rose. . . . In short, there has seldom, if ever, been a happier people upon the earth than the Church of the Saints now were.[32]

Idyllic or not, the system in Jackson County was plagued by two problems. One had to do with the nature of the property rights to be granted to the stewards; the second was concerned with the size of the "inheritance" to be given to each steward. In regard to the first, the bishop of the church in Jackson County, Edward Partridge, in the allotment of land purchased for the purpose, took the attitude that the inheritances ought to be tentative, entitling each settler to a right of use only, with a lease subject to cancellation on the order of the bishop. Considering the uncertainty in the number of converts for which he would have to provide land, the temporary nature of the allotments would make it possible for Partridge to make a reapportionment, if necessary, to provide for new arrivals. This plan would also discourage opportunists who might join the group to acquire an inheritance, and promptly withdraw. Finally, the non-title policy gave Partridge the power, under threat of the forfeiture of the entire stewardship, to enforce standards of workmanship, social behavior, and personal morality among those receiving inheritances. The wealth of the community would never be lost to apostates, "trouble-makers," or idlers.[33]

Several examples of the printed-form documents Partridge used in receiving consecrated properties and allotting stewardships have survived.[34] One-half of a large, folded sheet contained a deed of gift, granting to the bishop of the church an itemized schedule of property "for the purpose of purchasing lands, and building up the New Jerusalem, even Zion, and for relieving the wants of the poor and needy." In Mormon terminology, this would probably have been called a deed of consecration, but church leaders, in drawing up the documents, apparently sought to substitute the language of secular civil law for the usages in Joseph Smith's revelations. In the document the grantor bound himself and his heirs to release forever all rights and interest in the scheduled property. The bishop, acknowledging receipt of the gift, promised to use it only for the purposes stipulated in the contract and bound himself and his heirs to relinquish control of the property to his successor as bishop should he be removed from office by death or for other reasons.[35]

The six extant deeds of gift (see Appendix 1) list household furnishings and clothing as well as livestock, farming equipment, and artisan's tools. James Lee was the least affluent of those whose deeds have survived. He consecrated to the bishop "a number of saddlers tools, one candlestick & one washbowl valued seven dollars twenty five cents,—also saddlers stock, trunks and harness work valued twenty four dollars,—also extra clothing valued three dollars"—possessions totaling $34.25 in value. Among the wealthiest was George W. Pitkin, who gave "sundry articles of furniture valued forty seven dollars thirty seven cents,—also three beds, bedding and extra clothing valued sixty eight dollars,—also sundry farming tools valued eleven dollars and fifty cents,—also two horses, one harness, one waggon, two cows and one calf valued one hundred and eighty one dollars"—the total worth $307.87, according to the evaluation agreed upon by himself and the bishop.

Once the deed of gift was properly signed and witnessed, the grantor stood destitute before the bishop and the church. What the bishop accepted as a gift, however, he gave back in the same transaction as a "loan" together with a "lease" of real property— an inheritance in Zion. Mormons would probably have called this document, printed on the other half of the form, a deed of stewardship or a stewardship agreement. In civil law it would be described as simply a lease-and-loan agreement. Only four com- pleted land descriptions are known to have survived, leasing inheritances as small as carpenter Joseph Knight's village lot of 1.8 acres and as large as Levi Jackman's farm of 33 acres. Farmers were generally granted from twenty to thirty acres. In the four cases where deeds of consecration and stewardship for a single individual have survived, the steward was "loaned" by the bishop precisely the same scheduled possessions that he had given to the bishop in the deed of gift, nothing being withheld for the Lord's storehouse, a practice that obviously could not have been followed in all cases.

Responsibility for improving the stewardship was placed upon the individual who was to use the leased and loaned property "as to him shall seem meet and proper." He was to pay all taxes on the property and promised "to pay yearly unto the said Edward Partridge, bishop of said church, or his successor in office, for the benefit of said church, all that I shall make or accu- mulate more than is needful for the support and comfort of myself and family." The contract was to be binding during the life of the steward unless he left the church or was excommuni- cated. Were this to happen, he would forfeit the land and be ob- ligated to pay an equivalent for the personal property. The contract obligated the bishop to provide for the steward and his family in the case of disability so long as they were members of the church. If the steward were to die, the widow could claim the property on the same terms as her husband. If both parents were to die in the faith, the children would also have a claim upon the property for their support until they came of age, but no longer.

Under this system annual reconsecration of each year's surpluses would have prevented the accumulation of capital in the hands of single individuals or families. A central authority—the bishop, not the steward—decided how capital resources were to be allocated. A steward could not by his own decision expand the productive facilities of either farm or workshop, for each year his surplus would be taken into the common fund, unless the bishop decided otherwise. Children upon coming of age would enter the system on precisely the same basis as new converts, no matter how much or little their parents had consecrated to the Lord's storehouse over the years. Private accumulation of capital was impossible so long as one remained faithful to the Law of Consecration and Stewardship. The economic system Joseph Smith offered his followers, especially his system of land tenure, would have fit more comfortably into medieval England than into Jacksonian America.

As might be expected, the church encountered legal difficulties as the result of the "lease and loan" policy. Judges on the frontier viewed properties held in trust with noticeable disfavor. Some apostates successfully sued in the courts for the return of their consecrated properties. Moreover, Mormonism was being associated, in the minds of many, with such religio-economic movements as that of the Shakers—an association that Mormon leaders viewed with disfavor.[36] A leader of the church in Missouri finally wrote to Joseph Smith "on the subject of giving deeds, and receiving contributions from brethren." On April 21, 1833, the Prophet replied: "I have nothing further to say on the subject than to recommend that you make yourselves acquainted with the commandments of the Lord, and the laws of the state, and govern yourselves accordingly."[37] Ten days later, however, in a special letter to Bishop Partridge, he wrote:

Concerning inheritances, you are bound by the law of the Lord, to give a deed, securing to him who receives inheritances, his inheritance, for an everlasting inheritance, or in other words, to be his individual property, his private stewardship, and if he is found a transgressor and should be cut off, out of the church, his inheritance is his still, and he is delivered over to the buffetings of Satan, till the day of redemption. But the property which he consecrated to the poor, for their benefit and inheritance and stewardship [in other words, his surplus], he cannot obtain again by the law of the Lord. Thus you see the propriety of this law, that rich men cannot have power to disinherit the poor by obtaining again that which they have consecrated.[38]

Thus it became clear that the official church position had become one of requiring that a deed with no strings attached be made out at the time each inheritance was given out.[39] In commenting on this modification, or clarification, the editor of the church monthly later wrote that

they [the Latter-day Saints] have frequently been ridiculed in consequence of certain items contained in the one [revelation] setting forth their faith on the subject of bestowing temporal gifts for the benefit of the poor. . . .

Some have said, and still say, that this Church, *"has all things common."* This asserting is meant, not only to falsify on the subject of property, but to blast the reputation and moral characters of the members of the same.

The church at Jerusalem in the days of the apostles, had their earthly goods in common; the Nephites [inhabitants of ancient America described in the Book of Mormon], after the appearance of Christ, held theirs in the same way; but each government was differently organized from ours; and could admit of such a course when ours cannot.[40]

Because of the nature of prevailing state and national laws with respect to property, therefore, church authorities finally came to agree that a steward should hold legal rights to "the Lord's property" placed in his charge.[41]

After October 12, 1832, Bishop Partridge had a new form printed for receiving consecrations and granting stewardships, one copy of which (made out to Benjamin Eames) remains in the Church Archives. It has been suggested that this was an attempt to repattern the land-tenure system in Zion in accordance with the changed position of church leaders.[42] In the new form the deed of gift was essentially unchanged. The lease-and-loan agreement was altered considerably, but in a manner sufficiently ambiguous to leave room for at least two sharply divergent interpretations. As in the earlier document, the steward was initially "leased" a parcel of land and "loaned" the possessions he had consecrated. But the clause outlining the steward's rights to the property should he leave the church was given new emphasis by being moved from the fourth to the first sentence of a long paragraph setting forth conditions and qualifications of the agreement. Here the words "leased and loaned" were omitted from a phrase in the earlier document in which the steward had promised "to forfeit all claim to the above described leased and loaned property." Moreover, where the steward had earlier agreed "to give back the leased, and also pay an equivalent for the loaned," he now promised "to quit the said leased premises, and also to pay an equivalent for the loaned."

One explanation of these changes might be that they were a consequence of the Prophet's instructions in his May 2, 1833, letter to Partridge. By this interpretation the new reference to "above described property" was meant to apply only to the scheduled personal property and not to the real property or inheritance described in the document. The excommunicant's legal claim to ownership of the real property was not overtly contested. Possession of the property, however, was denied him, with the apparent optimistic hope that he would be willing to sell back to the church land rendered useless to him by an agreement denying right of possession. In this way the lands of Zion might be preserved intact for the faithful while at least the letter of the "law of the Lord" that a man's "leased" property remain his "private inheritance" was honored.

An alternative explanation would seem more plausible. It is altogether likely that the new form was made up before Bishop Partridge had received Joseph Smith's letter and thus was not meant to incorporate the new instructions. This would explain why the words "leased" and "loaned" were retained in the opening section of the document when, if full conveyance of title to property in fee simple were intended, other words could have easily removed any possible ambiguity. Deletion of the words "leased and loaned" in the later paragraph stating qualifications and conditions of the agreement could have been done to avoid redundancy. Unless the word "property" were commonly employed to describe personal property only, and not real property, the phrase in which the steward agreed to "forfeit all claim to the above described property, and hereby bind myself to quit the said leased premises" would seem to strengthen, rather than weaken, the bishop's hand against apostates' claims to their inheritances. Omission of the steward's promise to "give back the leased"

BE IT KNOWN, THAT I, *Levi Jackman*

Of Jackson county, and state of Missouri, having become a member of the church of Christ, organized according to law, and established by the revelations of the Lord, on the 6th day of April, 1830, do, of my own free will and accord, having first paid my just debts, grant and hereby give unto *Edward Partridge* of Jackson county, and state of Missouri, bishop of said church, the following described property, viz:— *sundry articles of furniture valued thirty seven Dollars,— also two beds, bedding and feathers valued forty four Dollars fifty cents,— also three axes and other tools valued eleven dollars and twenty five cents*

For the purpose of purchasing lands, and building up the New Jerusalem, even Zion, and for relieving the wants of the poor and needy. For which I the said *Levi Jackman* do covenant and bind myself and my heirs forever, to release all my right and interest to the above described property, unto him the said *Edward Partridge* bishop of said church. And I the said *Edward Partridge* — bishop of said church, having received the above described property, of the said *Levi Jackman* do bind myself, that I will cause the same to be expended for the above-mentioned purposes of the said *Levi Jackman* to the satisfaction of said church; and in case I should be removed from the office of bishop of said church, by death or otherwise, I hereby bind myself and my heirs forever, to make over to my successor in office, for the benefit of said church, all of the above described property, which may then be in my possession.

In testimony whereof, WE have hereunto set our hands and seals this   day of   in the year of our Lord, one thousand eight hundred and thirty

IN PRESENCE OF

[SEAL]
[SEAL]
[Seal]

Levi Jackman's Deeds of Consecration and Stewardship, executed in Missouri in the early 1830s, propose a form of land and property tenure more appropriate to medieval England than 19th century America. The

BE IT KNOWN, THAT I, *Edward Partridge*

Of Jackson county, and state of Missouri, bishop of the church of Christ, organized according to law, and established by the revelations of the Lord, on the 6th day of April, 1830, have leased, and by these presents do lease unto *Levi Jackman* of Jackson county, and state of Missouri, a member of said church, the following described piece or parcel of land, being a part of section No. *Sixteen* township No. *forty nine* range No. *thirty three* situated in Jackson county, and state of Missouri, and is bounded as follows, viz:— *beginning eighty rods E, of the N. W. corner of sd Sec. thence S. one hundred & four rods, thence E. seventy five rods 8 L. to a road thence N. 31° W. on the road sixty six rods 21 L. thence N. 7½ E. forty eight rods to the N. line of sd Sec. thence W. on sd line forty four rods to the place of beginning containing thirty three acres be the same more or less subject to roads and highways*

And also have loaned the following described property, viz:— *Sundry articles of furniture valued thirty seven Dollars, — also two beds bedding and feathers valued forty four Dollars fifty cents, — also three axes and other tools valued eleven Dollars and twenty five cents*

TO HAVE AND TO HOLD the above described property, by him the said *Levi Jackman* to be used and occupied as to him shall seem meet and proper. And as a consideration for the use of the above described property, I the said *Levi Jackman* do bind myself to pay the taxes, and also to pay yearly unto the said *Edward Partridge* bishop of said church, or his successor in office, for the benefit of said church, all that I shall make or accumulate more than is needful for the support and comfort of myself and family. And it is agreed by the parties, that this lease and loan shall be binding during the life of the said *Levi Jackman* unless he transgress, and is not deemed worthy by the authority of the church, according to its laws, to belong to the church. And in that case I the said *Levi Jackman* do acknowledge that I forfeit all claim to the above described leased and loaned property, and hereby bind myself to give back the leased, and also pay an equivalent for the loaned, for the benefit of said church, unto the said *Edward Partridge* bishop of said church, or his successor in office. And further, in case of said *Levi Jackman* or family's inability in consequence of infirmity or old age, to provide for themselves while members of this church, I the said *Edward Partridge* bishop of said church, do bind myself to administer to their necessities out of any funds in my hands appropriated for that purpose, not otherwise disposed of, to the satisfaction of the church. And further, in case of the death of the said *Levi Jackman* his wife or widow, being at the time a member of said church, has claim upon the above described leased and loaned property, upon precisely the same conditions that her said husband had them, as above described; and the children of the said *Levi Jackman* in case of the death of both their parents, also have claim upon the above described property, for their support, until they shall become of age, and no longer; subject to the same conditions yearly that their parents were: provided however, should the parents not be members of said church, and in possession of the above described property at the time of their deaths, the claim of the children as above described, is null and void.

In testimony whereof, WE have hereunto set our hands and seals this _____ day of _____ in the year of our Lord, one thousand eight hundred and thirty

IN PRESENCE OF

[SEAL.]

[SEAL.]

original forms were printed on one large sheet with the consecration agreement on the left half and the stewardship agreement on the right. (Church Archives) property from the original document would be a possible means of avoiding an interpretation of the phrase by civil courts as an acknowledgment on the part of the bishop that the property had at some point been given to him outright by the steward. Moreover, the injunction to quit the property was a means of building a case against apostates who sought, through stubbornly sitting on their inheritance, to gain right to legal title. In sum the document is more intelligible if read as an attempt on the part of the bishop to fortify his initial position—that title to lands and other property should, according to the Law of Consecration and Stewardship, remain with the church when a member apostatized or was excommunicated.

After receiving Joseph Smith's May 1833 letter, however, the leaders of the Missouri colony did change their position, issuing public statements in June 1833, declaring, among other things, that each family head had received, or was about to receive, "a warranty deed securing to himself and heirs, his inheritance in fee simple forever."[43] However, it is doubtful that the new policy was completely carried out because of the developing friction between Mormons and non-Mormons in Missouri.[44]

In regard to the second problem encountered in administering "the law" in Missouri—the amount of inheritance to be granted each steward—the revelation specified, in general terms, that each person was to have as much as was "sufficient for himself and family"; that every man should receive "according to his family, according to his circumstances . . . and his wants and needs."[45] What were a family's wants and needs? Who was to determine them? Evidently, there was some difference of opinion on the matter, for Joseph Smith found it necessary to direct a letter to Bishop Partridge in June 1833 explaining the procedure that was to be followed:

Every man must be his own judge how much he should receive and how much he should suffer to remain in the hands of the Bishop. I speak of those who consecrate more than they need for the support of themselves and their families.

The matter of consecration must be done by the mutual consent of both parties; for to give the Bishop power to say how much every man shall have, and he be obliged to comply with the Bishop's judgment, is giving to the Bishop more power than a king has; and upon the other hand, to let every man say how much he needs, and the Bishop be obliged to comply with his judgment, is to throw Zion into confusion, and make a slave of the Bishop. The fact is, there must be a balance or equilibrium of power between the Bishop and the people, and thus harmony and good will may be preserved among you.

Therefore, those persons consecrating property to the Bishop in Zion, and then receiving an inheritance back, must reasonably show to the Bishop that they need as much as they claim. But in case the two parties cannot come to a mutual agreement, the Bishop is to have nothing to do about receiving such consecrations; and the case must be laid before a council of twelve High Priests, the Bishop not being one of the council, but he is to lay the case before them.[46]

These instructions, like those pertaining to the granting of a deed, came too late to be applied in the Jackson County experiment.

Throughout the period of its operation, the active, on-the-job management and supervision of the system was vested in the bishop and his counselors. This imposed a heavy administrative task, since these men were also spiritual leaders. In April 1832 the Central Council was created. This was a group of five men, three from Kirtland, two from Independence, and later seven men, who were to serve as a board of directors for the supervision of business affairs in Kirtland and Zion. The Central Council, in turn, immediately created a "United Firm" or "United Order,"[47] which was a joint-stewardship of the members of the council with the responsibility of holding properties in trust,[48] assisting the poor, and supervising the establishment of merchandising stores in Ohio and Missouri.[49] The creation of this agency set the pattern for the assignment of responsibilities for the management of large companies and corporations; this was to be done by the method of joint-stewardship.[50]

While the creation of the Central Council removed overall temporal policy considerations from the province of the bishop, a thousand miles, mostly wilderness, separated Kirtland from Independence, and it is probable that the control of the Central Council was not very effective.

From a purely economic point of view, one fault of the Law of Consecration and Stewardship was the transferral of consecrated properties from the relatively well-to-do to the poor, when the latter were incapable of wise management of property. Theoretically, the bishop could offer greater stewardships to the more capable, thus placing capital in the hands of those who would be most likely to maximize the surplus. This was probably how the system was intended to work. But with many in dire need it became necessary, at the inception of the new order, to effect so drastic a redistribution of wealth that the possibility of greatly increasing the annual surplus through new production was kept to a minimum.

Another fault in the system was the diminution of incentive that might be brought about by the requirement that stewards consecrate all their surplus income. This eventuality need not have resulted among a zealous and faithful people, but was a probability without such stewards. We have Brigham Young's word for it that the system did not operate long enough, or successfully enough, to obtain much of a surplus:

> I was present at the time the revelation came for the brethren to give their surplus property into the hands of the Bishops for the building up of Zion, but I never knew a man yet who had a dollar of surplus property. No matter how much one might have he wanted all he had for himself, for his children, his grandchildren, and so forth.[51]

Whether these difficulties could have been surmounted, as they were in some contemporary American idealistic communities, or whether church leaders would have modified the system sufficiently to take these two factors into account, can never be known for certain. About a year and a half after Zion had been founded, and before the system was completely organized and put into running operation, the Latter-day Saints in Missouri ran into the stiff opposition of their gentile neighbors. Systematic persecution of the Mormons in Missouri commenced in April 1833.[52] In July 1833, the Mormon printing establishment was wrecked and the bishop and his companion tarred and feathered. The press was about to issue 3,000 copies of the Book of Commandments, the first edition of the revelations received by Joseph Smith, and also a quantity of hymnbooks. All of these were destroyed, with the exception of a few sets of signatures of the uncompleted Book of Commandments. On July 23, 1833, what came to be known as the "Missouri Mob" reassembled, thoroughly armed and bearing a red flag, and required the Latter-day Saints to leave the county within a fixed time. In November 1833, armed mobs drove the Mormons from Jackson County.

The condition of the Saints during these and succeeding months was not such as to make the administration of the Law of Consecration and Stewardship possible or effective. In December 1833, one of their number wrote Joseph Smith from Clay County, Missouri, describing their plight:

The condition of the scattered Saints is lamentable, and affords a gloomy prospect. No regular order can be enforced, nor any usual discipline kept up. . . . I should like to know what the honest in heart shall do? Our clothes are worn out; we want the necessaries of life, and shall we lease, buy, or otherwise obtain land where we are, to till, that we may raise enough to eat?[53]

After exhausting all peaceful means of repossessing their land, church leaders in Ohio organized a group called Zion's Camp to march to Missouri to "redeem Zion." While this group was preparing to leave Kirtland, a revelation was announced separating the Jackson County and Kirtland Orders.[54] Instructions were given in relation to the establishment of "the Lord's law" in Kirtland. A treasury was created into which the cash receipts of the late Jackson County Order were to be placed. This seems to have been particularly designed to receive the proceeds or "avails" from the sale of lands in Jackson County, if any such sales were consummated. The Saints were to draw out of this treasury for their needs in getting established in Clay County, Missouri, their new home. Thus, the treasury was a means of sharing the meager resources of the community among the needy.[55]

These matters arranged for, Zion's Camp, some 130 persons, with Joseph Smith as commander, left for Missouri. They were destined not to reach their goal or to accomplish their purpose.[56] An outbreak of cholera took a heavy toll of the little army and it was necessarily disbanded. Chastened and discouraged, his followers heard the Prophet announce a revelation on June 22, 1834, suspending the operation of the Law of Consecration and Stewardship until such a day as Zion could be redeemed by purchase rather than by blood. This suspension apparently applied to the Mormon settlements in Ohio as well as to those in Missouri.[57]

Zion—that is, Jackson County—was, of course, never "redeemed" by the Mormons, although some factions returned there after 1846; and the Law of Consecration and Stewardship was never reinstated, in its pristine form, by church officials in Missouri or in any of the subsequent habitations of the Mormons in the Mississippi Valley. However, an "inferior" system that bore considerable resemblance to "the Lord's law" was officially introduced by Joseph Smith in 1838 at Far West, Caldwell County, Missouri. Far West, approximately fifty miles north of

Independence, was the third Missouri gathering place of the Latter-day Saints, the first having been Jackson County and the second having been Clay County, from which approximately 10,000 Mormons were called to settle Caldwell County late in 1837. There they bought up most of the land claims of value and established Far West as their new Zion.[58] It was at this place, on July 8, 1838, that the following "lesser-law" version of the Law of Consecration and Stewardship was announced to the church:

Verily, thus saith the Lord, I require all their surplus property to be put into the hands of the bishop of my church in Zion,

For the building of mine house, and for the laying of the foundation of Zion [the purchase of lands?], and for the priesthood, and for the debts of the Presidency of my Church.

And this shall be the beginning of the tithing of my people.

And after that, those who have thus been tithed, shall pay one tenth of all their interest annually; and this shall be a standing law unto them forever. . . .

. . . all those who gather unto the land of Zion shall be tithed of their surplus properties, and shall observe this law, or they shall not be found worthy to abide among you.[59]

This "inferior" law, as it was called, was introduced because "the people had polluted their inheritances" while in Jackson County.[60] In principle, however, it was not greatly different from the so-called celestial law of 1831. First of all, the revelation required the consecration of surplus property at the time the convert joined the community of Saints. In this respect, the law was precisely the same in effect as the 1831 Law of Consecration. The 1831 law required that the convert, at the time he joined the community of Saints, consecrate all his property and receive back a stewardship measured by his wants and needs. The 1838 law obviated the transfer and reverse transfer by requiring that he consecrate only his surplus and retain the remainder. The equalizing effect was identical. While the gesture of placing all his property on the altar was not required in the later law, the principle of stewardship was still retained, at least as a religious principle. Furthermore, whereas the original law of consecration and stewardship required that all the annual surplus income or "residue" be placed in the storehouse for distribution to the poor and needy, the 1838 law required that a tithe or a tenth be universally paid on the annual increase. This might be regarded as a more precise definition of the "residue" or surplus income and resulted in the same transferral of annual savings to the church for community-investment purposes that was to have been effected under the Law of Consecration and Stewardship.

Because of the unsettled nature of the economic affairs of the Latter-day Saints at the time, it is difficult to determine to what extent the members complied with the Far West revelation and consecrated their surplus property. Less than three weeks after the revelation was announced, Joseph Smith mentioned in his journal that church officials, including himself, met at Far West "to dispose of the public properties of the Bishop, many of the brethren having consecrated their surplus property according to the revelations."[61] Brigham Young thought that the law "seemingly was not fully understood or practised."[62] In a pulpit statement that reflects his gift for hyperbole as well as the problems raised by the revelation, he explained:

When the revelation . . . was given in 1838, I was present, and recollect the feelings of the brethren. . . . The brethren wished me to go among the Churches, and find out what surplus property the people had, with which to forward the building of the Temple we were commencing at Far West. I accordingly went from place to place through the country. Before I started, I asked brother Joseph, "Who shall be the judge of what is surplus property?" Said he, "Let them be the judges themselves. . . ."

Then I replied, "I will go and ask them for their surplus property"; and I did so; I found the people said they were willing to do about as they were counselled, but, upon asking them about their surplus property, most of the men who owned land and cattle would say, "I have got so many hundred acres of land, and I have got so many boys, and I want each one of them to have eighty acres, therefore this is not surplus property." Again, "I have got so many girls, and I do not believe I shall be able to give them more than forty acres each." "Well, you have got two or three hundred acres left." "Yes, but I have a brother-in-law coming on, and he will depend on me for a living; my wife's nephew is also coming on, he is poor, and I shall have to furnish him a farm after he arrives here." I would [go] on to the next one, and he would have more land and cattle than he could make use of to advantage. It is a laughable idea, but is nevertheless true, men would tell me they were young and beginning in the world, and would say, "We have no children, but our prospects are good, and we think we shall have a family of children, and if we do, we want to give them eighty acres of land each; we have no surplus property." "How many cattle have you?" "So many." "How many horses, &c?" "So many, but I have made provisions for all these, and I have use for everything I have got."

Some were disposed to do right with their surplus property, and once in a while you would find a man who had a cow which he considered surplus, but generally she was of the class that would kick a person's hat off, or eyes out, or the wolves had eaten off her teats. You would once in a while find a man who had a horse that he considered surplus, but at the same time he had the ringbone, was broken-winded, spavined in both legs, and had the pole evil at one end of the neck and a fistula at the other, and both knees sprung.[63]

Whatever the status of the 1838 Law of Consecration in Far West, some Latter-day Saints took a further step at the time to consolidate their property by forming voluntary cooperative enterprises called United Firms. Joseph Smith mentions in his journal having attended meetings on August 20 and 21, 1838, at which groups of farmers organized the Western Agricultural Company, the Eastern Agricultural Company, and the Southern Agricultural Company.[64] In the case of one of these companies, at least, a decision was reached to enclose a field of twelve sections, containing 7,680 acres of land, for the growing of grain. According to other accounts, plans were underway to organize, in addition to these agricultural companies, three other corporations uniting mechanics, shopkeepers, and laborers, respectively. Thus, the land, machinery, and skills of the church members would be utilized "for the common good."[65] The four corporations, together with the modified Law of Consecration described above, were to implement the four goals of the Law of Consecration and Stewardship: economic equality, socialization of surplus incomes, partial freedom of enterprise, and group economic self-sufficiency. John Corrill, who observed these plans at Far West, wrote of them as follows:

Every man was to put in all his property by leasing it to the firm for a term of years; overseers or managers were to be chosen from time to time, by the members of the firm, to manage the concerns of the same, and the rest were to labor under their direction. . . . Many joined these firms, while many others were much dissatisfied with them, which caused considerable feeling and excitement in the Church. [Joseph] Smith said every man must act his own feelings, whether to join or not.[66]

Whether these plans, unofficial and voluntary as they seem to have been, would have materialized into a successful substitute for the Law of Consecration and Stewardship, or whether they would have run aground on the rock of human selfishness, can never be known. Late in 1838 the Mormons were once more driven from their homes and forced to leave Missouri and all their immediate cooperative hopes behind. According to one report, more than $300,000 worth of property was forcibly abandoned.[67]

The church took refuge in Illinois, with headquarters at Commerce (rechristened Nauvoo), on the banks of the Mississippi. It has seemed strange to many students of Mormonism that in seven years of comparative freedom and isolation there—years marked by growth and worldly affluence—no attempt was made to restore "the Lord's plan." When some church members living in Iowa undertook, in 1840, to establish the Law of Consecration and Stewardship, Joseph Smith advised, according to one source, that

the law of consecration could not be kept here and that it was the will of the Lord that we should desist from trying to keep it; and if persisted in, it would produce a perfect defeat of its object, and that he assumed the whole responsibility of not keeping it until proposed by himself.[68]

The views of the Prophet during his Nauvoo sojourn were perhaps expressed even more forcibly in a notation made in his journal on September 24, 1843: "I preached on the stand about one hour on the 2nd chapter of Acts, designing to show the folly of common stock. In Nauvoo every one is steward over his own."[69]

Actually, the circumstances surrounding the settlement of Nauvoo were sufficiently different from those attending previous settlements to account for Joseph Smith's seeming neglect of the Law of Consecration and Stewardship in that location. The church had to make far larger unit investments in land in Nauvoo than it had ever been called upon to do before, and its resources, financial and otherwise, were relatively fewer, partly because of forced property sales and partly because of the heavy expenses of frequent moving and establishing service enterprises. From the standpoint of economics, the Law of Consecration and Stewardship was simply not feasible. Because of basic economic necessity, then, property institutions in Nauvoo were undiluted except by such restrictions as those imposed by conscience and the principle of stewardship.

In 1841 the law of tithing was officially adopted as a substitute more suited to financial necessity and the weaknesses of human nature.[70] This law, which has been retained by the church to this day, contained no device for the reform of property institutions or for achieving a more equitable distribution of wealth and income. After 1841, church members were asked to participate in church programs by donating the equivalent of one-tenth of their possessions at the time of their conversion and one-tenth of their annual increase (or more) thereafter. Those who had no property, and therefore no annual increase, were expected to labor one day in ten for the church.

The stewardship phase of "the Lord's law" lapsed into an informal, voluntary, less-than-universal arrangement in which the faithful were urged to regard their property rights, however legal, as something less than absolute, and as subject to a measure of control by the priesthood. Church revenues came to depend to a considerable extent upon sources other than consecrations, such as borrowings, capitalistic business enterprises, and profit-making sales of property. In an account of the history and doctrines of the Latter-day Saints prepared shortly before his death, Joseph Smith made no mention whatever of the Law of Consecration and Stewardship.[71]

The failure of Mormon leaders to reinstitute the Law of Consecration and Stewardship in Nauvoo and elsewhere has led many to conclude that they regarded it as a practical failure, with little hope of succeeding even without gentile opposition. Several factors militated against its success during the short period of its operation in Ohio and Missouri. (1) Most of the converts to the early church were poor and had nothing to consecrate. Yet inheritances had to be provided for them. (2) Most of the consecrations that were made were in kind, while most of the church's investments (in real estate and so on to provide stewardships for those who needed them) required liquid resources. Conversion of the former into the latter was difficult on the Missouri frontier. (3) Constant persecution made property accumulation almost impossible. (4) The opposition of the courts to the Mormons, and to cooperative (and communal) ventures generally, made it easy for apostates who had made gifts to the church to disrupt the financial affairs of the system by demanding and securing the return of all their consecrated properties. (5) The converts were not faithful in making their initial and annual consecrations.[72]

Although all five of these factors have been recognized by Mormon writers, church leaders have consistently emphasized the last-named factor: selfishness, unfaithfulness, unrighteousness. In the revelation that counseled the suspension of the law, mention was made of "the transgressions of my people," who "have not learned to be obedient." They "do not impart of their substance, as becometh saints." Brigham Young, who was a member of the church during most of this early period, later explained that "persons would conceal from Joseph that they had any money; and, after they had spent or lost it all, would come to him and say, 'O how I love you, Brother Joseph!' "[73] On another occasion, many years after the system had been tried, George A. Smith said:

> The Lord endeavored to establish the order of Zion then, but while some considered it a privilege to consecrate their property to the Lord, others were covetous, and thought about looking after their own interests in preference to those of the Work of God.[74]

Since the plan provided that each steward voluntarily consecrate his annual surplus, the faithful gave much, the unfaithful little. A premium was placed on liberality and honesty. In the distribution of charity out of the surplus, some demanded much, others little, and there was not always correspondence between need and participation in the consecrated surpluses.

As a means of enforcing the plan according to the revealed standard, the rich were constantly exhorted to participate in this equalitarian plan.[75] Indeed, the rich who failed to participate would be damned:

> Wo unto you rich men, that will not give your substance to the poor, for your riches will canker your souls! and this shall be your lamentation in the day of visitation, and of judgment, and of indignation: The harvest is past, the summer is ended, and my soul is not saved!
> Therefore, if any man shall take of the abundance which I have made, and impart not his portion, according to the law of my gospel, unto the poor and the needy, he shall, with the wicked, lift up his eyes in hell, being in torment.[76]

At the same time, the unworthy poor were also exhorted not to take advantage of the plan:

> Wo unto you poor men, whose hearts are not broken, whose spirits are not contrite, and whose bellies are not satisfied, and whose hands are not stayed from laying hold upon other men's goods, whose eyes are full of greediness, who will not labor with their own hands![77]

That the plan must have been operating very imperfectly during the 1831-34 period is evident from the study of the revelations and correspondence of Joseph Smith during those years. J. Reuben Clark, Jr., who made such a study, concluded:

All of these communications, these callings to repentance, these reproofs against covetousness, light mindedness and the various other ills which were afflicting the brethren in Zion, indicate that Zion, as a whole, was not conducting itself in a way that the Lord could give unto them blessings. . . . It is perfectly clear from the kind of evils which it is indicated as having afflicted the brethren in Zion, that it would not be possible for such a group of Saints to live the law of consecration and the United Order as it had been laid down unto them.[78]

Joseph Smith apparently concluded after the Missouri failures that expansion and growth of his following and the building of an autonomous, powerful political base were his most pressing necessities. Turning his attention to these tasks, he sought to forestall any economic experimentation that might draw talent and energies away from his drive for rapid expansion of "the Lord's Kingdom." In counseling the faithful not to enter into communal economic ventures on their own, he placed himself in a position of apparent opposition to the principles that had recently held so high a place in his millennial vision. It would be wrong to conclude from this, however, that he had given up the Law of Consecration and Stewardship forever. He frequently couched his remonstrances against the communalistic stirrings of the Nauvoo Saints in terms that permitted a possible future renewal of the system. Brigham Young, who probably knew Joseph's mind as well as anyone, quite obviously hoped to effect within his lifetime a return to the ideal economic system announced in 1831. Apparently the command to live the "more perfect law of the Lord" was seen by Joseph Smith to be simply in abeyance until some future time when God should again speak on the matter.

CHAPTER 3

Becoming one:
Informal cooperation
after 1844

OSEPH SMITH'S economic system could have been realized only under favorable circumstances. A people driven as were the Latter-day Saints before the fury of their enemies, and ever uncertain of the duration of their sojourn in any area selected for settlement, must organize for immediate survival rather than for an idealized future. Nevertheless, group consciousness and group activity remained the foundation of Mormon achievement.

This chapter reviews several nineteenth-century cooperative undertakings of an informal or temporary nature that have been of importance in the establishment and preservation of Mormon group life and have served as steppingstones toward the more formal arrangements of the 1860s and 1870s. The examples given may be discussed under four headings: cooperation in migration, cooperation in settlement, cooperation in irrigation, and cooperative or group welfare.

Cooperation in Migration

In 1838 Governor Lilburn W. Boggs of Missouri issued his order to "exterminate" the Mormons, or drive them from the state. When it had become clear to the Mormons that further resistance would be futile, a covenant was entered into on motion of Brigham Young, president of the Council of the Twelve Apostles, to pool all material resources for the purpose of removing the Saints:

We, whose names are here-under written, do each for ourselves individually hereby covenant to stand by and assist each other, to the utmost of our abilities, in removing from this State in compliance with the authority of the State; and we do hereby acknowledge ourselves firmly bound to the extent of all our available property, to be disposed of by a committee who shall be appointed for that purpose, for providing means for the removing of the poor and destitute who shall be considered worthy, from this country, till there shall not be one left who desires to remove from the State with this proviso, that no individual shall be deprived of the disposal of his own property for the above purpose, or of having the control of it, or so much of it as shall be necessary for the removing of his own family, and to be entitled to the over-plus, after the work is effected; and furthermore, said committee shall give receipts for all property, and an account of the expenditure of the same.[1]

A committee of seven, later increased to eleven, was appointed to direct the removal and to provide for those not having means to care for themselves. An agent was appointed "to go down towards the Mississippi and establish deposits of corn for the brethren on the road and make contracts for ferriage."[2] The work of removal continued for several months, the means of those of substance becoming a common fund for the benefit of all, until the 12,000 members of the church had left Missouri and found refuge in neighboring states. The widespread suffering occasioned by this exodus was greatly reduced by the orderly manner in which it was conducted.

The exodus from Nauvoo seven years later was managed with similar spirit and similar arrangements. As before, there were many who unaided would have found it impossible to face the perils and hardships of removal. As it was, loss of life was heavy, but, again, joint action mitigated suffering and assured success. At a conference in the Nauvoo Temple October 6, 1845, Brigham Young proposed a covenant, "that we take all the Saints with us to the extent of our ability, that is, our influence and our property," which was accepted by all present at the conference. He prophesied that if the people would be faithful to the covenant, God would shower down means that it might be accomplished.

The wealth accumulated during the three or four years of peaceful industry at Nauvoo was largely sacrificed by conversion into portable form—wagons, cattle, food, and tools. Sales of real property were forced by the pressure of the state authority demanding the Saints' immediate departure. For example, a two-story brick house occupied only three months was exchanged for "two yoke of half-broken cattle and an old wagon."[3] No man was to regard his possessions as exclusively his own, and members who were disposed to act selfishly were warned they would be rejected. Losses caused by the haste of the Saints' forced departure made it necessary to postpone the pioneer journey to the Great Basin for a year.[4] Although the Twelve had departed from Nauvoo well outfitted for the long journey, intending to push through to a new site for permanent settlement during the summer of 1846, their provisions were soon exhausted by distribution to those in want.[5] So many were improperly equipped for travel that two Iowa settlements, Mt. Pisgah and Garden Grove, were established where, by cooperative efforts, the impoverished Saints might preserve themselves until they could be better outfitted for the long trek to the Great Basin.

Before they left Nauvoo, Mormon leaders adopted the organization that was followed by their emigrants year after year. A migrating company was divided into groups of ten families each, with a captain in charge; five groups of ten were led by a captain of fifty; and two such divisions were commanded by a captain of a hundred. Captains were responsible for the physical and material welfare of their groups. As a rule each family supplied its own equipment and provisions, but there was cooperation in hunting game, making camp, caring for livestock, gathering fuel, and numerous other camp duties. After colonies became established in the Salt Lake Valley and other western valleys, it became the practice to send back teams carrying food to meet the caravans and help them through the mountains. As many as five hundred teams were thus engaged in a single season.[6]

To assist members without means to migrate to Utah, the church worked out a plan of financial aid. Conceived in the fall of 1849, the Perpetual Emigrating Fund Company was given corporate form by the legislative assembly of the State of Deseret (the earliest name of Utah) in September 1850. The fund had four sources of income: voluntary contributions of church members, repayments from those assisted, interest on loans, and increments resulting from the sale of company property. Only the first two sources proved to be substantial. Nevertheless, the fund grew—on paper at least—to large proportions. Donations were received in grain, cattle, wearing apparel, jewelry, labor, cash, or anything convertible. The general assembly of the State of Deseret set aside Antelope and Stansbury islands in the Great Salt Lake as herd grounds for the company's stock. One of the earliest records shows that the amount subscribed in Deseret in 1849 equaled $5,857,[7] which was entrusted to Edward Hunter and expended in bringing poor Saints from Iowa in 1850 in fulfillment of the covenant made in the Nauvoo Temple in 1845. Contributions in the British Mission by July 1854 amounted to £6,832.[8] Scholars have not yet made a sufficiently detailed study to determine the total amount expended during the life of the fund, but it was placed by a contemporary observer in 1869 at five million dollars.[9] As the fund was turned over several times, the principal amount donated was, of course, much less than the total of advances.

The magnitude of the assistance given may be judged from the number of immigrants brought in by the fund. During the three years 1852, 1853, and 1854, the total Mormon emigration from the British Isles was 5,078. Of this number, 1,724 persons were carried at the expense of the fund at a cost of from ten to thirteen pounds apiece. In the following year 1,161 of a total of 4,647 traveled at the expense of the fund.[10] In addition, considerable assistance was given to Scandinavian and German immigrants. Gustive O. Larson concluded in his study that a majority of the 85,000 immigrants who came from Europe to the Great Basin received full assistance from the fund, but such estimates must remain tentative until recently available records have been subjected to careful examination.[11]

Under the plan of operation, donations were converted into cash and used by the agent in paying the expenses of the beneficiary from the point of departure to the Salt Lake Valley. All arrangements were made and paid for by agents of the company. Making every attempt to keep expenses at a minimum, agents under the management of the fund reduced the per capita cost from twenty British pounds to between ten and thirteen pounds.[12] The poverty of the beneficiaries constituted their chief claim to assistance. Those capable of financing their own passage were not expected to rely on the fund. Those shipped at fund expense were either designated by friends and relatives in the West who paid the passage money to the fund in Salt Lake City or they were chosen from among all applicants by the church agent in England. In consideration of the advance of expenses, the beneficiary signed an agreement to hold his time and labor subject to the appropriation of the company until the advance was repaid. This plan, however, was only partially effected; most able-bodied persons needed all they could earn to support their families in the New World, let alone repay the advances they had received.

The directors of the fund in Salt Lake City assisted the newly arrived immigrants in finding employment. Many were assigned to labor on enterprises of a public nature, such as the erection of buildings, the construction of the wall around Temple Square, and the building of a railroad to the rock quarries. Others worked for contractors engaged in the construction of the Union Pacific Railroad and turned over their surplus earnings to the fund.

Nevertheless, most of the beneficiaries of the plan were unable to repay their passage. By 1853 indebtedness to the fund was $56,000.[13] In 1880 the amount owed on principal account was $704,000, and accumulated interest at 10 percent equaled $900,000, making a total of $1,604,000. As that year was the fiftieth or Jubilee year of the church, its leaders followed the ancient Israelitish custom of canceling debts to clear the books and the consciences of thousands of debtors. On the recommendation of local bishops, worthy poor were thus relieved to the extent of one-half the book amount of the entire debt.[14] Most of the remainder was eventually lost. Accounts rendered three years before the company was finally ended, as a provision of the Edmunds-Tucker law in 1887, showed nominal assets of $417,968, almost entirely in uncollectable promissory notes.[15]

The failure of the fund as a business is not surprising. But whatever the bookkeeping status of the fund and those it assisted, the church's pledge to redeem the poor who had been driven from Nauvoo was fulfilled, and tens of thousands of others were brought from Europe to the Great Basin, where they could associate with those of their faith.

Cooperation in Settlement

In establishing settlements, whether permanent or temporary, the Mormons adopted cooperative procedures to economize labor. Though individualists in the ownership of land, they almost invariably fenced jointly. Just before the enforced exodus from Missouri, plans had been made for the enclosure of many sections of land by three different companies of Saints residing in Caldwell County.[16] Because of the ejection of the Mormons from that state, these plans were never realized, but a few years later a large number of Saints organized as the Big Field Association and enclosed a large tract six miles southeast of Nauvoo.[17]

The temporary settlements of Garden Grove and Mt. Pisgah, established during the Iowa crossing in 1846, sprang into being through cooperative labor. At Garden Grove one hundred men were assigned to make rails, ten to build fences, forty-eight to build houses, twelve to dig wells, and ten to build bridges. All others, except those required to herd cattle and to serve as camp guards, devoted themselves to clearing lands, plowing, and planting. Two farms, one of 390 and one of 325 acres, were quickly enclosed. At Mt. Pisgah a "Big Field" of about 1,400 acres was enclosed with a pole and rail fence on the east and north sides, the Grand River forming the boundaries on the west and south. Within the enclosure land was allotted according to the size of families, and rights were reserved for those to come later.[18]

In the Salt Lake Valley the companies of 1847 undertook to build twelve miles of fence to enclose more than five thousand acres of land selected for cultivation—the "Big Field." The first agricultural efforts were organized around the "tens" of the initial migration. To each ten and to each member of the ten was assigned as much land as could be successfully cared for with available manpower and equipment. The average was approximately ten acres to the man.[19] Though each man had his individual plot, he worked closely with his fellows in plowing, cultivating, and attempting to irrigate. In the spring of 1849 Salt Lake City was divided into nineteen wards, and each of these, under the direction of a bishop, became the administrative unit and nucleus of cooperative activity—getting out timber, building roads, establishing gristmills, and doing other necessary work. In subsequent years each city ward was enclosed by those residing within its boundaries, each man supplying materials and constructing fence in proportion to his acreage.

As with fencing and cultivation, so with the provision of shelter. The organization of labor at Garden Grove and the construction in 1847 of the Pioneer Fort in the Salt Lake Valley by the tens are two examples of providing cooperatively for the housing needs of the foundation colony. As additional companies of settlers arrived in the Salt Lake Valley in 1848 and succeeding years, the central fort or stockade was gradually broken up, and its inhabitants established themselves with the new arrivals on individual city lots scattered through the nineteen wards of the city and outlying settlements. Additional farm land was enclosed, and five- and ten-acre lots were apportioned to families by a drawing of lots. This principle of apportioning obligations according to anticipated benefits was subsequently applied to the digging of ditches and canals and other community efforts that could be thus divided. Quickly becoming an established step in the routine of settlement, cooperative work saved time in the early years when there was much to be done in clearing land, planting seed, and digging ditches; it also provided the most effective protection from hostile Indians. The log-cabin enclosure was simply a more substantial form of the circle of wagons in the nightly camp on the Great Plains, where for many long weeks the Saints had learned by hard necessity the advantages and the art of communal living.

In the colonies established in other western valleys, beginning in 1849, the cooperative foundational activities in Salt Lake City were imitated. Records of the settlement of Manti, in central Utah's Sanpete County, permit a preliminary judgment on how closely the Salt Lake City pattern was followed in other settlements. Late in October 1849, under the leadership of Isaac Morley, the hub colony for the opening of Sanpete Valley moved from Salt Lake City and entered upon Indian lands at the request of Ute Chief Walker (Walkara), who had gone to Salt Lake City in June to invite Brigham Young to send white men ("Mormonee") to teach his people the arts of agriculture and home building. Following exploration by Joseph Horne, W. W. Phelps, and others, who had reported favorably on the country, Morley was appointed to gather a company of about fifty families and open the region for settlement. About a month later he established camp on what is now Manti City Creek. Until 1851, when townsite surveys were complete and individual holdings subsequently given the settlers, they lived in dugouts and wagon boxes, holding out against heavy snows, severe cold, and a food crisis relieved by bringing in supplies on hand-drawn sleds.

The president of the Manti colony, always referred to as "Father" Morley, was an idealist in regard to "union and equality," themes that he often discussed before the Sabbath congregations. One of the first to move to Jackson County, Missouri, to try out the Prophet's system of stewardships, he had been living communally with a few families he had gathered around him at Kirtland when Joseph Smith first made his acquaintance.

Though he proved to be hesitant and ineffective as a colonizer, he was respected for his sincerity, humility, and spirituality. He followed Brigham Young's practice of allowing newcomers to enjoy the same blessings in regard to land and conveniences he himself had experienced.[20] Hence, in the apportionment of lands, water, and other resources, latecomers fared as well as those who preceded them until the community was "filled up."

In Mormon practice small holdings and intensive tillage was the rule; lands and other resources were not to be held for speculative purposes. Following the example of Salt Lake Valley pioneers two years earlier, the Manti group farmed a Big Field enclosure known later as the Old Field. Surveys were made of the townsite and fields in 1851 by Jesse W. Fox, and lots were increased in size from city lots of a little more than an acre to two and one-half, five, seven and one-half, ten, and twenty acres, with some even larger. The economy of fencing by joint enclosure commended itself to other groups as they joined the colony. Older settlers spoke of the various enclosures, in addition to the Old Field, as the Middle Field, Quarry Field (near the quarry), North Field, Cane Field, Danish Field (settled by Danes in 1853), and Brigham Field (a 282-acre tract at first set apart as a gift to Brigham Young).

Cooperation in Irrigation

The advance party of the Mormon pioneers was clearly concerned about the potential for irrigation as they reconnoitered the Salt Lake Valley on July 22, 1847. Orson Pratt recorded:

After going down into the valley about five miles, we turned our course to the north, down towards the Salt Lake. For three or four miles north we found the soil of a most excellent quality. Streams from the mountains and springs were very abundant, the water excellent, and generally with gravel bottoms. A great variety of green grass, and very luxuriant, covered the bottoms for miles where the soil was sufficiently damp, but in other places, although the soil was good, yet the grass had nearly dried up for want of moisture. We found the drier places swarming with very large crickets, about the size of a man's thumb.

This valley is surrounded with mountains, except on the north, the tops of some of the highest being covered with snow. Every one or two miles streams were emptying into it from the mountains on the east, many of which were sufficiently large to carry mills and other machinery. As we proceeded towards the Salt Lake the soil began to assume a more sterile appearance, being probably at some seasons of the year overflowed with water. . . .

[On the following day] the camp removed its position two miles to the north, where we camped near the bank of a beautiful creek of pure cold water. This stream is sufficiently large for mill sites and other machinery. Here we called the camp together, and it fell to my lot to offer up prayer and thanksgiving in behalf of our company, all of whom had been preserved from the Missouri river to this point; and, after dedicating ourselves and the land unto the Lord, and imploring His blessings upon our labors, we appointed various committees to attend to different branches of business preparatory to putting in crops, and in about two hours after our arrival we began to plow, and the same afternoon built a dam to irrigate the soil, which at the spot where we were plowing was exceedingly dry.[21]

As Wilford Woodruff arrived with the main body of the pioneer company, he observed that within two days of the establishment of the initial camp on July 24, 1847,

they had already broken five acres of land, and had begun planting potatoes in the valley of the Great Salt Lake. As soon as our encampment was formed, before taking my dinner, having half a bushel of potatoes, I went to the plowed field and planted them, hoping with the blessing of God, to save at least the seed for another year. The brethren had dammed up one of the creeks and dug a trench, and by night nearly the whole ground, which was found very dry, was irrigated.[22]

These earliest irrigations were merely a flooding of the land to facilitate planting. However, in dividing responsibilities among the earliest settlers, Brigham Young appointed Edson Whipple to "attend to the distribution of water over the plowed land," thus creating the office of watermaster, or "ditch-rider," an official who had become a familiar part of everyday life to farmers in regions of North America where irrigated agriculture is common.[23]

The problem of irrigation for the first season was soon made unimportant by killing frosts and then replaced by the larger one of preparing thousands of acres for winter and spring grains and for garden crops—crops which, once planted, had to be protected against Indians, cattle, crickets, and drought. Mormon leaders thought it probable but not certain that irrigation would be needed to mature winter wheat or crops planted early in the spring. When Brigham Young and the apostles, with a party of 108 persons, left Salt Lake City on August 26, 1847, to return to Winter Quarters, they left instructions that suggest how limited was the knowledge about the production of crops in the arid valley.

Should irrigation be found necessary, the City Creek will yield an abundance of water for that purpose, and it is wisdom that you should provide for any such contingency. We would therefore recommend that you prepare pools, vats, tubs, reservoirs, and ditches at the highest points of land in your field or fields that may be filled during the night and be drawn off to any point you may find necessary, through a tight and permanent gate prepared for that purpose when it shall have become sufficiently warm, so as not to check vegetation.[24]

In December of the same year apostle John Taylor, writing from the valley, mentioned the streams flowing out of the mountains as "valuable for the watering of stock, for water power, and the irrigation of land if necessary."[25]

Five months later, in May 1848, he reported to Brigham Young that there had been much rain, and grain crops were in promising condition. "It is the opinion of many," he said, "that wheat and early sown grain will not require irrigation."[26] But while he was writing, a withering siege of dry weather set in. The situation was compounded by failure of spring vegetable crops due to late frosts and by the relentless feeding of crickets upon the grain that was surviving the drought.[27] Many lost their crops that season but some harvests of grain and rye were secured without irrigation, and those who did irrigate raised double the quantity on the same amount of land. It had become clear that success in agriculture would require a considerable advancement in the arts of bringing water to the land.[28]

Nevertheless, the 1847 pioneers celebrated their harvest with a feast of thanksgiving on August 10. Wrote Parley P. Pratt:

We partook freely of a rich variety of bread, beef, butter, cheese, cakes, pastry, green corn, melons, and almost every variety of vegetable. Large sheaves of wheat, rye, barley, oats, and other productions were hoisted on poles for public exhibition, and there was prayer and thanksgiving, congratulations, songs, speeches, music, dancing, smiling faces and merry hearts. In short, it was a great day with the people of these valleys, and long to be remembered by those who had suffered and waited anxiously for the results of a first effort to redeem the interior deserts of America, and to make her hitherto unknown solitudes "blossom as the rose."[29]

More permanent arrangements for irrigation were made in 1849. The lands selected for cultivation lay on the level valley floor west of the bluffs and were crossed at intervals of two to three miles by the creeks flowing westward from the mountains into the Jordan River. Thus, it was a task of no great difficulty to divert the waters to the land through ditches from one to three miles in length of sufficient width and depth to carry the necessary volume of water. Water courses were made just as fences were built: the users of lands to be watered dug sections of ditch in proportion to acreage held. A few simple regulations touching division of the stream by volume or by hours of use were developed and adopted by common understanding. No large diversions were made in 1849 or the years immediately following; it was more feasible to water the lands from smaller channels or ditches, each under joint control of the users.

With established ecclesiastical wards serving as the units of administration in both spiritual and material affairs after the spring of 1849, the bishops became in practice watermasters, fence supervisors, and bridge builders. By instruction issued April 5, 1849, the bishops of Salt Lake wards were required to see that ditches were cut around their respective wards and that bridges were provided where ditches crossed open streets. Each ward of nine square blocks, that is, ninety acres total, was enclosed by a common fence as a means of saving time for cultivation.[30] Observers in the valley during the midsummer and fall of 1849 noted:

> The whole space for miles, excepting the streets and houses, was in a high state of cultivation. Fields of yellow wheat stood waiting for the harvest, and Indian corn, potatoes, oats, flax, and all kinds of garden vegetables were growing in profusion, and seemed about in the same state of forwardness as in the same latitude in the States. . . . All must cultivate the land or die; for the country was new and no cultivation but their own within a thousand miles. Everyone had his lot, and built on it, every one cultivated it and perhaps a small farm in the distance.[31]

> The system of irrigation is something new to our farmers, and it will require experience to enable them to cope with [irrigation as do] the Californians, native Indian races, or the inhabitants of the country of the Nile.[32]

The arrival of other companies of immigrants in the fall of 1849 and subsequent years occasioned further spreading of population and extended the area over which experiments with and development of irrigation could proceed in the Salt Lake and nearby valleys. At a public meeting held in the bowery on

An irrigation network near Mayfield, Utah—symbol of the
interdependence of individual and community in Mormon group life.
The cooperative nature of the various enterprises essential to settling the
Great Basin was made possible by a distinctly Mormon synthesis of the

inevitable tension between self and society. (Photo courtesy U.S.
Department of Agriculture—Agricultural, Stabilization, and
Conservation Service)

October 22, 1849, Brigham Young introduced a number of irrigation proposals, with the result that the group voted to bring water
from Mill Creek to the city, to divert Big Cottonwood Creek so as
to water the Big Field, to turn the waters of the Little Cottonwood
northward, and to take water out of the Jordan River.[33] Though
apparently some of the wards had not completed their irrigation
systems as planned in the preceding season, the ward system of
distributing water to the city lots was generally operative in 1850,
as described by Captain Howard Stansbury, U.S. Topographical
Engineers, who left Salt Lake August 27 after a year with the Mormons:

> Through the city itself [Salt Lake City] flows an unfailing stream of
> pure, sweet water, which, by an ingenious mode of irrigation, is made to
> traverse each side of every street, whence it is led into every garden-spot,
> spreading life, verdure, and beauty over what was heretofore a barren
> waste. . . . The irrigating canals, which flow before every door, furnish
> abundance of water for the nourishment of shade-trees. . . . The city was
> estimated to contain about eight thousand inhabitants and was divided
> into numerous wards, each at the time of our visit, enclosed by a
> substantial fence for the protection of the young crops; as time and
> leisure permit, these will be removed and each lot enclosed by itself as
> with us.[34]

Slowly, the early informal cooperative practices settled into
the institutional patterns generally followed throughout the rest of
the century. In Salt Lake City the residents of a ward became a
cooperating group to bring the water from the source of supply
and divide it among the inhabitants. The ward ditch was divided
at the boundary into branches from which each individual drew
his portion to his garden. The principle of ward responsibility
was recognized by an ordinance of Salt Lake City passed July 9,
1853, creating the office of city watermaster to distribute the
waters of City Creek, Red Butte, and Emigration canyons for irrigation, domestic, and other purposes, providing for assistant
watermasters in each bishop's ward, and making it the duty of the
inhabitants of the ward to construct and keep in repair dams,
gates, and sluiceways.[35] The principle of equality was carefully
applied, the water being measured out to each lot—eight to the
block—in turn.

This rigid adherence to equality had its defects, as Brigham
Young pointed out a few years later when the owner of a city lot
was permitted to use the stream only two hours a week and often

only during the night. An intensively farmed lot received no more water than one indifferently cultivated.[36] He favored storage reservoirs, daytime watering, and supply based on need, all of which Salt Lake City adopted only when ditches gave way to pipes and headgates to meter boxes.

As the Salt Lake City population grew, the insufficiency of water to irrigate all available land required a definition of established rights, which led to acceptance of the principle of priority. Departing from earlier practice, ecclesiastical and later civil authority began a policy of protecting an early appropriator against the encroachments of a later one. Early in February 1852, complaint was made to Brigham Young that a Brother Ward who had settled with sixteen families on Dry Creek (now Alpine) near the mountain represented a threat to the water supply of the earlier settlement (now Lehi) lower down the creek.[37] The answer of President Young, also governor of the Territory, is found in an act of the legislature granting to the inhabitants of Dry Creek the right to use but not to exceed one-third of the waters of American Creek. A further answer is found in an act of the same legislative session, approved March 3, which provides that a person may not survey land for the purpose of cultivation, "where to irrigate it would rob other previously cultivated lands of the needful portion of water."[38] No objection could be raised, of course, to the use of excess flow beyond the established needs of primary users. Recognizing the principle of secondary rights, the Salt Lake County Court granted a petition of fifty-two individuals for the use of water from the sect made to water the five-acre lots south of Salt Lake City, whenever it was not wanted for irrigation by original users.[39]

Adjudication of disputes over water rights was commonly done through ecclesiastical machinery. Within the wards, a decision by the bishop was usually final. If further authority were desired, the stake president, an apostle, or a member of the First Presidency could be appealed to. If yet more formal consideration was advisable, the dispute was discussed in the bishop's court or before the stake high council. In 1855, for example, a dispute over water in the Taylorsville settlement (southwest of Salt Lake City) was brought before the county court; the court declined jurisdiction and advised the disputants to take the matter before the church high council.[40] Disputes were common enough and multiplied with the increase of population. In years of scanty rainfall the allocation of water, upon which the fortunes and very lives of families depended, became a matter of intense concern.

It was commonly assumed that Mormons could pass through such emergencies with less difficulty than non-Mormons, as the following extract from a letter written in a year of acute water shortage illustrates:

City Creek is distributed to about the finest thread. Gentiles could not possibly live here, for they would kill each other with their hoes, and as it is, Mormons have protracted civil discussions day and night at the head of the water ditches.[41]

Though such statements tend to gloss over the fact that acrimonious disputes over water rights did break out at times among Latter-day Saints, the Mormon failure to make distinctions between secular and religious affairs encouraged a degree of cooperation not readily obtained in communities where a common religious commitment was less pronounced. Mormon leaders often made a secular pursuit, such as the settling of a new area, a religious obligation. Many Mormons cheerfully obeyed the advice of church leaders even when it was clearly not in their own material interest to do so. Given this tendency to see compliance with the advice of church authorities as a moral obligation, whether the advice touched upon religious or secular concerns, it is not surprising that the frequency and intensity of disputes over water were kept at a relatively low level. A local bishop was considered to be a mouthpiece of God in matters involving members of his congregation. A communicant who ignored his advice in the use of water risked an ostracism far more enduring and formidable than just the momentary loss of the good will of members of his ward community. The advice of leaders and the common practice of church members over the first few decades is summed up in a few words of counsel given to the Mormons of Sanpete Stake in 1878: "In water disputes, let the Priesthood rule."[42]

A weakness in the practice of settling disputes by church decree was the absence of power to draw upon the sanctions of common law in compelling acceptance of the terms laid down. The degree of compliance to a bishop's decision was ultimately a function of faith of the parties involved. At first this was not a serious problem, but as time went on it became clearly evident that in many cases finality could be attained only in decisions made and enforced by the civil power. Decrees made in the present century by the district courts, however, are often based upon and carry into effect the terms of settlement made long before by ecclesiastical tribunals.

It has been said that the Mormon pioneers were merely actuated by the fundamental law of self-preservation in developing their system of water usage.[43] Of northern-European descent and familiar with the riparian-rights doctrine prevalent in humid regions, they might have been disposed to accept that doctrine in their new environment, but to do so would have meant complete defeat of their social and religious objectives. According to the law of riparian rights, "each owner of land bordering upon a stream or through which a brook flows is protected against any change in the course or behavior of the stream, except from natural causes; and he in turn is prohibited from bringing about any modification which may affect other landowners below or above."[44] That any individual should have or should acquire rights that would conflict with the best interests of the group was repugnant to Mormon philosophy. Strongly impressed with the doctrine that man is only a steward over his material possessions, Mormons applied the principle of beneficial use to land and water alike. No man was to take more land than he could till, nor was he to claim more water than his reasonable needs required. Moreover, church leaders attempted to apply the same principles in the use of timber, grazing lands, and other natural resources in limited supply. Cooperating for the common good, the Mormon people, despite disappointments and failures, achieved irrigation successes that have been both significant and lasting.[45]

Cooperative or Group Welfare

Many of the 1,800 Saints who spent the first winter in the Salt Lake Valley soon found themselves short of food supplies. Early in the spring of 1848 Bishops Tarleton Lewis and Edward Hunter arranged for exchanges and donations to provide for all as far as the rapidly diminishing supplies would permit.[46] In 1850 a farm was located for the poor and sixteen houses were provided. In the famine year of 1856 it was suggested that the poor be permitted to glean the fields as in the days of Boaz, and all who possessed bread grains restricted their daily rations to provide more for distribution to others.[47] Brigham Young states that an average of 600 were fed through the central tithing office for the four years, 1851 through 1854; Heber C. Kimball is reported to have fed about 100 beyond his own extensive household.[48]

Most relief programs were planned and administered by the bishops of the various wards. William Hepworth Dixon, editor of the prestigious British magazine *The Athenaeum*, spent several days among the Mormons and left a vivid account of the bishops' role in administering relief:

The unpaid functions of a bishop are extremely numerous; for a Mormon prelate has to look, not merely to the spiritual welfare of his flock, but to their worldly interest and well-being; to see that their farms are cultivated, their houses clean, their children taught, their cattle lodged. Last Sunday, after service at the Tabernacle, Brigham Young sent for us to the raised dais on which he and the dignitaries had been seated, to see a private meeting of the bishops, and to hear what kind of work these reverend fathers had met to do. . . .

The old men gathered in a ring; and Edward Hunter, their presiding bishop, questioned each and all as to the work going on in his ward, the building, painting, draining, gardening; also as to what this man needed, and that man needed, in the way of help. An emigrant train had just come in, and the bishops had to put six hundred persons in the way of growing their cabbages and building their homes. One bishop said he could take five bricklayers, another two carpenters, a third a tinman, a fourth seven or eight farm servants, and so on through the whole bench. In a few minutes I saw that two hundred of these poor emigrants had been placed in the way of earning their daily bread. "This," said Young, with a sly little smile, "is one of the labours of our bishops."[49]

As they arrived in Utah, immigrant poor were distributed among the various wards and settlements, so that no bishop would have an undue burden of responsibility in affording necessary care. Dixon described the operation of the system as follows:

A special fund is raised for the relief of necessitous Saints; and [Brigham] Young himself, the servant of all, discharges in person the troublesome duties of this trust. I went with Bishop Hunter, a good and merry old man, full of work and humour, to the emigrants' corral, to see the rank and file of the new English arrivals; six hundred people from the Welsh hills and from the Midland shires; men, women, and children; all poor and uncomely, weary, dirty, freckled with the sun, scorbutic from privation; when I was struck by the tender tones of his voice, the wisdom of his counsel, the fatherly solicitude of his manner in dealing with these poor people. Some of the women were ill and querulous; they wanted butter, they wanted tea; they wanted many things not to be got in the corral. Hunter sent for a doctor from the city, and gave orders for tea and butter on the Tithing office. Never shall I forget the yearning thankfulness of expression which beamed from some of these sufferers' eyes. The poor creatures felt that in this aged bishop they had found a wise and watchful friend.[50]

Since overland transportation was limited to summer months, each fall brought an incoming tide of immigrants for whom food and shelter had to be provided. Covered wagons brought by the immigrants could be readily renovated to serve as temporary shelters, but food had to be saved locally each season to provide for those whose time of arrival did not permit them to participate in food-producing labors. Church leaders were faced with the problem of accumulating and maintaining a surplus and finding an equitable means of distributing it. Tithing payments in foodstuffs and staple commodities from established church members provided the bulk of the supply.

The strong bias of Brigham Young in favor of work relief over direct relief dictated the underlying philosophy governing distribution of the surplus to the poor. He told a Utah audience in 1867:

My experience has taught me and it has become a principle with me, that it is never any benefit to give, out and out, to man or woman, money, food, clothing, or anything else, if they are able-bodied and can work and earn what they need, when there is anything on the earth for them to do. This is my principle, and I try to act upon it. To pursue a contrary course would ruin any community in the world and make them idlers.[51]

Accordingly, wherever possible, work on public projects was found for the poor in exchange for which they were given sustenance from church storehouses.

One of the earliest such public works projects in Salt Lake City was the building of the Council House, an assembly hall for public and church gatherings, begun in February 1849. At the same time, work was begun on a bathhouse at the Salt Lake Warm Springs and on a storehouse and a granary. A bowery on Temple Square served for public gatherings for two or three years until the completion of the first tabernacle in 1851. In that year workers began enclosing the temple block, a project requiring several years, and fencing the church farm and the tithing pasture. An account of the disposition of church funds up to the spring of 1852, reported at the semiannual general conference of the church, affords a glimpse at public works completed and in progress:[52]

The report of the financial affairs of the Church, by the
Trustee in Trust, showed that, from the commencement of
tithing in the Valley, on the 6th of November, 1848, to March
27th, 1852, there had been received at the office, on tithing,
mostly in property valued at $244,747
Received in loans, and from other sources 145,514

Total $390,261

Expended, during the same time, on Council-house, storehouse, stores rented, old bowery, blacksmith's, carpenter's,
and paint shops, Church-barn, Tabernacle, Bath house,
trench round Temple lot, railroad, farms, city lots, paper
factory, pottery, water ditches, the poor, houses for Elders on
missions, superintendents, clerks, public labour, grain, hay,
provisions, assisting emigrants, cattle lost by Indians and
wolves, stationery, etc. 353,766

$ 36,495

Now on hand in grain, vegetables, merchandize, cut stone,
lumber, shingles, printing press, obligations, horses, mules,
and stock of various kinds .... $ 74,512

Other major undertakings during the fifties and begun sub-sequent to the above report were the beet sugar factory in southeast Salt Lake City, the Social Hall, the Salt Lake Temple, the Endowment House (a building temporarily housing temple ceremonies), the Church Historian's House, and the "Spanish" wall around the city. In addition to the employment provided by these and similar construction projects, the church maintained several shops where those skilled in various trades were steadily employed. All the public works were directed by a general superintendent, Daniel H. Wells, a member of the First Presidency.[53]

The progress of public works and the amount of labor pro-vided were limited by the volume of church income through tithes and other offerings. The theoretical tenth fluctuated with good and bad times and with the ebb and flow of faith. In 1852 the superintendent of public works discontinued an advertise-ment in the *Deseret News* offering cash for lumber and shingles,

stating that the public works were threatened with suspension unless those able to do so were more prompt and liberal in supplying all kinds of building materials and clothing and food for the
public hands.[54] There was a serious shortage of tithing funds in
1855, a year of crop failure through drought, and in the famine
year that followed public works were temporarily suspended. Yet,
whenever possible, public works were continued as a recognized
means of providing employment for the Mormon poor.

It was inevitable, in such an effort, that church leaders could
not always satisfy the public's estimation of what constituted
needed projects of lasting value. Criticized for the make-work nature of some public works projects in the early 1860s, Brigham
Young responded with a rebuke that, hyperbole forgiven, set a
distinctly modern standard of societal priorities in the use of
public funds.

Some have wished me to explain why we built an adobie wall
around this city. Are there any Saints who stumble at such things? Oh,
slow of heart to understand and believe. I build walls, dig ditches, make
bridges, and do a great amount and variety of labour that is of but little
consequence only to provide ways and means for sustaining and
preserving the destitute. I annually expand hundreds and thousands of
dollars almost solely to furnish employment to those in want of labour.
Why? I have potatoes, flour, beef, and other articles of food, which I wish
my brethren to have; and it is better for them to labour for those articles,
so far as they are able and have opportunity, than to have them given to
them. They work, and I deal out provisions, often when the work does
not profit me.[56]

A distinctive aspect of nineteenth-century life in the Great
Basin that reinforced the community pattern of cooperation was
the practice of plural marriage. Mormons have been reticent to
discuss the difficulties encountered in developing and maintaining harmonious family relationships within the many polygamous
families in early Utah. Such families strove to perfect the art of
cooperation, both in organizing the labor needed to sustain the
household and in sharing the collective product of household
endeavors. Only in recent years have scholars given attention to
the innovations in social and economic relationships that the institution of polygamy required. The creation of large family units
permitted greater individual specialization among family
members and a higher degree of family self-sufficiency. Since

land was usually allotted on the basis of families—i.e., one lot and farming acreage for each wife and her children—plurality also created larger units of operation and greater play for managerial skill. It also resulted in greater equality in levels of living, since most plural households provided homes for the poor and unfortunate.[57]

A final phase of informal cooperation was prompted by the policy of the church to foster industries designed to support struggling communities. This is not the place to detail this activity, which involved early attempts to produce sugar, iron, leather, textiles, paper, and the basic materials of the building trades.[58] Though favoring private enterprise as a general policy, the church was for several decades the chief source of the capital required to meet the heavy expense of experimental manufactures and was liberal in offering advice as to where private capital could be best invested to secure the greatest collective benefit. The effort to combine capital and labor in the development of industries essential to a self-sufficient regional commonwealth forms the background of the social and economic experiments described in the chapters that follow.

CHAPTER 4

Property on the Altar:
The consecration movement
of the 1850s

ARLY STUDENTS of Mormon communitarian experiments were struck by the long interval between failure of the Missouri experience and the revival of such experiments in Utah in the 1870s. Hamilton Gardner was typical in pointing out that "nothing is more remarkable than the fact that during this time the Mormons found no time in their activities for the United Order."[1] More recently, however, attention has been called to the fact that Brigham Young in the 1850s did attempt to secure a general consecration to the church of all property of the members—an effort that clearly sought to revive the Law of Consecration and Stewardship established earlier under Joseph Smith. Curiously, this movement, eliciting scores of sermons, causing the recording of hundreds (perhaps thousands) of deeds, and occupying the attention of the Great Basin Mormons for several years, has escaped the notice of many historians.

T.B.H. Stenhouse, one writer who did notice the consecration movement, depicted it as a machination of Brigham Young designed to aggrandize himself at the expense of his credulous followers. Stenhouse quoted a deed executed by Jesse W. Fox, as follows:[2]

BE IT KNOWN BY THESE PRESENTS, That I Jesse W. Fox, of Great Salt Lake City, the county of Great Salt Lake, and territory of Utah, for and in consideration of *the sum of one hundred ($100) dollars and* the good-will which I have to the Church of Jesus Christ of Latter-day Saints, give and convey unto Brigham Young, Trustee in Trust for said Church, his successor in office and assigns, all my claim to and ownership of the following-described property, to wit:

One house and lot being lot 6, block 60, Plat C, Great Salt Lake
    City, value of said house and lot $1000
One city lot, as platted in plat E, being lot 2, block 6, value 100
East half of lot 1, block 12, 5-acre, plat A 50

Lot 1, block 14, Jordan plat, containing nine acres value	75
Two cows, $50; two calves, $15	65
One mare, $100; one colt, $50	150
One watch, $20; one clock, $12	32
Clothing, $300; beds and bedding, $125	425
One stove, $20; household furniture, $210	230
Total	$2127

Together with all the rights, privileges and appurtenances thereunto belonging or appertaining. I also covenant and agree that I am the lawful claimant and owner of said property and will warrant and forever defend the same unto the said Trustee in Trust, his successors in office and assigns, against the claims of my heirs, assigns, or any person whomsoever.

(Signed)   Jesse W. Fox

Witnesses:
Henry McEwan
John M. Bollwinkel

Territory of Utah
County of Great Salt Lake

I, E. Smith, Judge of the Probate Court for said county, certify that the signer of the above transfer, personally known to me appeared this second day of April A. D. 1857, and acknowledged that he, of his own choice, executed the foregoing transfer.

E. Smith
Notary Public

The words in italics were added by Stenhouse to give the document the appearance of conformity to ordinary legal conveyances of title. In not one of hundreds of deeds of the period 1855-65, known in the records as church deeds or deeds of consecration, was there evidence of monetary consideration in exchange for conveyance of property.

Although it may never be known exactly how many deeds were recorded, it is certain that the movement was churchwide. Books of record containing official copies of these deeds have been found in Box Elder, Weber, Tooele, Utah, Sanpete, Summit, and Millard counties in Utah. Record books for Cache, Davis, Salt Lake, Juab, Beaver, Iron, and Washington counties are missing, but there is positive proof that deeds were recorded in all these counties except Cache and Beaver, where it is nevertheless presumed that deeds were made by residents. It appears to have been a rule that recorded deeds were sent to the office of the Trustee-in-Trust of the Church. There are 363 deeds carrying numbers and dates of recording and signatures of several county recorders on file in the Church Archives and very possibly more will be found as classification of materials in the archives progresses.

Brigham Young's consecration deed is found in Book A of Deeds, Pioneer Records, Salt Lake County Recorder's Office, p. 249. No other deed of this kind appears in the same record book, but there are thirty-two references to such deeds in other recorded transfers. For example, Wilford Woodruff, in transferring a piece of land to John P. Smith, September 17, 1857, includes the following words, "which was consecrated to the Trustee-in-Trust July 9, 1856," thus establishing the fact that he had executed a deed of consecration to the church.[3]

The exact number of deeds recorded for counties where books of record are still preserved has been easily determined. And by finding the highest serial number of existing deeds for counties such as Salt Lake, where official record books are missing, at least the minimum number of deeds presented for record may be ascertained.

Table I presents the available data and shows the extent of participation in the making of deeds in comparison with the estimated number of heads of families. The deeds are uniformly made on printed forms, worded exactly as the Fox deed reproduced above with the omission of words in italics. The maker had only to fill in name and schedule, sign in the presence of two or three witnesses, and acknowledge before a notary.

An examination of the schedules shows that it was ordinarily the intent of the maker to transfer title to all his possessions, including personal property such as firearms, tools, and bedding. Frederick Rowlett of Brigham City made one particularly unusual contribution:

One five (5) acre lot of farming land bought of William
    Davis in the Big Field, Box Elder Survey, not numbered .... $ 50.00
One city lot in Brigham City and improvements 120.00
Household furniture and kitchen furniture, including bedding
    and clothing of all kinds, cooking and farming apparatus
    and utensils 200.00
Also my daughter, Fanny Charlott Rowlett, born in Geneva,
    Switzerland, October 26, 1844 A.D.   _____
                                  Total $370.00

The shortest schedule discovered is that of Soren Andersen of Manti:

Household furniture	$20.00
Mechanical tools	10.00
One gun	3.00
One sword	3.00
	$36.00

Table I

DEEDS OF CONSECRATION
BY COUNTIES AND YEARS OF RECORDING
Prepared by Feramorz Y. Fox

County	Estimated Population 1858(a)	Estimated No. of Families 1858	No. of Deeds Recorded 1855-1858
Cache	2,500	500	140(b)
Box Elder	1,300	260	34(c)
Weber	3,300	660	226(c)
Davis	2,700	540	200(d)
Salt Lake	10,700	2,140	628(e)
Tooele	900	180	99(f)
Juab	600	120	40(g)
Utah	7,200	1,440	865(c)
Summit	-	-	- (h)
Millard	600	120	83(c)
Sanpete	3,200	640	197(c)
Beaver	600	120	40(i)
Iron	900	180	100(j)
Washington	500	100	30(k)
TOTAL	35,000	7,000	2,682

(a) Based upon U.S. Census of 1850 and 1860 and an enumeration by ecclesiastical wards, October 1853.

(b) No data available. The figure given is a guess. Cache County was not organized until April 4, 1857.

(c) Exact. Taken from records in office of the County Recorder.

(d) Estimated. Thirty-eight original deeds are on file in the Church Archives, mostly in surnames beginning with B.

(e) Minimum as indicated by the highest serial number of existing deeds.

(f) The total of 100 for Tooele County includes two deeds recorded in 1862. No recording of deeds of consecration has been found for the years 1859, 1860, 1861.

(g) Estimated. Eight deeds are on file in the Church Archives.

(h) No data available. Though created in 1854, Summit County remained unorganized until 1861.

(i) Estimated. The County Clerk of Beaver County states that the Recorder's office was first opened December 8, 1857.

(j) Estimated. Seventeen original deeds are on file in the Church Archives.

(k) Estimated. Four original deeds are on file in the Church Archives.

The longest schedule is that of Brigham Young (Appendix II) totaling $199,625, dated April 11, 1855. In all probability President Young's schedule as given in his deed of consecration includes a complete inventory of his possessions, for on April 7, 1855, in the Salt Lake Tabernacle, Orson Pratt stated that on the same day President Young had expressed his intention of consecrating "all that he has unto the Church."[4]

Practice was not uniform in the transfer of property by a person owning land in more than one county. President Young's deed, recorded in Salt Lake County, includes a house and farm at Manti, while Ezra T. Benson made separate deeds for the transfer of title to his properties in Tooele and Salt Lake counties respectively. Charles C. Rich, who owned property in both Davis and Salt Lake counties, also made separate deeds.

White Mormon settlers were not the only ones to embrace the Order of Stewardships. Soon after the settlement of Manti, Mormonism was preached to Indians in Sanpete County; and the tribal chieftain, Aropeen (Arropine, Arapeen), and scores of his followers were baptized and confirmed as members of the church. Following the example of his white brethren, Aropeen executed and recorded his deed of consecration using the regular form provided for the purpose. As Indians did not recognize individual ownership of lands, Aropeen's deed conveyed all the tribal claims, as well as his personal belongings. This interesting document, not a treaty as some have supposed, is presented in full to show its identity in form with all other deeds of consecration:

BE IT KNOWN BY THESE PRESENTS that I, Siegnerouch (Arropine), of Manti City, in the County of Sanpete and territory of Utah, for and in consideration of the good will which I have to the Church of Jesus Christ of Latter-day Saints, give and convey unto Brigham Young, Trustee in Trust for said Church, his successors in office and assigns, all my claim to and ownership of the following described property, to-wit:—

The portion of land and country known as Sanpete County

together with all timber and material on the same	$155,000.00
Ten horses $500, 4 cows $120, total	620.00
One bull $40, 1 ox $50, 1 calf $5, total	95.00
Two guns $40, farming tools $10, total	50.00
	$155,765.00

Together with all the rights, privileges and appurtenances thereunto belonging or appertaining. I also covenant and agree that I am the lawful claimant and owner of said property and will warrant and forever defend the same unto the said Trustee in Trust, his successors in office and assigns against the claims of my heirs, assigns or any person whomsoever.

His
Siegnerouch (Arropine)   X
Mark

Then follow names and witnesses and notarized acknowledgment.

Although the earliest located deed was recorded in Millard County January 1, 1855, the movement began almost a year earlier. The first public announcement was made in the general conference of the LDS Church in April 1854. In his remarks on April 8, 1854, President Young referred to the principle of consecration and emphasized the importance of union in everyday affairs. On the following day the theme of consecration was further discussed by apostle Orson Hyde.[5] It was also the subject of bishops' meetings in April. Bishop Joseph L. Heywood of the Salt Lake City Seventeenth Ward was especially pleased with the proposed application of the principle of consecration, "which would put the presiding bishop in his true position and so also the bishops of the wards."[6] Presiding Bishop Edward Hunter reminded the bishops that under the stewardship system each man would have as much to manage as he was able to take care of, and wished that he could give to some double what they already had. Bishop Joseph Harker reported that the brethren of the West Jordan Ward were favorable to the law of consecration.

After the adjournment of the conference, the First Presidency, as was customary, issued a statement in the form of an epistle to the world:[7]

In union there is strength; but how can a people become united while their interests are diversified. How can they become united in spiritual matters, and see eye to eye, which they can only partly understand, until they become united in regard to temporal things, which they do comprehend? It was given in a revelation unto brother Joseph Smith, in the early days of the Church, that all the Saints should consecrate their substance unto the Church, and receive their inheritances at the hands of Bishop [Edward] Partridge, who was then officiating in that office. . . .
During the conference the teachings turned upon this subject [consecration] and the doctrine of being united in the things which could be understood by all, and concentrating our interests in things in which

we could see eye to eye was considered; being the first step towards effecting that union so desirable to be accomplished; which would give us that power to put down iniquity and drive every evil and pernicious influence from our midst. This principle manifested itself to the understanding of the brethren in all its plainness, beauty, and simplicity. The people seemed to feel a strong desire to comply with every commandment and requirement that had been given, and appeared to feel as though now there were no obstacles to a full and frank compliance with the law of consecration as first given to Brother Joseph [Smith].

The sequel thus far proves their sincerity in this thing; for they flock by hundreds and thousands to give in their names, devoting and deeding all and everything which they possess, unto the Church, receiving their inheritances, and so much of their property as is needful for them from the hands of the Bishop.

In view of the fact that no deed of record has been found with a date earlier than that of January 1, 1855, it is difficult to understand this reference to deeds "by the hundreds and thousands" nine months earlier. However, a clue may be found in the Twelfth General Epistle issued in April 1855, which stated that "the consecrations of the Saints have been delayed for a time in order to obtain the form of a deed which should be legal in accordance with the laws of the Territory. This has now been accomplished and many are deeding their property to the Church."[8] Another explanation might be found in the statements of James H. Martineau of Parowan, who reports that toward the end of April 1854, Elder T. D. Brown came from Salt Lake City to teach the principle of consecration and that he (Martineau) was appointed to make out the deeds. Elsewhere he reports that he was so appointed in May 1855, subsequent to the date of the Twelfth General Epistle referring to the legal form of deed.[9] The deeds were probably drawn during the year 1854, perhaps without regard to uniformity of wording or arrangement of subject matter. If presented at all to the bishop or other agent of the church, they were withheld from record and finally exchanged for deeds drawn in proper form. All of the deeds were conveyed to Brigham Young, Trustee-in-Trust, and not to Edward Hunter, Presiding Bishop of the Church, thereby departing from the letter of the revelations and from the practice in Jackson County, Missouri, twenty years earlier.

Since none of the property described in the schedules was ever actually transferred, it has been questioned why the deeds were made at all, and why in 1855-65 rather than at some other time. Mormon history and theology hold the answers. The Mormons who colonized Utah were largely those who had been thwarted in Missouri and expelled from Illinois, and they carried with them the conviction that they must, to please God, observe his commandments as revealed through the Prophet, although not all were in complete agreement on the meaning of the Prophet's words. The most vigorous and scholarly exponent of Joseph Smith's ideas was Orson Pratt, whose sermon on the principles of consecration, printed in July 1854, began with an exhortation to the Saints from a revelation Joseph Smith had received early in 1841. "Be one; and if ye are not one, ye are not mine." Temporal as well as spiritual unitedness were commanded in this revelation, Pratt maintained, pointing out examples in the Book of Mormon as well as in Acts where the uniting of temporal assets was a distinguishing practice of the earliest Christians. Pratt reminded the Saints of their failure to live the Law of Consecration and Stewardship in Missouri, with the result that God had put them under "preparatory laws given because of the hardness of our hearts, and the blindness of our minds, and our covetousness." This did not end the matter, however, for "nothing is more certain," Pratt asserted, "than that the Saints must eventually become perfect enough to consent to the great principles of equality in regard to property." Temporal equality was not to be introduced by a division of property, but

by a *union* of property. Let all the property of the Church be united instead of divided: and then let each person in the Church possess the whole; and let this joint possession be under strict and impartial laws; and let each individual and family have their stewardship; some in one branch of business and some in another; some having more capital under their charge and some less, according to the nature of their callings and business; and let each one give an account of his stewardship to those whom God has appointed as judges in Israel; and let each family receive a sufficient portion of the avails of their stewardship to supply their proper wants and necessities, according to the magnitude of the joint fund, and the amount of population to be supplied from it.[10]

Pratt thus refreshed the Saints' memory of the three steps necessary to enter the Law of Consecration and Stewardship as practiced under Joseph Smith: first, the transfer of all the property of the member to an agent of the church; second, the allotment of a stewardship to the member by the bishop; third, the periodic transfer to the bishop of the surpluses realized from the operation of the stewardship. The consecration of properties was the first step in a renewed attempt to realize such a system, and there is reason to believe that President Young in 1854 planned to establish the system in its entirety. The collapse of the program in Jackson County in 1833 had been followed by futile attempts to repossess Zion both by a show of force and by appeals to government. There was insufficient stability during the Clay County, Caldwell County, and Nauvoo periods to warrant renewal of the experiment. For two years after the murder of Joseph Smith, Brigham Young and the apostles had to contend with dissension from within the church and bitter opposition from without, leading eventually to the expulsion of the Mormons from Illinois. Compelling circumstances favored the maintenance of a spirit of close cooperation during the migration to the Great Basin and the first two or three years of settlement. The allotment of land was controlled by church leaders; holdings were small; differences in wealth were insignificant. The earliest settlers gave generously of their labor and products to provide public improvements, to support immigration, and to help establish the poor.

Until after 1850, in other words, there was little reason except in theory for a system of consecration. By that time the California gold rush had revealed the worldliness of many of the Saints. Although Brigham Young held most of the faithful by appeals to their good sense and their belief in the destiny of the church, some sold or traded their holdings and joined the caravans headed for Eldorado. Believing that consecration of properties might hold more of the wavering ones in check, he admonished the settlers at Parowan:

> If the people had done their duty and consecrated all their property to the Church of Jesus Christ of Latter-day Saints, they could not have gone away and lost their souls. . . . I want to have you consecrate your property if you wish it, if not, do as you please about it. If any man will say, "I am going to apostatize," I will advise him to consecrate all he has that he might be kept with the Saints and saved, so that if you are tempted to go away, you may feel it best to stay where your treasure is.[11]

On the heels of the gold rush appeared another threat to the cooperative commonwealth that church leaders were striving to establish: non-Mormon merchants from the Midwest had brought alluring stocks of goods for which some Latter-day Saints were willing to part with their cash or to exchange their staples at unfavorable prices. Counter to the church plan of building a self-sufficient economy, the profits of the merchants were a measure of the impoverishment of the Saints; the amounts paid for imported goods limited the growth of home industries. Already a matter of concern in 1852, this issue grew in magnitude as time went on, leading to important countermoves by church leaders. The consecration of one's property to the church signified its possessor's willingness to yield control over its use to the authority of church officials.

A third influence that may have had a bearing on the revival of the principle of consecration was the activity of apostates who by 1852-53 had become a source of annoyance to the Mormon establishment. The dissenting group denounced Brigham Young and other church leaders from the street corners as the Saints passed to their homes from services in the Tabernacle, and were excoriated in turn from the pulpit. Following an emphatic warning to the apostates by President Young, Parley P. Pratt expressed his own feelings in the following words:

> In all the general persecutions, . . . I do not recollect of a single instance, that the general storm was not brought about by men from among ourselves, professing the name, membership, and Priesthood of the Latter-day Saints, traitors to the cause that they professed to believe. This was the direct means of the suffering, and the breaking up, of the community in Kirtland; of the breaking up of the community in, and the expulsion of them from, Missouri. It was the direct means of this last persecution which led to the martyrdom of the Prophet [Joseph Smith] and the . . . plundering of millions, the burning of our Temple, and our migration to this country. We came here for peace. . . . Sooner than be subjected to a repetition of these wrongs, I, *for one,* would rather march out today and be shot down. . . . People have the privilege of apostatizing from this Church. . . . But they have not the privilege to disturb the peace, nor to endanger life or liberty. . . . [12]

If any of the Saints were on the verge of being led astray by the attacks of apostates, the call to consecrate their property was at once a challenge to self-examination and a pointed test of faith.

The consecration movement offered a means of checking the undesirable effects of the gold rush, a growing gentile influence, and apostate criticisms of church leaders. But it was not entirely defensive in conception, offering a means of achieving bold positive objectives of the church leaders as well. With imaginations

Deseret Store and Tithing Office, 1861. These buildings were the nexus of early Utah's economy, serving as a warehouse and distribution center for foodstuffs and other commodities donated to the Church as tithes and offerings. (Photo by Charles W. Carter, Church Archives)

stirred by the prodigious material achievements of the first few years and by the contemplation of vast stretches of unappropriated lands capable of sustaining an immense population, the leaders drew plans on a broad scale. Until 1861 the area of Utah Territory was nearly three times that of the present state of Utah. To possess and people this inland empire was a challenge to the brain and brawn of every man, woman, and child in the church, whether already settled in the valleys of the mountains or awaiting the opportunity to migrate from the various centers of missionary activity where they had cast their lots with the Saints. Major phases of the work of empire building, proselyting, immigrating, colonizing, and making of public improvements required the pooling of immense amounts of labor and capital.

The cost of missionary work, though it bore heavily in the first instance on the family of the traveling elder, was largely passed on in the missions and at home to those who assisted—by cash and labor—the missionary and his dependents. Consecration would result in a pooling of resources and spread the burden of supporting missionary activity.

Gathering the Saints from afar was a heavier burden. While many emigrants were able to meet their own expenses, thousands who had little or nothing were anxious to join the Saints in their Promised Valley. During the 1850s while the Perpetual Emigration Fund was in its earliest stages, the necessity of augmenting its resources was a matter of constant concern. Both the disappointing slowness with which those indebted to the fund repaid their obligations and the departure of some for California spoke loudly in favor of the system of consecration of all property. Just two months before the conference convened in which the principle of consecration was urged, a list of 277 debtors to the Perpetual Emigrating Fund was published in the *Deseret News* over an appeal for immediate settlement. General consecration would place all material wealth and all labor time at the disposal of church authorities and would solve the problems both of collecting debts and of enlarging the Emigrating Fund.

Colonization, like missionary work and immigration, required the closest kind of cooperation. The establishment of far-flung settlements over the broad stage of pioneer activities presented other problems in addition to attacks from the Indians. The tendency for strong individualists to reach out for themselves and take more land than they could use limited the opportunities of those who were to come later, weakened the community, and placed in jeopardy the lives of those who made habitations at a distance from the town site. Again, the pooling of all property would be advantageous; there would be less incentive for individual personal aggrandizement.

Finally, the support of public works required a heavy draft on both labor supply and resources. Tithes alone seemed inadequate to construct the mighty works expected of those who were building the Lord's kingdom. Consecration would place at the disposal of the church everything acquired or produced beyond current subsistence.

These considerations alone cannot account for the consecration movement of the middle 'fifties although they make more apparent why the attempt occurred at that time rather than at some other. Out of a desire to honor through practice the principles taught by Joseph Smith came the effort to establish a new social order in Jackson County in 1833, the movement for consecration in the period under discussion, and the United Order movement inaugurated by Brigham Young in 1874.

The first step in the institution of the Law of Consecration and Stewardship was taken in the period under review by hundreds of individuals whose deeds of transfer were recorded over a period of nearly eight years. The records indicate that the movement was practically terminated in 1858. No records of consecrations have been found for the period 1859-61 and only a few for the 1860s. Making generous allowances for the number of deeds recorded in counties where records are missing, it is apparent that the total number of people consecrating was less than half of the 7,000 heads of families residing in Utah in 1858. Acceptance of the principle of consecration was equivalent to saying, "Take not my tenth, but my all."[13]

Undoubtedly disappointing to President Young, the results confirmed the judgment of apostle Orson Pratt that the Saints were worshippers of "the Gentile god of property." Among General Authorities of the Church, Pratt was the strongest advocate of the principle of consecration and frequently expounded it from the pulpit and in the press. In 1854, even before the standard form of deed had been made available, he said, "I long for the time to come when I can consecrate everything I have got; all the cattle I have; . . . also my books, and the right and title I have to publish my works, also my wearing apparel, and my houses."[14]

Not every apostle was equally enthusiastic. Orson Hyde confessed that at first he was negligent and had departed on his mission to Carson Valley, Nevada, without complying. Later he experienced a change of heart and made a partial consecration.[15]

In accounting for the comparatively limited response to the call to consecrate, it may be taken for granted that some took alarm at President Young's vigorous statements from the pulpit. Annoyed by the slowness of response to the appeal to members still owing to the Emigrating Fund, he scolded church debtors soundly, not only those owing the fund, but tithing delinquents as well. Addressing his words to the latter, he said:

> I want to have you understand fully that I intend to put the screws upon you, and you who have owed for years, if you do not pay up now and help us, we will levy on your property and take every farthing you have on the earth. I want to see if I can make some of you apostatize; I will if I can by teaching sound doctrine and advocating correct principles; for I am tired of men who are eternally gouging their brethren and taking the advantage of them, and at the same time pretending to be Saints until they gain an advantage over this people, and then they are ready to leave. . . . If I had the money due to the Church by a few individuals, I could pay every one of our individual debts and the Church debt, and have a few scores of thousands lying by me to operate upon.[16]

An apostle, Lorenzo Snow, explained the limited interest in consecration by saying that President Young was indifferent about it; that is, though he saw in the observance of the principle a safeguard against temptation, he thought the members must exercise the greatest freedom of choice in the matter. The speaker observed that the youth were more ready to consecrate than those older in the faith, perhaps because of the relative amounts of property held.[17] Those having little would be sure to get that little back as a stewardship, and there was a chance that they might get more out of the surpluses of the better-to-do. Some appear to have expected a redistribution of President Young's vast holdings, but he rejoined by condemning the principle of equality. "The superior is not to be directed by the inferior, consequently you need not ask me to throw that which the Lord has put into my hands to the four winds."[18] It is probable that some held back because the deeds were transferred to the Trustee-in-Trust instead of to the bishop as provided in the revelations. No doubt as many or more would be influenced contrariwise, depending on the degree of confidence inspired by their respective bishops.

According to the revelations and the interpretation given to them by such authorities as Orson Pratt, the transfer of title to the church should have been followed by a formal return of all or part of the property, or of some other, as a stewardship to be used first to supply the needs of the member and his family and next to support the work of the church. In the absence of action by an agent of the church to take control and designate a portion or the whole as a stewardship, the donor would stand in the relationship of steward or manager for the church of that which he formerly possessed, and it would be his duty to place all surplus income at the disposal of his bishop. Assuming that he did so, it is doubtful that the surplus turned in to the bishop would exceed the tithing or tenth that the member was accustomed to pay. Needs normally outrun income.

There are several possible explanations for the failure of President Young to formulate a program for the control and use of consecrated properties.

1. Congress had not, as expected in 1854, passed a law by which title to land in Utah Territory could be conveyed by the federal government to Utah settlers. All of the Saints were in the position of squatters on the public domain. The national opposition to Mormonism was such that if the church had taken possession of the consecrated lands of its members, Congress would almost certainly balk at the confirmation of land titles to the church. It would be wise for the church to wait to institute the Law of Consecration and Stewardship until Congress had established a General Land Office in Utah, as it eventually did in 1869, and conveyed titles to the current owners.

2. Response to the call for the consecration of property, being neither general nor wholehearted, made subsequent steps inadvisable.

3. Any practicable program would have had to recognize the bishops as overseers of property, and President Young was quick to see what might happen under weak or incompetent management. His expressed intent of maintaining control over his own possessions on the ground of his superior ability to utilize it is consistent with the doctrine of stewardship, but points to a practical difficulty in its observance.

4. Finally, conflict with the federal government culminating in the Utah War of 1857-58 soon came to occupy all the time and energies of church leaders. A new type of consecration was called

for. Speaking of the approach of the Utah Expedition, Brigham Young said, "I suppose a few have urged upon the brethren to consecrate, but do you not see that we are coming to where the Lord will make us consecrate."[19]

Since the first step in the plan, that of consecration, was taken by a minority of Latter-day Saints, and the second, the assignment of stewardship, was not taken at all, tithing and other donations and contributions continued to be the chief source of church income. The movement for the observance of the principle of consecration in the 1850s proved to be a symbolic gesture—faith and the willingness of the Saints literally to lay all they possessed upon the altar.

The uniting of means:
Cooperative mercantile
and manufacturing associations

OMMITTED from the first to a policy of self-sufficiency for his people, Brigham Young, with his associates, did everything possible to promote the development of manufactures so that traffic in goods from the eastern states would be limited to an irreducible minimum. He abhorred trade, particularly when it was carried on, as in most frontier communities, at what he regarded as outrageous prices. He was impatient with his brethren who engaged in it. Yet he was forced to seize upon it as a potent weapon in maintaining Mormon business supremacy in the territory won from the desert by the cooperative industry of his people. During the decade following the conflict between the Mormons and the federal government—the Utah War—he was forced to recede from his position as an opponent of trade; at its close he found himself directing one of the most powerful mercantile institutions in the West—the hub of a cooperative system that attracted nationwide attention.

Non-Mormon traders appeared early in Utah. Taking advantage of the demand for goods that appealed to palate and pride, these merchants, lacking competition from Mormons fearful that church leaders would charge them with profiteering, amassed fortunes in just a few years. In addition to the demand for such staples as tea, coffee, tobacco, and sugar, which could not be produced in the Great Basin, there was a large and steady demand for hardware, leather goods, and silk, wool, and cotton fabrics.

George A. Smith, a pioneer church historian, left this account of the first non-Mormon merchants:

> The first commercial house established here by strangers was Livingston and Kinkead's. Mr. Livingston had about eight thousand dollars, which was all the money the firm had to invest. Kinkead was

taken in as a partner, and they obtained credit in the East for twenty thousand dollars' worth of goods, freighted them here and opened their store. They reported to their creditors that on the first day of opening they received ten thousand dollars in gold. They remained here until they made themselves fortunes, and carried gold from this Territory, perhaps to the amount of millions, and established themselves elsewhere.[1]

The eagerness with which the people exchanged their means for the goods of this firm was described by Brigham Young himself:

I recollect once going into the store of Livingston and Kinkead, and there being a press of people in the store. I passed behind one of the counters. I saw several brass kettles under it, full of gold pieces—sovereigns, eagles, half-eagles, etc. One of the men shouted, "Bring another brass kettle!" They did so and set it down, and the gold was thrown into it, clink, clink, clink, until in a short time, it was filled. I saw this: the whole drift of the people was to get rid of their money![2]

In addition to Livingston and Kinkead, several other substantial firms, some owned by Mormons, were established in Salt Lake City in the decade of the fifties.[3]

Preparation for an exodus in anticipation of the invasion of Johnston's Army, and the cutting off of imports by a military order to intercept wagon trains headed for Utah, caused all stores to close in 1857-58. In one of his straight-from-the-shoulder sermons on home industry, Brigham Young expressed his satisfaction with the disappearance of the traders.

But now, thank God, there are no stores in which to buy; and I hope there will not be any more here, for it is the conduct of traders who have fattened in our midst that has brought an army into our Territory. I would rather see every building and fence laid in ashes than to see a trader come in here with his goods. I want you to understand that we are in favour of home manufacture in good earnest. Raise sheep and flax, and make cloth, and raise cotton, as fast as you can, and we will try to improve.[4]

Brigham Young's wish was not fulfilled. As soon as it became apparent that there would be no war between the army and the Mormons, the traders resumed their lucrative business. In retaliation, certain influential Latter-day Saints began to voice the feeling that the trade should be taken over by members of the church. At a meeting of leading citizens called July 4, 1860, William H. Hooper, a man of wide experience in trade, presented a plan for the formation of a mercantile association with shares of $100 each to operate "on the wholesale principle" for three years. At the end of that time, profits would be distributed. Most of those present were favorable.

E.D. Woolley arose and remarked that it was time something was done to stop the bleeding of the people in regard to means. Said there was a prejudice existing against any "Mormon" who will embark in the business of merchandising, but there was no prejudice against any person who did not belong to us. No matter how much they imposed upon the people, and when trouble came upon them, they would pack up their goods and the immense fortunes they had made, and leave us to ourselves to bear the burden. He approved of the plan suggested by W. H. Hooper—set forth the advantages that would arise from our own merchants bringing goods, in tithing, taxes, clerk, etc.[5]

A committee was appointed to lay the matter before Brigham Young, and at a subsequent meeting eleven of the eighteen present voted to sustain the proposal with their own means.

One week following the initial meeting, Brigham Young vetoed the plan with the following explanation:

The plan was a good one, but from the experience he had had with this people, he believed that the people would not be willing to trust their means in the hands of the Association. He said, he did not think they would trust him, and he thought his credit was as good as any other person's. He said that the brethren could do more good by putting the sheep's grey upon their backs and upon the backs of their families than by bringing goods into this country; and if the people had not given [him] clothing, he would have worn sheep's grey for years; it was good enough, and it was only for the respect of his friends. He also said that he would have to repulse the operation as that kind of business was not for us; the Kingdom was for us, and if we went into it, would not prosper, but it would be like the mail contract, it would be a disastrous business.[6]

Though disapproving the plan as a profit-seeking venture, President Young advocated that the Saints purchase directly at Missouri River landings such goods as must be imported. He had decided to send teams to bring in the immigrants and advised the people to withhold expenditures from the stores and buy for themselves through those who would be engaged in this undertaking.

We can raise cattle without an outlay of money, and use them in transporting the Saints from the frontiers, and such freight as we may require. Brethren and Sisters, save your fives, tens, fifties, a hundred dollars, or as much as you can, until next spring, (considering yourselves, as it were, a thousand miles from a store,) and send your money, your cattle, and waggons to the States, and buy your goods and freight them. Twenty dollars expended in this way will do you as much good as several times that amount paid to the stores here.[7]

The advice was excellent for the far-sighted and the thrifty, but the "hand-to-mouth" buyers continued to patronize the stores. Heber C. Kimball, who agreed fully with President Young on the issue, set a fine example of household economy.

If you want to know my views in reference to merchants and their goods coming here, I will tell you that I wish there could not any more goods be brought here. Why, can you get along without them, brother Kimball? I can, by the help of God; I want but little to be independent of every merchant that comes into this city. Why, this last year my family have made over eight hundred yards of cloth, and that will clothe a great many people; and dresses made of that kind of cloth are as far ahead of those you buy in the store as your silks are of the Indian blanket.[8]

Brigham Young's motives seem, in retrospect, to have been clear and consistent. He opposed trading of all kinds because he recognized that if the Mormons became integrated into a national economy they would become mere suppliers of raw materials, forced to repurchase their own products in manufactured form at a comparative disadvantage. His supreme goal for Utah economic life was self-sufficiency. Insofar as the Mormons became accustomed to purchasing superior quality goods from the East, the development of the home manufactures needed for self-sufficiency would be impeded and the people impoverished. His answer was to condemn all trading from whatever source.

The consequences of his attitude were predictable. Faithful Mormons heeded his advice and avoided involvement in mercantile pursuits. The demand for manufactured goods continued, however, leading enterprising non-Mormons to enter the breach. His policies had effects similar to those of medieval monarchs who prohibited faithful Christians from usurious lending and thus encouraged the engrossment of non-Christian banking firms, laboring under no such inhibitions. The kings, however, enjoyed considerable control and private advantage, since the non-Christians' very presence in the realm depended upon their grace. Such was not the case with Brigham Young. His policies had the consequence of permitting the non-Mormons to gain the initiative in establishing the foundations of trade in Utah. It seemed to be expecting too much even of Saints to demand that they refrain

Salt Lake City street in late 1860s. The proprietors of the establishment on the left have indicated their dislike of the ZCMI system by displaying their own alternative to the "Holiness to the Lord" standard used as identifying mark of Church-sponsored cooperatives. (C. W. Carter photograph, Church Archives)

from trade in eastern goods. The merchants had the advantage of a monopoly market without the disadvantage of having to curry royal favor.

As Hooper's plan for associative effort was not acceptable to President Young, individuals belonging to the church seized the opportunity to increase their private mercantile activities. In 1864 the firm of Hooper and Eldredge purchased in the East goods to the amount of $150,000, the freight on which increased the cost for Utah delivery by $80,000 more. William Jennings purchased goods worth a quarter of a million dollars in the Salt Lake Valley and in the following year bought in New York a half-million dollars' worth of goods, upon which he paid $250,000 in freight.[9] Apparently to their eyes the issue was between Mormon and non-Mormon control of trade rather than between self-sufficiency and trade. Accordingly, they risked the President's wrath and opened their own establishments. The burden must have been considerable, for once trading was condemned to the faithful and hence consigned to noncommunicants, the latter provided justifiable objects for hostility previously directed against trading in the abstract. Since gentiles (Mormon term for non-Mormons) were in trade, Brigham Young's opposition to trading was reinforced.

By 1864 Mormon as well as non-Mormon merchants were becoming objects of the Church President's criticism. That summer he visited the settlements north of Salt Lake City to advise the Saints concerning their temporal welfare. About trade he cautioned:

I want to say a word or two with regard to brethren here taking goods from merchants to sell. Watch and learn the spirit of the man who does this, and in nine cases out of ten his faith, feelings, and affections are wholly to benefit his employer, to get all he can from the people, and really commit the riches of the Saints to his employer, no matter whether he be Jew or Gentile. Such a man will, sooner or later, apostatize.[10]

In Salt Lake a few months later he attacked the price policy of Mormon merchants, which, he thought, was unconscionable.

What their goods are worth is not a question with them, but what they can get. They will get sorrow—the most of them will be damned, there is no doubt of it, unless they repent. You will excuse me for talking thus of my brethren, but what else can I say about them? I am not speaking about my individual feelings towards them, but upon principle. My individual feelings are nothing but good towards them.[11]

Despite efforts of church leaders to control prices and maintain independence from "the merchants of Babylon," both Mormon and gentile merchants increased in number and influence. Partly as a consequence of Brigham Young's attitude, many of the latter came to be among the bitterest enemies of the Mormon people, not only opposed to Mormon policies at home, but also suspected of generating anti-Mormon feeling throughout the nation and in Congress. In the gentiles' own newspaper, the *Union Vedette,* the case for the non-Mormons on political and economic matters was presented often with considerable hostility and bias against the Saints. Indignant that those who profited by trading with the Mormons should use their gains to feed the fires of malice, President Young became persuaded by 1865 that he must adopt new tactics. To suppress the non-Mormon merchants he did a complete turn-about, urging his followers for the first time to engage in trade. At October general conference he announced:

I wish the brethren, in all our settlements, to buy the goods they must have, and freight them with their own teams; and then let every one of the Latter-day Saints, male and female, decree in their hearts that they will buy of nobody else but their own faithful brethren, who will do good with the money they will thus obtain. I know it is the will of God that we should sustain ourselves, for, if we do not, we must perish, so far as receiving aid from any quarter, except God and ourselves. If we have not capital ourselves, there are plenty of honorable men whom our brethren can enter into partnership with, who would furnish and assist them whenever they should receive an intimation to that effect. I know it is our duty to save ourselves; the enemy of all righteousness will do nothing to help us in that work, neither will his children; we have to preserve ourselves, for our enemies are determined to destroy us.[12]

A few weeks later a *Deseret News* editorial advocated cooperative merchandising on the plan that had proved successful in England and in a few places in the Eastern States.

Working men and others of limited means unite, put their pittances together, stock a store, and, while that store undersells the regular retail dealers, receive a fair percentage of interest on this invested capital, however little that may be. Why should we not have such cooperative action here? By putting together what means they could spare for this purpose, there is nothing to hinder the people from becoming their own store-owners.[13]

During 1866 the antagonism between Mormon and gentile

was fanned into high heat. Two gentiles were killed, one for violating Mormon standards of propriety and the other for attempting to "jump" a land claim. Insinuations that Mormon leaders had encouraged violence followed. Soon, under the increasing conviction that the gentile menace must be rendered impotent, a vigorous campaign for a boycott of non-Mormon merchants was carried on throughout the church. Reaction to the boycott was voiced by twenty-three Salt Lake merchants in a jointly signed conditional agreement to leave Utah Territory:[14]

December 20, 1866

TO THE LEADERS OF THE MORMON CHURCH

Gentlemen:

As you are instructing the people of Utah, through your Bishops and missionaries, not to trade or do any business with the Gentile Merchants, thereby intimidating and coercing the community to purchase only of such merchants as belong to your faith and persuasion, in anticipation of such a crisis being successfully brought about by your teachings, the undersigned Gentile Merchants of Great Salt Lake City respectfully desire to make you the following propositions, believing it to be your earnest desire for all to leave the country that do not belong to your faith and creed, namely:

On the fulfillment of the conditions herein named, First—The payment of our outstanding accounts owing us by members of your church.

Secondly—All of our goods, merchandise, chattels, houses, improvements, etc., to be taken at a cash valuation, and we to make a deduction of twenty-five per cent from total amount.

To this fulfillment of the above we hold ourselves ready at any time to enter into negotiations, and on final arrangements being made and terms of sale complied with, we shall freely leave the Territory.

Respectfully yours,

Gilbert & Sons	S. Lesser & Bros.
Walker Bros.	Klopstock & Co.
Bodenberg & Kahn	John H. McGrath
Wm. Sloan	Glucksman & Cohn
C. Prag, of firm of Ransohoff & Co.	Wilkinson & Fenn
Ellis & Bros., by J. M. Ellis	Morse, Walcott & Co.
McGrorty & Henry	J. Watters
J. Meeks	J. Bauman & Co.
F. Auerbach & Bros.	M. B. Callahan

Siegel Bros. Morris Elgutter
Oliver Durant Thos. D. Brown & Son
L. Cohn & Co.

To this offer Brigham Young rejoined that the profit in such a sale would be greater than that received by any merchant who ever traded in the territory, that it was a matter of indifference whether they stayed or left, and that the attack of the church leaders was directed only at those who used their gains from sales to members of the church to "encourage violations of institutions, to oppose the unanimously expressed will of the people, to increase disorder, and to change our city from a condition of peace and quietude to lawlessness and anarchy."[15] That the church boycott was directed only at those merchants who were the known enemies of the Latter-day Saints was reiterated in a *Deseret News* editorial appearing in the same issue with President Young's reply. Other gentiles were assured that the church had no quarrel with them. As for the rest, the article concludes:

> But there have been and there are those here, who have labored for years unintermittingly to make us trouble. These we desire to have no fellowship, communion or dealings with. They can leave the Territory or stay, as it suits their pleasure. If they go, none will lament their absence; if they remain, they will change very much if they do not continue to be the objects of contempt which they now are. We would not trade with them, would not associate with them, would not willingly be brought into contact with them, would not injure them in the slightest degree; but we would let them alone—severely alone—and give them uninterrupted freedom to associate, trade, and mingle with those of kindred dispositions, while guaranteeing to them the fullest enjoyment of every constitutional right of which they would rob the people who for years have been filling their coffers.[16]

One effect of the boycott was to enhance the prosperity of Mormon merchants through trade diverted from the gentiles. Mormon merchants were quick to take advantage of the operation of laws of supply and demand, making in some cases reported profits of 500 percent on goods sold. Brigham Young, who had little tolerance in any case for the involvement of healthy men in soft-handed employments, flatly maintained that he "could not be honest and do as they do," taking such profits "from an innocent, confiding, poor, industrious people. . . . If they do not repent," he threatened, "they will go to hell."[17] Contemplating the evils of trade as they affected his people, he slowly

formulated plans to bring about a revolution that would correct
them all. He intimated in remarks at the April conference in 1867
that major changes were afoot:

> I do not know how long it will be before we call upon the brethren
> and sisters to enter upon business in an entirely different way from what
> they have done. I have been an advocate for our printing to be done by
> females, and as for men being in stores, you might as well set them to
> knitting stockings as to sell tape. Such business ought to be done by the
> sisters. It would enable them to sustain themselves, and would be far
> better than for them to spend their time in the parlor or in walking the
> streets. Hardy men have no business behind the counter; they who are
> not able to hoe potatoes, go to the kanyon, cut down the trees, saw the
> lumber, &c., can attend to that business. Our young men in the stores
> ought to be turned out and the sisters take their place.[18]

It seems apparent that the approaching completion of the
transcontinental railroad was the decisive factor in bringing about
the consummation of the new trade policy. There were some who
feared the impact this new force would have upon Mormon institutions, but Brigham Young was not among them. Always a
staunch advocate of mechanical progress, he consistently
encouraged the railway project. "Speaking of the completion of
this railroad," he remarked, "I am anxious to see it, and I say to
the Congress of the United States, through our Delegate, to the
Company, and to others, hurry up, hasten the work! We want to
hear the iron horse puffing through this valley. What for? To
bring our brethren and sisters here."[19] That it might also bring
more non-Mormon merchants, lawyers, gold-seekers, gamblers,
land jumpers, and others who constituted a menace to Latter-day
Saint objectives was obvious; the success of these had to be
blocked. Moreover, the railroad would assure even more trade
with the East. To Brigham Young it seemed imperative that this
trade be controlled by Mormons and in the interest of the community.

These circumstances determined the time of action, but not
the form. It was likely, however, that some form of consumer
cooperative would be initiated by church leaders to meet the
situation. A succession of experiments in Europe had reached
their culmination in England in 1844 with the founding of a consumers' cooperative at Rochdale by Lancashire textile workers.
Knowledge of the success of this cooperative came to the Latter-
day Saints through missionaries working in England and through

converts who emigrated from the area to the Great Basin. One of the territory's earliest cooperative stores, organized in Lehi in 1868, was founded at the instigation of a returned Mormon missionary, Israel Evans, as a direct result of his observations in England.[20] There was, however, little influence from American cooperative movements outside of Utah. The major instrument in establishing such cooperatives throughout the United States in the nineteenth century was the Grange movement. Founded in 1867, the year before Mormon leaders initiated their cooperative movement, the Grange had not yet had time to foster cooperatives on a scale significant enough to have come to the attention of the Mormons in Utah.

A Mormon cooperative institution was founded in 1864 at Brigham City. The Brigham City cooperative is of such importance that it merits a detailed examination in a later chapter, but it undoubtedly served as a model to Brigham Young and other church leaders as they cast about in 1868 for a means of averting the threat posed to Mormon sovereignty in Utah by the coming of the railroad. It must also be recognized that the Mormons by the 1860s had successfully established and perpetuated a tradition that made cooperative endeavor of all kinds especially appealing to them. They thus rapidly adopted the idea of cooperative retail merchandising when recommended by their leaders. Within six weeks after the opening of the parent institution in Salt Lake City eighty-one Mormon cooperative stores were in actual operation.[21] Hamilton Gardner was undoubtedly correct in his judgment concerning the founding of Mormon cooperatives that "the real proximate cause, which fully and logically accounts for establishing the [cooperatives] . . . , is found in the experience of the people with cooperation and its palpably evident fitness for the existing conditions."[22]

Finally, it is important that Brigham Young believed strongly in social equality. Ideologically opposed to gradations of wealth and status among his people, he sought instinctively for a scheme that would prevent aggrandizement of a few at the expense of the many. His opposition to the first association of Mormon traders proposed to him in 1860 was based partly upon these grounds. He consistently encouraged the widest possible ownership of the new cooperatives, to prevent the establishment of a wealthy privileged class. The cooperative movement was, thus, wholly consistent with his own social philosophy.

By 1868 the time was ripe for mercantile cooperation. A few days before the October church conference there appeared in the official newspaper an editorial by apostle George Q. Cannon, supporting a movement for the establishment of cooperative retail stores and a central cooperative wholesale house in Salt Lake City. The plan, if realized, would mean the displacement of the establishments of Mormon merchants and ruin to those operated by non-Mormons, for it appeared that the latter could not all thrive on the limited trade available through exclusively gentile channels. After a full discussion by church authorities, the plan was presented to the Saints at the conference. First, the evils of prevailing methods of trade were reviewed, and the advantages to be expected from a concerted effort to build up Zion were emphasized. Apostle George A. Smith denounced the practice of patronizing the enemies of the church and advocated a more exclusive program.

I do not fellowship Latter-day Saints who thus use their money. I advise the Saints to form cooperative societies and associations all over the Territory, and to import everything they need that they cannot manufacture, and not to pay their money to men who use it to buy bayonets to slay them with, and to stir up the indignation of our fellow men against us. Our outside friends should feel contented with the privilege of paying us the money for the products of our labor, and we should exact it at their hands, as a due reward for our exertions in producing the necessaries of life in this desert.

Some may say, "We are afraid the brethren are making money too fast," or, "We do not like to trade with them, they charge us too high." Suppose they do, you need not buy of them; but do not go and buy of men who would use that money to cut your throats, or to publish lies about you, and endeavor to induce all men to come here and dispossess you of your homes.[23]

Brigham Young was equally emphatic.

How our friends, the outside merchants will complain because we are going to stop trading with them! We cannot help it. It is not our duty to do it. Our policy in this respect, hitherto, has been one of the most foolish in the world. Henceforth it must be to let this trade alone, and save our means for other purposes than to enrich outsiders. We must use it to spread the Gospel, to gather the poor, build temples, sustain our poor, build houses for ourselves, and convert this means to a better use than to give it to those who will use it against us.

We have talked to the brethren and sisters a great deal with regard to sustaining ourselves and ceasing this outside trade. Now what say you, are you for it as well as we? Are we of one heart and one mind on this subject? We can get what we wish by sending to New York for it ourselves, as well as letting others send for us. We have skill and ability to trade for all we need; and if we have to send abroad we can send our agents to buy and bring home what we need. My feelings are that every man and woman who will not obey this counsel shall be severed from the Church, and let all who feel as I do lift up the right hand. [The vote was unanimous.] That is a pretty good vote.[24]

As part of a publicity campaign undertaken to preserve sentiment favorable to the gigantic new program, the *Deseret News* reported a meeting of October 13 at which it was decided that a cooperative wholesale store to control prices and effect a wider distribution of profits was feasible. High church officials were scheduled to present the plan in detail to local congregations throughout the region during the next week.[25] Other articles appeared in the *Deseret News* and the *Utah Magazine*. Apostle Orson Pratt, the most able spokesman for church officials, in a powerful sermon appealed for support of the movement as a step toward the Law of Consecration and Stewardship revealed by Joseph Smith.[26]

On the fifteenth of October, 1868, a meeting of merchants and prominent citizens was held in the City Hall with Horace S. Eldredge as temporary chairman. At this first meeting George A. Smith declared that those who would enter the proposed cooperative society should do so with the spirit and zeal of a missionary, and Brigham Young expressed himself as favoring the admission of only those who were regular tithe payers. Others could qualify by paying back tithing and making regular payments in the future.[27] This stringent principle was actually applied, as evidenced by a provision to that effect incorporated as Section 20 in the constitution of the new institution.[28] Yet Section 25 provided that "all certificates of stock. . . . shall be deemed personal property and as such subject to sale and transfer," with no stated limitations as to tithing status of the buyer. An effort was made at a subsequent meeting to rectify this inconsistency, but the proposed amendment did not prevail.[29] Accordingly, it was inevitable that in time stock would find its way into the hands of non-Mormons and nonpayers of tithes, thus bringing about a fundamental change in the nature of the association. The constitution as adopted provided for an association of the corporate form,[30] to be known as Zion's Cooperative Mercantile Institution (ZCMI), with an authorized capital of $3,000,000, increasable to $5,000,000 in shares of a par value of $100. Stockholders were to have voting power in proportion to stock held, one vote for each share, and the private property of shareholders was exempt from institutional liabilities.[31] The new corporation differed from the consumers' cooperative of England, which stressed the one-man, one-vote principle and adhered strictly to the ideal of decentralized control. Apparently noting this divergence, one of the organizers proposed unsuccessfully that the term "cooperative" be dropped from the corporate name.[32]

The minutes of meetings, which continued at intervals for several months, reflect both Brigham Young's impatience to get underway and a desire on the part of the merchants involved in the enterprise to delay the consummation of his plans. Some thought it better to begin modestly and within a limited field such as wholesale dry goods, allowing the established merchants time to work off their stocks and come into the new business gradually. There were differences of opinion about the relationship of retail stores to the ZCMI, about the maintenance of uniform prices, and about the threatened displacement of existing stores owned by Latter-day Saints. The question was also discussed whether there should be one central wholesale in Salt Lake or wholesale stores in other centers as well.

The latter question was answered by enterprising men in Provo who, while Salt Lake merchants hesitated, undertook to capture the central wholesale firm for that city. At a meeting held December 4, 1868, a preliminary organization was effected with subscriptions amounting to nearly $5,000, which was rapidly increased to $12,000. It was decided to name the undertaking the Provo Cooperative Institution. Brigham Young, accompanied by Henry W. Lawrence and others from Salt Lake City, attended a meeting of shareholders held on February 8, 1869, and gave the proposed institution his personal approval and support. He advised the promoters to obtain their goods directly from the East and to undersell the Salt Lake merchants, who presumably would thereby be brought to see the folly of their long delay in organizing the proposed ZCMI. President Young subscribed for $5,000 stock in the venture. Lawrence, of Provo's Kimball and Lawrence Company, offered to turn over the stock of his new store and to accept as partial payment $3,000 in shares. The President then returned to announce to the recalcitrant Salt Lake City group that if they did not move at once, Provo would become the trading center of the new system. All Mormon opposition to the ZCMI vanished and local merchants flooded the promoters with offers to turn over their goods to the new institution.[33]

ZCMI was finally launched as a wholesale store on May 1, 1869, when the dry goods department opened for business in the Eagle Emporium, formerly occupied by William Jennings, who turned in his merchandise as a subscription to the capital stock of the new cooperative. President Young offered an impressive dedicatory prayer and made the first purchase in the sum of $1,000. Ten days later wholesale grocery and hardware departments opened in the Old Constitution Building. With the purchase of the business of Ransohoff and Company, a retail department with a line of men's furnishings opened in April, 1869.[34]

Concurrently a number of Mormon merchants retired and sold their stocks to the new institution for cash or to pay for their subscriptions to capital. Table I lists the source and amount of such transfers to the end of March 1869 and the distribution of shares among the original promoters of the institution.

TABLE I
A

SOURCE AND VALUE OF PURCHASES OR MERCHANDISE OF ZION'S CO-OPERATIVE MERCANTILE INSTITUTION FOR THE FIRST MONTH'S OPERATION (MARCH, 1869)

Company	Value of Merchandise
William Jennings	$200,000
Eldredge and Clawson	75,000
N. S. Ransohoff and Co.	75,000
Bowman and Co.	15,000
H. W. Lawrence	30,000
David Day and Co.	10,000
Woodmansee Bros.	5,000
Sundry Purchases	40,000
Total	$450,000

B
DISTRIBUTION OF SHARES AMONG PROMOTERS OF ZCMI AT ITS FOUNDING

Shareholder	Number of Shares	Value of Shares
William Jennings	790	$79,000
Brigham Young	772	77,200
William H. Hooper	110	11,000
David Day	100	10,000
Brigham Young, Jr.	53	5,300
Joseph Woodmansee	50	5,000
Fifteen Others	115	11,500
Total 21	1990	$199,000

Sources: Arden B. Olsen, "The History of Mormon Mercantile Cooperation in Utah," Ph.D. diss., University of California, Berkeley, 1935, p. 130; and "Zion's Cooperative Mercantile Institution: Agreement, Order, Certificate of Incorporation, and By-Laws" (Salt Lake City, 1870), p. 7.

It has been noted, as Tables IB and II indicate, that Brigham Young failed to achieve the wide distribution of shares in ZCMI that was his avowed aim. Certainly the fact that four men possessed 1,772 of 1,990 shares lends credence to the argument of one scholar that "on account of its organization and the method of dividing profits, we must deny the Zion's Cooperative Mercantile Institution its [legally] cooperative character."[35] Efforts made by Mormon leaders during 1869 to broaden the ownership of the corporation were partially successful. By September the number of shareholders had been increased to 347, most of whom had subscribed for twenty-five shares or less, bringing the paid-up capital to a total of $279,500. In March 1870 there were more than six hundred shareholders.

It is nevertheless true that in the Salt Lake City ZCMI, which conducted a major portion of its operations as a wholesaler to local cooperatives, the Rochdale form of consumer cooperative was not followed. In the Rochdale institution the customers owned the retail stores, which in turn eventually formed a wholesale store from the same capital pool, so that the profits of both wholesale and retail trade were distributed to consumers proportionate to purchases. Consumers were given with each purchase a small metal token, which was saved and used as the

TABLE II

TOTAL AMOUNT OF PAID UP CAPITAL CONTRIBUTED TO ZION'S COOPERATIVE MERCANTILE INSTITUTION AS OF SEPTEMBER 30, 1869

Amount of Individual Contributions	Number of Shareholders	Total Amount Contributed
$75,000	2	$150,000
25,000	1	25,000
15,000	1	15,000
10,000	2	20,000
5,000	2	10,000
3,000	2	6,000
2,300	1	2,300
2,500	2	5,000
2,000	3	6,000
1,600	1	1,600
1,500	2	3,000
1,150	1	1,150
1,000	2	2,000
900	1	900
600	1	600
500	25	12,500
400	2	800
300	5	1,500
200	10	2,000
150	6	900
125	2	250
100	66	6,600
75	4	300
50	44	2,200
25	151	3,375
20	2	40
Unknown	6	505
Total	347	$279,520

Source: Arden B. Olsen, "The History of Mormon Mercantile Cooperation in Utah," Ph.D. diss., University of California, Berkeley, 1935, p. 12.

basis for distributing dividends when annual accounts were closed. Each shareholder had but one vote in corporate meetings, however great his investment. Such consumers' cooperatives had been praised in the *Deseret News* as early as 1865. In October 1868, a series of articles on the Rochdale system was published in the *Salt Lake Daily Telegraph*.[36] Had the Mormons followed the English pattern, retail associations would first have come into existence;

after the lapse of several years, these associations would have united in establishing a wholesale agency to secure the advantages of quantity buying. But the exigencies of the situation in Utah required immediate action to forestall any strengthening of the non-Mormon position that might follow the completion of the transcontinental railroad. It was Brigham Young's determination to wrest from gentile traders whatever power they possessed to insure the dominance of his own people.

Three factors differentiated the Mormon endeavor from those of other initiators of cooperatives: the great scale of the undertaking, the negative feelings toward many local sources of wholesale supply, and the long distance from outside wholesalers. The leaders were planning to establish not just a single cooperative store or even a single community of cooperatives, but rather to reform an entire regional economy upon cooperative principles. The immediate need, of course, was to find sources of wholesale goods with which to stock the hundreds of local retail stores being planned. In England cooperatives could continue to purchase from local retailers until they gradually saved sufficient capital from their earnings to establish their own wholesale stores. In Utah this was not possible. Sufficient capital and stocks of goods had to be found to accomplish the setting up of both wholesale and retail organizations at one time. Young's only recourse was to entice local merchants who possessed both goods and capital to pool their resources with the ZCMI. His success in this endeavor is indicated by the fact that the beginning stock of ZCMI goods consisted of almost half a million dollars worth of goods acquired from Salt Lake merchants for stock or cash (see Table IA). Local merchants were, in effect, partially compensated for their loss by being given the opportunity to become major shareholders in ZCMI.

It seems likely that Brigham Young found it necessary to remove the limitations on permissible returns to capital and on the voting power of those owning multiple shares of stock so his plans would be acceptable to Latter-day Saints of substantial means. The consequence was inevitable. The legal ownership of ZCMI became such that it gave every appearance of being a "combine," as Albert Wilson has charged. Such a view overlooks, however, a fundamental fact operative in the ZCMI situation. Unlike most merchants, the ZCMI organizers were committed above all to operating their enterprise in the public interest. In a frontier economy where difficult problems of supply tended to favor scarcity prices and windfall profits, the Mormon consumers had been vulnerable to exploitation. There is no reason to doubt the veracity of a public statement issued by the ZCMI founders in 1895 that "from its foundation until the present it has never advanced the price of any article because of its scarcity."[37] Brigham Young claimed in April 1869, shortly before the tying of the transcontinental railroad, that the cooperative system, because of lower markups, had already reduced prices for retail goods in Utah twenty to thirty percent.[38] Thus, though ZCMI's dividends and policy were not shared or determined by its consumers, the store was nonetheless managed as a public enterprise and at great material benefit to its consuming public. It retained the aims, if not the form, of a true cooperative. This was assured by its ecclesiastical sponsorship.

Initiation of the cooperative system obviously tended to alter the existing distributive system. Several Mormon merchants exchanged their stocks for share capital, and with time the loss of sales impelled others to request that they be bought out. Walker Brothers, who claimed their business declined from $60,000 to $5,000 a month,[39] offered to sell all their real estate and merchandise and move out of the territory. ZCMI directors did not want the real estate and were of the opinion they could get better merchandise in New York. Walker Brothers proceeded to undersell. Discussing means to wage the price war, a ZCMI director suggested about thirty men could close out the Walkers in about a month by purchasing everything offered below the common price level.[40] Whatever was done about it, Walkers survived through trade with non-Mormons. The Auerbachs were saved by trade developed with the growing mining centers.[41] Other non-Mormon merchants moved to Corinne, a town founded in March 1869 as an exclusively gentile commercial city. In Mormon communities outside of Salt Lake City, however, the appearance of the community co-ops was a signal of doom to noncooperating local merchants.

Despite strong advantages enjoyed by ZCMI in Salt Lake City, a steady sequence of problems was to plague the institution. Shortly after its founding a director resigned because of unwillingness to surrender his own mercantile business. Brigham Young answered the deed at a meeting of the directors February 15, 1869, expressing his opposition to the continuance of retail stores on

Main Street. Two-thirds of those in trade, he thought, should be retired and go into the field preaching.[42] At the ensuing April conference he presented his views in detail and with characteristic emphasis.

I know that many of our traders in this city are feeling very bad and sore over this. They say "you are taking the bread out of our mouths." We wish to do it, for they have made themselves rich. Take any community, three-eighths of whom are living on the labor of the remaining five-eighths and you will find the few are living on the many. Take the whole world and comparatively few of its inhabitants are producers. If the members of this community wish to get rich and to enjoy the fruits of the earth they must be producers as well as consumers.

As to these little traders, we are going to shut them off. We feel a little sorry for them. Some of them have but just commenced their trading operations, and they want to keep them up. They have made, perhaps, a few hundred dollars, and they would like to continue so as to make a few thousand dollars; and then they would want scores of thousands and then hundreds of thousands. Instead of trading we want them to go into some other business. Do you say, what business? Why, some of them may go to raising broom corn to supply the Territory with brooms, instead of bringing them from the States. Others may go to raising sugar cane, and thus supply the Territory with a good sweet; we have to send to the States for our sugar now. We will get some more of them to gathering up hides and making them into leather, and manufacturing that leather into boots and shoes; this will be far more profitable than letting hundreds and thousands of hides go to waste as they have done. Others may go and make baskets, we do not care what they go at provided they produce that which will prove of general benefit. Those who are able can erect woolen factories, get a few spindles, raise sheep and manufacture the wool. Others may raise flax and manufacture that into linen cloth that we may not be under the necessity of sending abroad for it. If we go on in this way, we shall turn these little traders into producers, which will help to enrich the entire people.

Another thing I will say with regard to our trading: Our Female Relief Societies are doing immense good now, but they can take hold and do all the trading for these wards just as well as to keep a big loafer to do it. It is always disgusting to me to see a big, fat, lubberly fellow handing out calicoes and measuring ribbon; I would rather see the ladies do it. The ladies can learn to keep books as well as the men; we have some few, already, who are just as good accountants as any of our brethren. Why not teach more to keep books and sell goods, and let them do this business, and let the men go to raising sheep, wheat or cattle, or go and do something or other to beautify the earth and help to make it like the Garden of Eden instead of spending their time in a lazy, loafing manner. . . .

I want to impress one thing on the minds of the people, which will be for their advantage if they will hear it. When you start your co-operative store in a ward you will find the men of capital stepping forward, and one says "I will put in ten thousand dollars;" another says "I will put in five thousand." But I say to you, bishops, do not let these men take five thousand, or one thousand, but call on the brethren and sisters who are poor and tell them to put in their five dollars or their twenty-five, and let those who have capital stand back and give the poor the advantage of this quick trading. This is what I am after and have been all the time. I have capital, and have offered some to every ward in the country when I have had a chance. I would take shares in such institutions. I am not at all afraid; but nobody would let me take any except in Provo and in the wholesale store here. I will say to Bishop Woolley, in the 13th Ward, do not let these men with capital take all the shares, but let the poor have them. I say the same to the 14th Ward and to every ward in the City; and you bishops, tell the man who has five thousand or two thousand to put in, to stand back, he cannot have the privilege, we want the poor brethren and sisters to have the advantage of it. Do you understand this, bishops and people?

The capitalists may say "What are we to do with our means?" Go and build factories and have one, two or three thousand spindles going. Send for fifty, a hundred, or a thousand sheep and raise wool. Some of you go to raising flax and build a factory to manufacture it, and do not take every advantage and pocket every dollar that is to be made. You are rich and I want to turn the stream so as to do good to the whole community.[43]

Brigham Young exercised considerable resourcefulness in helping the institution through financial problems that developed in the 1870s. During the winter of 1871-72 heavy snows delayed the arrival of nearly $120,000 in merchandise from the East. Payment for the merchandise fell due long before the goods had arrived in Utah and before profits from anticipated sales could be realized. He responded by lending church assets to ZCMI and by purchasing capital stock to increase the operating reserves of the institution. Assuming the presidency of ZCMI for several months following the Panic of 1873, the Mormon leader used the credit standing of the church to solicit loans from eastern financial establishments sufficient to weather the difficulties caused by the panic. The retail departments of the central store were especially hard hit, leading superintendent William H. Hooper, in his report of May 1, 1874, to recommend that they be disposed of to friendly interests. As a result some of the merchants who had retired at the inception of ZCMI became purchasers. William Jennings purchased the retail dry goods department, and Day and Company acquired the retail grocery and hardware departments. The retail clothing department was closed and the goods transferred to the wholesale dry goods department. By 1875, however, affairs had been put sufficiently in order to reopen several departments. Major building programs took place in 1875, 1880, and 1891, resulting in a facility large enough to house the bulk of ZCMI operations until the mid-twentieth century.[44]

Further difficulties arose as a result of the practice of paying wages to employees partly in scrip redeemable for goods at ZCMI or cooperating institutions. Counterfeiters began to exploit the system, necessitating a recall of the first issue and the printing of lithographed scrip. As much as $20,000 in scrip was circulating at one time—providing occasion for harassment of ZCMI by federal officials in the late 1870s. Acting under a provision of the 1863 National Banking Act, the collector of U.S. Internal Revenue for the Utah area, O.J. Hollister, in 1878 imposed taxes upon ZCMI scrip to the amount of $9,500. ZCMI officials decided to pay the sum under protest, and at the same time initiated action against the United States Treasury to recover the payment. Taxes on further ZCMI issues brought the total paid to the federal government to almost $17,000 before lawyers employed by the firm in Washington succeeded in securing a judgment in favor of the institution. In 1884 the entire amount was returned to ZCMI.[45] Successfully overcoming its early growing pains, ZCMI survived subsequent depressions and increasing competition, remaining a leading merchandising establishment in the intermountain region into the twentieth century.

ZCMI was by no means the only achievement of Brigham Young's cooperative movement, and in many respects it was not typical of other establishments formed during the period. Though the parent store remained in its organizational structure more a joint stock company than a cooperative, many of the retail stores established throughout the Mormon commonwealth came close to the cooperative ideal represented by the Rochdale model.

The plan to have a cooperative store in every ward and settlement developed during 1868 discussions of the proposal for a gigantic wholesale institution. Brigham Young himself raised the question whether such stores should be established.[46] Except among merchants whose business would be curtailed, the idea met with ready response and the people of various wards took steps to organize. The distinction of having the first "ward store" in Salt Lake City belongs to the members of the Tenth Ward, who completed the organization of the Tenth Ward Co-op before February 2, 1869.[47] Within a short time one hundred fifty retail cooperatives were organized in Utah alone, including ZCMI and its branches,[48] with others in Idaho. Following the advice of Brigham Young, organizers made restrictions on stock ownership. It was common to place shares of stock at five dollars each, permitting even the poorest members of the ward to become shareholders. The Twentieth Ward association in Salt Lake City decided in addition that no one could hold more than one share of stock, though each member of a family could be a shareholder. In this ward stockholders were limited to one vote per member and dividends were paid on purchases as well as upon capital stock, following the Rochdale pattern, except that in Rochdale the dividend to stockholders was a prearranged, fixed amount. Each quarter all customers received a discount on purchases during that quarter. Profits remaining after this division were paid out to the two hundred stockholders of the association. The Seventeenth Ward Cooperative Mercantile Institution followed nearly the same plan except that shares were set at twenty dollars each. Since many ward members could not afford that amount, however, half and quarter shares were offered for sale. Anyone who contributed as much as five dollars received the same percentage of dividends as those with full shares.[49]

In accordance with President Young's vigorous expressions at the April 1869 conference, a number of co-ops were conducted by women. The prominent and influential leader Eliza R. Snow founded a Women's Cooperative Store and Exchange in Salt Lake City in 1876, an establishment that continued operations into the 1890s. Similar stores were founded in Ogden, Brigham City, Provo, Parowan, and St. George. All succeeded for a time, providing employment and a sense of independent achievement for the women who sustained them.[50]

Financially the retail cooperatives were independent of ZCMI. Although the larger company held no stock in the ward stores, at least one of the latter and very possibly more invested in the shares of ZCMI.[51] Regardless of this corporate independence of the central or parent store and the retail co-ops, they together constituted a distributive system much like that of a modern chain store. But the system, in addition, was bound by ties much stronger than mere financial interest—ties based on religious faith and obedience to authority. The local units purchased all their eastern goods from the central wholesale and continued to do so when it may have been advantageous to do otherwise.[52] To facilitate its service to the local stores, the parent company established branches at Provo, Ogden, and Logan, Utah, and at Soda Springs, Idaho.

Thousands of Mormon villagers became stockholders in their local cooperative stores. The Spanish Fork Cooperative, though founded before the inception of the ZCMI, may be taken as typical in its formation of the many that later sprang up like magic on the word of Brigham Young. It was established in January 1867, following consideration of a plan laid before the local bishop by Thomas C. Martele and Charles Monk. A constitution was formulated by local promoters and submitted to Brigham Young in that year. According to one account, he replied "that the system entered upon was very commendable, suggested one amendment to the constitution, and advised the company to go ahead, promising that God would add His blessing." Though in its first year the business was not prosperous, it gained impetus in 1868 and received patronage from residents over a wide area.[53] The original capital stock amounted to $450. In a community where cash was at a premium, much of the stock was paid for in produce and labor. Hannah E. Babcock paid for most of her stock in eggs; James Anderson did blacksmithing work for the institution; William Jex contributed lumber. Hay, grain, butter, bacon, and many other commodities were accepted as payment for subscriptions. The co-op in 1869 absorbed the business of James Miller and William J. Warren, who took stock in exchange for the merchandise turned in. By December 1872, the capital had been increased to more than $6,000. Outstanding capital stock in 1935 equaled $140,000.[54] The Spanish Fork store, unlike most local retail co-ops, prospered well into the twentieth century.

As the cooperative system was established to confine the trade of Mormon people within channels controlled by themselves, all stores within the system were identified by a special sign. Having taken stock in the wholesale store and agreed to buy from it, owners of stores existing when ZCMI was in the formative stages erected the insignia over their doors. The *Deseret News* noted the appearance of the first one.

Yesterday evening we saw the first of a series of signs which will be placed over those stores the owners of which are shareholders in the Co-operative Mercantile Association lately organized. The sign is over the store of Eldredge & Clawson, and is artistically painted. It is the work of Midgley & Evans; "Holiness to the Lord" occupying the top of the sign, arching an all-seeing eye; and underneath "Zion's Co-operative Mercantile Institution."[55]

Some merchants who withdrew early from the system or bought goods elsewhere than at the parent store were soundly denounced for continuing the use of this trade-pulling emblem. Eventually the signs came down or the offending merchants mended their ways.

In the first few years of their existence, many of the co-ops, including the retail businesses, reported profits of almost incredible amounts. The Salt Lake City Twentieth Ward cooperative paid a 30 percent dividend the first year, increasing its capital stock at the same time by a remarkable 22 percent. At Fountain Green, in Sevier County, dividends of 68 percent were paid in 1870. The Fillmore cooperative paid a semiannual dividend the same year of 30 percent. The community co-op of Gunnison, in Sanpete County, paid $3 per quarter on each $5 share during its first three quarters of business operation.[56] Obviously such profits were possible only by a rapid turnover of stocks at a liberal margin between buying and selling prices. Three years after the opening of ZCMI, the superintendent reported that the institution was doing an annual business of four million dollars on a capital of $466,000, necessitating a complete turnover of capital every six weeks. The president of ZCMI pointed out in the spring of 1872 that any reversal of business would, owing to the use of credit, find the institution in an embarrassing condition.[57] Such proved to be the case; within eighteen months the effects of the Panic of 1873 made themselves felt in Utah, causing representatives of the store to request that creditors in the larger trading centers of the country give extensions of time for the payment of obligations amounting to more than half a million dollars. Interest was paid on these extensions at from 7 to 12 percent. ZCMI in turn tightened up on the co-ops, with the result that for a time dividends were reduced or passed altogether.

In 1875 there appeared an apostolic circular that summarized clearly considerations that led the church into cooperation and praised its progress. Cooperation, the leaders explained, had been a means of countering "a condition of affairs . . . which was favorable to the growth of riches in the hands of a few at the expense of the many." Fearing that a wealthy class might arise with interests "diverse from those of the rest of the community," the church officials concluded that such an occurrence "was dangerous to our union; and, of all the people, we stand most in need of union and to have our interests identical." The ZCMI had been opposed by the wealthy and the established, but since its founding had established a solid reputation while paying substantial dividends and paying a church tithe on all its profits.[58]

The elation over impressive dividends and continuing growth of the system concealed the fact that forces were working against continuation of the cooperative principles which had inspired it. The original intention of having all Latter-day Saints acquire stock in a retail co-op and as far as practicable in the parent institution was frequently emphasized, and no doubt a wide distribution was effected in many communities. Following the usual corporate pattern, however, two fatal provisions were usually included, one granting voting power according to shares and another permitting the transfer of stock. Unsuccessful cooperatives languished and eventually closed. Those paying good dividends supplied every inducement for the increase in the number of shares in the hands of those who had inside information and means to act on it. Gradually, ownership became more and more concentrated and much of the original cooperative character disappeared.

For a time the network of cooperatives continued to enjoy the benefits of church sponsorship in spite of the increasing trend toward private ownership and concentrated control. Recognizing this trend, John Taylor and other Mormon leaders issued a general letter in 1882 opening the field of merchandising to all Mormons. "Under existing circumstances," the letter read, it had been thought best to throw open the field of trading, under proper restrictions, but that we should do all we could to confine it as much as possible in the hands of our own people, who were honorable and upright, and good Latter-day Saints. All should be subject to the principle of co-operation, and not recede a particle from it; but we should put our own business people in the place of outsiders, and sustain them, inasmuch as they sustained the principle of cooperation themselves by acting honorably in their dealing, paid their tithing and donations, were willing to be counselled and advised, and had at heart the interest of the work of God.[59]

In response to the new church policy there was a rapid expansion of private merchandising firms. The cooperatives had been protected, through the semi-monopoly they enjoyed, from the need to develop efficient marketing and accounting techniques. Suddenly faced with competition from private firms, many were unable to survive. The consequent partial decay of retail cooperation was lamented in a ZCMI trade paper of 1886.

The great drawback of narrowed cooperative, as of combined or personal stores, is that the primary object is to make money. It is not a percentage simply on the investment that is expected or desired; big profits and fortune is the ultimatum [sic]; and the closer we come to cooperation, if this selfish spirit prevails, the greater the evil, for the assumption and presumption is, that such a store or organization possesses a claim upon the town or settlement and so if illy regulated it becomes a monopoly as grasping and avaricious as the most exacting could desire. Is it not because of this that so-called co-ops have lost prestige and that in little towns where one jealously guarded store would have been ample for necessity, there are now from ten to twenty, dividing the interests, feelings, and working against the progress of the body temporal in almost every sense?[60]

By the time of the onset of the Great Depression of the 1930s only eight of the one hundred fifty or more cooperatives organized by Latter-day Saints in the Great Basin remained free of outside control.[61]

In the same way, the character of ZCMI has substantially changed with lapse of time. No longer can it be considered a Mormon institution in the same sense that it was in 1875. Anyone having the means may acquire stock; church membership is not a requirement for holding a directorship or a position on the staff. The all-seeing eye and the words "Holiness to the Lord" have long since been removed from the facade. If the LDS Church has any influence in molding policies, it is only that of the leading stockholder.

Brigham Young's passionate desire to achieve self-sufficiency for his people had caused him initially to oppose trading in whatever form. It was this same impulse that led him, pressed by growth of gentile establishments and by the impending arrival of the railroad, to establish a system of merchandising cooperatives throughout his far-flung kingdom. It is not surprising, then, that this movement was accompanied by sporadic efforts to turn these cooperatives to the cause of home manufactures. He employed two means to his end. First, the cooperatives were instructed, whenever possible, to stock products manufactured in the Great Basin, and to urge them upon their customers over imported goods. In addition, however, experiments of a more far-reaching nature were attempted, aimed at the much more difficult task of founding successful producing cooperatives. It was Brigham Young's wish that the profits secured through cooperative retailing would be used to build up regional industry.

ZCMI pursued this objective both by purchasing for resale the products of home manufacture and by entering into production on its own account. A boot- and shoe-making enterprise was begun by the firm in 1870 shortly after its founding. The superintendent's report for April 5, 1873, states that the store had sold homemade goods to the amount of $20,000 in six months and had manufactured $23,096 worth of boots and shoes. More could have been sold if goods had been available. The manufacture of boots and shoes increased rapidly during the decade, and both the shoe factory and the trunk factory are mentioned as departments in the report of the secretary issued in September 1871.[62] The advent of the railroad resulted in the suspension of all the tanneries in Mormon settlements and played havoc with the leather industries generally. In the spring of 1874, in an attempt to create employment for themselves, about twenty-five shoemakers pooled their meager capital and incorporated the Workingmen's Cooperative Association. Three years later William H. Rowe, then the manager of the shoe and leather department of ZCMI, bought for himself the capital stock at ten to twenty cents on the dollar and assumed all liabilities, saving the corporation from bankruptcy. This establishment merged with another firm, the Deseret Tanning and Manufacturing Association, and was finally added to ZCMI at the instigation of a "committee on Cooperation, Home Manufactures, and Industries," appointed by Brigham Young's successor, John Taylor, in 1878. The committee recommended that producing cooperatives be founded to supplement merchandising cooperatives, determining that ZCMI should use its profits "for the development of home manufactures, the making of machinery, the introduction of self-sustaining principles and the building up of the Territory generally."[63] Pursuant to this recommendation ZCMI took the Deseret Tanning and Manufacturing Association into its operations in 1879. By 1888 the factory had expanded to an annual output of 160,000 pairs of shoes and employed 180 workers.[64]

During this period the ZCMI also initiated clothing manufacture, building by 1881 to an annual production of 50,000 finished items, including overalls, lined coats and vests, overshirts, undershirts, and men's pants. Cloth for the enterprise came primarily from a cooperative woolen mill in Provo. Local cooperatives followed the ZCMI lead, restricting dividends in order to promote cooperative sawmills, tanneries, molasses mills, furniture shops, butcher shops, and other such establishments. Though these were small affairs, within a valley or region they did contribute considerably to local self-sufficiency. In some localities most co-ops had three or four such subsidiary industries.[65] The largest of these so-called cooperative manufacturing institutions was the woolen mill at Provo, built by substantial capitalists who organized the Timpanogos Manufacturing Company June 1, 1869. Secretary L. John Nuttall refers to the undertaking May 28, 1870, when the cornerstone was laid for the Provo Cooperative Woolen Factory. In the spring of 1872 the buildings, erected at a cost of $155,000, were completed. Brigham Young, who became the president of the association, advanced $70,000 to purchase the machinery. The first wool was carded in October 1872 and the first cloth manufactured on June 1, 1873. Incorporated in the fall of 1873 under the territorial statute of February 18, 1870, the company then adopted the corporate name, Provo Manufacturing Company.[66] Other concerns included a cooperative cotton and woolen mill at Washington, built by Brigham Young in 1870, which was sold in 1871 for $44,000 to the Zion's Cooperative Rio Virgen Manufacturing Company. The stockholders were chiefly residents of Washington, Iron, and Kane counties. Perhaps the best example of the application of the cooperative principle to production is the system developed at Brigham City, an account of which is the subject of the next chapter.

Small textile mills were erected, in addition, in Hyrum, Ogden, Brigham City, Grantsville, Salt Lake City, Springville, Kingston, Beaver, Parowan, Washington, and Orderville, Utah, as well as at Franklin, Idaho; Afton, Wyoming; and Tuba City, Arizona. Most of these mills operated successfully, though on a small scale until the turn of the century. In 1880, according to census records, twelve mills with $402,000 capital were manufacturing woolen and cotton goods; they employed 306 wage earners, who added a value of $136,763 to the materials they worked with. It should be noted that many of these enterprises were not full cooperatives in the sense that they were founded at the initiative of local residents who worked in the factory, retained collective control of the enterprise, and shared in its profits. People in the locality were urged to purchase stock by furnishing labor and local materials, but it was necessary to rely heavily upon the resources of the church and local capitalists in order to obtain machinery and supplies from the East.

Both voting and distribution of dividends were based upon stock ownership. Not only the inclination but also the expertise needed to establish a successful factory had to be built from the ground up, with many errors and failings along the way. Newly arrived immigrants, who had been familiar with textile manufacture in England, were often called upon to supervise these establishments, and on at least one occasion special efforts were made to convert a body of textile workers in England and bring them to the Great Basin, where their skills could assist in the launching of a southern Utah factory.[67] The shortage of trained personnel meant that the initial capital fund must be sufficiently large not only to set up plant and equipment, but also to sustain the enterprise while its managers and workers were learning to efficiently produce a marketable product. Such a burden made it difficult for local residents to launch a major enterprise on their own and made necessary the joint stock form of establishment. Other establishments founded during the period bearing the cooperative aim, if not always its form, were Salt Lake City's Bank of Deseret, founded in 1869 as Zion's Cooperative Banking Institution, and the Union Iron Works, set up near Cedar City, Utah, in 1870.[68]

In addition to its wide application to trade and industry, the cooperative principle was adopted quite generally for the management and improvement of livestock. Requiring very little cash and little technical knowledge to operate, such associations could readily be formed by the pooling of stock and the employment of competent herders, with resulting economy of labor. A score of companies came into existence in the 1870s, assuming, in the spirit of the times, such names as Utah County Cooperative Stock Association, Heber City Cooperative Sheep Herd, and Canaan Cooperative Stock Company. The process of organization departed from the complicated earlier practice of each rancher putting stock bearing his brand into a collective herd and then attempting to sort them and their progeny out at the end of a season.

Acting on the advice of church leaders, stockmen in 1869 moved to a more fully cooperative arrangement. Abandoning individual ownership of animals, the stockmen made capital subscriptions in cattle, horses, or sheep and entered these in the books at a value determined by a committee on appraisal. The cooperatives successfully took advantage of economies in the use of labor and of range lands, and in addition improved the quality of the herds by the importation of breeding stock. A number proved so rewarding that they have continued in successful operation into the twentieth century.[69]

The Mormon enthusiasm for cooperation became so widespread during the late 1860s and early 1870s that the name was given to virtually every new enterprise, whether it represented a cooperative effort on the part of the local community or not. Those who have chafed at the indiscriminate use of the term have failed, however, to consider a fundamental aspect of the situation. Through the medium of the Mormon Church most residents of the Great Basin saw themselves as part of a far-flung commonwealth that set its boundaries only where church membership ended and where church authority and discipline were lost upon the individual man. The small settlements comprised intimate communities that entered collectively into a larger community of communities, embracing the entire body of the church. Cooperation for them meant the willing pursuit of any enterprise, in whatever form that promised to benefit the whole body. The form of the enterprise was not so important as the extent to which it could contribute to an early self-sufficiency of the Mormon commonwealth. The effort demanded of community members a degree of cooperation that made precise form and structure unimportant.

In encouraging the cooperative movement in 1869, Brigham Young had stressed to the Saints that it was a step toward that "more perfect union" abandoned in the fall of 1833 amid their ruined and plundered hope in Missouri. At the same time other apostles dwelt upon the relationship between the cooperative plan and the order revealed to the Prophet Joseph Smith.[70] Within five years Brigham Young would launch an effort to bring the Saints yet closer to the realization of this perfect society. His wish to move beyond consumers' cooperatives, with their occasional manufacturing centers, into fully integrated economic communities was encouraged by the successful development of a nearly sulf-sufficient community-wide economic order at Brigham City, under the leadership of apostle Lorenzo Snow.

CHAPTER 6

The Brigham City Cooperative: Steppingstone to the United Order

COOPERATIVE COMMUNITY established in 1864 by Lorenzo Snow in northern Utah's Brigham City may well have served as a model not only for the cooperative movement begun by Brigham Young later that decade, but also for the more ambitious United Order movement that succeeded it. In the fall of 1864 Brigham Young counseled Snow on what future course might best insure "the moral, spiritual, and financial interests of the Saints in Brigham City." During that conversation, as the two traveled north together, President Young suggested "all the elements and principles of what [was later to be] . . . called the United Order." As Snow recalled in an 1875 letter to the Mormon leader,

One thing has been a source of consolation—that you were ever with me in spirit—that I was "in you and you in me" in my efforts to carry out your program. I stripped myself and put on the harness for the conflict, so I could say to this people, Come and follow in my footsteps. They have felt the influence of this until prejudice and opposition have been gradually giving way, and moving along, step by step, we have succeeded in arriving at a position of some prominence in spiritual and financial union.

I do not for a moment consider that we are worthy to be called a people of the United Order, but we are slowly progressing toward that position.

He explained further that his main objects in the cooperative had been "to unite together the feelings of the people by cooperating their interests with their means and make them self-sustaining according to the spirit of your teachings and to make them independent of Gentile stores."[1]

Lorenzo Snow was born in Ohio of Yankee stock and attended college at Oberlin before his conversion to Mormonism. He subsequently became a close associate of Joseph Smith and of Brigham Young, helping to build their burgeoning young move-

ment as an early missionary to England. He was ordained an
apostle in 1849 and five years later was asked by Brigham Young
to assume the leadership of Box Elder, a remote struggling community sixty miles north of Salt Lake City.[2] A new body of settlers for the community was selected with special care to include
a schoolteacher, mason, carpenters, blacksmiths, shoemakers, and
other skilled craftsmen and tradesmen who would insure its economic success. Many of these were recent emigrants from
Europe, some with previous experience in cooperative movements. The group was specifically instructed to grow and manufacture all that they consumed.

The construction of a fort, canal, gristmill, sawmill, and other
primary tasks of colonization occupied the settlers until 1864,
when a considerable influx of Scandinavian immigrants permitted
(and made necessary) the establishment of small manufactures,
retailing, and other crafts and trades. Lack of transportation
facilities and good roads prevented the development of a specialized economy. The community, renamed Brigham City, was
not connected by railroad with Salt Lake City until 1871.

In 1864, the year of his conversations with Brigham Young,
Apostle Snow supervised the organization of a cooperative
general store. It was his intention to use this mercantile cooperative as the basis for the organization of the entire economic life of
the community and the development of the industries needed to
make the community self-sufficient. He detailed the origin of the
movement in a letter to the Church president, as follows:

> Some ten years ago and upwards, a number of small mercantile
> establishments were located in our city, owned principally by
> speculators, who possessed no interest in common with the people. I
> proposed to such as were inclined to do so, to unite on some co-operative
> system for the general welfare and interest of the community. Some
> consented, whereupon we organized the Brigham City Co-operative
> Association, giving all an opportunity of taking stock and enjoying equal
> rights and privileges. At first we limited our operations to mercantile
> business, and as it progressed it gained the confidence of the people, and
> gradually increased in number of stockholders, till about the fifth year
> from its commencement [1869] it consisted of some two hundred
> shareholders, with a capital stock of twenty thousand dollars. Our
> dividends were paid in merchandize at the selling price rates, and
> averaged about twenty five per cent per annum.[3]

This original association, it is to be noted, was nothing more than a joint stock enterprise to which Apostle Snow and three others subscribed three thousand dollars. It was an immediate success, and other stockholders were attracted by persuasive sermons, by the generous commodity dividend policy, and by the reduction of shares to five dollars each. The profitability of the concern (by 1870 it was the only store in town) and the policy of giving no dividend in cash or imported merchandise made possible the accumulation of sufficient savings to establish home industries. This, of course, had been part of the original intention. Some stockholders, as one would expect, objected that this reinvestment would cut dividends. As the apostle later related:

It required some effort on the part of our stockholders to reconcile their feelings with a knowledge of their duty and obligations as elders of Israel and servants of God. A good spirit, however, prevailed, and a desire to build up the kingdom of God and work for the interest of the people, outweighed all selfish considerations; hence, consent was granted by all the stockholders to establish home industries and draw dividends in the kinds produced.[4]

Utilizing the labor of the community available after the fall harvest of 1866, the group built, at a cost of $10,000, a two-story tannery building, 45 by 80 feet. Virtually all the labor and materials were furnished in return for capital stock, although one-fourth wages were paid out of the store in merchandise to "those who needed it."[5]

Snow wrote that "we gained by this measure additional capital as well as twenty or thirty new stockholders without encroaching much on anyone's property or business."[6] The construction of the tannery, the selection of the equipment, and the procuring of the workers and supplies were under the direction of a Mormon convert who had tanning experience in England, Cincinnati, and Salt Lake City.

A visitor to the tannery in 1872 reported:

Mr. Hillam, the gentlemanly and efficient superintendent in charge, took us through the building, and exhibited some valley-tan that is pronounced by competent judges equal to the best Eastern oak-tanned leather. The greatest difficulty that this department has to contend with appears to be the short-sighted policy of some of our stock-dealers in selling their hides to exporters, instead of supplying tanneries for home consumption, and for the reason that a meagre cent or two can be made by so doing.

The shoe shop came next in order of establishment, on the principle that one branch of business begets another in co-operative work, the same as in private enterprise. Mr. Kelly, the business manager of the shoe shop, exhibited a first-class article of manufacture in the shape of brogans, boy's shoes, and fine boots, which for the wear of our territory are undoubtedly superior to Eastern manufacture and sold at Eastern prices. The shop is supplied with an abundance of machinery for all common purposes, and works from eight to twelve hands, is centrally located, and bids fair to supply a long-felt want. . . .[7]

The growth of the leather and leather-goods departments was rapid. In 1875 the weekly output of the shoe shop was valued at $500 and at $700 two years later. A total of $132,000 worth of goods had been produced.[8] With these enterprises all the leather needs of the community were met, and some leather products were sold for cash in the Salt Lake City, Ogden, and Logan markets. Dividends to the stockholders of these and other enterprises consisted of goods produced by the jointly owned cooperatives.[9]

After incorporating these enterprises under the name "Brigham City Mercantile and Manufacturing Company" in 1870, with 7 directors and 126 stockholders,[10] the group then planned the construction of a woolen factory. Using, as with the tannery, the winter labor of the community, materials contributed in return for capital stock, and the profits of enterprises already established, a $35,000 woolen factory was constructed in 1870-71 and equipped with machinery purchased in the eastern states.[11] The 44-by-88-foot building was two stories high. The factory originally contained a spinning jack with two hundred spindles, four broad looms, and three narrow looms, and other facilities for washing, drying, carding, and dyeing. The factory came to employ thirty-two hands and eventually did a $40,000 annual business in yarns, blankets, men's and women's wear, and similar products. Machinery in both the woolen mill and the tannery was powered by water.

Simultaneously, the association began to build up the sheep herd from 1,500 head to 5,000 head by retaining the natural increase and by banding together additional sheep contributed for capital stock by those joining the organization. In this way a "dependable supply of wool" for the factory was guaranteed. The sheep were wintered on two farms near Bear River City, Utah. By 1879 the herd had grown to well above 10,000. Soon afterward, a horned-stock herd of a thousand cattle was established that, together with the sheep, supplied an association meat market. A hog enterprise also served the same purpose.[12]

By 1874 virtually the entire economic life of this community of 400 families was owned and directed by the cooperative association. Some fifteen departments, later to be expanded to forty, produced the goods and services needed by the community, and each household obtained its food, clothing, furniture, and other necessities from these departments.[13] Almost complete self-sufficiency had been attained, and some textile products, leather, furniture, and dairy products were "exported" to other northern Utah settlements.[14] The paid-up capital of the Brigham City co-op in 1874, which amounted to $120,000, was owned by 372 shareholders.[15]

Food enterprises in 1874 included a model dairy at Collinston—"perhaps . . . the finest, best and most commodious of any dairy in this Territory"—consisting of five hundred milk cows. Established in 1871, it was reputed to be the first commercial dairy in Utah. In addition to fluid milk, the dairy department produced nearly $8,000 worth of butter and cheese annually. Almost 40,000 pounds of cheese were produced for exportation alone in 1875. Some one hundred hogs were raised in connection with the dairy to consume the waste products of the dairy and to supplement the supply of beef and mutton. A butcher department prepared the meat for sale. Several molasses mills were operated, providing food for both man and milk cow. A number of farms, including a dry farm at Portage, Utah, were operated by the agricultural department for the production of food, feed, and other supplies. A horticultural department planted and cared for flowers, shrubs, vines, and orchards. Farm machinery and equipment, to the tune of $12,500 yearly, were manufactured or repaired by a special machine and repair shop. The group also maintained an "Indian Farm" upon which Indians in the vicinity were established and taught to farm.[16]

Textile enterprises included, in addition to the woolen factory, a hat and cap factory or millinery shop, employing up to twenty-five girls and producing fur, wool, and straw hats, together valued at $5,000 annually; tailor and "fancy work" shops, employing nine hands and turning out $14,000 annually; a silk department, which planted several thousand mulberry trees, raised silkworms, and manufactured silk; and a 125-acre cotton farm in southern Utah, 300 miles away, to which a dozen or more young men were called in 1873 and thereafter for a period of two years at a time to raise cotton for use in the woolen factory. A letter from the first superintendent, James May, reflects the spirit of the men and reveals the extent of this enterprise in its early stages.

> We are five miles east of Washington on the Virgin river. We have about 100 acres of land on the west side of the river, and 300 on the east side. We have dug a ditch one and a half miles long, three feet wide; blasted through a point of rocks 55 feet long, five feet wide; 11 feet deep; built a dam across the river, 150 feet long, 40 feet wide, 4 $\frac{1}{2}$ feet high; cleared the brush off fifty acres of land, plowed thirty acres, put out 625 grape vines and 1800 grape cuttings, planted 100 peach trees; and are all well at this time. The Lord has blessed us in all our labors, for which we feel truly thankful. There has been no swearing in camp. I have not heard an oath since I left home. We have no smoking, chewing, or card playing, but we have plenty of books and quite a variety, so we need not get lonesome for the want of amusements. Is not this a good showing for thirteen young men? We expect to plant 35 acres of cotton, 10 of corn, and 5 of lucern.[17]

The yield of cotton that first season produced about 70,000 yards of warp; double the quantity was produced in the second season. The cotton farmers also maintained a farm on which to grow their own food and produced raisins, wine, and sugar cane for transporting north to Brigham City. In addition, Lorenzo Snow called a group of people to settle a valley ten miles east of Brigham City, originally called Flaxville and now called Mantua, for the purpose of raising flax. Predominantly Danish, these colonists produced grain sacks and sewing thread.[18]

Construction enterprises in Brigham City included a shingle, lath, and picket mill; three sawmills, including a large steam sawmill; brick and adobe shops; a lime kiln; a blacksmith shop; a furniture or cabinet shop, which dressed white pine to make baby carriages and other furniture; a large two-story factory fitted with machinery for wood turning, planing, and working mouldings; and architecture, carpentry, mason, and painting departments. During the years 1874 and 1875 these departments employed 46 hands and built 46 houses, plastered 163 rooms, and did work valued at $21,000. A public works department built roads, bridges, dams, canals, and public buildings. The latter included church, civic, and cooperative buildings.

By 1874 the cooperative mercantile establishment was doing $30,000 worth of business annually. It was the only store in the city. According to apostle Lorenzo Snow,

Several parties have set up stores at various times since the organization of our Co-operative, and entered into competition but could not obtain sufficient patronage to make it a success, and while they received the sad experience of disappointment the city treasury received the benefit of their licenses. All the business men and the majority of the people have more or less interest in this co-operative association, and the profits arising from their patronage, in room of going to individual hands, to be applied for private aggrandizement, or perhaps spent outside of the interests of the community, goes to support home institutions, therefore, the people generally feel to sustain their own mercantile establishment.[19]

So profitable had the Brigham City business become that officials contemplated opening branch houses in Logan and in Salt Lake City for the sale of their productions.[20] Undoubtedly, the competition with ZCMI operations in both cities would not have been welcome, and perhaps for this reason the plan was abandoned.

Other enterprises, in addition to those already mentioned, included a tin shop, a rope factory using hemp grown on the co-op farm, a pottery shop, a broom factory, a cooperage, a greenhouse and nursery, a brush factory, and a wagon and carriage repair shop. An education department supervised the school and seminary. There was even a "tramp department," which utilized the labor of tramps who sought handouts by putting them to work chopping wood and doing other odd jobs.[21]

Because virtually the entire town worked for the cooperative, the opening and closing of the departments were uniformly regulated by the ringing of a bell in the courthouse tower. "At fifteen minutes to seven the department doors were opened and the ringing of the triangle told the workmen to begin the labor of the day."[22]

The cooperatively owned departments were expected to comprise the economic life of the community. Indeed, city growth was planned around the cooperative enterprises. All the shops and factories of the various departments were to be located on a twelve-acre square around the center of the town, and street cars were to run from this square to various parts of the town and to the railroad station.[23] This arrangement was never quite completed.

Each department or enterprise had clearly delineated responsibilities and was operated by men and women of all ages under

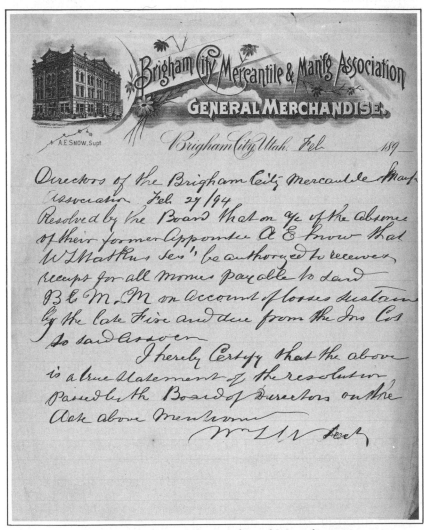

Letterhead of the Brigham City Mercantile and Manufacturing
Association, with a note referring to difficulties encountered the year
prior to final dissolution of the cooperative. (Church Archives)

the supervision of an overseer or superintendent. Typically, the superintendent had learned his skill in Europe. A general superintendent (Lorenzo Snow) was in charge of the operations of all departments. The bookkeeping was described by Apostle Snow as follows:

The accounts of each department are kept separate and distinct, in stock taken annually, separate statements and balance sheets made out and kept by the secretary of the association, so that the gain or loss of each may be ascertained and known at the end of the year, or oftener if required.

At the close of each year a balance sheet is made from the several statements, giving a perfect exhibit of the business.

From this exhibit, a dividend on the investments or capital stock is declared.

The profit or loss of each department, of course, is shared equally by the stockholders.[24]

Superintendents and workers alike were paid wages that appear to have been commensurate with those being paid elsewhere in the nation at the time. Wages in 1873 ran as follows: secretary and bookkeeper, $1200 per annum; chief clerk, $900; overseer of sheep herd and farm, $1200 per annum; overseer of the tannery, $3 per day; overseer of the boot and shoe shop, $3 per day; carders, spinners, and weavers, "the same as is paid in other factories." Wages at first were paid in merchandise, one-fourth in imported goods and three-fourths in home products. Later the proportion was changed to one-sixth in merchandise, the remainder in home products.

The general superintendent, Lorenzo Snow, reported himself as working "for nothing." Since he was the largest stockholder, his dividends were presumably sufficient for his support. Undoubtedly, members of his five families worked in some of the departments. He added:

I have labored to inspire the overseers of the various departments with a proper sense of their obligations to the people, to be satisfied with a reasonable wage, and be willing that their abilities should be employed, to a certain extent, for the building up of Zion. I endeavor to influence all our laboring hands not to be greedy for high wages, and also those who furnish the capital, to be satisfied with reasonable dividends, and thus work together in harmony on principles of equal justice, that the Lord may take cognizance of our works, and bestow blessings of prosperity and salvation in the hour of necessity.[25]

To facilitate the division of wages into home-produced and imported goods, employees were paid each Saturday in two types of scrip. One type was redeemable at the various industrial and agricultural departments and was known as "Home D" (for home department) scrip. It would buy furniture, pottery, boots, hats, brushes, dairy products, meat, and other locally produced products. The other type was stamped with the word "Merchandise" in red letters and was redeemable at the cooperative store or mercantile department, at which the purchaser might obtain imported goods. (These might be imported from no farther than Salt Lake City.) Both types of scrip bore a resemblance to currency, being two by three inches in size, and were in denominations ranging from five cents to twenty dollars.[26] They were also the medium of exchange for admission to concerts, plays, and other community productions. More than $160,000 of this scrip was paid out in wages and dividends in 1875, and the total production of all the departments in the same year was valued at $260,000. Thus, in that year some $100,000 can be said to have been reinvested in cooperative enterprises. (These figures would have to be multiplied by about five to obtain 1976 equivalents.) The operations of the various departments required $30,000 in cash in 1874, of which half was paid to employees in imported merchandise and the other half devoted to the purchase of such imported materials as iron, horseshoes, nails, furniture, boot and shoe trimmings, paints, dyestuffs, and warps.[27]

When Brigham Young initiated his region-wide consumers' cooperative system in 1868, the Brigham City Co-op had already demonstrated the viability of such an undertaking. Apparently he saw the establishment of the consumers' cooperatives as a first step toward a regional economy composed of many nearly self-sufficient communities. By 1868 the Brigham City Co-op had already begun to move toward full cooperation.[28] From the building of the tannery in the fall of 1866, the first major step in this direction, the small community had by 1874 proliferated its home industries to the point where it was approaching self-sufficiency. In that year Brigham Young began his drive to organize United Orders in every Mormon settlement, a step that would follow logically, if the Brigham City example were pursued, from the prior establishment of retail cooperatives in the settlements. He himself later observed that "Brother Snow has led the people along, and got them into the United Order without their knowing it."[29]

There was apparently some concern that the United Order as Brigham Young spoke of it might necessitate changes in the Brigham City system. On July 3, 1874, Lorenzo Snow allayed such fears, informing the seven-member board of directors that he had met with the Mormon President several times and had discussed the nature of the Brigham City venture, and that Brigham Young approved their course and did not recommend any alterations.[30] Though the Brigham City United Order was organized in that year, it brought about no essential changes in the operations of the cooperative. The able secretary of the board of directors, William L. Watkins, never varied through 1895 from his accustomed designation of the organization as the Brigham City Mercantile and Manufacturing Association. In fact, the term United Order of Box Elder County was superficially attached to the older community without effecting substantial change in the spirit or manner of its operations. The only notable change, besides altering the name, was the creation of a "United Order Council," consisting of "sixty influential citizens" of the county, which was supposed to function as a kind of congress for the determination of policy.[31] Each member was made a steward over all his possessions, including his home, farm, livestock, and shares of capital stock in the cooperative institution. A man saved simply by accumulating credits or certificates of indebtedness, which could then be used to make additions or improvements on his home or farm, or for any other purpose. One observer noted that:

> If [any Brigham City] brethren should be so unfortunate as to have any of their property destroyed by fire, or otherwise, the U. O. will rebuild or replace such property for them. When these brethren, or any other members of the U. O., die, the directors become the guardians of the family, caring for the interests and inheritances of the deceased for the benefit and maintenance of the wives and children, and when the sons are married, giving them a house and stewardship as the father would have done for them. Like care will be taken of their interests if they are sent on missions, or are taken sick.[32]

The management of the Brigham City cooperative was in the hands of a board of seven directors, a president, a secretary, and a general superintendent, all of whom were elected annually by the stockholders. Lorenzo Snow was the president and general superintendent throughout all of the life of the association. Ecclesiastical influence was strong throughout, and the motto in business transactions was said to be "as with the Priest, so with the people."[33] Co-op officials attempted to provide suitable work for every person desiring employment, and by 1874 approximately 250 persons were furnished employment in the various departments.

Interesting glimpses into the mixing of spiritual and temporal affairs by the Brigham City Mormons can be seen in minutes of the General Council of the United Order of Box Elder County, organized in 1875. On April 22, 1877, the clerk recorded: "Bro A Baird said I cannot do good without Gods help nor forsake and overcome my weaknesses. I am determined to carry out what I am counseled and to be one with you." Without apparent interruption, the pious Baird was followed by A. Hillam, who "spoke on the various industries established by the UO."[34] It is apparent, from statements in minutes of meetings held by various councils of the Brigham City Co-op, that unities in temporal and in spiritual affairs were thought to be mutually reinforcing. Yet one senses in the documents left by these people a strong preoccupation with the business—a tendency to see their union as primarily an agent of economic, rather than social and religious, amelioration. The minutes of the United Order Council meetings suggest that the sixty male leaders gathered primarily to reiterate and reinforce their devotion to the higher goals. But temporal concerns kept intruding themselves upon the group, as the quotation above indicates. Minutes of the board of directors meeting are almost entirely taken up with problems of management, procurement of supplies, raising of capital, apportioning of dividends, and other such secular concerns.

It would seem paradoxical that Lorenzo Snow, a man of great piety and spiritual conviction, should have built a community strikingly lacking in those qualities. One is struck by the fact that comparatively few warm memories of the oneness of the community have survived, compared with many from the Missouri period and from the Orderville United Order. Perhaps the experiment was too successful for too long, failing to gather to itself the nostalgic glow with which we remember noble youth and beauty cut down in their prime. The Brigham City Co-op, after all, was an important factor in the community's economy for nearly thirty years. Moreover, its history followed an almost perfectly symmetrical cycle, beginning as a retail general store, expanding into a complex and powerful net of producing, manufacturing, and retailing relationships, then divesting itself one by one of its various branches until it was once again a retail store. There is little drama in such an evolution, and much familiarity. The co-op was for its members a fact of life that they accepted matter-of-factly. They did not remember it as a brief moment in Utopia.

During the mid-1870s the town must have been a hive of industry. One correspondent to the *Deseret News* stayed eight days in Brigham City observing the working of the United Order and reported: "I did not see a loafer, or an idle man, boy, woman, or girl during my visit; industry, prosperity and contentment seemed to characterize the entire community."[35] Publicity concerning the Brigham City Order even reached England, as Edward Tullidge wrote:

> It was in review of just such a social problem as that which this apostle [Lorenzo Snow] brought to a promising issue [at Brigham City] which caused the learned socialist, Brontier O'Brien, a quarter of a century ago, to proclaim to his class in Europe that the Mormons had "created a soul under the rib of death." The article was published in *Reynolds' Newspaper*. At that time the attention of the socialists of England was attracted to the social problems of the Mormon people. Reynolds, Bradlaugh, Holyoak, Barker, O'Brien and others held the Mormons up to admiration.[36]

The community attracted the attention of Edward Bellamy in 1886 while he was writing *Looking Backward,* and he spent several days in Brigham City observing the system and conversing with Lorenzo Snow.

Most of the observers of the system thought the chief advantage the so-called cooperative system gave to the city was in its promotion of home industry. One correspondent wrote to the *Salt Lake Herald* in 1876, in regard to the Brigham City system, that:

> If the example of the inhabitants of this town was more generally followed, Utah would be far more prosperous and her people much better off. Our present suicidal policy of exporting raw materials and importing manufactured articles would be stopped, we would be far more independent of our sister states and territories; the financial panics of the east or west would not affect us; our people would all have good homes and enjoy more of the comforts of life than they can hope for under present regulations; and our children would stand a much better chance of receiving good educations and becoming useful members of society.[37]

Other writers gave similar emphasis to the manner in which

Brigham City industry could "bid defiance to the fluctuations of trade, or commercial depressions":

A visit to the various departments of this institution will at once convince a person . . . , how a community can control their own industries, and live independent of commercial disasters, so fearful in their effects, especially to the dependent classes of France, England, and America.[38]

Nevertheless, Brigham Young's successor as president of the Church, John Taylor, did not want to put the final stamp of approval on the Brigham City organization, just as a few years later he did not want to give official sanction to the Orderville United Order. Said he:

There are some things that Brother Lorenzo Snow is doing that are very creditable; but it is not the United Order. He is working with the people something after the same principle that our sisters teach the little ones to walk. They stand them in a sort of chair which rolls along, and the babies appear delighted; they think they are walking. But we have not learned how to walk yet. . . .[39]

The Brigham City Order seemed to be functioning beautifully in 1877; it was attracting widespread attention in Utah and elsewhere. Not only was it maintaining a high rate of investment, but the 500-odd employees were as well paid as elsewhere in Utah, where the prospects of future development were not so bright.

It was apparent, however, that further growth would bring incalculable management problems. The build-up of the cooperative through reinvestment, the multiplication of enterprises under central direction, and the assumption by the corporation of responsibility for many decisions that are normally made by families and individual business units magnified the problems of the spiritual-temporal leader, Lorenzo Snow. Decentralization became an evident preference, and once the process began, it was almost inevitable that a larger and larger share of community activity would be delegated to private enterprise. That church leaders were aware of this problem is indicated in a letter from Snow to Brigham Young shortly before the latter's death in 1877. He revealed the anxieties that plagued him as he witnessed the little voluntary cooperative store burgeoning into an immense community enterprise employing hundreds of people in diverse tasks, and reflected on the meaning of his creation.

In working up to the principles we call the United Order we have shouldered very serious responsibilities. Over one thousand persons, little and big are depending entirely upon the Institution for all their supplies, for their food, their clothing, and all their comforts and conveniences. Over one thousand more living in our City are more or less dependent upon this Institution because in its progress it has gradually monopolized and gathered to itself all the main arteries and channels of business. . . .

We have been now twelve years engaged in this business, striving to unite the people in their business affairs, classifying and assigning them severally to such departments of industry as would best promote individual and general interest and of building up the Kingdom of God.

I guard against adopting the principles faster than the virtue, faith and intelligence of the people will sustain them lest I be left alone, and I think I move quite as fast as can be done with safety. I try to keep two objects in view — to amalgamate the feelings of the people and to establish a financial system in which everybody can secure necessaries and conveniences of life through their labour and be preserved from the evils and corruption of outside influences.

These two objects have already been achieved to some extent and the prospects for the future are very encouraging; but the care, the anxiety and the excessive mental toil and labor are quite sufficient to subdue any feeling of pride and vanity if any such existed for any outside applause.

A greater weight of responsibility comes upon us to supply necessities and conveniences by furnishing employment to those who have accepted the Order and classification (of labor) than we otherwise would feel if each pursued his own course, and this is expected by the people.

When Israel left their leeks and onions by the direction of Moses they looked to him for their supplies, and became very quarrelsome and troublesome whenever they failed. This is a feature in the United Order which I contemplate with no small degree of anxiety, viz. concentrating a multitude of individual responsibilities upon one man or a few men. One man may assume the responsibility of looking after the general interest of a community but to be required to provide for their daily wants, their food and clothing, one might do very well in prosperous times, but not very desirable in a financial crisis unless abounding in resources. . . .

I confess, in the solemn silence of the night, that I have sometimes inquired of myself, where are we drifting, in following this untrodden path for many generations, and in sailing upon a sea so little known and unexplored? Is there not danger of getting an elephant on our hands (to use a common phrase) that our wisdom and ability cannot manage or support? In other words, may we not drift into responsibilities that would be difficult or even impossible to discharge? I have sought to avoid such a dilemma as much as I could consistently with a knowledge of what was required of me.

I thought it necessary to establish some industries and to classify the people in their labors and to assign them to their several departments of business as fast as they were organized and as fast as the people could be brought to a willingness to comply with counsel. This was a gradual work but it has been progressing since its inauguration by three individuals with myself.

We invited the people to invest, as capital stock, in labor, money or property such portion of their surplus as they felt disposed to part with. This surplus labor or property was used to start, from time to time, these departments of industry, at the same time without diminishing any one's actual resources or means of living.

We have gradually, imperceptibly, and without calculation or previous design, drifted into possession of all the principal channels, and main arteries of business, trades, manufacture, and all industries which are carried on in Brigham City and in many of the surrounding settlements. Most of these, however, have been created by the energy of the Institution, or very greatly improved and enlarged, and this in a manner that could not have been done by allowing things to have gone on in the old way of private enterprise, everyone doing in his own way what seemed right in his own eyes. If it could have been done in some other settlement, it could not in Brigham City, for the men with the necessary ability and capital were not here. But this amalgamation, absorption, monopolizing and gathering into one, and centralizing of all our industries, thrown upon myself, is a responsibility that I should never dared to have assumed. In fact I never anticipated such a result, though I have felt it gradually approaching, but yet could not see how to escape and be justified.[40]

As this account suggests, the path of progress was not altogether smooth: the experiment had its difficulties. Scarcity of cash was a cause of increasing worry and became a source of embarrassment as the nationwide depression beginning in 1873 continued. It was impossible to wholly dispense with imports. Peddlers supplied the demand for finer fabrics than the local factory could produce and for imported shoes, since competing stores were rigorously suppressed.[41] It is said that $19,000 worth of boots and shoes was peddled among the people of Brigham City and surroundings. The co-op had to send out cash for tea, coffee, tobacco, cotton goods, ribbons, leather bindings, tools, machinery, and other goods that could not be provided at home.

As the number of industries grew and payrolls expanded, cash needs increased rapidly. Needs, reported at from $10,000 to $12,000 a year in 1873, more than doubled by the end of 1875, in spite of a reduction in the proportion of store-pay from one-fourth to one-sixth of total wages. In the latter year cash outlays greatly exceeded cash returns. Interesting and sometimes costly expedients were adopted to meet cash requirements. Wheat was used as a money equivalent, but the harvest from co-op farms fell short of the consumption requirements of the factory hands.[42] The deficiency had to be purchased in exchange for the products of home industries at a discount of 40 percent from established trade prices, leading to complaints from those who were unfamiliar with the necessities of the situation. Attempts were made to pay obligations to ZCMI. Home products and limited amounts were thus exchanged, but ZCMI objected to Brigham City cheese because it was not packaged like eastern cheese. And after the completion of the Provo woolen mill ZCMI also ceased to receive the products of the Brigham City woolen mill.[43] The greatest single source of cash was from taxes which, by common consent, were exchanged for the local mercantile and factory scrip with which county employees were paid. Lorenzo Snow explained the procedure as follows:

The railroad brought us Corinne and a host of thieves which threatened to demoralize and overthrow our city, and to clear our ranges of all our stock. To balance against these evils it also brought us about ten thousand dollars as a yearly revenue in taxes. One-fourth of this goes to the Territory, which has been promptly paid, the balance has been appropriated by the County Court for roads, bridges, jail and general improvements in the County. It has never been used for private purposes or for private schemes.

These appropriations have been expended in precisely the same manner as we had always done before, viz.: we hired men by the day or job and paid them reasonable wages until the amount of means was expended. We have never been in the habit of advertising and letting out contracts to the lowest bidder.

When a bridge was to be built, or a certain amount of lumber furnished or any particular job or work done, we would consult those who understood the value of such work, then let it out to some responsible party to do it at such prices. . . .

We paid for most of this public work from our Woolen Factory and our Boot and Shoe Shop, and one-fourth in merchandise and reserved the cash to assist our home manufacturing institutions. All this money, with the exception of what we used to buy machinery, went to Zion's Cooperative in Salt Lake City to purchase goods. The advantage which our cooperative gained in this transaction was simply the marketing of these home products for cash at their retail prices. The advantages gained went for the general good instead of going into the hands of speculators, and the work called for by the appropriations was well and honestly done and met the approval of the court, the selectmen and gave general satisfaction.[44]

It appears further that in the use of cash, there was an exchange of favors between the county and the co-op. As Lorenzo Snow wrote:

In some instances public work has been required on roads, bridges, etc. When there were no means in the treasury, our Co-op, on several occasions of this kind, has advanced the means, sometimes to the amount of two or three thousand dollars, and in some cases, our Co-op has borrowed the means and paid afterwards. At present we owe the County between three and four thousand dollars. I am superintendent of the County means, also of the Co-operative institution and have done by both as I thought right and just.[45]

Obtaining cash became more and more difficult as the co-op expanded its departments and added to the number on the weekly payroll.

The year 1877 marks the peak of the expansion phase of the history of the Brigham City Mercantile and Manufacturing Association, followed by a series of circumstances that eventually wiped it out of existence. That year there were heavy losses of farm crops to grasshoppers, typical of raids that once devastated portions of the arid West every few years. The loss was estimated at $4,000 but was considered a small matter, quite to be expected in the course of agricultural operations. A staggering blow, however, was the destruction of the woolen mill by fire in December. Within half an hour the building, machinery, wool warps, and cloth were destroyed, representing a loss of about $30,000. Though momentarily disheartened, leaders of the community began immediately to build another factory, putting operatives who had been thrown out of work by the fire to the task of erecting a building to house machinery for the new mill. The work was pushed vigorously; the weather was mild and masons were able to work nearly every day. By March they had completed the walls of the main building, and in anticipation of future expansion, had laid a massive foundation for another. By July the machinery was installed and the new mill was running regularly.[46]

Another disaster occurred in consequence of a contract undertaken by the association to provide lumber products for the building by the Utah Northern railroad of a line into Idaho. After purchasing a new sawmill and shingle mill in Marsh Valley, Idaho, the cooperative added to the capacity of the new establishment by moving its own steam mill to Marsh Valley from Box Elder County. For several months a camp of more than one hundred persons supplied the railroad while adding needed cash reserves to the cooperative fund. But in the late summer of 1878 the mill was raided, and a grand jury, sitting in non-Mormon Malad City, Idaho, indicted fifty-three mill workers for unlawfully cutting timber. They were eventually freed and their fines remitted through the intervention of President Rutherford B. Hayes at the behest of the unsavory railroad titan Jay Gould. But the association had no heart to continue the enterprise, and the Marsh Valley mills were sold.

Eliza R. Snow, the apostle's sister, wrote of the incident that, "irrespective of the anxieties, disappointments, and embarrassments resulting from that unhallowed onslaught, the financial loss which the association suffered amounted to from six thousand to eight thousand dollars."[47]

The words of Shakespeare, "when sorrows come they come not single spies, but in battalion," find exemplification in the history of the Brigham City Co-op. In July 1878, hardships already detailed were compounded by one yet worse, when the United States Collector of Internal Revenue levied a penalty tax on the circulating medium of the co-op just as he had attacked the issue of the ZCMI in Salt Lake City. Concerning the co-op currency, Snow explained:

> Before the tax law was so amended as to affect co-ops, we issued to employees and stockholders unrestricted bills but found serious trouble by persons not interested in our institution receiving them and requiring payment in the articles that were nearest to cash, and which we could scarcely supply ourselves. . . .
>
> To remedy this difficulty, we called in all that class of bills, determined in future to keep them at home. Therefore, when we commenced the new issue, we printed upon the face, "Good only to employees and stockholders." These bills are, among us, called "Home

D;" that is, good for articles made in our home departments. . . . Our store scrip is . . . used to pay employees and is good only for just what it calls for. A great distinction exists between these two classes of bills, the store bills being good for any imported article in our store, while the Home D. is not presentable in this department and in no instance has it ever been redeemed in such articles.[48]

Both the levy and the arrest of the mill hands at Malad were part of the "Crusade," a persistent program of non-Mormon officials to break the Mormon power. The association had only the immediate choice of paying the tax or being found in contempt of federal law. In a series of meetings of the United Order Council, several methods of raising $10,200 cash were carefully considered before an assessment on the capital stock was decided upon. Lorenzo Snow suggested that the stock of those who could not raise the assessment be pledged with "three wise men" who would borrow against the stock and allow a reasonable time for redemption. His proposal received unanimous support of those present.[49] The money was paid under protest in 1879. Later it was found that the levy was illegal and the money was remitted in 1884—too late, unfortunately, to relieve the strain that brought about great curtailment of the cooperative business.

In reporting to President John Taylor and the Council of the Twelve the hardships that had befallen the Brigham City Mercantile and Manufacturing Association, Lorenzo Snow took occasion to complain of the absence of the cooperative spirit in the dealings of ZCMI with his institution. Since the organization of ZCMI, the Brigham City Co-op had purchased all its merchandise from that institution, amounting to about $400,000; and except for $3,000 or $4,000 worth of cheese accepted by ZCMI, cash had been paid during the last two or three years. Attempts to induce the parent co-op to stock the products of the industrial departments at Brigham City had been futile. Only a feeling of religious obligation and motives higher than considerations of profit prevented the Brigham City organization for a time from making purchases in cheaper markets and thus saving itself thousands of dollars. Because of recent difficulties, indebtedness to ZCMI had mounted to nearly $23,000, for which the Brigham City leaders had given their notes, and they were being charged 20 percent on goods purchased on credit, as compared with cash prices. To meet present emergencies, Snow asked in behalf of his company for the privilege of operating on a strictly competitive basis, buying wherever savings could be effected and selling on margins close enough to discourage the entrance of other merchants into the territory served by the co-op.[50]

At that time ZCMI was having troubles of its own. Hoping to improve relations with its loyal customers throughout Mormon territory, church president John Taylor set up a central board of trade with branches in the stakes of the church for disseminating information, establishing fair trade practices, and adjusting grievances.[51] In accordance with this policy, the Brigham City debt was cancelled in an amount (about $5,200) sufficient to bring the remaining debt to $17,500. Of this amount $10,000 was to be repaid immediately in cash and the balance in three interest-free notes of $7,500 each falling due at six-month intervals after April 6, 1880.[52] But the relief brought by these concessions was relatively minor compared to the financial distress in which the co-op found itself. Other measures were needed to help save the situation. Lorenzo Snow explained their plight to Franklin D. Richards in a letter of November 1, 1879.

Thus there appeared but one course left for us to pursue, viz: curtail our business, close several of our departments, lessen the business of others, and dispose of such property as will assist in discharging our cash obligations; thus using every exertion to outlive our misfortunes and save ourselves from being totally wrecked.

Accordingly, we have labored faithfully to this end, and, although no one has made any abatement of his claims against us, except Zion's Co-operative Mercantile Institution, in cancelling the interest on what we owed them, we are now nearly out of debt, having but one cash obligation to discharge of $2,500 to Z. which will be paid this fall.

Our checks in the hands of employees or other parties have now all been redeemed, with the exception of a very few, which we are prepared to settle whenever possible.

We now have eleven industrial departments in operation; the business, however, is not carried on quite so extensively as formerly.

The mercantile department is doing three times the business it was previous to the curtailing of our home industries; and has the patronage of nearly the entire people of Brigham City and surrounding settlements.

It has been our uniform practice to submit all business matters involving important interests of the people to the council of the United Order, where the most perfect liberty and greatest freedom of expression of thought and opinion have always been allowed and always indulged.

The council is composed of sixty members, those most influential in the community, selected on account of their integrity, faithfulness and

willingness to labor and assist in promoting the cause of union and
brotherhood.

Notwithstanding our severe reverses and the fiery ordeal through
which we have passed, the confidence of the people in our principles of
union has been preserved and they feel that we have worked earnestly
and unselfishly to secure their interests and promote their general
welfare.[53]

The report proved to be over-optimistic. As affairs became worse,
the United Order apparently ceased its function as an advisory
body to the cooperative.

The last entry in the minute book of the Brigham City United
Order on July 20, 1880, attributes to Lorenzo Snow these words:

Because of many losses and disasters . . . we have discontinued some
of our enterprises and curtailed others. Yet for a period of fifteen years,
our union has prevented division in mercantile business; say nothing
about many other things which have been done by our union, and I have
nothing to regret of all we have accomplished. We have kept out our
enemies, and in all these matters we did them by common consent.[54]

Though the United Order faded out, several of its leading figures,
as directors of the Brigham City Mercantile and Manufacturing
Association, continued their struggle to keep the co-op alive. That
year the co-op sold Hansen's Dairy. The annual dividend, once in
the mid-twenties, and often 10 to 13 percent, declined to 3 percent
on a capital stock which, by vote of the stockholders, had been
reduced one-half in value. In 1881 the woolen mill was shut
down. At the same time the directors noted that the tannery had
been operating at a loss for the past two years. Finally, in January
1888 it was conceded that "our manufacturing departments were
. . . lying comparatively useless and throwing the burden of
profits almost entirely on the merchandising and sheepraising departments."[55] That same winter severe storms decimated the
sheep herds, leaving the surviving sheep in such poor condition
that the clip was reduced from an anticipated four or five pounds
per head to three and one-half. In February 1892 the directors
found it necessary to borrow $5,000 from the Deseret National
Bank in Salt Lake City. Liquidation of company assets continued,
with the sale of the machine shop, sheep herds, woolen mill, and
various parcels of real estate. The next year the directors had to
borrow another $10,000. In 1894 two different fires damaged the
store, apparently administering the death blow to the ailing

association. In November 1895 the Brigham City Co-op went into receivership. A carbon copy of the procedures to be followed in settling affairs of the co-op is the last item in the directors' minute book, signed in pencil by Lorenzo Snow.

It has been questioned whether the later history of the co-op would have been different if the extraordinary losses beginning with the 1877 fire in the woolen mill had never occurred. It seems likely that other factors—the railroad, and the taste for finer fabrics and footwear than could be produced at home—could account for the decline of cloth and leather manufacturing. The nature of the capital structure would have made the gradual concentration of stock and the disappearance of the cooperative nature of the undertaking inevitable. In addition, management problems helped lead to the disposal of many other departments. Had the store itself weathered its third period of depression and continued indefinitely, it would have survived as a co-op in name only.

During the growth of the cooperative movement church authorities frequently advocated it as a stepping-stone to a larger, finer, and more comprehensive system: the Order of Enoch, the ultimate economic goal. It was planned that the co-ops would be absorbed into the more comprehensive scheme. Late in 1873 Brigham Young launched at St. George his drive to organize the Saints into his ideal system. In Brigham City the co-op was touched only remotely by the development of the Order and outlasted it. Elsewhere the United Order displayed great vitality and for a time at least superseded or swallowed up the co-ops.

CHAPTER 7

The United Order
of Enoch:
The order of heaven

N 1875 Brigham Young and other directors of ZCMI found occasion to reflect upon the broad principles and conditions that had led to the cooperative movement:

> Years ago it was perceived that we Latter-day Saints were open to the same dangers as those which beset the rest of the world. . . . Then it was that the Saints were counseled to enter into cooperation. In the absence of the necessary faith to enter upon a more perfect order revealed by the Lord unto the Church, this was felt to be the best means of drawing us together and making us one.[1]

The apostle Orson Pratt saw in the organization of ZCMI the beginnings of a new unity that would culminate in the redemption of Zion and the realization of an ideal social system.[2] Similarly apostle George Q. Cannon voiced the opinion of many when he found in the success of the cooperative institutions, after three and a half years of operation, a lesson pointing to the more general and more salutary results to be expected from the Order of Enoch.[3] Brigham Young himself said in 1869 that "this cooperative movement is only a stepping stone to what is called the Order of Enoch, but which is in reality the order of Heaven."[4]

Undoubtedly Brigham Young continued to see as an attainable goal the Law of Consecration and Stewardship outlined by Joseph Smith. Every subsequent cooperative effort of a material nature seems to have been intended to teach and lead the Saints closer to the more comprehensive system that ultimately was to be realized in the Order of Enoch. Concerned with immediate as well as with remote objectives, Brigham Young adhered to his policy of Mormon isolation and independence that required arrangements much broader in scope than a cooperative system based on a combination of monetary capital; it was obvious that an association of stockholders excluded the rank and file of the church—small farmers, mechanics, and laborers, whose subsistence needs left little for investment. To consolidate the interests of all Latter-day Saints, he inaugurated in 1874 the United Order, a system that from one perspective may be regarded as his supreme effort to check disintegrating forces developing within and without the church, forces that threatened the economic and political independence of the Mormon people. Though his motives derived in part from these immediate considerations, it is also evident that he hoped through the organization of the United Order to achieve before his death, as a tribute to the memory of his beloved friend and prophet, Joseph Smith, the ideal society that had escaped them in Missouri.

It is important in understanding the origin and progress of the United Order to review the bitter political conflict that characterized the period under discussion. A succession of bills before Congress that were designed to curtail the rights and privileges of Mormons and to reduce them to a subordinate position in political and economic affairs through the extension of federal power provoked leaders of the church to seek legitimate and effective means of thwarting the apparent designs of their enemies. Brigham Young's desire to retain the maximum degree of economic independence for the Mormon commonwealth was spurred by the political persecution to which he and his people were subjected. For example, in October 1871, he was arrested following a grand jury indictment based on charges of unlawful cohabitation. Released on bail, he went to St. George as he had done in previous winters, was accused of fleeing from justice, and made a midwinter return to Salt Lake to present himself in court. He was promptly arrested on a new charge of murder and kept for many weeks as a prisoner in his own home, a concession made to his age and importance.

The general unease caused by such persecution was aggravated by a disruptive chain of events in the wake of the Panic of 1873, which no doubt suggested that the time was right for a more radical reconstruction of the economic institutions of the Latter-day Saint commonwealth. The depression hit first the mining industry—an industry completely dependent on the whims of national and international markets. The industry was obviously an enclave of non-Mormons. While considerable numbers of Latter-day Saints were employed in mining in 1873, virtually all the mines and banks that sustained them and depended upon them were owned by non-Mormons. Bank deposits dropped by one-third during the twelve months following the panic. With a shrinkage of national markets, the mines were shut down. Unemployment and economic stagnation were the result, and Mormons lost both their jobs in the mines and their market for foodstuffs and other commodities used in the mining camps. It seemed obvious to Brigham Young that the "outsiders" had been vectors of the plague visited upon Utah in the wake of the panic.[5]

Local conditions also influenced the organization of the United Order, especially the disruption of Mormon village life in southern Utah caused by the mining industry at Pioche, Nevada. Cash wages in the camps and an insatiable market for building materials, vegetables, fruit, grain, and meat had led to serious shortages of labor, lumber, and foodstuffs in the Mormon communities from Parowan to St. George. In 1870 Erastus Snow, resident apostle in the Southern Utah Mission, advised Brigham Young in Salt Lake City that because of a shortage of labor, the fields south of St. George had been abandoned, and he urged that a hundred men from northern settlements be sent to the area.[6] The St. George Temple, undertaken on the initiation of President Young, required large supplies of lumber, which was difficult to get because of the strong demand at Pioche, Nevada. At this same time Brigham Young was bringing to completion the $50,000 cotton and woolen mill at Washington, which he turned over to the Zion's Cooperative Rio Virgen Manufacturing Company in exchange for its notes bearing interest at ten percent.[7] The views of church and community leaders in regard to conditions in southern settlements are reflected in contemporary records. Brigham Young's counselor, George A. Smith, in dedicating the St. George Temple site, called upon God to

hasten the redemption of the center stake of Zion in this land; overrule the discovery of minerals in this land for the good of Thy people. Control the President of the United States and those in authority who purpose evil against Thy people.[8]

Erastus Snow, ecclesiastical leader of the area, complained that

many had gone away to earn money in the mines and elsewhere leaving at home comparatively few to do the farming and most necessary work. ... He had given permission to a few to go for a short time and earn a little money to supply their immediate wants on condition that they would be faithful while absent and pay their honest tithing on their return.[9]

Another leader, Joseph W. Young, openly told the southern Utah Saints that they "had no right to go to Pioche and trade off . . . lumber, chickens, eggs, and grain unless . . . told to do so."[10] Prospering from supplying and servicing the mining camps, many Latter-day Saints contracted considerable indebtedness in order to expand their profit-making ventures. To these people, closing of the mining camps spelled disaster. A bishop in the Parowan area lamented that because of the heavy lumber trade with Pioche "the brethren doing the hauling [have] got into debt to the Gentiles and since the falling off of the . . . trade, those debtors have been at the mercy of the Gentiles who are their creditors."[11]

The condition of the southern settlements was of special concern to Brigham Young. He had hoped that the mild climate in the St. George area would make possible the production of tobacco, silk, and cotton sufficient for home consumption. He had invested in livestock, farmlands, and industrial enterprises in the region, and had built a winter home there. The mines were seen by Young and local church leaders as unwanted pockets of gentile infection that threatened to contaminate the whole region, setting awry their plans for its economic development and sapping the spiritual strength of the settlers. In a sense, the situation presented a prototype of what might happen to the entire Mormon commonwealth if steps were not taken to bind the Saints into an economic and spiritual unity that left no interstice for entry of outside influence. Accordingly, his plans for a broader cooperative system took shape in St. George, and the first of the United Orders was organized there.

The United Order was by no means, however, exclusively an outgrowth of what church leaders observed happening at St. George. The need to further unify the interests and labors of the Saints throughout the Great Basin had for some time been a theme of continual discussion. At the 1872 general conferences in April and October, several speakers dwelt upon cooperation; apostle George Q. Cannon in the fall session predicted its early extension.

The time must come when we must obey that which has been revealed to us as the Order of Enoch, when there shall be no rich and no poor among the Latter-day Saints; when wealth will not be a temptation; when every man will love his neighbor as he does himself; when every man and woman will labor for the good of all as much as for self. That day must come, and we may as well prepare our hearts for it, brethren, for as wealth increases I see more and more a necessity for the institution of such an order. As wealth increases, luxury and extravagance have more power over us. The necessity for such an order is very great, and God, undoubtedly, in his own time and way, will inspire his servant to introduce it among the people. I do not wish to foreshadow when it will be done, or what the circumstances will be that will call it forth, for this is not my province; but I feel led to talk upon it, and to prepare my own heart, and to seek, with all the faith and influence I have, to prepare the hearts of my brethren and sisters for the introduction of this order.[12]

Taking up the theme, the following day Brigham Young described at length an ideal community such as might exist among a people disposed to live according to the principles of the Order of Enoch.

Now suppose we had a little society organized . . . after the Order of Enoch—would you build our houses all alike? No. How should we live? I will tell you how I would arrange for a little family, say about a thousand persons. I would build houses expressly for their convenience in cooking, washing, and every department of their domestic arrangements. Instead of having every woman getting up in the morning and fussing around a cookstove or over the fire, cooking a little food for two or three or half a dozen persons, or a dozen, as the case may be, she would have nothing to do but to go to her work. Let me have my arrangement here, a hall in which I can seat five hundred persons to eat; and I have my cooking apparatus, ranges and ovens, all prepared. And suppose we had a hall a hundred feet long with our cooking room attached to this hall; and there is a person at the further end of the table and he should telegraph that he wanted a warm beefsteak; and this is conveyed to him by a little railway, perhaps under the table, and he or she may take her beefsteak. . . . No matter what they call for, it is conveyed to them and they take it, and we can seat five hundred at once, and serve them all in a few minutes. And when they have all eaten, the dishes are piled together, slipped under the table, and run back to the ones who wash them. We could have a few Chinamen to do that if we did not want to do it ourselves. Under such a system the women could go to work making their bonnets, hats, and clothing, or in the factories. . . .

What will we do through the day? Each one go to his work. Here are the herdsmen—here are those who look after the sheep—here are those who make the butter and the cheese, all at their work by themselves. Some for the Kanyon, perhaps, or for the plow or harvest, no difference what, each and every class is organized, and all labor and perform their part. . . .

Work through the day, and when it comes evening, instead of going to a theatre, walking the streets, riding, or reading novels—these falsehoods got up expressly to excite the minds of youth—repair to our room, and have our historians, and our different teachers to teach classes of old and young, to read the Scriptures to them; to teach them history, arithmetic, reading, writing, and painting; and have the best teachers that can be got to teach our day-schools. Half the labor necessary to make people moderately comfortable now, would make them independently rich under such a system. Now we toil and work and labor, and some of us are so anxious that we are sure to start after a load of wood on Saturday so as to occupy Sunday in getting home. . . .

If we could see such a society organized as I have mentioned, you would see none of this waste. You would see people all attending to their business having the most improved machinery for making cloth, and doing every kind of housework, farming, all mechanical operations, in our factories, dairies, orchards, and vineyards; and possessing every comfort and convenience of life. A society like this would never have to buy anything; they would make and raise all they would eat, drink, and wear, and always have something to sell and bring money, to help to increase their comfort and independence.[13]

A few months later Orson Pratt reviewed at length the revelations of Joseph Smith on the Order of Enoch, pointed out the evils of grasping individualism, and called upon the Saints to conscientiously apply the principles of the gospel in regard to property.[14] He returned to the theme at the April 1873 general conference and was followed by President Young, who announced to the people that those who wished to "live as a family" and could arrange legally to do so would have his blessing. "The Lord almighty has not the least objection in the world to our entering the Order of Enoch," he maintained.[15]

At a conference in October 1873 Lorenzo Snow also urged adoption of the system: "It is more than forty years since the Order of Enoch was introduced, and rejected. One would naturally think, that it is now about time to begin to honor it."[16]

Brigham Young had explained that summer to residents of the northern Utah community of Logan that

the only reason why we do not . . . enter into the organization of Enoch, . . . is simply because we have not yet been able to find every item of law bearing on this matter, so as to organize in a way that apostates cannot trouble us. This is the only reason. It is a matter that I am paying particular attention to, with some of my brethren, to see if we have skill enough to get up an organization and draw up papers to bind ourselves together under the laws of the United States, so that we can put our means and labor together and join as one family. As soon as we can accomplish this, and get an instrument that lawyers cannot pick to pieces and destroy, and apostates cannot afflict us, we expect to get up this institution, and enter most firmly into it.[17]

By late winter church leaders were apparently persuaded that the needed legal structure had been sufficiently developed to permit inauguration of the program. Actual organization got underway at St. George early in the year 1874. After a series of discussions aimed at enlightening the people on the operation of the Order of Enoch, the United Order of the City of St. George was organized on February 9 of that year. The following Sunday, after further discussion and a promise by Brigham Young of blessings to the faithful, three hundred enrolled for membership in the Order. A preamble and articles of agreement were presented for adoption at a public meeting held the latter part of March. Prepared with painstaking care by President Young and his associates, the document is of considerable importance and is printed in full in the appendix to this volume. It was used, in substantially its original form, as a model for the hundreds of United Orders founded in virtually every Latter-day Saint community over the next several months. The preamble bespoke familiarity with the rhetoric of agrarian dissent stirred by the Panic of 1873, employing this rhetoric to advance the continuing church goal of self-sufficiency.[18]

Noting the conflict between capital and labor, the distress and uncertainty occasioned by extravagant speculation, and the abuse of the credit system, the preamble stated that the objectives of association would be to establish a self-sufficing economy through cooperation in labor and simplification in consumption. The first ten articles of the full document gave the name of the co-partnership, the place of business, and its objectives. It also created a board of management consisting of a president, two vice-presidents, a secretary with two assistants, a treasurer, and three directors. It defined the duties of these officers and provided further for a committee to appraise property invested in the Order and fix wage rates. Duties of foremen who were to manage various branches of business for the Order were clearly defined. Article 11 provided for an annual meeting for the report of business and election of officers. Voting was to be in person, by letter, or by proxy, and the support of two-thirds of the membership was required for elections. The board could propose by-laws, which would become binding if sustained by a two-thirds vote of all members. The board was empowered to buy and sell real and personal property and transact all business consistent with the interests of the Order. Article 12 was a pledge of the members to place in the Order their time, labor, energy, and ability, and such property as they may feel disposed to transfer for the use of the Order. Article 13 provided for a declaration of a dividend at the end of each period of five years, the dividend to be credited to the capital holdings of each member in proportion to his investment. A member could withdraw at the end of any five-year period by accepting one-half his capital and dividend in full settlement of his claim. The article stated further that the greater potency of labor under the system would make the half greater than the whole would have been if individually managed. Article 14 declared that the Order would not assume the debts of members unless property were transferred to offset them. Article 15 was a pledge to limit trade with those outside the Order to absolute necessities not otherwise obtainable, and Article 16 enjoined temperance, frugality, and the avoidance of imported luxuries. Similarly, Article 17 bound the members to simplicity in dress and to a preference for homespun materials. Article 18 concluded the document with a pledge of industry, faithfulness, and unselfishness in seeking to promote the welfare of each other and of all mankind.

Brigham Young and George A. Smith also prepared a letter of instructions for circulation among the communities of southern Utah embodying suggestions for care and economy in the planting and gathering of crops and for the promotion of home manufactures. Fourteen rules of conduct, cast in the form of pledges, were read, adopted, and subsequently presented with very slight amendment wherever branches of the United Order were established. Adapted from regulations originally drafted as requirements for members of the "School of Prophets," the rules were similar in tone to the United Order agreement itself, as this sampling illustrates.

1. We will not take the name of Deity in vain, or speak lightly of His character or of sacred things.

2. We will pray with our families morning and evening and also attend to secret prayers.

6. We will observe the Sabbath day and keep it holy in accordance with the revelations.

10. We will not knowingly patronize any person engaged in any business who is not a member of the Order, unless our necessities absolutely require us to do so.

12. We will be simple in our dress and manner of living, using proper economy and prudence in the management of all entrusted to our care.[19]

Convinced that the time was ripe and the people prepared for general acceptance of the plan, President Young sent church leaders and special agents as organizers into all the southern settlements. The president himself presented the plan to the settlements through which he passed on his return from St. George to Salt Lake City. Delayed by severe weather and bad roads until it was too late to reach the city in time for the April conference, he sent directions to his associates to adjourn the conference for one month. At the single session held on April 6, 1874, Orson Pratt delivered a sermon designed to prepare the minds of those present for the acceptance of the new social order even though it might involve departures from the system described in the revelations to Joseph Smith. He reminded the congregation that revelations are applicable to particular times and peoples and are not necessarily binding after the circumstances to which they apply have changed. Even without detailed information concerning the United Order then being established in the southern settlements and intended to become churchwide, he was sure that modifications of the Jackson County system would be necessary. He anticipated division among the Saints and opposition to the system from men of wealth, but pleaded for tolerance until all could be brought in by conversion to the merits of the plan.[20] On the same day, April 6, President Young and apostles George A. Smith and Erastus Snow began the two-week journey toward Salt Lake City, organizing branches of the United Order in towns along the route.

In Beaver, Utah, on April 12, according to one report, "President Young showed very clearly that it [the United Order] was not a personal speculation; that himself with the rest would put in all he possessed for the accomplishment of the work he was engaged in, and it would all become common stock. The intention is to elevate the poor, and make them comfortable and happy as well as the rich. He wanted no poor in our midst, nor would there be any when the Order got fully established."[21] A report in the local paper on April 20 showed that in response to

Brigham Young, second president of the LDS Church and founder of Utah's United Orders. (Church Archives)

Brigham Young's speech, two-thirds of the citizens had already joined the Order, stock was being turned into common herds, and great activity prevailed in getting the plan underway.[22]

The report of a non-Mormon in Beaver at the same time, however, suggested that at least some dissent existed. "Mormons [some of them presumably disaffected members] say here," the man wrote,

that he [Brigham Young] wishes to get hold of their property, then he will compel them to do anything he orders or excommunicate them. A number of the faithful are distressed over this matter. They dislike to give up their fellowship in the church, and they dislike to give up their property.[23]

Meanwhile an amendment to the territorial general incorporation law of 1870 was passed and approved February 20, 1874, permitting subscriptions to capital to be made by conveying by deed of trust property other than money at valuations to be determined in accordance with properly defined rules.[24] According to Erastus Snow, this amendment was passed to meet the needs of mining interests, but it suited the purposes of those who wished legal safeguards for properties invested in the Order.

Reaching Salt Lake City on April 20, Brigham Young lost little time in effecting an organization there. Preliminary meetings had already been held in some of the wards. The Twentieth Ward was organized on the twenty-ninth of April, and stake organizations were effected early in May in Cache Valley and Ogden. At Ogden 1,200 people handed in their names for membership, an evidence to church leaders that the time was ripe for the establishment of the Order.[25] Places not reached before the reconvening of the postponed conference were visited by members of the Council of the Twelve Apostles as promptly as possible afterwards, and by the early part of July, few wards, if any, remained unorganized (see Appendix VII).

The purpose of the reconvened conference, which continued in session four days, was to convert members to the plan already launched by President Young and the general authorities of the church. At least a dozen sermons were preached favoring the United Order and covering the entire range of arguments in its favor. It was emphasized that the Saints' destiny was to realize a complete spiritual and temporal unity, enjoying all things in common. The designs of the Lord as revealed to Joseph Smith for the observance of the principles of consecration and stewardship had been frustrated by disobedience and selfishness among the Mormon settlers in Jackson County, Missouri, leading to their expulsion from the land of Zion. Later, in Utah, the scramble for individual gain had become a serious obstacle to the progress of the church and the fulfillment of its mission. However, the cooperative enterprises of the preceding decade had pointed the way to the complete severance of trade with the gentiles and the development of a program of complete self-sufficiency in every Mormon community. Now the time was ripe and the Saints were ready for the acceptance of the revelations and the redemption of Zion that could be accomplished only by a righteous and unselfish people. The United Order, unlike the co-ops, contemplated the pooling of labor as well as capital and would realize the economies theoretically possible by the pooling or joint use of capital and by the division or classification of labor. Taking full advantage of the productive capacity of every member under the direction of wise leadership, the organization of labor was expected to multiply the wealth of the Saints beyond all expectations and leave ample time for study and recreation. Retrenchment in the use of imports and luxuries would make possible the accumulation of capital for the establishment of new industries, at the same time banishing pride and ostentation and breaking down social distinctions that conflicted with the ideals of Mormonism. In short, the United Order would provide the material and social conditions essential to individual and collective happiness and progress.[26]

The one aspect of the Order ignored or treated only briefly by the several speakers was the precise manner of its operation. Erastus Snow, who, next to President Young, had most to do with the work of the organization in the south, advised, "As to the minutia of the workings of the various Branches of this Order, the details of the business and the relations of life, one meeting of this kind would not suffice to tell, nor could the people comprehend it if we were able to tell it; but it will be revealed to us as we pass along, line upon line, precept upon precept, here a little and there a little, and everything necessary will appear in its time and place, and none need be over-anxious to pass over the bridge before they reach it."[27]

The sermons of the adjourned conference and provisions of the St. George articles of association defined the general procedure as follows: Each community or ward would constitute a branch with a board of directors to determine policy and assign responsibility. On coming into the Order, a member would transfer control of his economic property to the board and agree to assume such responsibilities and to perform such labors as might be decided upon by the central authority. Laborers would be assigned to specific specialized tasks, and nominal wages would be agreed upon. Superintendents selected by the directors or by the laborers in each class would direct the work of the respective trades and the operation of farms and stores. Products resulting from the operations of the Order would be drawn against for the sustenance of the members and their families, while any surplus to the credit of an individual arising from the production of more than the amount of his withdrawals was recorded as increased capital in his favor. A member withdrawing after five years could take out one-half of the capital standing to his name, the balance being both a penalty against withdrawal and a return to the combined labors of the remaining members of the cooperating groups.

On the third day of the Salt Lake City conference, May 9, 1874, the names of the general officers of the United Order of Zion were presented and sustained by show of hands. The organization ran parallel to that of the church. Brigham Young was named as president of the United Order in all the world wherever established. His associates in the First Presidency were made vice-presidents of the Order, and the twelve apostles became assistant vice-presidents. The first vice-president, George A. Smith, also held the office of treasurer, with Edward Hunter, presiding bishop, as assistant treasurer. Capable businessmen were included within the organization as the board of directors.[28]

On the last day of May President Young issued a compilation of suggestions similar to those that had been issued at St. George, in which the following principles were presented:

1. By consolidation and cooperation in farming, surplus equipment could be released and sold or stored.

2. The exportation of raw material, such as hides, pelts, and wool, should be checked and manufactures should be expanded to work up these materials for the home market.

3. By retrenchment on the one hand and diligence on the other, imports should be restricted to indispensable articles impossible of local manufacture.

4. Simple but accurate accounts should be kept.

5. Each organization should determine the price of labor.

6. Each branch of the Order should be legally incorporated.[29]

While there was no voice of dissent at the conference, many did not accept the program with enthusiasm. Brigham Young's remark that the new system would be all-inclusive, and that the cooperatives would be absorbed into it, did not please those who had enjoyed ten to twenty-five percent dividends on their investments in cooperative stores and livestock companies. Open opposition found voice in the Third Ward of Salt Lake City when the bishop and his associates questioned the plan.[30] Frederick Kesler, bishop of the Sixteenth Ward, himself a warm advocate of the new order, lamented the appearance of opposition. "I am sorry to see so much opposition manifested towards the United Order as there is in this city. It betokens no good and in consequence we may be made to see much sorrow and affliction."[31] The general failure of the people of Salt Lake City and in scores of other communities to go actively into the Order indicates that opposition was much more widespread than appeared when votes were taken in assemblies of the Saints. Gentile opposition was expressed in the Salt Lake *Daily Tribune,* which carried correspondence and editorials ridiculing the movement as a "gigantic fraud" and "an insatiable monopoly" for the benefit of church leaders at the expense of the people.

Doubtless the people would have been much more ready to go into the Order if a clear-cut plan of operation had been presented to them. As was to be expected, men of greatest means were the most reluctant to place their tangibles into a common stock. Some questioned to what extent Young himself intended to enter the Order. His sincerity in launching the plan cannot be questioned. He had originally intended to put all his possessions into the collective enterprise. At the Third Ward in Salt Lake City, two months after the Beaver meeting, he said: "Ask me if I am going into the Order with all that I have. Yes, as I told them in a meeting not long ago, I am going in with hat, coat, vest, pants, shirt, boots, and all I have. . . . I want it [his property] appropriated for the salvation of the human family, to build Temples, to sustain the families of the Elders who go abroad to preach; I want it to be used for the good of the poor and for the establishing of truth and righteousness on the earth. That is all it is for."[32] Unless he was misunderstood, however, his later actions did not bear out his original intentions. He had always maintained that men of superior abilities should direct others in the use of time and of property. Before another two months passed he made the following admission at Lehi: "I am laboring under a certain embarrassment and so are many others, with regard to deeding property, and that is to find men who know what to do with property when it is in their hands. . . . When this factory at Provo can go into the hands of men who know what to do with it, it will go; when my factory in Salt Lake County can go into the hands of men who know what to do with it, it will go."[33] Such men apparently were never found.

The reluctance of Brigham Young and other Mormon leaders to put their own interests wholly under management of the United Order provided a field day for the anti-Mormon press in Salt Lake City. A satirical journal, *Enoch's Advocate*, was founded for the specific purpose of ridiculing the program. Chiding the Mormon leader on the issue, the editors of the anti-Mormon *Salt Lake Tribune* offered a bit of unsolicited advice:

If the Profit [*sic*] don't make the rich men fork over as well as the poor, we shall think him an unjust, discriminating Profit, and shall tell the world that he is afraid of the strong rich men and is an oppressor of the weak and the poor. Brother Brigham, sail in, and show a fair hand in this Euchre Business. Don't slight Brothers Jennings, Hooper or any of the gilt-edged. One big pot, Brother Brigham, and no favoritism.[34]

Meanwhile, consideration of articles of incorporation that were, in accord with territorial law, to supersede the St. George draft proceeded in a series of meetings, the first of which was held in the old tabernacle in Salt Lake City on June 19. A committee of twelve was chosen, which reported a "new constitution" to a second gathering on June 27. After discussion, the draft was adopted.[35] Brigham Young, who had presided at the first meeting, was absent from the second; he was attending a conference with several of the Council of the Twelve at Brigham City, where the revised form of the articles was presented. The Brigham City branch of the United Order was the first to be organized under the revised articles.[36] The many attempts to operate under the United Order plan, accompanied by a stream of questions directed to the First Presidency, prompted the publication of a pamphlet intended to be a manual or guide for members and officers everywhere. After the material for the guide was presented at a conference of church leaders August 11-13, members of the Twelve were sent to all parts of the territory to effect reorganizations under the revised forms.[37]

In addition to the articles of association and by-laws, the new pamphlet contained instructions for members. Church leaders had slightly amended the fourteen rules of conduct worked out at St. George, providing, in addition, a series of questions and answers likely to arise in every community where serious attempts were made to make the United Order a success. Reprinted in the pamphlet (see Appendix V) was correspondence between the officers of the Order at St. George and the First Presidency of the church, containing valuable suggestions on meeting difficulties that had developed in the actual operation of the Order over a period of several months. Although the pamphlet stated that the purpose of organizing under the statutes of the Territory of Utah was not the perpetuating of individual interests, but to take advantage of the protection thus afforded, the nature of that protection was not explained.

The articles of association followed customary forms, stating name, duration, general objects, place of business, capitalization, official set-up, powers of the board of directors, and so forth. Article VIII provided for election by ballot, unless it was decided by a majority of eligible voters present to make the election *viva voce.* The person receiving a majority of the votes cast was to be declared duly elected. The article did not clarify whether voting power was dependent on amount invested, but when the question was raised later, the answer was given that the legal way of voting was by shares, a departure from the parallel provision in the original articles drawn at St. George in which the one-man, one-vote principle prevailed. Article XIII was the usual limited liability clause, exempting private or individual property from liability for the debts or obligations of the company. Article XIV permitted subscription to capital by the transfer of real or personal property at a value determined by the appraisal of competent parties, and Article XV permitted the directors to declare dividends and pay them to stockholders in cash or in stock as they deemed necessary.

The duties and responsibilities of officers along with rules governing the time and place of meetings and the keeping of records were set forth in fifteen by-laws, the last of which permitted amendments or alterations by a two-thirds vote at any general meeting. Section I permitted the transfer of stock by endorsement and return of certificates to the company. Though the original St. George articles permitted withdrawals only at five-year intervals and pledged the member to accept as payment in full one-half the amount credited to him in the books of the company, no other safeguards were designed to protect the company against the membership of undesirable persons who might acquire stock by purchase. In brief, the casting of the articles and by-laws in legal form for purpose of incorporation removed every distinguishing characteristic that made the contemplated order different from any other business corporation.

Following the articles and by-laws in the pamphlet, the fourteen rules of conduct and behavior were reprinted substantially as in earlier articles of association. In the revised draft, Rule 10 was tempered to read: "We will patronize our brethren who are in the Order."[38]

The decision to organize the branches of the Order under the territorial law of incorporation provoked regret, if not dissatisfaction, among those who longed for a system cemented by unselfishness and brotherly love. A legally corporate Order controlled by stock-voting, seemingly similar to the co-ops, stood in stark contrast to their expected "family-type" Order with all working for all and no account kept in terms of money wages. The presidency answered that although all communities would eventually take that form, people were not yet ready for a perfect system; consequently, accepting the legally incorporated form meant a move toward the goal. In rare cases where the members were willing and eager to adopt the family pattern, it was advised that account should be kept by a credit and debit system of the contributions in goods and labor and of the consumption of each individual. Thus, misunderstandings over supposed inequality and discrimination would be avoided. In further defending the corporate form, Brigham Young expressed his regret that "we have to bow to the whims and caprices of the ignorant, and to the prejudice of wilful, ignorant sectarianism." In consequence, he explained, "we are under the necessity of getting up our constitution or the articles of our association so that they will agree with existing statutes and be legal, that we can carry on business as we wish without being infringed upon or molested by anybody."[39]

At the October 1874 general conference John Taylor, senior apostle, spoke in favor of the corporate principle: "We have been trying, since God moved upon his servant Brigham, to get things into order, but the ship moves very slowly; there seems to be a good many snags of one kind or another in the way." A point of dispute overlapping the issue of gospel vs. legal form was the question of how closely Brigham Young's Order approached that revealed by Joseph Smith. In answer, Elder Taylor explained that it would not be practicable to follow the pattern outlined in the Doctrine and Covenants because of the necessity of conforming to the laws of the land. Answering the query "where does the principle of stewardship come in?" he said that "the voice you have in selecting your officers, and in voting for them and the stock you hold in these institutions is your stewardship." When asked if labor as well as capital would have a vote, he replied, "They ought to have, and will have if the law will let them; the great trouble is that the law will not allow us to do everything we would like; but whenever we can get at it we shall vote on all these things as you have voted here today. But we have to evade these things a little now, because the law will not allow us to do otherwise." Pointing out the ordinary imperfections of humanity, he argued that the common treasury from which members might draw freely to assist in the operations of their stewardships could not presently be made operative. He was sure that many who were advocating the adoption of the plan outlined in the Law of Consecration and Stewardship would change their minds after further consideration. "For all men are not capable and all men are not honest and conscientious; if they were we should be nearly ready to be caught up, but we have not reached that point yet, and consequently we have to do the best we can."[40]

Obstructed by the stubborn wall of human nature, Brigham Young's plans for a church-wide United Order had already gone awry. The people, contrary to what he had thought a few months earlier, were not ready for unity in temporal affairs. When practical considerations were squarely faced, it was obvious that to place property in the control of the inexperienced or the incompetent was a waste. On the other hand, many were mistrustful either of the integrity or the ability of the boards of control set up over the branches of the Order, and therefore were in some cases unwilling to transfer title to their property. The leaders in many localities, being men of affairs and of property, were less willing to join the Order than those of small means.[41] Under these circumstances the notion of stewardships as used in the revelations of Joseph Smith was revived, and those who feared to transfer their holdings to the Order were to be regarded as stewards over their own property.[42] While this arrangement fell short of the requirements of the revelations that called for a transfer of everything to the bishop and an allotment from him of an "inheritance," the alternate plan made it possible for some who would have hesitated to enter a more exacting system to assert allegiance to the Order. News that the stewardship plan had been inaugurated in Salt Lake City disturbed many who had already undertaken to adhere to more difficult standards. Answering an inquiry from Sevier Stake, President Young upheld his original plan as superior to that of stewardship.[43]

The editors of the *Tribune* maintained that in Salt Lake City the order had received an "icy reception" and that of seven or eight thousand who attended the meetings in the Tabernacle, only three hundred were willing to join the order.[44] Official records show that only four Orders were incorporated in Salt Lake County. The United Order of Big Cottonwood Ward filed articles in March 1875 and disincorporated in 1881. Only one year longer in duration, the United Order of West Jordan was incorporated in June 1876 and dissolved in 1883. Taking advantage of the prestige value of the United Order drive, twenty-four Salt Lake City tailors organized in February 1875 the United Order of Tailors to engage in the merchant tailoring and outfitting trades.[45] This was a departure from the prevalent use of the term and was analogous to the organization of shoemakers a year earlier into the Workingmen's Cooperative Association. Not unlike the latter, the tailors' association was of comparatively brief duration, the latest filing of directors' names being in July 1878.[46] Though United Orders were organized in all twenty of the Salt Lake City wards, the only city ward to incorporate was the Nineteenth, articles for which were filed in January 1875. Among the enterprises included within the activities of this branch was that of making soap and axle grease, a business begun by J. B. Maiben. With the general decline of interest in the United Order movement, the stockholders of the United Order of the Nineteenth Ward revamped their articles by filing two sample amendments, one changing the title to the Utah Soap Manufacturing Company and the other substituting in place of Article III the simple declaration that the objective of the association "is the making of soaps, concentrated lyes, sal soda and axle grease."[47]

Even the editors of the *Tribune* were willing to concede that the United Order fared much better in rural villages. "Either the novelty of the thing," they wrote, "or its quasi-agrarian character suddenly introduced and seconded by the satellites of the Presidency met with much temporary approval in the villages and small towns."[48] In southern Utah especially, an overwhelming majority of the people accepted the call to join the Order and underwent a special ritual of rebaptism to signify acceptance of its principles. At Ephraim on June 27, 1875, the thirty-first anniversary of the martyrdom of Joseph and Hyrum Smith, seven of the twelve apostles were baptized. In the course of the next few weeks thousands followed their example. The officiating elder used the following words: "Having authority given me of Jesus Christ I baptize you for the remission of your sins, the renewal of your covenants, and the observance of the rules of the holy United Order, in the name of the Father and of the Son and of the Holy Ghost."[49] It has been suggested that the purpose of the ordinance was to revive needed support for a system already on the decline.[50] Be that as it may, as time went on less and less was said about the United Order in the general conferences and other assemblies of the Saints. The efforts to realize it in a few communities, however, were persistent and heroic. When the movement was referred to in later years, its departures from the system of consecrations and stewardships outlined in the Doctrine and Covenants were generally pointed out and the latter held up as the ideal toward which the Saints must move. In one of his last sermons reiterating the central thought of the system advocated by Joseph Smith, Brigham Young declared that an equal division of property was not essential to the establishment of the United Order, but the prime requisite was the same type of unity in temporal affairs as had been achieved in things spiritual, whereby the labors of all are subject to the direction of those endowed with wisdom and ability.

With the death of Brigham Young on August 29, 1877, the reins of church government passed into the hands of John Taylor and others whose views on cooperation and practicable means of attaining a unity of the Saints, if previously in accord with those of their departed leader, had been modified with experience and adjusted to changing circumstances. An account of the changes introduced by the new leadership will be better understood after the most significant experiments with the United Order have been reviewed.

CHAPTER 8

St. George:
Oneness
in heart and hand

RIGHAM YOUNG was obviously in a jubilant mood when he sent the telegram to Salt Lake City on February 28, 1874, announcing that he had initiated the United Order movement from his base in southern Utah. "We have organized six companies after the order of Enoch," he told the waiting brethren in Salt Lake City. "We go up the river next week to organize the settlements." Mixed with the jubilation in his message, however, was a clearly discernible outpouring of relief—of the release that comes when bold action has been taken after the anxiety of a long, expectant hesitancy. "The brethren and sisters all seem ready to go into this order of oneness, heart and hand," he continued. "Thank the Lord the people are so prepared for it. With the fire of the Gospel burning thus brightly, we need not fear the efforts of our enemies."[1]

The enunciation had been long awaited. Since the fall of 1872 church leaders had sermonized extensively on the need for greater unity, promising a time "when there shall be no rich and no poor among the Latter-day Saints; when wealth will not be a temptation; when every man will love his neighbor as he does himself; when every man and woman will labor for the good of all as much as for self."[2]

The Saints in St. George and surrounding areas had been the objects of a particularly assiduous preparation, through many sermons delivered by President Young and his colleagues during their winter residence in the south. A year prior to the organization of the United Order in St. George the aging president had preached on unity among the Saints, calling upon those present to raise their hands if they were willing to build up Zion and nothing else. No one was willing to risk the displeasure of Brigham Young by raising his hand in dissent.[3]

The anticipatory sermons at St. George were, no doubt, directed toward specific problems the church leaders perceived in

the community. Nearby Nevada mining camps were drawing settlers from their fields, setting awry the careful plans Brigham
Young had laid for a self-sufficing commonwealth. St. George had
been founded as the capstone of the Mormon economy, to supply
the northern areas with commodities that could be grown only in
its mild climate. Pursuit of the new wealth to be gained through
servicing the mining operations was preventing the southern area
from fulfilling its crucial role within the planned system. The
building of a temple there, which commenced at the time of the
founding of the Order, was no doubt a part of a broad design to
build up faith and commitment among the members, so their
efforts as a community might be more effectively turned to the
good of the greater Mormon commonwealth. These conditions no
doubt determined the place and time for the initiation of the
United Order, but not the idea itself. There is ample evidence that
before the founding of the United Order in the south, President
Young planned that the movement would be churchwide—a
general effort to bring the Mormons closer to the original economic order envisioned by Joseph Smith.

The sermons of preparation were clearly directed toward both
the spiritual and the immediate practical goals. A favorite theme
at the church gatherings was the necessity of economic unity. Oft-
quoted was the text, "Except ye are one, ye are not mine." Brief
summaries in St. George Stake records show that in meeting after
meeting a succession of speakers with varying emphasis, and
from several points of view, enlarged upon the subject and
pointed out the implications. One expounded the principle of
stewardship: God is owner; man, his agent. Another explained
consecration of property as the first step toward stewardship. He
saw in the principle of cooperation as applied in the livestock
business a means of enrichment through controlled prices. The
principle, it was inferred, could be and should be applied to other
affairs of the Saints. President Young, consistent with his policy
of exclusive trade, urged cessation of traffic with the gentiles. The
sisters should keep their chickens and eggs at home and use them
to sustain workers on the temple. Pine Valley lumbermen should
withhold their products from export for use by gentiles at the
mines, and to meet requirements for the temple.[4]

At St. George in the fall of 1873 Brigham Young expressed his
desire to see the people begin to prepare to enter into the Order
of Enoch.[5] He further developed the theme on January 24 in urg-

ing the Saints to practice retrenchment (doing without imported goods). Two days later he led a discussion at the home of Erastus Snow, the ecclesiastical leader of the area and a distant cousin to Brigham City's Lorenzo Snow. At this meeting he explained to a small group of local church leaders his plans for realizing the Order of Enoch.[6] Shortly thereafter, he asked one of these men, Robert Gardner, to prepare a list of ten or twelve men who were willing to work together in a United Order.[7] A meeting was called February 9, at which the president discussed the principles of the new order, and then officers were elected, with Gardner as president. At a special meeting of the priesthood of the stake on Saturday, February 14, Brigham Young declared that "the time had arrived when we should conform to the Revelations contained in [the] Book of Covenants, to be one. To enter into this friendly, brotherly labor is the present duty of the Saints, and has been during the past forty years. 'The question,' he said, 'is are we ready, and are we willing?' 'The answer is with the people themselves.'" Erastus Snow ended the evening meetings by telling the assembled men of St. George that "I have spoken much to the people of the south during the past twelve years and during the past four or five years especially, on co-operation. . . . I want to see action now instead of talk."[8] Sunday meetings the next day were spent introducing the United Order to the general membership. President Young ended the emotion-charged meetings by reiterating that "now is the accepted time and blessed are the Latter-day Saints, but if we are not disposed to enter into this Order, the curses of God will come upon the people. I cannot help it. I will not curse them, but the time has come for this work to be commenced." About three hundred came forward to subscribe their names on the United Order roll.[9]

Following the initial steps of organization in February and March 1874, Young called a meeting at St. George "especially for the sisters" to instruct them in the first principles of the Order of Enoch. He stated that he had contemplated the Order for years but had never felt that the people were ready until the present time. "If the people are faithful the citizens of this city will have the honor of being the first to enter into the holy Order of Enoch." Reverting to the subject of retrenchment, he advocated strict economy on the part of the women of the church. He gave specific examples of the application of the principle of retrenchment. To avoid importing leather, he recommended the use of wooden-bottomed shoes, which would prove better for damp weather and for very hot weather when the ground became intensely heated. Their use would save from $10,000 to $15,000 a year in St. George alone. The making of caps from old trousers would save from $5,000 to $8,000. The sale outside the district of preserved fruit, and especially of wine, which he thought the people of St. George should make but not consume, would realize about $20,000 a year.[10] No doubt his recommendations for retrenchment were easier to accede to in public meeting than to apply in the home, but many of the Saints nevertheless took them up without reservation, resenting subsequent attempts at dilution, even by the prophet himself.

The term "United Order," once it came into popular use, was applied to a bewildering variety of organizations, sometimes different in jurisdictional levels, in organizational structure, and even in objectives. The problem of understanding the differences among the various United Orders is compounded by the fact that the same men often served concurrently as officers in more than one Order, making it difficult at times to determine from a given record exactly which United Order is being referred to. At St. George there were several organizations bearing similar names and overlapping in personnel.

The United Order of St. George Stake was the first of many similar organizations in the various stakes of the Church. Its membership consisted of all who joined local (ward) branches of the United Order within the stake. Its board of management consisted primarily of the ecclesiastical officers of the stake and bishops of wards as far north as Kanarra and as far east as Kanab. When fully organized, the board of the United Order of St. George Stake had twenty-seven members.

The United Order of the City of St. George was the local unit in the community whose name it bore. This association was succeeded after a life of about seven months by the United Order of St. George, incorporated in October 1874 and an active force for five years.

The United Order of St. George First Ward came into existence as an incorporated cooperative on February 3, 1876. The authors have found no evidence that the other three wards in the city of St. George formed separate units in the Order. If they did so, they apparently did not file articles of incorporation. Though not likely to be confused with the Orders already mentioned, two other branches of the United Order of the City of St. George were founded, the Price City United Order and the Mt. Trumbull United Order. In St. George Stake there were organized, in addition, fourteen or more local associations, many of which were remote from the central office.

As it turned out, stake organizations were largely administrative and were not functioning cooperative communities. They served in theory to supervise and to coordinate the work of the local units. At first, when interest was high, the monthly meetings of the stake United Order board were well attended, but as interest waned attendance dropped. During its first year of operation, 1874, the United Order of St. George Stake held a number of meetings and transacted several important items of business. One of its earliest acts was the appointment of a superintendent to direct the transportation of goods to and from the northern settlements. The control of freighting had long been a problem, and the haphazard manner in which it was carried on had occasioned several plans for more economical methods. In 1869 Erastus Snow had organized the Southern Utah Cooperative Mercantile Association to haul merchandise to and from California, a venture that proved very profitable.

In a circular announcing the arrangements for the control of traffic with the north, plans were reported for similar control of traffic with Nevada settlements. The letter also offered suggestions for such cooperative economies as the maintainance of central yards for poultry and pens for pigs, and for the division of the labor of women as well as of men so that skills might be efficiently utilized. A great saving of labor could be effected, it was pointed out, if all sewing were done by the most skillful. "One skilled cutter will generally be enough for a neighborhood."[11]

The lack of the minutes of the monthly meetings makes it impossible to give a detailed account of the activities and problems of the stake board of management during the summer months of 1874. There was plenty to worry about, as is evident from correspondence between the board and Brigham Young in August. This correspondence was thought to be important enough to be circulated throughout the church, providing insights into problems that undoubtedly arose in every community. After assuring the general church leaders that "the Order is established and working in every settlement in the St. George Stake, though with

varying success," the board launched into a set of questions that
touched upon thorny administrative problems threatening to stop
the experiment at its inception. One set of questions was directed
toward the difficult problem of determining scales of wages acceptable to those working in the Order. Neither farmers nor
teamsters had been assigned wage scales as late as August 4.
Tradesmen, however, were working at well-established pre-
United Order wages and were already withdrawing from the
Order the maximum amounts due them. Others, who had committed only part of their possessions to the Order, were taking
time to care for their private concerns, causing dissent among
those who had committed all their possessions to the community
and devoted all their labor to it. It was found also that some, such
as teamsters, could bring into the Order more than needed for the
support of their families, while others with large families did not
earn sufficient for the needs of their own households. Again the
question arose as to how an equitable adjustment could be made.

Other questions arose over proper administrative procedures,
particularly the amount of centralization considered optimal by
the general church leadership. Those from local settlements were
lax in attending monthly board meetings, because of a feeling that
each settlement "considers itself empowered to do its own business to suit its own convenience." Moreover, individual departments within the local orders had been organized by activity—
farming, mechanical, manufacturing, and stock-raising—and the
question was raised whether these departments should be
allowed "to do each their own business, set their own prices,
make trades and exchange to suit themselves, and receive the full
benefit of their own labors."

The problem over fair allocation of wages and time and the
proper degree of centralization raised more fundamental questions concerning the Order. "Can the United Order be conducted
on the system of a well regulated family," the board asked,
"where each member of the family, according to ability, works to
accumulate means for the family; doing so without so much per
day or per month for such accumulation, and letting each eat and
wear what is needful, consistent with the circumstances of the
family, without bringing charges in dollars and cents for what is
eaten and worn?" The board members were concerned about
reports that efforts were being made in Salt Lake City to incorporate the United Order under the Territorial Incorporation Act,
thus "re-establishing the old cooperative system." Those who had

put their all into the Order had announced that "if it is only the old system of cooperation with a dividend perpetuating individual interest, they do not want anything to do with it." Such a system, they maintained, "is not the spirit of the Order, nor in keeping with your instructions of last winter."

The response of the church authorities to the questions from St. George was less than satisfying. In many particulars they threw the questions back to the local leaders, straddled the issue, or gave evasive answers. "We do not wish to say anything upon the subject of wages," they responded. "Each stake, where there is an organization, must appraise its own produce and labor." The task of assigning value to labor should be done by local men selected as appraisers, men "in whom the people have confidence and whose decision they will abide." In explaining that "we do not wish to accept a portion of a man's person and a portion of his substance . . . until he is ready to enter himself with all that he has," they seemed to be countering the general rules setting up the Order the previous winter. The original articles of association, though committing members to the contribution of all their "time, labor, energy and ability," permitted them to offer "such property as . . . [they] may feel disposed to transfer to the Order." Each settlement was to be free to conduct its own business independent of interference from the stake board, the general leaders decided, except in cases "where there is business of a general nature in which the stake is interested." Proceeds and prices of individual departments within an Order were to be controlled and disbursed through a central treasury under the board of management, which also could regulate prices and wages.

The wish to conduct a United Order like a "well regulated family" could hardly be carried out at the present, the leaders wrote, but "this system of living will eventually be reached." If practiced in the meantime, however, "care must be taken in the keeping of books to have every member . . . charged with the amount he or she may draw." Articles of incorporation were, indeed, being prepared, but "not for the purpose of perpetuating individual interest." The main purpose is "to protect ourselves by law and that it may be a shield to us." Use of the troublesome words "stock" and "dividend" was "necessary to carry out the law."[12]

Some of the ambiguities in the reply were products, no doubt, of sound judgment and wisdom on the part of the central authorities. The setting of wages by local persons who commanded the respect of the community offered the double advantage of permitting flexibility to accommodate local conditions and imposing the social control that comes from assent to the judgment of familiar peers. Other ambiguities seem simply to be products of uncertainty among the leaders as to the most promising and beneficial course to follow. The main fault, however, must lie in the ambiguous position of the leaders themselves, who recognized that their will must at many points be compromised to the demands of those enforcing national and territorial law within the Mormon commonwealth. As the destruction of the Brigham City cooperative sawmill project at Marsh Valley, Idaho, illustrates, Mormons were subject to harsh, arbitrary applications of the law at the hands of hostile federal appointees. Church leaders wanted to break with traditional economic and social usages, inaugurating a new, more just order, but were hindered by the knowledge that hostile judges were scrutinizing their every act, prepared to bring the full weight of the law to combat any activities contrary to accepted American practice. Wanting to break out of the world, they knew that they were yet in the world and must accordingly scale their designs to the limits worldly authorities could impose. Certainly a large measure of the ambiguity of their response to the questions from St. George must be attributed to difficulties arising from their territorial status within the United States. One needed only look to the southern states, then being reconstructed in the wake of the Civil War, to see how willingly federal officials trampled on local autonomy if they sensed among the populace a disloyalty to traditional American values.

Much of the substance of the questions and answers just quoted, of course, applies primarily to the local active branches of the Order. The problems were no doubt common to several branches and were perplexing enough to prompt the stake board of management to seek guidance from the highest possible authority. The inquiry was of little avail to many of the settlements in which the Order had been indifferently accepted and where its termination was already contemplated. In September a report of the experiences of the local societies at Pine Valley, Kanarra, Santa Clara, Pinto, Long Valley, Hebron, Washington, and Mt. Trumbull was made by their presidents at a meeting of the stake board of management. In general, farm labor had been more productive, the fields had been better tilled, crops were better,

One of the tangible fruits of the United Order of St. George was the St. George Temple, the first Mormon temple to be completed in Utah. Much of the work done on the temple was organized under United Order auspices. (Church Archives)

and labor had been more economically applied than under individual methods. There had been carelessness in the use and care
of tools and implements and disaffection over the disposal of
crops. Harvest hands in the St. George-Santa Clara field "felt as
though they ought to feed all the grain their animals could eat."
At Pinto many had been dilatory and some had applied their
labor in building their own homes. When the draft of the
proposed articles was received, property ceased to come into the
Order. At Santa Clara there was grumbling from those who were
partly in and partly out. In a few places all members were pleased
with the Order, offering no complaints. Seven men were in the
Order at Mt. Trumbull and were reported to be as interested as if
attending to their personal affairs.[13]

When Brigham Young suggested that the stake board with
representatives from various departments should adjust wages
and prices, a convention assembled in St. George in November
1874. The task was a great one and required several days. Committees were appointed on farm labor and field products, horticulture and its products, livestock and its products, team and
common hands' labor, and mechanical labor and its products. A
sixth committee on modifying and harmonizing lists was to iron
out inequalities in the recommendations of the committees.
Altogether about one hundred items appeared in the final
schedules, which included wage scales for all kinds of work and
prices for products of all sorts, from glue to goat meat, and from
wine to Windsor chairs.[14] These became the bases of the
allowances and charges in the accounts of individual members in
the books of the local associations.

An examination of the account books of the United Order of
St. George shows how individuals were compensated for the use
of land and for labor during the year 1874. Land owners who
turned in acreage for the use of the Order received a credit
designated as a dividend on land. For their work they were
credited at the agreed wage rates. All credits for the labor of
minors were included with those of the family head. For example,
William Carter, superintendent of St. George-Santa Clara field,
received $3.00 a day; his twenty-year-old son, $2.00 a day; his
fifteen-year-old son, $1.50; and his ten-year-old son, 75 cents.
Against the credits thus established, food, clothing, and other
supplies were obtained from distributing agencies and charged to
the family account. A good deal of scrip in the form of meat scrip,

bread scrip, and orders on the Tithing Office were used in making settlements. Accounts were not systematically kept, however, and a good deal of confusion resulted. Attempts to strike a balance at the end of the year were futile.[15]

When Brigham Young returned from Salt Lake City for his winter sojourn at St. George the following year (1874-75), he found much to disappoint him. The anticipated revolution in the economic system had run into unforeseen difficulties and obstructions. Both leaders and people were at fault. It was already apparent that in some communities no attempt would be made to continue the Order for a second year. The president's rebuke and appeal for continued efforts to realize the objectives of the Order were incorporated in a circular letter issued January 10, 1875, in which he made clear his belief that excessive individualism was inhibiting the success of the Order:

Brethren, with regard to the United Order: You are my witness that we did not ask for your gold, nor silver, nor houses, nor lands, goods nor chattels, nor anything else of property kind; but we asked for you, your time, your talents and all the ability that God has given to you, to enter into the United Order after the pattern of Heaven to build up the Zion of God upon this land. . . .

You may not understand one fact that is before our eyes; that this temple in St. George is being built upon the principle of the United Order; and when we cease our selfishness, and our whole interest is for the building up of the Kingdom of God on earth, we can then build temples and do anything that we want to with united voice and hands.[16]

Notwithstanding this appeal, many communities returned to individual ownership and responsibility. Harmony, Toquerville, Washington, Pinto, Panaca, Pine Valley, and Rockville abandoned attempts to preserve the Order after a year's trial.[17] There is little available in the records to show how these withdrawals affected the organization of the United Order of St. George Stake, but it is certain that board members who attempted indifferently when the Order was in process of formation would not become active after the cessation of operations in their own wards. It may be therefore taken for granted that the stake organization found its duties more and more circumscribed until its activities became practically identical with those of the United Order of the City of St. George, which, with one or two other branches, struggled on for two or three years.

In one of the early organization meetings at St. George Brigham Young, seeking to overcome the hesitancy of property owners, had asserted that he would prefer to accept members without property "who were willing to be dictated in the application of their labors and talents" than to take men worth thousands. By wise application of labor on the one hand and the exercise of prudent economy on the other, it would be possible, he declared, to acquire a fund without initial investment of capital.[18] And so it came about that the articles of association for the United Order of the City of St. George pledged the member to give all his time and ability to the Order, but made property subscriptions optional. This proved to be a mistake, as shown in the statement of problems presented to President Young in the August letter. It required only a short experience to confirm the New Testament dictum that "where your treasure is, there will your heart be also."

There were in fact two classes of people among the adherents of the United Order: the idealists, who believed the system could be made to work, and the realists, who, if they hoped it might, were reluctant to risk the loss of any substantial portion of their possessions without setting up safeguards to protect them. The idealistic attitude is apparent in the articles of agreement adopted in March, and the realistic in the October articles of incorporation. The former, in the words of Erastus Snow, set up the gospel plan; the latter, the legal plan. The first was communal and recognized the equality of individuals; the second was capitalistic and recognized wealth as the measure of importance.

The fundamental change effected by the Order was the substitution of centralized planning and control of production for individualistic methods.

Farming offers an example. The lands within the Order were tilled under the direction of department supervisors, and the acreage allotted to different crops was fixed either by them or by the board of management. Because the farm labor force had for several years been lured to the mines, leaving the farms uncultivated, it had been necessary to import wheat from outside counties with money borrowed from the Trustee-in-Trust of the church at 1 $\frac{1}{4}$ percent a month.[19] An April 2, 1874, report maintained that under the Order the situation had been corrected, and more land had been planted than ever before.[20]

Some interesting details of the farm departments are instructive. The cultivated land lay principally in four fields: the St. George-Santa Clara field, the Virgin field, Copper bottom, and the

Price City field. The latter area, five miles south of St. George, was operated by a group organized as a branch of the United Order of the City of St. George, a group deserving something more than passing mention, since they were the first to assume the family form of organization. Brigham Young may have had Price City in mind when he described his ideal community before the general conference in Salt Lake City (October 9, 1872). "I have a splendid place," he said, "large enough for about five hundred or a thousand persons to settle upon, and I would like to be the one to make a donation of it, with a good deal more, to start the business, to see if we can actually accomplish the affair, and show the Latter-day Saints how to build up Zion."[21]

The area had been opened under the name of Heberville by a company in which Brigham Young was interested, and prior to 1869, improvements consisting of a ditch and the leveling of the land had been made to the value of $4,500. When the wave of cooperation swept over the church in that year, a company on the cooperative plan had been organized, with Robert Gardner as president, which purchased the land and improvements from its previous owners. By 1873 all the stock was held by eleven men who had bought out others and assumed the debt. When the United Order movement was begun, these men turned their stock into the Order. Accordingly a company was formed of farmers from St. George and Santa Clara as a department of the United Order of St. George, with George Baker as superintendent.

During his visit to the southern settlements in the fall of 1874, apostle George Q. Cannon took pains to get first-hand information about this branch of the United Order. He reported his visit at the general conference in Salt Lake City. Members of the group were all living as a single family, eating at a common table. There were forty-four men, women, and children. The women cooked for the entire company on three small stoves, quite inconveniently situated, but adequate for their needs. In the beginning, they did their washing collectively, but having no machinery, they found it advantageous for each family to do its own.

The superintendent reported no friction in allotting the labors among the men. In the morning they would meet in one room together and have prayers; then they sat down to breakfast, during which period the superintendent made the arrangement of labor for the day. They assembled at noon for luncheon and again in the evening for supper and prayers. They spent the remainder of the evening in social conversation or in discussing the business of the group.[22]

For reasons not made clear in the record, this particular experiment in the United Order was terminated at the close of its first season. It is possible that they too were displeased with the Order as reorganized under the articles of incorporation. In any case, members of the old Heberville Cooperative Farming Company voted on February 16, 1875, to receive back the farm. It was decided to continue operating the farm with William F. Butler as foreman, the name of the company being changed to the Price City Co-operative Farming Company.[23] Thus was brought to a close the first attempt to establish the United Order after the family pattern. Though detached from the Order after 1874, Price City continued as a cooperative farm for three years with unsatisfactory results. In January 1877 the St. George United Order Board received a petition from the members of the Price City Farming Company, expressing the wish to become a department of the United Order "with our farm and all that we possess, our time and talents to be controlled by the Priesthood." It is not recorded what action the United Order Board decided to take in the matter. Eventually, the lands, buildings, and equipment were divided among the members.[24]

Other departments of the United Order of the City of St. George made at least temporary progress toward achieving Brigham Young's aim of an ideal community. One objective of the Order was to supply lumber for the temple as well as for general needs. A road was built to Mt. Trumbull sixty-five miles southeast of St. George and two mills were set up, the larger one supplied by the Trustee-in-Trust (Brigham Young) at a cost of about $10,000. In this remote spot workers called to serve the Order seem to have escaped the dissension that developed sooner or later in most branches of the association. As late as August 1877, a member of the group reported that "we have a most perfect organization here, and I believe we have actually got a living branch of the United Order."[25]

In the United Order of the City of St. George, there were at least eleven departments in addition to those already mentioned. They included a carpenters' department, a teamster department, a vineyard, a meat department, a western trading department, and departments for making brooms, shoes, hats, and wine.

The Order transacted a good deal of business with the co-ops —the St. George Cooperative Mercantile Institution, Zions Cooperative, Rio Virgen Manufacturing Company (the textile mill at Washington), and others—but these were not departments of the Order. Young had hoped that the cooperative institutions would become absorbed into an all-inclusive United Order, but this did not come about at St. George.

The United Order of the City of St. George, a co-partnership, was succeeded in October 1874 by the United Order of St. George, a corporation framed according to the pattern worked out at Salt Lake City by church leaders. Misgivings among the idealists were strong when rumors reached St. George that incorporation was contemplated. Their complaint to Brigham Young in August 1874 was unusually assertive in its insistence that if the proposed articles of incorporation represented a return to the old system of cooperation, they did not want "anything to do with it." They even went so far as to accuse the president of inconsistency, pointing out to him that incorporation "is not the spirit of the Order nor in keeping with your instruction of last winter."[26]

Meetings were called at St. George in September with apostles George Q. Cannon and Erastus Snow present to persuade the members of the Order that they should accept the corporate form. Cannon, after a stirring appeal for all to dedicate time, talent, and substance to build up the Kingdom, presented the prescribed articles of incorporation for the United Order and explained certain important features. Speaking to the question "Why were we not incorporated under the law last spring, and if not then, why are we called upon now to do so," Erastus Snow said he had favored incorporation at the beginning and that he and George A. Smith had approached President Young in the matter. He did not state what the reply had been. Presumably President Young had not yet been ready to make a decision, since nothing was said publicly on the matter and the St. George organization was entered into as a co-partnership. The president's attitude, said Snow, had been that of a father, gentle, easy, and kind. Now after a summer's experience it was considered best to organize so as to get the advantage of the law. Certain amendments made by the legislature in the interest of the mining business were found to afford greater latitude for the organization of the United Order than was possible under the earlier general incorporation act. "We began with the gospel," said Snow, "and now we will continue by organizing under the law." Within three years he was advocating a return to the gospel plan.

Answering questions in the minds of some who looked for the inauguration of the stewardship plan and the allotment of land to individuals, apostle George Q. Cannon said such an arrangement was not to be entered into, unless to a very limited extent. "Combination of labor," he asserted, "is decidedly more profitable than individual exertion has been." On the same subject Erastus Snow said:

> We should guard against the disposition manifest by some to set stakes to fence in the Lord and his servants. Some have referred to stewardships. What is said in the Doctrine and Covenants is but little given to a small branch of the Church from Colesville and in Jackson County; it forms but a part of the line upon line, and precept upon precept. What was given to Joseph was given for that time and for the people then in the Church. Why not equally honor the word of the Lord through Brigham? There is no revelation as to how we shall manage cooperative institutions, cotton factories, Mt. Trumbull lumber interests. How shall we manage these? As the spirit of revelation shall manifest. Wherever a man is appointed to labor there is his stewardship. Beware of entertaining the idea of individual stewardships without being amenable to a directing controlling power.[27]

Incorporation accomplished exactly what the idealists had feared. It placed control in the hands of property owners. Some, like Erastus Snow, who had been "slow, doubtful, hesitating, in receiving the establishment of the United Order," now came in as stockholders.[28] The stockholders' ledger shows that seventy-three individuals subscribed a capital of a little more than $25,000. The form of capital subscriptions is illuminating. Only $170 in cash was invested. Orders on the Tithing Office amounted to $696. The most abundant form of wealth was livestock, the subscription in animals and in the capital stock of cooperative livestock companies totaling $8,554. Teams, wagons, and harness came next with a total value of $6,276. Merchandise and shares in the cooperative store equaled $2,284. Then followed stock in the Washington cotton and woolen mill, $1,940; wine, $1,150; lumber mill stock and lumber, $1,131; growing crops, $1,019; labor, $536; and various miscellaneous classes of property of smaller significance.

The importance of individual investors, as measured by amount of investment, varied greatly. The dominant shareholder was James W. Nixon, who held 384 shares valued at $7,680. He held the office of treasurer throughout the life of the corporation and was at different times vice-president and president as well. He held more than a fourth of all the capital stock. Five men out of the seventy-three held more than half. Since, by the articles of incorporation, the right to vote was the privilege of stockholders only, members without stock, who under the co-partnership or gospel plan had a voice and a vote in the business of the enterprise, were now, under the legal plan, deprived of active participation in the councils of the Order.

The change in the structure of the organization was accompanied by a weakening of loyalty to its objectives. Farmers for the most part returned to their accustomed arrangements, planted what they wished, and minded their own business. A few became stockholders in the Order by subscribing the value of their growing crops. The greatly reduced number of individual accounts in the books in 1876 reflect the changes that were taking place. The waning interest in the Order was regarded as evidence of a lack of spiritual fervor and of loyalty to the interests of the church. It may be on this account that at St. George, as elsewhere, the ritual of baptism was invoked, and in the fall of 1875 several hundred men, women, and children accepted rebaptism as a sign of willingness to observe the rules of the Order.[29]

Notwithstanding the continual exhortations of ecclesiastical leaders, differences increased and were given an airing at a meeting in the St. George Tabernacle, December 18, 1875. One man favored the classification of labor but thought that an individual should control his own property. Another thought that the Order had been launched on too great a scale; a better beginning would be to have each family practice the united plan of labor until perfect and then to join with another, and thus gradually enlarge the circle of united effort. Another, taking his cue, perhaps, from reports from Salt Lake City, thought that most of the people were unready for anything higher than individual stewardships. A member of the board opposed the idea of stewardships and favored organizing companies within the Order. He probably had in mind cooperative groups similar to the prevalent livestock and mercantile companies. Another who favored stewardships sup-

ported his stand by referring to the revelations in the Doctrine
and Covenants. Against this contention Erastus Snow appealed
for support for the plan of the "living priesthood," declaring the
United Order as it was practiced in St. George to be in advance of
the stewardship plan, and offering, in support of this position, a
letter prepared by Brigham Young for the members of Richfield,
where opinion was similarly divided.[30]

Turning toward the gospel plan, members of the St. George
First Ward early in 1876 organized and incorporated the St.
George First Ward United Order. Of the twenty-five incorpora-
tors, eight were stockholders in the United Order of St. George.
The members of this group rejected the principle of apportioning
power according to shares held, maintaining instead that "the
stockholders shall be entitled to one vote each at all meetings of
the stockholders without regard to amount of their capital stock."
In this respect the new association was patterned after the original
United Order of the City of St. George. In other particulars the
articles were similar to the original standard form. It is not known
how great a financial investment the members made in the Order.
The largest subscriptions reported at the time of incorporation
were for ten shares of ten dollars par. The association seems to
have been financially successful. At the end of the first year a
profit of 22.25 percent was reported.[31] There is no record of how
long the St. George First Ward United Order remained active, nor
are we informed of the branches of business in which it engaged.
The latest date on which a director's qualifying bond was filed in
the county recorder's office is July 5, 1877. The organization of the
St. George First Ward United Order was but one example of a
mounting protest, from the right and from the left, against the
forms and practices of the United Order of St. George. Apostle
Brigham Young, Jr., speaking at St. George in May 1876,
predicted that apostates would bring about the destruction of the
Order. Whether he was referring to opposition generally wherever attempts to realize the Order were being made, or to opposition at St. George, his observation was no doubt based on the
open recalcitrance of lukewarm members of the church who
remained outside the Order and had nothing to gain by its continuance.[32]

There is some evidence that even Brigham Young's faith in
the St. George United Order as an efficient economic agency was
weakening. On May 17, 1876, the Board of Directors of the Order

received a letter requesting that the steam sawmill at Mt. Trumbull be relinquished to the exclusive use of providing lumber for the temple, after which it was to be sent to the Mormon colonies in Arizona. As the Order had been established to make possible a more economical utilization of labor and capital, the withdrawal of this $10,000 investment by the Trustee-in-Trust is significant. By an adjustment a few months later, the church accepted a loss by depreciation of $3,000.

During its third year (1876) the United Order of St. George was managed primarily to the end of conserving the assets of the original investors in the capital stock. Contrary to legal assumptions, properties subscribed in the beginning were regarded as the private property of original owners, and income received from such property was paid out to the original owners, as though they still retained possession. Especially was this true of shares in the several co-ops. Dividends from these, instead of being regarded as income to the United Order, were merely passed through the hands of the treasurer of the Order to original subscribers. This appears on the face of it to have been unequal treatment of stockholders according to the nature of the property turned into the Order in exchange for its own shares.

The Order had obviously fallen far short of the full cooperative community it was originally designed to be. Little wonder that the number of those who wished to continue in it steadily diminished. Finally, at a meeting of stockholders in March 1877, more than the legally necessary two-thirds of the stock was voted in favor of disincorporation. The process of liquidation was slow, however, and the business was not finally wound up until early in 1880. The capital stock was paid off at 91.5 cents on the dollar.

Meanwhile, those who still considered cooperative efforts superior to individualistic methods set up new forms of association to replace the old. The dissolution of the corporation did not of itself signify an abandonment of the principles of the United Order. Mormon ideology, based as it was on the teachings of Joseph Smith, would not be abandoned because of one, or even a few, disheartening failures. Brigham Young and his associates had, in a hundred sermons, transformed the Saints' attitude toward union from a distant millennial hope into a desire for immediate realization. The agreement to disincorporate was regarded by many as simply the removal of a major obstacle to the success of a program that in its first and most successful year had operated without legally sanctioned forms. The change now proposed meant merely a return from the letter of the law to the spirit of the gospel. Apostle Erastus Snow so defined it in Richfield, where at the same moment the Order was collapsing.[33]

A reorganization of the St. George Stake occurred in April 1877, a month after the stockholders of the Order had voted to disincorporate. Shortly thereafter the new stake president, J.D.T. McAllister, having qualified by acquiring a nominal amount of stock, became vice-president of the United Order of St. George. At the annual meeting in February 1878, he became president, thus again giving local priesthood holders authority in the councils of the Order. As additional steps toward the return to an order based on the gospel plan, two organizations were effected on the principles of true brotherhood. The first included all church members in good standing engaged in the building trades, and the second, the farmers. In these associations there were to be no returns to capital, no extravagance in consumption, and no individual claim to surplus.[34] Regrettably we have no account of actual operations under these agreements, except evidence in the account books of the United Order that the Builders Union made small purchases of lumber over a period of one year.[35] Aside from this there is nothing in the record to show that these final attempts to bring about a new order of economic and social unity were long maintained. Nevertheless, it is apparent that with the disincorporation of the legal Order some persons hoped to return to an association that would still realize the idealistic hopes on which the United Order was first founded. Such must have been the intent of President McAllister, who announced that he was still ready to receive into the Order all who were willing to fall into line.[36] Apparently little came of the invitation. Instead, pent-up feelings broke into open hostility in a Sunday meeting, scarcely six weeks after the death of Brigham Young. One resident attributed the movement to priestcraft instead of to priesthood. Another, avowing his belief in the United Order, was sure that the system they had attempted to realize in St. George was not the plan of the Almighty.[37] The remarks appear to have gone unchallenged. The stake historian, in his journal for the last day of the year, expressed regret that "for months past there has been a decadence in United Order affairs."[38] Except for the redistribution of capital the Order was history.

To the disillusioned adherents of the United Order Erastus Snow, resident apostle, gave wise counsel: "Murmur as little as possible; complain as little as possible; and if we are not yet advanced enough to all eat at one table, all work in one company, at least feel that we all have one common interest and are all children of one Father; and let us each do what we can to save ourselves and each other."[39]

CHAPTER 9

Richfield:
Combatting the feeling
of "mine"

ATTER-DAY SAINT SETTLERS in central Utah's Sevier County organized a second major United Order shortly after the St. George Order was begun. Joseph A. Young, eldest son of Brigham Young, was the leading light in this Order, centered in the town of Richfield, about midway on a direct line between Salt Lake City and St. George. Young had been sent from Salt Lake City two years earlier to preside over the Mormon settlements in Sevier County and the surrounding areas. Associated with his father in a large railroad contract, he had accumulated a small fortune that he converted into land, water rights, mills, and livestock in the Sevier area, becoming by right of ecclesiastical position and wealth the most influential man in the county. A former missionary and fully in accord with his father's religious and social plans, he was indefatigable in his efforts to establish and maintain a spirit of unity and devotion among the people in Richfield.

In December 1873 Brigham Young presided over a two-day gathering of the Saints at Richfield, where he expounded the material advantages to be expected by a group willing to work together and to yield strict obedience to counsel.[1] At this meeting discussions preliminary to the founding of a United Order in Sevier County no doubt took place. The actual organization was not attempted, however, until Joseph Young made firsthand observations of the initial steps taken at St. George, where on April 5, 1874, he testified in public of the beauty of the Order and expounded some of its advantages. He saw in the Order the remedy for poverty, a condition prevalent in his own jurisdiction.[2] Two weeks later, with the St. George articles of association as a guide, he effected the organization of the Sevier Stake United Order on April 19 and in rapid succession set up local units in every community in the stake.

Rosy pictures were painted at organization meetings. It was expected that the Order would result in greater production, more economical consumption, lower costs for goods produced, higher prices for goods sold, and equalization of incomes at continuously higher living standards. For example, freighting by team, which because of competition had become a starvation job, would be controlled to yield adequate returns. Twenty thousand dollars a year would be saved in Richfield and $10,000 in Monroe by the more economical use of teams. Even such household drudgery as the family wash would be largely eliminated by the cooperative use of machinery and the release of nine-tenths of the labor.

On the other hand, there were misgivings. One brother wisely remarked that "it takes pure people to live pure principles." In every community there were dissenters; in some places as many as half the total number of families refused to join. At the farming settlement of Joseph, fourteen miles southwest of Richfield (and named after Joseph A. Young), the bishop demurred, saying that though he expected to die in the church, "he could not see the Order." He was immediately released and succeeded by one who was in harmony with the plan. Finally Young, after strenuous argument and admonition, won a unanimous vote of support from those present.

Members were permitted to enter local associations by the subscription of all or part of their property, and in the record many of the names are followed by the phrase, "With all I have." Debtors were advised to clear their obligations before subscribing encumbered property, but as a gesture of good intent they were permitted to place their names on the lists.

The stake organization, like that at St. George, was concerned primarily with the encouragement of intercommunity exchange of products, the development of manufactures, and the opening of roads to Cove Creek and other nearby valleys. The stake United Order also constructed and operated a tannery, later incorporated as the Sevier County United Order Tannery. However, the United Order was basically a community movement, and the emphasis was upon community self-sufficiency, rather than on intercommunity exchange.

The heart of the Order—the level at which citizens participated in founding and sustaining a full cooperative community—was in Richfield. Settlement of Richfield had begun in the mid-1860s, but during the Black Hawk Indian Wars of 1865-

67 Brigham Young had recalled the group. Families began returning in the fall of 1870, after which settlement continued at a lively pace. By the time the Order was initiated the village had a population of 753 persons constituting 145 families, most of whom had so recently arrived from Denmark that all important instructions presented in public meetings were repeated in Danish.[3] The material possessions of most of these families consisted of the few necessities that could be brought in by team and wagon. Though a few one-room houses had been built, many settlers were still crudely sheltered in their covered wagons or in dugouts.

In a sense the Richfield Order got off to a bad start. There was little time for ripening of ideas or maturing of plans. Though Joseph A. Young had brought back some firsthand observations of beginnings at St. George and a copy of the articles of association for the Order at that place, he remarked at the organization meeting in Richfield that all speculation about the Order was vain, and that the only way to comprehend it was to get it into operation and to profit by day-to-day experience. Thus, the first year was one of intense idealism, but also of hasty preparations and tentative decisions. In the making of decisions, all members possessed equal voting power, regardless of property contributed. This setup, said Erastus Snow, leader of the Mormons in southern Utah, was characteristic of "the Gospel Plan," as distinguished from the corporate plan that was adopted later in Richfield and elsewhere in the church.

Four-fifths of the residents of Richfield entered the Order, and the door was kept wide open for the admission of new settlers who cared to come. After the harvest, teams were sent to bring in those who had no means of their own to make the journey from northern settlements. "We have sent our teams," said a member, "for emigrants and for poor, whenever they have desired to come here, and Saints even from Bear Lake to St. George have come here to join the Order."[4]

The articles of association, modeled after the St. George United Order, required all the time, labor, energy, and ability of a member and such property as he wished to invest. The members at Richfield decided to retain as individual stewardships homes and such domestic animals as the family cow, pigs, and chickens. All else was turned in at appraised values. Much of the spring planting had been done when the Order was organized on April 19. Since there were as yet no legal titles to land, appraised values were agreed upon at $3 an acre for prepared land and $1 an acre additional for seed. A farmer who turned in to the Order ten acres planted to grain received a book credit of $40. Horses, cattle, and sheep were turned in at appraised values, or if a member had previously invested his surplus livestock in one of the several cooperative herds, his shares were transferred to the Order.

In the spirit of equality on which the Order was founded, a first concern was to provide creature comforts to all, as far as the resources of the association would permit. Cows were supplied to every family. An inventory revealed that among them all they possessed 9,150 pounds of flour, barely a month's supply. It was necessary to borrow grain from northern settlements. This was done on the credit of the Order and charges were made on the books for family requisitions. Joseph A. Young set a fine example by distributing his extra clothing, and a supply of ducking was purchased for distribution to those in greatest need. Even so, many were shabbily and inadequately clad, though better off, no doubt, than they would have been outside the Order. An attempt to obtain on credit $500 worth of cloth from the Provo Woolen Mills, to be paid indirectly by labor on the St. George Temple, failed. After harvest, exchanges were made for grain—always an equivalent for cash. Meat was supplied from the co-op herds, at the rate of two beefs a week.

Every family without adequate shelter wanted a house, and those that had provided a room or two by their own exertions wanted more. There were many who needed fences, pig pens, poultry houses, and outdoor privies. It was one of the dreams of the advocates of the Order that such requirements could be provided more economically and more promptly through systematic utilization of labor than by the old individualistic methods. Combined farming would, it was thought, release labor for mechanical pursuits. Joseph A. Young had a steam sawmill that went with the rest of his property into the association and became the basis of a lumber department that was feverishly busy until winter closed the hastily constructed roads.

The demand for construction was particularly acute. A committee of the board, made up of representatives of the building trades, carpenters, rock layers, and adobe layers, looked after all building requirements. The three members of this committee began by making a survey of needs and an inventory of materials. The responsibility looked forbidding and there were frequent disputes within the membership, followed by resignations and reorganization. Stability was temporarily achieved within six weeks and the committee continued to function as an arbiter of needs, a commissary of supplies, and a coordinator of labor. But the problems were insuperable. In approving plans for houses, the committee was expected to be guided by considerations of taste, comfort, and economy. But the first applicant had to modify his plans and accept a less expensive shelter; other applications were filed, the sawmill worked at capacity, and delays became longer and longer. Counting roadbuilders, haulers, and the mechanics used in construction, about thirty-five men were used in providing shelter. Yet, from the viewpoint of the Order, houses were "dead property" and added nothing to the ability to produce more grain, wool, and hides.

The principle of equality required the adjustment of wages, piece rates, and prices, so that farmers, unskilled laborers, and mechanics would receive approximately the same credits and work approximately the same number of hours. Accordingly, the eight-hour day was accepted as standard, with $1.50 a day for a man and $3.00 for a man and team. Mechanical work, it was thought, could be done under a contract system, but the problem proved so difficult that specific recommendations were deferred. The sawmill was operated as a cooperative business and delivered the finished product to the Order at agreed rates per thousand feet. Piece rates per thousand were to be agreed upon for stockers, sawyers, haulers, and sellers. Similar arrangements were planned for other activities, including farming and herding.

Meanwhile, the members were urged to be diligent in their labors, though they had only the vaguest idea as to what they would realize from it. Most of them were willing to accept the situation on faith, and pairs of local priesthood holders—ward teachers— were sent to all the homes to urge diligence. Special difficulty was met in irrigation, as running water is not amenable to eight-hour rules. Much may be guessed from a note in the minute book requiring ward teachers to see if the Order members would "give all their time, and if not, why not."[5]

At harvest time, particularly with threshing, the eight-hour day interfered seriously. The Order had purchased a threshing machine in Salt Lake City in late August; even so, threshing proceeded slowly because of the indifference of the laborers assigned to the task. A competing machine came in from Fillmore, the owners taking a portion of the grain they threshed as payment for their service. Despite the need of the Order to avoid loss of grain, members, laying claim to stacks from their own farms, brought work to the owners of the Fillmore thresher. At the end of the season it was stated that the Order thresher had not done a very good business, but no blame was attached to the overseer.

It was foreseen that there would be attempts at withdrawal. In the original agreements, therefore, capital was entered for five years and withdrawal penalized by the retention of one-half its book value. This procedure was without legal sanction and was enforceable only by the good faith of the members. In the phraseology of the church's Doctrine and Covenants, the members entered the Order by a "covenant that could not be broken." Nevertheless, there were those at Richfield who took these arrangements lightly, helping themselves at harvest time to what they judged was a fair share of the grain. Encouraged by these high-handed actions, still others undertook to recover the yields of their lands after the threshed grains were in the bins. Following the order of the church, these actions were taken before the Quorum of Teachers, which found in favor of the Order and demanded a settlement from the offending brethren who otherwise would be branded as covenant-breakers. Later, the United Order board summoned the chief offender to appear—a man who, though he had been a member of the original board and had placed all his possessions into the Order, pleaded in defense ignorance of its rules and requirements. His position was emphatically pointed out to him, as one board member after another spoke against his actions and labeled him as a covenant-breaker whose offense was like that of the betrayer of Jesus. To regain the confidence of his brethren he was required to restore what he had taken.[6]

While the Order at Richfield and those at other places were gaining significant though perplexing and painful experience, general church authorities in Salt Lake City were engaged in revamping the plans for the various orders and molding the system into a stock company with legal protection for capital. On his way south to St. George in August 1874, Erastus Snow visited Richfield and explained the standard articles of incorporation. These were discussed in subsequent mass meetings in both English and Danish. Schedules of property to be invested were prepared, and the Order was duly incorporated November 9, 1874, with two-thirds of the village folk supporting the plan. The authorized capital was $1,000,000, with shares valued at $25 par. Shareholdings were indicated as capital credits according to appraised values, and fractional shares were recognized. The articles of incorporation show that 159 took stock in the corporation, most offering property in lieu of cash for their capital subscriptions.

The stewardship principle observed at the inception of the Order was still applied, so that homes and farmyard stock, exclusive of teams, were omitted from invested capital. Most of the members had little else and it is not surprising to discover that about half of the subscribers invested $50 or less. Joseph A. Young and his Richfield wife—he had another family in the Order at Gunnison and a third in Salt Lake City—held $30,000 in capital stock, more than all other stockholders combined. Joseph A. Young's schedule is significant in what it reveals of the nature of productive property at the time, and of the absorption of local cooperatives by the Order:

Capital Stock in Sevier Co-op Horse Herd $4,500
Capital Stock in Sevier Co-op Cattle Herd 3,200
Capital Stock in Richfield Co-op Mercantile Institution 700
Capital Stock in Richfield Co-op Sheep Herd 800
Capital Stock in Richfield Co-op Grist Mill 7,600
One Griffith and Wedge Steam Sawmill; one shingle
    machine and lazy saw. One set of blacksmith tools
    including anvil and bellows—said machinery all set
    up with buildings, sheddings, and all appurtenances 5,000
Miscellaneous harnesses, teams, wagons, office furniture, etc. ... $1,100
Amount of water-right paid for and not applied including that
    for land south of the City Survey 2,600

Total Value $25,000

In general, a subscriber who was well enough off to turn over a span of mules with harness and wagon—an outfit valued at around $500—was a comparatively large stockholder. Many were permitted to acquire a share of stock in exchange for labor, a means adopted to bring into the Order those worthy of admission but too poor to have any surplus property.[7]

Few changes were effected in the nature and operation of the Order by incorporation. The most important change was the power granted to the board to prevent the withdrawal, at any

Threshing scene, photographed near American Fork, Utah, was typical of those at harvest time in Mormon towns throughout the Great Basin. (G. E. Anderson photo, Church Archives)

time, of invested capital. Though the articles provided for voting by shares, the *viva voce* method was invariably followed at Richfield. With few exceptions it was the rule to choose the ranking church leader, usually the bishop, as president of the Order. In Richfield Joseph A. Young, president of the stake and the heaviest stockholder, was elected to this office. When he died in August 1875, he was succeeded by the bishop, William H. Seegmiller, who served until the fall of 1876, when he declined reelection because he was in disfavor with President Brigham Young. He was succeeded by Lars P. Christiansen, but continued to be the real leader of the Order in the capacity of general superintendent.

The board functioned through committees appointed to supervise the various activities and interests of the Order, the duties of which were modified as experience dictated. Board meetings were held every two or three days and required hours of the directors' time. At first, every request for cash or equivalent was acted on by the board. A member could not go fishing, visit his relations a few miles away, or attend the general church conference in Salt Lake City without a grant of released time by the board. A few quotations taken from the Richfield United Order Record indicate the extent of control that the board deemed it necessary to exercise:

Bro. Swen Borgquist met with the Board and stated his circumstances and wished to be assisted in his present destitute condition or released to go off and earn means to clothe his family.

Moved by Bro. H. P. Miller that Bro. Borgquist be instructed to be patient and trust in the Lord and share with us. Motion seconded and carried.

Bishop Seegmiller stated the reasons of Bro. Brandley's going to Salt Lake; said F. W. Ellerbeck had telegraphed for him to come and assist in laying the city waterpipes—had written him previously and offered him three dollars per day in cash. Bishop Seegmiller had sanctioned his going and had instructed him that what means he had left, over and above his board bill and necessary expenditure, be deposited with the Z. C. M. I. to our credit on their account against us. Action approved of.

Resolved that all persons whose labor is not entirely directed by the Board furnish an itemized and explanatory monthly report to the secretary in writing to be presented to the Board.

Moved by H. P. Miller that G. Ence's pigs be taken to the gristmill to be fed there for the use of the Order, he having credit for the same and being allowed to retain and feed one for his extra trouble; motion carried.

Bishop Seegmiller stated that Godfrey Hafen desired to go north to procure mulberry trees. Moved by H. M. Petersen that the request of G. Hafen in regard to going to the City for mulberry cuttings be laid over till spring, motion carried.

Simon Christensen met with the Board, said last season he desired to get a pig, applied to the brethren in the Order, but did not succeed, he therefore purchased one from H. C. Holdensgaard, promising to pay grain after harvest, namely four bushels of wheat for the same, which he would like to have paid.

Moved by R. Ramsay that the debt of Simon Christensen to H. C. Holdensgaard as stated by him be paid, with the understanding that no more such debts be contracted without the consent of the Board; motion carried.

Bro. Swen Borgquist met with the Board; stated that his brother in the city desires him to come to Salt Lake City and take charge of his harness shop the beginning of the following month for one month; stated that he needs a stove very much, which he could procure by going to the city.

Resolved, that if on inquiry Bro. Borgquist can make satisfactory arrangements, he be permitted to go.

A note was read from T. S. Kenner, stating that as he had now returned, he desired employment, having been absent to Beaver for a short time, without the consent of the Board.

Resolved, that T. S. Kenner be required to appear before the Board and give an account of his absence before we give him any more employment.[8]

There are other examples. One George Frazer was granted in January 1875 an order for $100 to assist him in starting housekeeping. Five weeks later he asked for $15 more to pay debts in Provo and redeem his watch. Request denied.[9] In April a brother who petitioned for $10 was disgruntled at receiving only $3 and another who wished to go away to earn cash was advised to stick to the Order and trust in the Lord.[10] The petition of another for a new hat so that he might make a visit to the temple in Salt Lake City was granted (February 1876). Another was allowed 50 cents a week for hired help for his sick wife during his own necessary absence from Richfield.

Later the board used the device of an executive committee to expedite business and economize time. The practice of holding frequent discussions of problems with all the stockholders was inaugurated during the final year of the Order's existence. These semimonthly meetings provided disgruntled members an opportunity to release a good deal of pent-up emotion, but the device was inadequate to turn sentiment against the dissolution that members eventually demanded.

In 1875 Bishop L. J. Nuttall of Kanab, seeking advice in managing his own troubled organization, wrote to officials of the Richfield United Order for advice. Their reply gave a detailed picture of the principles and policies followed at Richfield. Houses, lots, and barnyard animals were held by owners as stewardships, but all other property was turned into the Order by bill of sale, for which shares of capital stock were paid. Originally, title to real property was transferred to the Order by quit-claim deed. After incorporation title was reconveyed to the original owners and back to the Order by trust deed or lease.

Farming lands were divided into 150-acre farms, each managed by a foreman appointed by the board of directors and four workers selected by the foreman. The Order furnished teams and implements needed for farming the land. The farmers turned all they harvested in to the Order and drew their support from the common storehouse, as any other member did.

Wherever possible work was done by the job at low wages, which were nearly equal for all workers. Low wages limited the amount of credit that malcontents could claim against the Order should they decide to withdraw. The heads of large families, which could not strike a balance with the Order at such low wages, received advances that they could make up when the children were old enough to work.

A single superintendent coordinated the work of all the different branches, holding regular meetings with the board of management for that purpose. Where property was invested in cooperative institutions the shares were transferred to the Order, which drew the dividend. The board attempted to find useful employment for the aged and infirm, but these persons were provided for whether work could be found for them or not. The Order received all who came to it well recommended and willing to turn in their property according to its rules. Finally, the board of directors sought to avoid "sinking live capital into dead property," such as houses, which did not increase the productivity of the community.

The difficulty of translating Brigham Young's vision into a practical, working community is evident in the record of the Richfield United Order. Spring planting was well advanced when the Order was launched in 1874. To realize the promised economies it was necessary for the board of management to immediately effect a division of the community's labor force. Craftsmen, such as carpenters, adobe layers, blacksmiths, and shoemakers, were relieved of any farming operations in which they may have been engaged, and farming was carried on as a full-time specialized occupation. Farming lands were divided into three zones, and a superintendent for each zone directed the agricultural laborers. Like their co-partners in the trades, the farmers adopted the eight-hour day and were credited with wages at the agreed rates of $1.50 a day.

Though farm labor was in general much more efficient than previously, there was complaint about indolence and indifference. The assurance of regular wages without regard to intensity of application proved to be a great temptation to those disinclined to hard work. Accordingly, the board changed the plan for the second and subsequent years and organized eight large farms of 150 acres, with a foreman and crew of four men for each, chosen by lot. The crews were supplied with teams, equipment, and seed, and were allowed a share of the yield as credits on the Order books. The incentive thus provided was weakened by delay on the part of the board in fixing the basis of division between the Order and the farm crews. The board struggled with the problem but delayed the answer pending a study of the wage and price structure to be set up to establish comparative equality among the various classes of labor. It was more than a year before the rates were fixed. Impatience for a definite understanding was met by exhortation to cultivate faith in the Order plan and unselfishness in adherence to its principles. Meanwhile, despite the uncertainties surrounding their wage rates, farmers in general worked with diligence and showed improving results each year. In 1875 12,000 bushels of wheat were harvested, compared with 5,000 in 1874. The harvest increased even more in 1876. Oats, barley, and potatoes were raised, in addition to wheat. Despite the dramatic gains in wheat production, it was necessary to supplement the local supply from outside in 1874 and 1875.[11]

Hay lands were attended by a separate company, and in 1875 ten four-acre plots of sugar cane were planted, each cared for by a manager with necessary help. The yield of hay is reported to have been adequate, the cane crop a failure. One member, Godfrey Hafen, was charged with the responsibility of setting out a nursery, but the Order was terminated before it could benefit from his efforts. It will be recalled that each family had its own lot (1.05 acres) and raised garden vegetables. No reckoning was kept of the products of the home garden, it being assumed that approximate equality was attained by the possession of equal areas by all families. There must have been in fact great differences in such incomes due to differences in ability and size of family.

Though standard wages were set at $1.50 for an eight-hour day, no wages were actually paid. Instead, earnings were entered on the books as credits to be drawn against for necessary supplies. But even with crop yields improving, it was impossible to pay the credits earned with crops produced and goods and services available from departments of the Order.

The majority of the Order members apparently were willing to curtail present consumption as the price of ultimate success, but there were many who demanded the book value of their earnings in store-pay. The board of management was harassed with requests that it could not justly meet. Accordingly, at a general meeting held at the beginning of the year 1875 it was agreed on recommendation of Joseph A. Young that the ten-hour day become the standard.[12] Some jobs were changed from a day wage to a piece-rate basis of remuneration. The herder who took the cows out to graze was allowed one cent a head per day; he hired two boys to assist and was charged for the use of horses. Farmers in 1875 were allowed $7/8$ cent a pound net for grain produced and $1/3$ cent a pound net for potatoes. This proved to be relatively excessive, and the next year they were allowed one cent a pound on grain and $1/3$ cent a pound on potatoes, but were required to bear half the expense for repairs of equipment and shoeing of teams. In 1876 the sawmill gang worked on a contract and received $11 on every $25 of lumber produced, meeting breakage expense below $15. Where piece rates were impracticable, day wages were fixed by the board but not with absolute uniformity. The best or most skilled workers were credited with $2.00 a day, and others as the board decided. The harness maker, the chief blacksmith, and the schoolteacher received the maximum and their assistants $1.50 a day.

Against the credits members were charged for withdrawals. There was always a shortage of cash and its equivalent, store-pay. Grain was readily convertible and was, in fact, frequently used in making cash exchanges, but the Order was a borrower of grain in

1874 and in 1875 and was later making a heroic effort to fall in line with the counsel of Brigham Young to store grain for future security. Even in a year of heavy yield, the grain could all have been exhausted in exchange for store goods and cash.

There were numerous requests from Order members for grain or other payment sufficient to make special personal purchases, such as a new hat or clock. Most of the petitioners had book credits for work performed and wished to draw only a part of their earnings. Many, of course, either because of the size of family or because of infirmity, or occasionally because of sheer indolence, overdrew their credits. The haphazard and unequal dispensing of store-pay led to an attempt at uniformity in December 1876, when board members voted to limit community withdrawals to a stipulated percentage of book earnings and to demand that complete and accurate records be kept.[13]

Despite strenuous effort, the board found it impossible to keep a reserve of grain, the best exchange medium. For years, Brigham Young had vigorously opposed the sale of grain to outsiders, and the Richfield United Order had accepted the storage of wheat as a cardinal principle. But the pressure for its conversion was uncontrollable. As with other communities, Richfield had an insistent demand for imported goods—goods that could be had directly or indirectly only for cash. Much attention was given in board meetings to the importance of moving toward community independence, and the tannery with its associated shoe shops was regarded as a step forward. Plans made for a dairy farm and cheese factory at Rabbit Valley (near Loa, western Wayne County) could not be carried out, however, and eventually were terminated by the dissolution of the Order. Some homespun was made and tailors belonging to the society were kept busy.

But the Order from the beginning was in debt to Zion's Cooperative Mercantile Institution (ZCMI) in Salt Lake City and was constantly scheming to get cash to settle. It has already been observed that Joseph A. Young in 1874 distributed his extra clothing to those in need to avoid immediate purchasing. In the same year a contract was taken by the several Orders of Sevier County, including Richfield, to do grading for cash wages for the Utah Southern Railroad. In the fall of 1875 the Richfield Order contracted to herd 300 head of stock for the church and some for ZCMI, with earnings to be applied on account. The Order was a borrower of grain in 1874 and 1875 but held a surplus after the harvest of the latter year. Some wheat was traded at 80 cents a bushel for cloth from the cooperative cotton factory at Washington, Utah. Some was traded in the spring at $1.50 a bushel to increase the Order's holdings in the Richfield Cooperative Sheep Herd.

The needs of Joseph A. Young's families at Richfield and at Gunnison proved a heavy draft on the cash and grain resources of the Order. Requests could not be denied, as there was always the possibility that the Young property might be withdrawn from the association; indeed, this was finally the case. In mid-January 1877, ZCMI made demand for payment for goods purchased by the Order for the co-op store. Grain was the only cash equivalent and there was a good market at the mines, but because of Brigham Young's attitude and the rules of the Order, the directors seriously debated before finally deciding to send grain on consignment to an agent at Kanarra. So much grain was disposed of that by the middle of May it was necessary to put the members on rations of eight pounds of flour a week to all over ten years old, six pounds to those between five and ten, and four pounds to children under five. A Brother Ence, whose task was to deliver the flour, thought the plan was justified as a check on those families that habitually drew unnecessarily large amounts.

As an additional means of relief, men were sent to earn cash wages at the Horn Silver Mine at Frisco, near Beaver, Utah, which they turned in to the Order for book credits. They were allowed 15 percent for personal use as encouragement. Two who had saved money by boarding themselves instead of paying $8 a week were allowed the difference, but, like the rest, they turned in the balance.

The attitude of these men at a time when the Order was crumbling is indicative of the high degree of loyalty that they and many others exhibited toward this experiment in communal living. It was stated in a general membership meeting on August 27, 1877, that in sending men out to work for cash wages the board had "gone against counsel," by which was meant that working at the mines for the gentiles had been strongly condemned by President Brigham Young. It was also stated that during the year grain had been sacrificed to get cash articles, a policy also condemned. "But," said the speaker dejectedly, "whichever way we turn is against counsel." Though approving the wisdom of the church policy of storing grain, the Richfield United Order had over a four-year period found it impossible to do so.[14]

It was well-established Mormon policy to occupy irrigable lands as fully as possible and head off the influx of non-Mormons. New communities were expected to receive Mormon immigrants freely and local leaders were ambitious to build up their own settlements rapidly. After the establishment of the Orders, operating branches were glad to welcome those who avowed their faith in the system and whose motives were apparently honest. Although at first the door to admission at Richfield was wide open, experience revealed the importance of selection based on the possession of property or of occupational skills needed by the community. On October 26, 1874, for example, the board decided to send teams after harvest to bring in people who had applied for membership in the Order. This policy continued through the year and into 1875, when it was decided to accept single young men under twenty-one "if they were their own masters and in good standing in the Church." On February 26, 1875, the board voted "to accept the Milford family, though destitute, after they declared to the board that they wished to join the Order on principle and not for support." By fall, however, there was evidence of a more restrictive policy, an applicant being "refused because the Order could not use another blacksmith." Though the Order agreed early in 1876 to accept the whole membership of the Prattville United Order "if they settle their debts first," the open-door policy was on the way out. Rigid restriction of admissions was advocated in a general meeting of stockholders on November 7, 1876. By February, 1877, the board had decided not to bring more immigrants to Richfield for an indefinite period.[15] Clearly, the leaders drew from three years of communitarian practice the lesson that the poor and infirm could be accepted only at the peril of the whole endeavor. Admission became contingent upon the potential contribution of the applicant either in skills or capital. Idealism was compromised by the desperate need to keep the enterprise afloat.

One of the great difficulties in operating a planned society is to regulate labor and consumption so as to achieve at least a rough approximation to economic equality. Under the competitive system the forces of demand and supply are always at work to adjust production to consumption and wages generally, and in the long run represent the product of the laborer. The United Order, in obedience to the implications of church teachings that "it is not given that one man should possess that which is above another, wherefore the world lieth in sin," aimed at relative equality of effort and of consumption and a steady elevation of the general level of living. The proponent of the system was under no illusion concerning the necessity of initial sacrifice, but he and his followers anticipated ultimate and comparatively early prosperity.

One weakness in the Richfield experiment was the failure to work out a schedule of prices. The directors no doubt felt that since all were (theoretically) working with the same intensity and consuming in the same amount, delay in rendering account on the books was relatively unimportant. That too little had been produced and too much consumed was painfully obvious by the end of the first season. Much of the difficulty was attributed to the eight-hour day, and some to laziness. In any event, some felt that the shiftless were riding on the backs of the thrifty and the industrious and that the cure for this evil lay in exhortation and better system. A special committee consisting of a chairman, a farmer, a mechanic, and a laborer was appointed in July 1875 to recommend a schedule of wages and prices, but apparently the committee was unable to agree. Nor did the foremen promptly or completely report the labor of all their subordinates. Thus, it was impossible for the secretary to keep a current record of individual labor credits, and it was impossible for an individual to find out where he stood, or for the board to find out if he were not already overdrawn.

In the year 1874, when the Order had operated on the gospel plan, living as though all were of a family, accounts were of small importance. But they were absolutely essential under the requirements of the corporate plan. It was a regular occurrence for the president of the board to express regret to the members at general meetings that accounts were far behind and to attribute the delay to the procrastination and ignorance of foremen. The members for the most part accepted the explanation with composure and confidence in their leaders; and when a faultfinder publicly stated, in June 1876, that many were becoming impatient, he found no support from the audience. By November 1876, the books had been brought up to March 1, covering the operations of the first crop year under the corporation. Some excitement was occasioned by the discovery of some members that they were in debt to the Order. Whether the situation had become worse or better since spring could not be known for an indefinite time.

A member of the board stated that the Order was carrying 100 nonproducers, by which he doubtless meant those whose charges exceeded their credits; he favored rigid limitations on supplies furnished to those in debt. Bishop Seegmiller, more kindly disposed, remarked that it would not be right to cut off supplies so abruptly. The disappointing revelations of the incomplete books created an insistence for more and prompter record keeping, but the poor secretary toiled over his thankless task in vain, always months behind. Finally, when from this agitation and other causes the Order was cracking up, a visiting church dignitary, John W. Young, whose advice was desired, urged extra help for the secretary, and a crew of clerks worked day and night to complete the record of individual accounts.[16]

Meanwhile, the directors were learning much about individual differences. That some would work for the glory of God and others only when hungry was quickly apparent. For example, one member demanded store-pay to purchase shoes, as he could not get them at the shoe shop (orders in the shoe shop were always months ahead of output). He threatened to seek work outside the Order unless his requests were granted. This challenge to the board was met by a motion to cut off his supplies until he should conform to Order rules. In exactly three months he was back expressing his willingness to work and requesting a little store-pay in advance. The board told him he must first bring vouchers for work performed.

There are many such instances in the records. Indolent members were often cited before the board. One had earned only $10 credit in six weeks. The board took great pains to bring such members into line. They first urged, then commanded, at last expelled.

In addition to difficulties arising from human frailty, and common to all working branches of the Order, the Richfield society had to face a disastrous loss in the sudden death of Joseph A. Young on August 5, 1875. Half of all the capital in the Order had been subscribed by him, and his business acumen and leadership had sustained the hope of ultimate success. To have control of his property without his active participation seemed a heavy responsibility. A letter was dispatched to his father, Brigham Young, asking if it would be proper to make all stewards over their own property, as had been done in Salt Lake City. In his reply President Young underscored his faith in the original United Order principles:

> For you to change your method of doing business to that of stewardships would be taking a step backwards and would not be in accordance with our feelings. So far as we know concerning your operations you have been doing well, and the prospects before you are encouraging. What can you possibly gain by changing your system? . . . what end can be accomplished by your turning back? We cannot perceive any good that will result. It is a union of the people, their means, and their efforts that are wanted, and the shortest cut to that is the best.[17]

Shortly after the church president wrote these words, disaffection appeared in the Richfield Order that eventually came to his attention in such a way as to occasion a break between him and the officials of the Order and to aggravate the spirit of discouragement that was beginning to weigh upon them. The issue grew out of the desire of L. M. Farnsworth to withdraw his capital, consisting of a recreation and dance hall that he had built and operated for two years before the organization of the Order, and that he had transferred as a subscription to capital stock. With some alterations it was used by the Order for general meetings and for recreation. The board had good reasons for refusing to "buy in" the Farnsworth capital stock; it could not easily spare the hall, and it was furthermore committed to the church policy of holding its grain, the principal source of cash. Moreover, the successful withdrawal of so important a stockholder would set a bad precedent and lead to no end of trouble. Farnsworth carried the matter to Brigham Young and induced him, by representations that were possibly one-sided, to advise the Order to make a settlement. It is probable that the church president, in addition, was beginning to suspect the competence of the general president of the Order, Bishop W. H. Seegmiller, for he must have known that the families of Joseph A. Young, along with others in the Order, were having difficulty securing ordinary necessities. The condition of the records of account made matters worse, and it was rightly suspected that the Order capital was being slowly consumed. An adjustment was finally negotiated by which the Farnsworth capital stock was purchased for $1,250.[18]

Meanwhile, Brigham Young had let Thurber and Seegmiller know that he expected to dictate in regard to the Joseph A. Young property.[19] In August 1876, B. T. Young, a son of Joseph A. Young, made a request in behalf of his mother at Gunnison for $1,000 at once and $2,000 in the spring, to make repairs and alterations on her home and meet other expenses. The board decided to do the best it could and notified the applicant that the Young family would be treated fairly, as with other members' families. In October Bishop Seegmiller reported that Brigham Young was dissatisfied with the treatment accorded his daughters-in-law and their families and that he had said that he would withdraw the Joseph A. Young property from the Order. "We must do as he says, and be loyal," Seegmiller advised his colleagues.[20]

At general meetings in November the members were apprised of the dark cloud hovering over the association and of President Young's expectations that the Joseph A. Young property should yield enough to support the family. His notion that the property was being squandered was correct, it was pointed out, insofar as members were busying themselves with pigs and chickens and gardens to the neglect of the needs of the Order. At the annual stockholders' meeting on November 30, Bishop Seegmiller and stake president A. K. Thurber declined renominations to the board, because, as Seegmiller said, his honesty had been questioned by President Young. The members, however, gave ample evidence of their esteem for the two brethren by voting that they make the nominations to fill vacancies and by prompt certification of their selections. The newly elected board members likewise honored them by requesting that they name the officers, by inviting them to attend all meetings, and by reappointing Bishop Seegmiller general superintendent.

The new officers undertook to close the breach between Brigham Young and the Richfield board of management and to compose the feelings of the members. The president, Lars P. Christiansen, reminded the people that though the Order was beautiful in theory, there were practical difficulties that could only be surmounted by experience. He was sure that President Young had been misinformed by mischief makers. Clara F. Young, widow of Joseph A., expressed the opinion that President Young questioned the ability rather than the integrity of those who had managed the Order. On the authorization of the board, Christiansen and Thurber went to Saint George to interview

President Young at his winter residence and to get his views on questions that had arisen in Richfield but had not been conclusively answered. They were empowered by the board to agree to the withdrawal of the Joseph A. Young property on a legal basis if President Young so desired. On their return the brethren read a letter prepared by President Young in answer to the questions submitted and reported that as a result of their visit he felt much better disposed toward the Order. He had for the time at least deferred any intention previously entertained of withdrawing the Young family property.[21]

Nevertheless, from that date (January 26, 1877) forward, requisitions of the Young family for store goods, livestock, equipment, and other provisions were honored with greater liberality, though they were still meager compared with the $3,000 requested by B. T. Young a few months earlier. These requisitions, detailed in full, were a heavy burden to the Order with its very limited liquid resources. And it must not be overlooked that many others were petitioning the board for like consideration.

Nevertheless, the majority of the board still had faith unshaken in the Order and were determined to save it. As a means of economy in living, they proposed the organization of family associations within the Order. The idea met with favor and "The United Family Organization A" came into being, with eight families and forty-two individuals as members. What they did and the spirit of the attempt may be given in the words of one participant:

Without any or but little help from the outside, they have, while fulfilling their duties to the United Order of Richfield, and amidst many difficulties, been able to erect a dining room and six sleeping rooms, and are prepared to build more as soon as time and means permit. So far as the experiment is concerned, it has been highly successful, and although our fare is humble, yet we all feel contented and happy, and feel the spirit of love, order and unity among us. We feel that we have been greatly blessed thus far in having been, by the providence of our Heavenly Father, able to accomplish so much with so little. Our little community numbers about 42 souls, although not all as yet living together on account of want of room. There is also in Joseph City a few families living together on the same principle. . . .

Let me say for my part that, as in my youth in the old country, it was given to me in answer to my prayer that the Gospel as preached by Joseph Smith and the Latter-day Saints was true from heaven, so also, when President Brigham Young preached the principles of the United

Order, it was given unto my understanding that it emanated from heaven for the benefit of the Latter-day Saints. This is the testimony of your humble servant, Henry Edward Desaules.[22]

The last glimpse we have of this little group was three months later, on the eve of the dissolution of the Richfield United Order, when they were granted a supply of lumber to finish their community edifice.

For months the semimonthly meetings designed to let off steam and acquaint the members with the decisions and activities of the board had been growing more and more vociferous. The explosions of the cantankerous members were not nearly so disheartening as the growing convictions of some who had been strongest in their support that disunion had gone too far to be repaired. "I am leaving the Order," said one member of the board, "because there is no order in it." Into this atmosphere came apostle Erastus Snow with advice to disincorporate. Two conflicting interests had met in the Order, he said, the poor and those of property. Without disincorporation it would be illegal for the directors, who were under bond, to permit the withdrawal of capital.[23]

With four negative votes, the assembly in which apostle Snow had suggested disincorporation voted to maintain the association in its existing form at least until after harvest. In the interim there was time for deliberation and, though among saints it should not have been so, for vituperation. Unfortunately, nobody would know until the books were brought up to date and balanced just how well or just how poor the Order had gotten financially. Many were sick at heart at the thought of surrendering the program. They had seen in the Order the beginning of fulfillment of the most cherished dreams of a devout people. Undismayed by cloud or storm, they had fervently wished to press on toward the new day. Convinced that the Order had been established to realize the purposes of the Almighty, they regarded continuance as inevitable and preferable, even though difficult and uncertain, to any form of retreat. Opposing these were the wranglers and the wreckers who had lost "the spirit of the Gospel" and with almost undisguised malice and bitterness seized every occasion to attack the men who had accepted the thankless task of managing the society's affairs. With some cause, such members maligned the movement and declared that the framework of the Order was the work of scheming lawyers who had distorted the original plan to serve "the god of the Gentiles." Between these extremists stood the men of calm, practical, conservative disposition who aimed to pacify feelings, to keep the boat on even keel, and to get it to port with as much of the cargo as could be saved.

After a meeting with John W. Young on August 8, 1877, it was decided to bend all efforts to completing the accounts, and extra clerks were employed and extra shifts served in the endeavor. The chief lack lay in the determination of labor credits. Several members of the board who had served from the beginning had not yet been credited with wages. Whether due to modesty, indifference, or downright procrastination, this neglect is suggestive of the difficulties that made correct bookkeeping impossible. Now, however, a committee was appointed to recommend a scale of wages. The report was submitted to the board, revised downward and approved, then carried to a meeting of the stockholders, revised a second time, and ratified. This process required two months. In most instances lump-sum settlements were arranged, but when day rates were applied the prevailing wage was $2.00. As an example of the standard that was followed, Bishop Seegmiller was granted $1,500 total for the two years, 1875 and 1876, and $1.75 a day for 1877. The secretary, J. A. Hellstrom, was granted $1,450 for two years of service and $2.00 a day thereafter.

Meanwhile, though legal steps to dissolve the corporation had not been taken, the property of the Order was in process of distribution. B. T. Young met with the board on September 8 and arranged terms for the release of his father's holdings, agreeing to leave the sawmill for the time being as a pledge against the Young share of any shrinkage in assets. Five percent was added as a dividend to capital over the entire period of the corporation's existence. Dissolution was ratified on September 20, and an attempt was made to return to each member the actual property he had subscribed on coming into the Order. It was voted to rescind debts of those who had served as missionaries during the existence of the Order, to cancel debts of the poor on the recommendation of the bishop, to collect debts from all others, and to pay tithing on crops for 1877 as had been done in each preceding year. Mischief-makers registered their disapproval and added to the general impoverishment by burning the stacked hay and the machinery.

It was irregular to distribute property before paying labor, but the procedure was generally considered equitable inasmuch as the owners would share labor losses along with the two-thirds who had no property to begin with. Following the precedent in the settlement with the Young estate, the board voted that six percent (per annum in this instance) be allowed as a dividend for the use of property. Whether it was paid or entered as a credit is not recorded. At the end of the year a financial report was made showing liabilities (labor and other credits) of $23,000 and resources of $10,000. It was explained that $8,000 had been paid as tithing and $12,000 contributed to the building of temples. These amounts should, it was suggested, be broken down and charged to individual accounts. If this were done the deficit would equal $3,800.

Except for the making of collections and final disbursements over the next few months, the Richfield United Order had closed the last chapter. Joseph A. Young, Brigham's son, had been the first to sign the United Order roll in April 1874. "With all my property," he added behind his name in the record book.[24] That fall he admitted that "when the Order came along it was a trial to him." He had been a businessman and realized that the United Order would "shut down on speculation." He told the faithful of his village that in building a more perfect order, "The feeling 'Mine' is the greatest feeling we have to combat." Moreover, he had noticed "classes forming among the saints, some feeling themselves above their brethren." It was his hope that "this Order will check such, will make us move on an equal standpoint."[25] Four years later he was dead and his heirs were quarreling with the Order, seeking a return of part of the property he had selflessly given for the common good in 1874. The last president, Lars P. Christiansen, urged the members not to assume that because the Young estate had drawn property from the Order it was permissible for others to do so also. He suggested they not look "at the legal or technical part of business and take advantage of [the] same, but regard the moral part and be actuated thereby." Those who had entered into the Order, he advised, should not allow selfishness

to have sway or room in our hearts, but if it is deemed necessary to agree to disagree and every one to labor himself, that we should manifest the same good spirit we enjoyed when we embraced and entered upon the principles of the U.O.

Already discerning the end of a fervent hope and years of strenuous effort to put into detailed practice Brigham Young's celestial order, the leader offered the villagers his hope "that the Lord would bless and enable us to prove faithful to the end."[26] If the ideal was lost as a community endeavor, it was nonetheless hoped that its principles and spirit might remain with the people as they left their common fields, divided their common properties, and went, each to his own way.

CHAPTER 10

The proliferation of United Orders:
Utah Valley, Cache Valley,
Bear Lake Valley, City Orders

RIGHAM YOUNG described the ideal United Order on numerous occasions and in explicit terms. The model for his vision was the "well-regulated family," an institution characterized by sharing of resources according to need, contributions of labor according to ability, and a concern for the welfare of others in the group that transcended selfishness and promoted harmony and unity. The physical environment of an ideal Order would be similar to that of a family as well, with a common kitchen serving both as a symbol of equality in consumption and labor and as a hearth, the center of the family social and spiritual life. Private apartment houses or rooms would accommodate the members for sleeping and more personal aspects of their lives, but the social experiences of Order members were to take place in the community environment rather than within the nuclear family.[1]

This was the ideal—a perfect expression of Brigham Young's compelling interest in the family and family life. Indeed, the ideal Order as described by the president bore a striking resemblance to his own family. The perfected Mormon society would possess the social dynamics, the economic structure, and the physical appearance of his own sizeable domestic establishment. Mormon society was to be his family writ large.

This ideal, sometimes called the "gospel plan" of the United Order, or the "big family," was seldom achieved in practice for an extended period, though many communities attempted for a time to make it a reality. The inevitable problem of protecting community resources against dissidents and laggards made a detailed accounting necessary—militating against the spirit of the sharing that was fundamental to that vision. The hostility of the federal territorial courts to any aspect of Mormon life departing from greater American norms loomed as a constant threat, making incorporation advisable as a protection against suits by

apostates. Moreover, many Saints found such all-embracing communalism repugnant to their own values and ambitions and
refused to accept it without modification. Brigham Young was too
much a realist to believe that such would not be the case, and on
March 11, 1874, he telegraphed instructions covering such
eventualities to the apostles in Salt Lake City from his winter
residence at St. George.

We want the Twelve and other brethren that wish to take hold in the
organization of the Order of Enoch . . . [to] commence in the several
wards by getting the brethren and sisters together to see who wishes to
take hold of this order of Zion. Take the names of such brethren both
male & female as wish to enter into this order of their own will & choice
for we do not wish any one to enter upon this holy order against their
own choice. . . . If there are not more than a dozen in a ward, whatever
there is organize them. They can commence farming in the Order this
spring & other branches as they get ready and go to work unitedly
together as one family. . . . Such as do not wish to join, treat them with all
the kindness and fellowship as though they were in the Order for many
will wish to wait & see what the result of our acts will be. But those who
have been preaching this order for thirty or forty years need not wait any
longer.[2]

Most saints, as Brigham Young had anticipated, were unwilling to enter into the more "advanced" communal life, creating a
situation that, if unresolved, threatened to divide rather than unite
the faithful. He had to anticipate either a following comprised of
two distinct and possibly hostile groups—a few Order members
and a much larger group of non-Order members—or a compromise of the ideal, permitting community leaders to amend the
Order to whatever extent necessary to gain general acceptance.
He chose the latter course, encouraging local innovation and
adaptation according to the desire of the Saints and the judgments
of local leaders. In consequence, the name United Order was applied to associations of all kinds, from full communes to loose
cooperatives. It was not uncommon for a single Order to run the
gamut from one to the other of these extremes (and sometimes
back again) as it struggled to find a viable form of association.

The many varieties of United Order seem to fall logically into
four distinct classes. Perhaps most followed the pattern set at St.
George, in which members contributed all their property to the
Order and received differential wages and dividends depending
upon their contributions in labor and capital stock. Work
performed and dividends were credited to families on the account

books of the organization. Withdrawals of consumer goods and services could be made as needed. Hostility between members of such Orders and townsmen not joining the Order compounded difficulties caused by the indolence of a few and confusion in procedural matters, leading to dissolution of perhaps half of such Orders within the first year of organization.

Another type of United Order was aimed primarily at increasing community ownership of manufacturing and agricultural enterprises, permitting individuals to retain their own property and to act as free agents in the disposition of their labor. Brigham City provided the model for this type of Order. The form was characteristic of communities where the cooperative movement had been particularly successful, and already formed a large part of the industrial and commercial life of the town. In such localities the United Order served only to reinforce and extend the cooperative organizations already in existence. In addition to Brigham City, the Orders at Hyrum, Utah, and Paris, Idaho, took this form. In purely economic terms these may have been the most successful types of United Order.

Brigham Young's ideal United Order seemed most adapted to small rural villages, where the social and economic life of the community already were closely intertwined and limited in scale. In larger cities, such as Salt Lake City, Ogden, Provo, and Logan, an alternative form of Order emerged, similar in many respects to the twentieth-century Mormon welfare plan. A single cooperative was organized in each ward, usually directed toward the development of one enterprise. The enterprise was chosen for its possible contribution to territorial self-sufficiency and was financed and run by ward members, who were rewarded by the creation of new employment and through dividends declared in proportion to initial investment. Several of these, such as the Salt Lake Nineteenth Ward soap factory, were successful for a considerable period of time, though the antipolygamy "raid" of the mid-1880s caused the bulk of them to fail or pass into private hands.

Finally, there were several Orders that came close to the communal ideal envisioned by Brigham Young. The best-known of these was Orderville, in southern Utah, but others were established as well, including, most notably, those at Price City, Springdale, and Kingston, Utah; Bunkerville, Nevada; and in several Mormon settlements on Arizona's Little Colorado River. A number of these Orders survived into the 1880s.

Partly because of the continuing reputation of Orderville as the supreme achievement of the United Order movement, it has been assumed that the Order was chiefly a southern Utah phenomenon. In fact, the Order in some form was initiated with notable success in a number of the northern settlements, including Paris, Idaho, and Hyrum, Pleasant Grove, and Spanish Fork, Utah. The most communal Order form does seem, however, to have been limited almost exclusively to southern settlements. It must be remembered that southern Utah in 1874 was still in name, and to a considerable degree in fact, mission territory. Indian uprisings in the mid-60s had caused abandonment of many of the smaller settlements, and resettlement in the early 1870s amounted virtually to new settlement. With the Indian presence still evident in many localities, settlers felt a need for collective effort to insure community survival. In addition, the massive labors involved in the building and maintenance of new dams, canals, mills, and homes made cooperation a logical, and perhaps necessary, choice. The more arid climate in the south made settlements especially dependent upon the caprice of nature for their harvests, leading many to believe that the economic advantages of division of labor and pooling capital that the Order was intended to accomplish would favor the success of the settlement. Finally, and perhaps most importantly, southern settlements, being newer, seemed more open to innovation and less established in their economic and social patterns. In fact, the most idealistic of the United Order towns were those founded during the peak period of Order activity. In such communities mercantile and manufacturing patterns were not yet set and the Order threatened less to disrupt community life. Nevertheless, as the painful experience in Kanab illustrates, there were striking failures in the south, just as there were notable successes in the north. As the Order began to be preached throughout the Mormon kingdom, there was a proliferation of United Orders—north as well as south, urban as well as rural—each developing significant variations on the communal theme emphasized by Brigham Young.

Utah Valley

Since the eighteenth century, visitors to Utah Valley, just south of the Great Salt Lake, have described it as among the most pleasant and potentially fruitful sites for agricultural enterprise in all of the Great Basin.[3] Mormon pioneers were quick to recognize the area as a promising site for settlement and began colonization early in 1849. By 1874 small, well-established farming communities dotted the landscape, stretching in a rich crescent along the eastern edge of freshwater Utah Lake from Lehi in the north to Santaquin in the south.

The commercial and ecclesiastical capital of the region was the town of Provo, and it was there that the Order was first preached in Utah Valley. Late in March 1874, regional church leader and bishop of Provo, Abraham O. Smoot (father of the late United States Senator Reed Smoot), conducted a three-day conference "attended by people from all the settlements of the county as well as in Provo." Speeches and testimonies were given during the three days on "the necessity of the people being self-sustaining, in producing what they consume, the organization and classification of labor, etc."[4] Though the United Order was not mentioned by name, Bishop Smoot had almost certainly heard via telegraph of the organization in St. George and called the conference to prepare the people for the new doctrine.

Residents of Pleasant Grove, ten miles north of Provo, and of Spanish Fork, about the same distance south, were among those attending the conference. After three days of spirited exhortation in Provo the sturdy farmers from these towns, with those from other Utah Valley settlements, returned to their lands and waited for church leaders to take further action. It was another month before Smoot began visiting the settlements, holding meetings to organize the Order in each village. By that time spring planting was underway and the tempo of another annual cycle of agrarian life established. Though the Order was imposed after spring work was largely completed, church members earnestly attempted to integrate it into their established pattern of production and consumption. If Pleasant Grove and Spanish Fork are typical, however, the Utah Valley Saints would brook no wholesale overhaul of their economic activities. They accepted the United Order of Enoch, but on practical terms.

Pleasant Grove was the smaller of the two settlements. In 1870 there were 286 families in the village, about half of them engaged in farming 2,140 acres of improved land. Holdings were small, in the typical Utah pattern, but the average farm, 22 acres, was worth about $636, and a family working the land with about $64 worth of machinery and $256 in livestock produced goods worth $360 annually.

About 80 percent of the 286 families in Spanish Fork were farm families. Their farms averaged slightly larger than those in Pleasant Grove, about twenty-four acres, but the land was much less productive. An average farm in Spanish Fork was worth only about $236, and a farmer normally worked with machinery and livestock valued at $54 and $191, producing annually but $236 worth of goods, much less than the average annual production in Pleasant Grove. In both towns the main crops were wheat, barley, oats, Indian corn, molasses, and potatoes. Though a significant part of the communities' wealth was invested in livestock, apparently most of these were draft animals, as production of meat, wool, and dairy products was not strikingly high. Spanish Fork was the more densely populated of the two communities, supporting 3.8 persons upon each acre of farm land, compared with 2.7 in Pleasant Grove.[5]

The Order was introduced in Pleasant Grove on April 27, 1874. As was the custom on important church occasions, representatives of the general church leadership were present, apostles Wilford Woodruff and Erastus Snow. Under their instruction, officers were chosen and the Pleasant Grove branch of the United Order founded.[6] The next day officers were discussing the need to employ members in opening a road into Pleasant Grove Canyon and working on the Provo canal. Over the next few weeks further steps toward organizing the community were taken. On May 3, the farming land was divided into three districts with a foreman to supervise the work of the men in each district.[7] The practical was unusual in that members were asked to assign land use, rather than the land itself, to the Order. The farmer was to pool his labor with that of others in his district in tending and harvesting crops on lands owned by members of the district. He was also to surrender his draft animals, tools, and machinery to Order use. The question of whether or not to deed real property was raised in July 1874 and deferred until the next year on the advice of a higher authority, presumably Bishop Smoot, who advised the Saints "not to do any thing with land titles at present but to Unite and work together all the same—to unite our labors and personal property."[8] The records do not indicate if individual farmers had prior claim on crops harvested from their own fields, but the infrequency of disbursals of grain in Order account books suggests that this was the case. Apparently only a surplus was taken into the Order granary for feeding the indigent and town-dwelling tradesmen who did not own farm lands. In neither community were there references in minute books of the need to borrow foodstuffs in the spring to tide the community over until harvest—a common occurrence in the south.

During May 1874 the Pleasant Grove Order began seeking out a sawmill to rent, appointed a beekeeper, and organized plasterers, masons, and carpenters. As many as 130 men became members of the Order, representing about 70 percent of the families in Pleasant Grove.[9] An Order farmer with approval by proper authority could requisition an Order plasterer or carpenter to help repair his home, the tradesmen charging the labor to the Order account books. The carpenter could in turn draw honey, wheat, and cheese from the Order, products of the farmer's fields. Presumably both farmer and tradesman were permitted a certain leeway for independent operations—a tradesman was allowed, when no Order work was needed, to hire himself out to nonmembers for pay; the farmer might sell some commodities, such as eggs or garden vegetables, to nonmembers for cash.

Almost to the time of the Order's demise in 1880 the board of directors was exploring possible new areas of enterprise. In the fall of 1874 there was discussion of the possibility of exploiting commercial fishing opportunities in Utah Lake. Though the fishery was not established, an apiary was set up with considerable success. Order members surrendered their beehives to central management in 1874 and 1875, the collective apiary totaling 62 colonies—rendering a sufficient annual yield to pay a manager for his services, increase the stock by eight colonies, and net 800 pounds of honey.[10]

Less successful was the Order's mining enterprise. In the winter of 1875-76 a Brother Golding persuaded the board of directors to join with him in developing a coal mine. Though he kept assuring the board that the discovery of a rich pocket was imminent, there is no evidence that the Order ever received a return from its substantial investment in the venture.[11] Helping to make up for such losses were the profits from the sawmill, a standard money-maker for many United Orders. The Pleasant Grove group purchased their mill in June 1876. During the summer they sawed enough lumber to pay wages for workers at the mill and fully repay the three- or four-thousand-dollar debt. Grain harvests were sufficient in 1876 to justify the building of a granary, to which a second story was added in 1877.

That summer the board discussed plans for expanding Order activities with a tannery and a silk-producing department. These optimistic plans never came to fruition. It was perhaps a portent of the fate of the Order that in November 1878 the board decided to remodel the upper story of their granary and make it into a dance hall. For reasons not indicated in the record, the board of directors decided that autumn to return the Order bees to their original owners. In March 1879 the board decided "after considerable conversation" that it was "advisable to abandon farming as a corporation and return to original owners all teams and farming implements as far as practicable." By August the board ordered further that "all stocks and other property held by the Order be returned to the original owners, wherever the accounts of such owners would justify such return." The only properties of any significance still held by the company were the sawmill and the granary. At the next meeting of the board, a year later, the sawmill was appraised at $4,000 and the granary $2,000, presumably in preparation for a final liquidation of the assets of the Pleasant Grove United Order.[12]

There were no high church dignitaries present when the Order was initiated in Spanish Fork. The regional leader, Abraham O. Smoot, drove to Spanish Fork from Provo on May 2, 1874, taking with him a business associate and civic leader, L. John Nuttall, who was later called to be arbiter and pacifier of hostile United Order factions in Kanab. After a prayer by Nuttall, Smoot proceeded to allay the fears of doubters by explaining that the United Order "was nothing new. It is only part of that gospel we embraced at the Waters of Baptism or part of our religion." Officers were elected in the afternoon and President Smoot (the title apparently from his position as president of the high council in Provo) closed the meeting by cautioning the Saints "against vain Speculations and Street arguments" concerning the Order.[13] Apparently citizens of the village, having had ample time to amplify rumors of changes to be introduced in their lives, were not entirely docile in their acceptance of the proposed economic system.

Nevertheless, activities began at once, and, on paper at least, the town was organized by the end of the summer in a manner similar to that of Pleasant Grove. Spanish Fork residents were by no means guilty, however, of moving too hastily into the new system. As board member William Creer put it, they "desired to be very cautious and move slow and if they see a wrong step turn round and retrace and get right again." The board, he maintained, "did not pretend great wisdom but felt their weakness and to look to God for light and the Brethren for their cooperation and etc."[14] The brethren did cooperate that summer sufficiently to operate a sawmill, cultivate molasses cane, rehabilitate an old threshing machine, get a woodworking shop into production, and collectively tend and harvest some of the season's crops. As many as 172 persons had active accounts with the Order in 1874, representing about half of the population.[15]

Though citizens of nearby Pleasant Grove were convinced by fall that "we were the only ones hereabouts who were doing much in the United Order," members of the Spanish Fork group were not yet willing to let their enterprise die. Early the next spring a general meeting was called to determine "whether we quit or go ahead." After a lengthy discussion a consensus emerged that it was "a duty to unite if we could only strike on the right system."[16] Though the sawmill was not run and the cane field not cultivated in 1875, the board of directors began a protracted series of negotiations leading eventually to the establishment of a large dairy. Order books at the end of the year showed a positive balance of $3.14. Dairy operations brought the balance to a still small, but more comfortable, $314.41 in 1877. The dairy continued to be the main enterprise of the Order until records ceased in 1880.[17]

If the communities of Pleasant Grove and Spanish Fork are typical, the Order in Utah Valley was confined to a more limited sphere than was the case in many of the southern settlements. There were, nonetheless, sincere efforts to place the producing and consuming activities of the citizens in Order hands, a goal accomplished more fully in Pleasant Grove than in Spanish Fork. The reported Order assets in Pleasant Grove in 1876 were larger than the producing wealth of the whole community (machinery and livestock) as listed in the 1870 census.[18] It is difficult to assess the meaning of such figures without better information as to how they were collected, but they suggest that in Pleasant Grove, at least, a significant amount of the community wealth was placed under Order management. Perhaps the word "management" is the key to understanding United Order operations in Utah Valley. There was no leveling in Spanish Fork or Pleasant Grove—no effort to take all resources into the Order and redistribute them according to need. Real estate was never deeded to the Order. Tools, machinery, and animals were placed under Order direction, but when dissolution came in 1880 there was apparently no difficulty identifying the former owners of the property. The Order served in Pleasant Grove, and less extensively and for a shorter time in Spanish Fork, as a means of providing efficient central direction for the local economy. This task quickly became tedious, however, and was quietly abandoned. The Orders in both communities were more successful in operating specific enterprises. Through profits from sawmills and dairy farms the Orders managed to remain solvent and to build cooperative home industries in the fashion of Brigham City. When the zeal for cooperation began to die out in 1876-77 these specific enterprises extended the life of the Orders into the next decade. Though such efforts were far from the "big family" ideal Brigham Young had hoped to see, the Order movement no doubt altered for the better the shape of local economies, providing jobs and producing commodities that otherwise would not have been realized.

Cache Valley and Bear Lake Valley

In the alpine valleys of northern Utah and southeastern Idaho the Order took a form that departed even more sharply than in Utah Valley from the ideal Brigham Young had envisioned. Lorenzo Snow's model cooperative community of Brigham City lay on the major route between settlements in the north and Salt Lake City. Leaders from Bear Lake and Cache Valley, passing through the city several times a year, could not escape being impressed with its successes. When Brigham Young preached the Order to them, the living example of Brigham City no doubt dominated their vision of what the church leader wished them to build. From the outset, the United Order in Cache Valley and in Bear Lake Valley was a producer's cooperative, or set of cooperatives, supplementing and stimulating, but not supplanting, the private economic activities of the citizens. In the north there was little talk of putting all one's possessions in the Order or living as a big family.

The geographical setting of both Cache Valley and Bear Lake Valley settlements limited and defined the role of agriculture in the local economies. The high altitude and mountainous terrain brought hard winters and a short growing season. Hardy grain and hay crops proved most successful, and ranching and dairying were the main activities. The mountains, in addition, provided an abundant timber harvest, opening alternative opportunities to those discouraged by limited agricultural potential. Oats, corn, potatoes, hay, butter, and cheese were the main products of the region in the 1870s. Farms ranged from ten to eighty acres, with the average just over thirty acres. In Paris, Bear Lake Valley, the value of livestock on farms exceeded that of the land itself, and in the Cache Valley town of Hyrum nearly so. Census enumerators reported that only about 25 percent of the residents of Paris and the surrounding area were land-owning farmers, while in Hyrum the figure was only 4 or 5 percent.[19] Apparently the bulk of the populace in Hyrum was engaged in grazing cattle on public lands and timber cutting, farming only the two-and-one-half-acre plots surrounding their village homesites.

Hyrum, ten miles south of Logan in Cache Valley, was settled in 1860 under the leadership of Ira Allen. A decade later there were 145 families in the settlement, totaling 708 persons. The Swedish-born bishop, Ola N. Liljenquist, had enthusiastically supported the cooperative movement begun in 1869, encouraging the settlers to advance beyond a retail store founded in that year to the cooperative ownership and management by 1874 . of sawmills, a livestock ranch, and a dairy. When the Order movement began it served only to encourage the expansion of cooperative enterprises already well established in the community.[20]

The citizens of nearby Bear Lake Valley had not been so successful at cooperative endeavor. Paris, capital of the region, was settled in 1863-64 under the leadership of apostle Charles C. Rich. By the 1870s the village had grown to just over half the size of Hyrum. Ninety-two families lived there in 1870, totaling altogether 491 souls.[21] Despite exhortations from church leaders in 1869, the cooperative movement did not really begin until Brigham Young visited the community in 1873, entering the valley through a newly opened canyon road built in record time by the cooperative labors of the Hyrum saints. The absence of cooperative institutions in Paris contrasted sharply with successes in Hyrum, setting the major theme of a sermon delivered by the church president during his visit. "Get a good co-operative store," he advised the Paris saints,

and operate together in sheep-raising, store-keeping, manufacturing and everything else, no matter what it is. By and by, when we can plant ourselves upon a foundation that cannot be broken up, we shall then

proceed to arrange a family organization for which we are not yet quite
prepared. You now, right here in this place, commence to carry on your
business in a co-operative capacity.

Preaching on the economic advantages of the division of labor, he
assured the group that if they followed his counsel, "by and by,
when we can, we will build up a city after the order of Enoch. . . .
A city of one-hundred thousand or a million of people could be
united into a perfect family, and they would work together as
beautifully as the different parts of the carding machine work
together. Why we could organize millions into a family under the
order of Enoch."[22] Acting on the Prophet's advice, the Paris community organized a mercantile store the next year and then
proceeded rapidly, under United Order auspices, to extend
cooperation in scale and scope.[23]

Paris was still launching its cooperative economic development when the Hyrum United Order, organized in March 1875
with Bishop Liljenquist as president, became the governing institution of the latter community's cooperatives, initiating a period
of further expansion and diversification. Another sawmill,
powered by water and specializing in railroad ties, was put into
operation. A sheep ranch was established, and a community
slaughter pen and meat market. In the town a blacksmith shop
was set up with two furnaces and a full set of tools. In addition,
the Hyrum residents built two lumberyards; planing, lath, and
shingle mills; a furniture shop; and a new two-story co-op general
store. By 1887 the firm was annually sawing almost 650,000 feet of
lumber, making up to 1,000,000 shingles, turning out 6,000 cross
ties, milking some 200 cows, and manufacturing some 24,000
pounds of cheese and 1,500 pounds of butter. Charles C. Shaw
reported to the *Deseret News* of October 28, 1877, that as the direct
result of the establishment of the United Order enterprises,
Hyrum had become, in three years, "a thriving little city."

> Handsome and commodious dwelling houses have been erected.
> Good barns and picket fences take the place of old sheds and willow
> fences, and all classes of the community, as well as many of our
> neighbors, are benefited by the labors of our little company of United
> brethren.

Under Order direction Hyrum became a virtually self-
sufficient community. There was no unemployment in the town
during a decade when the population nearly doubled. "As a result
of co-operation," wrote Bishop Liljenquist in 1881, "more than

one hundred and twenty thousand dollars have been extracted from the mountains in the shape of lumber, shingles, and cheese and butter from the cows." And this, despite two damaging fires that wiped out valuable properties.

By 1881 the once heavily timbered Blacksmith Fork Canyon, which was the basis of their prosperity, was pretty well "lumbered out," and Hyrum's economic opportunities began to decline. Residents found it increasingly necessary to find employment outside the town and valley. The company decided to dispose of the mills, dairy, and herd grounds to private interests, and by the end of the 1880s nothing was left under cooperative ownership but the store. This went into private hands before the end of the century.[24]

Though slower in getting started, the United Order of Paris experienced a similar evolution. Shortly after he organized the Order in Pleasant Grove, apostle Wilford Woodruff journeyed to Bear Lake Valley, where he supervised organization of both stake and community orders during the latter half of May 1874. The first fruit of his effort was the establishment that year of the Paris cooperative institution with an initial capital subscription of $3,057. This was apparently the only successful Order enterprise in the village until after a further visit by church officials in the summer of 1875. Apostles John Taylor and George Q. Cannon accompanied Wilford Woodruff on the subsequent visit, and the apostles spoke at a regional conference of church members on August 15. After sermons on the United Order the entire company retired to a nearby stream, where members and local leaders, including resident apostle Charles C. Rich, signified their willingness to support the Order by undergoing a ritual rebaptism performed by George Q. Cannon.[25]

With the fires of cooperation thus freshly fanned, the United Order of Paris began in earnest. Early in 1876 a dairy business was developed as part of the cooperative movement. Suitable pasture land was obtained eighteen miles north of Paris, and a herd of more than 120 dairy cows was gathered in exchange for stock in the cooperative association. When the Swiss cheese produced by the dairy proved expensive and unpopular, the community dispatched a delegate to Brigham City to learn the art of making American cheese. He returned with a former manager of the Brigham City cheese plant, and after ordering new equipment from the East in 1877, the Paris dairy began to produce an excellent quality product. The same year a tannery went into production and a leather-working shop was established to utilize the leather produced by the tannery. In addition, the Order acquired possession of a shingle, lath, and planing mill.[26]

Suffering, as do all young growing businesses, from lack of capital, the Paris United Order continued nevertheless to expand. The mercantile store remained the nexus of the institution, marketing the products of the various branches and helping to provide capital for new industry on the expectation that eventual freedom from outside sources of supply would more than make up for momentary deficits. The cooperative system minimized the problems created by an outflow of currency from the valley. Scrip was issued by each enterprise for labor performed and goods contributed. The bearer could then trade the scrip of tannery or cheese factory for those of meat market or sawmill, according to his needs. Though no central clearinghouse for scrip was established, individual bartering worked well enough to permit most to fill a substantial portion of their consumer needs within the system. Certainly this relative independence from extreme fluctuations in business activity and money supply on the outside was among the benefits Brigham Young hoped the United Order would achieve. Although the citizens of Paris preferred to build a cooperative rather than a communal Order, the prophet must have found some satisfactions in his last years from the successes attending their efforts.

Something of the scope of the Order enterprises in Paris is suggested in a report made to the *Deseret News* by Robert Price, one of the managers, in 1879. The principal properties of the organization in February of that year were store buildings in Paris, various land claims, buildings and improvements in Nounan valley, a tannery, cows, oxen, horses, wagons, agricultural equipment, dairy equipment, tannery tools, machinery and tools in the shoe shop, and a shingle, lath, and planing mill. There remained, in addition to the mercantile store, four industrial departments. The amount of business transacted during the year 1878 was given by Price as follows:

Amount of retail business done in boots and shoes	$ 6,500
Amount of retail business done in harness	750
Amount of retail business done in merchandise	35,000
Manufactured 36,000 lbs. of cheese @ 14¢ per lb.	5,040

Raised 3,500 lbs. pork @ 10¢ per lb.	350
Raised 650 bushels of oats	320
Manufactured leather	3,900
Manufactured shingles, lathe, etc.	1,500
Sold of beef 25,000 lbs.	1,500
Total	$54,860

During the year $13,000 had been paid for labor. In the first nine months a dividend of 40 percent was declared and applied on capital stock. On increased capital amounting to $5,000 the dividend for 1875 was 42 percent, which was paid out in merchandise and amounted to about $2,000 after tithing was deducted, as required by the by-laws of the company. The dividend in 1876 was 34 percent, half of which, following company regulations, was reserved and applied on capital stock. Within a population of 649 Latter-day Saints, 190 were shareholders, according to a report of February 28, 1882. There were more shareholders than there were heads of families.[27]

A significant tribute was paid to the residents of Paris when the *History of the Idaho Territory* was published in 1884. "Probably nowhere in the civilized world is cooperation carried on so successfully as it is among this peculiar people," the authors wrote. Reviewing the history of the Paris cooperative, they concluded that the United Order was

virtually a business of the people, comprising today 200 shareholders with a capital of $25,000. Shares are $5.00 each and no one shareholder can hold more than $400 worth.

It pays annually $20,000 for labor and has paid its shareholders, since establishment in 1874, $27,000. . . .

This institution has demonstrated that by judicious management, cooperative institutions can be made the means of increasing the wealth of the people; that the citizens of moderate means, and even the poorer classes can, by a combination of their efforts, do their own merchandising and manufacture their own necessities and share the profits among themselves, and thus prevent the growth of monopolies, which become, in many instances, the tyrants of their patrons.[28]

The Paris cooperative was in decline, however, at the time these words were written. The Oregon Short Line Railroad, later a division of the Union Pacific Railroad, completed a branch line through the valley in 1882. In consequence, the tariff on outside manufactures caused by high transportation costs was greatly reduced. Outside products of superior quality suddenly cost only a small amount more than items of home manufacture. Building their enterprise in a small, captive, local market with a bare minimum of capital investment, Order managers had never successfully upgraded the quality of their products beyond a serviceable minimum. With "Valley Tan" leather products scorned by fashionable people throughout the commonwealth, it is not surprising that the tannery failed first, taking with it the shoe shop and the harness shop. It was found that shingles made of Oregon red cedar would lie flat on the roof without curling as the local "yellow pine" (Pinus ponderosa) shingles did. After the coming of the railroad they cost but $1 more per thousand, an extra expense well worth it for those who could afford the small extra initial investment.[29]

In addition, the ready supply of a much greater variety of goods caused several individuals to begin competitive merchandising establishments, drawing business from the mercantile store, which had been the heart of the Order system. When reorganization of the co-op store in 1888 failed to put it into a more competitive position, the company began gradually to lease out or liquidate its assets. By 1900 only agricultural enterprises remained, particularly those associated with livestock and dairying.[30] The Bear Lake Valley was becoming in its relationship to the rest of Utah what the territory was becoming in its relationship to the other states—a supplier of raw materials to wealthier, more populous and industrialized regions.

The examples of Paris and Hyrum suggest that cooperation in the north represented an entirely different order of experience from cooperation in the south. In Hyrum, where cooperation was well-advanced when the United Order movement began, and even in Paris, where cooperation was made successful under Order auspices, involvement did not at any time become a symbol of exceptional selflessness and faithfulness. Individuals there were not asked at any point to declare themselves for or against the Order of Enoch. Purchasing stocks, working at day wages for a tannery, or purchasing goods at a cooperative store required little in the way of personal commitment. The Order in the north did not upset a social system. It only modified an economic system. The personal lives of individuals could pass in and out of the realm of Order activities without a prick of conscience or a moment of self-doubt as to orthodoxy and faithfulness.

UTAH
SOAP
Manufacturing Company.

U. O., 19th WARD, S. L. CITY,

OFFER TO THE MERCHANTS OF THE Territory and vicinity several brands of first-class SOAPS, including

PALE SAVON,
CASTILE,
WALNUT OIL SHAVING,
VARIEGATED TOILETS,

Including the celebrated
THOMAS PATENT SOAP,

Which we guarantee to be equal to any others in the market.

Having secured the service of **Mr. Joseph Ellis**, a practical soap maker, who has manufactured all kinds for a period of twenty-five years in the Eastern Cities and Canada, thus supplying these markets with the above articles and all Standard Soaps known to the market.
We would especially call the attention of Woolen Factories and Wool growers, that we are manufacturing the celebrated

SCOURING OR FULLER'S SOAP,

Also **Adamantine or Miners' Candles**, which we offer as cheap as the cheapest.

☞ A liberal price allowed for all boxes returned.
The Highest Market Price paid for all kinds of GREASE delivered at our Factory.

☞ Our soap can be had at the Factory and at the Scandinavian Store, next door to the Great Western Hotel, near the corner of Second South and First East Streets.
All orders to be addressed to Mr. John South, Assistant Secretary, P. O. Box 716.

A. H. RALEIGH, *Prest.*
A. W. CARLSON, *Secty.*
w50

Advertisement from the *Deseret News*
for United Order soap, guaranteed
"to be equal to any others in the market."
(Church Archives)

Brigham Young had hoped this type of cooperation would lead people gradually, imperceptibly, into the more perfect, communal Order of Enoch. Clearly, it did not. In fact, the most striking aspect of the Order in the north compared with that in the south is that it seemed, in the memory of those who participated, to have imparted little, if any, spiritual direction to the community. In both Hyrum and Paris old-time residents continued to refer to their collective enterprises as "the co-op" rather than the United Order, in spite of the fact that the Order made the Paris effort viable and greatly stimulated Hyrum's enterprises. The term "United Order," with its compelling call to conscious pursuit of social perfection, seems almost deliberately to have been avoided. Paradoxically, where the Order brought the greatest economic benefit it seemed to lift men's spirits least. Those leaders who dared great things and failed greatly seemed to move the Mormon people more than did those who attempted less and found a modicum of success. It is perhaps for this reason that the United Order seems, in the collective memory of present-day Mormons, to have been primarily a southern Utah phenomenon. The United Order as a hortatory symbol persisting in time derives from the dramatically unsuccessful experience in the south.

The ideal communal form of United Order envisioned by Brigham Young was best adapted to the conditions of life in small agrarian villages, where religious, social, and economic life overlapped to a considerable degree. Variations in the form Orders took in different farming villages were probably determined more by the attitudes of local church officials and their judgment as to how organization could be best achieved within their jurisdiction than by differences in the communities themselves. Also important in northern Utah was the influence of Brigham City, an eminently successful cooperative community led by a popular and greatly respected leader, Lorenzo Snow. When Brigham Young preached the Order in the north, local Latter-day Saints took as their model the city that bore his name. The more communal forms attempted in the south were not contemplated in the north, except as a possible end in the remote future. In the larger towns and cities, however, such as Logan, Ogden, and the territorial capital, the communal Order was, at least at the outset, patently unworkable. More complex patterns of social and economic life were well established, involving gentiles and miscreant Mormons in a structure that did not permit the ready clustering of the faithful into discrete "big family" units. These conditions made adaptation of the United Order a necessity rather than an option of local leaders.

Salt Lake City and Logan Orders

The pattern of urban adaptation emerged as the Salt Lake City ward United Orders were organized in the early summer of 1874. Brigham Young initiated the movement in the Salt Lake City Twentieth Ward on April 29. By June 14 all but one of the twenty-seven wards in the city and suburbs had completed at least a paper organization.[31] There was, of course, no prospect of building, as in Hyrum and Paris, largely self-sufficient economic communities in each ward, with several departments producing goods to be marketed in a local cooperative store. Typically, ward members were asked to join in providing capital for the launching of a single enterprise, the products of which could be marketed through the central ZCMI wholesale and retail outlet. The several United Orders in a city were, in effect, to accomplish collectively in the larger urban economy what a single Order with several departments was to accomplish in a smaller community like Hyrum. Though communal life was not attempted in the cities, regional self-sufficiency at least could be promoted by cooperative funding and management of new industries. Only a few of the Salt Lake City Orders got beyond the initial election of officers. The Eighth Ward operated a hat factory; the Eleventh Ward, a tailor's shop. In the Nineteenth Ward a soap factory was established, and in the Twentieth Ward a boot and shoe shop.

Independent from these individual ward enterprises was the central United Order of Zion organized May 9, 1874, in Salt Lake City, with Brigham Young and his two counselors, George A. Smith and Daniel H. Wells, as chief officers and the apostles as assistant vice-presidents. The board of directors was comprised almost entirely of wealthy businessmen, bankers, contractors, and ranchers.[32] An apparent successor to this organization was the "United Order of Salt Lake City Number One" organized in Brigham Young's office on August 4, 1875. At the founding meeting of this Order, the church president "obtained an expression from each of those present of his willingness to abide the law of the Lord through the Priesthood and his desire to enter into further bonds of union for the building up of the Kingdom of God."[33] The thirty-one prominent religious and financial leaders present also voted to bring a schedule of their properties to the board at a subsequent meeting. Upon presentation of the schedules, George Q. Cannon, following instructions from the president, "interrogated the new members as to whether they were willing to hold themselves and all they had subject to the direction of the Priesthood."[34]

It is not known precisely what role the church president expected this and its parent organization to play in the greater United Order movement. Apparently the Order was to build a large capital pool as a special resource in promoting local industry and achieving regional self-sufficiency. At a meeting of August 19, 1875, he expressed his dissatisfaction with time spent devising United Order constitutions that would withstand legal assaults. Now, he told the men, he "wanted to reach something that the people could live up to." It would not be necessary for members to give all their possessions to the bishop, as had been done in Missouri, "but each man should act as a steward over his own property" and "should be subject to the board of directors in the course he should take with his means. The board would also direct what should be done with the profits of our labors or surplus means." On the last day of August 1875, he addressed the wives and families of this group on the waste caused by the aping of eastern fashions and luxurious and ostentatious manners of life and dress.[35] It was the last meeting recorded in the minute books. Apparently Brigham Young's United Order Number One, though representing a laudable effort to make sure that all classes, rich as well as poor, were committed to the United Order goals, accomplished less than many of the ward United Orders.

Also organized in Salt Lake City were a Tailors' United Order and a Tanners' United Order. Virtually nothing is known of these institutions other than the fact that they existed. In all probability they were associations uniting tradesmen in the setting of wages for their labor and in apportioning work fairly among members. One suspects that the religious sentiment that was an integral part of the entire United Order movement was important in these associations as well, making them more like medieval craft guilds than the American labor unions, then in their infancy. (The Knights of Labor had been organized nationally in 1869; the American Federation of Labor was founded in 1881.)

United Order organization in the Cache Valley capital of Logan was similar to that in Salt Lake City, though the successful Logan ward Orders tended to be more diverse in their undertakings. The United Order Manufacturing & Building Company was organized in the Logan Second Ward on December 2, 1875. The first enterprise was the importation of a turning lathe and other machinery to make broom, hoe, rake, and pitchfork handles. Two Second Ward firms, Card & Son Sawmill, Lath and Shingle Mill, and P. N. Petersen & Sons Planing Mill, each having advantageous water power rights, were united in the general ward cooperative. The company formally commenced business on January 10, 1876, with a paid-up capital of $10,410. The group put up several small buildings, sent for new woodworking machinery, and prospered handsomely. Within a year it determined to construct a general store, called the "U.O. Store," which reputedly did the largest retail business of any store in Cache Valley. Since the enterprise did not do an export business, and there was little cash to be had in the valley, the general store made it possible for the United Order to pay its employees in merchandise.

Ultimately, a second store was opened and a United Order currency was introduced and circulated. By 1880 the capital stock had increased to $26,000, the company had paid out 99 percent in dividends, and "constant and profitable employment had been furnished to 65 men and 35 teams." The enterprise built homes, manufactured much of the furniture sold in the valley, and sold over $100,000 worth of "States goods" at retail. They supplied 53,000 railroad ties to the Oregon Short Line in 1881. In February 1877 the Logan Third Ward joined with the Second Ward and turned in their cooperative dairy on the west side of Bear River for equivalent capital stock in the Second Ward store. Thus, at its peak in the early 1880s, the company produced sashes, doors, moldings, brooms, furniture, cheese, butter, and shingles. The institution continued to expand and operated as many as seven sawmills at one time in Logan Canyon. It was the leading enterprise of its kind in the valley until 1909, when it sold out to George Cole & Sons.

The United Order Foundry, Machine and Wagon Manufacturing Company was organized in the Logan First Ward on January 5, 1876, with a paid-up capital of $2,500. The company did not prosper at the start and earned only $279 the first year.

Business picked up, however, and by the end of four years, the company had turned out eight complete shingle mills, seven complete sawmills, fifty feed cutters, one planing machine, one turbine water wheel, "and a vast amount of castings, embracing mill irons, shafting, morticing machines," and many other tools, implements, and machine parts. This foundry was the first full-time foundry in Cache Valley. In fact, the historian Tullidge wrote that before the establishment of the United Order Foundry, blacksmiths were forced to unite farming with their work at the shop, and "frequently those who brought their work to be done would find the sons of Vulcan absent on their farms, which of course occasioned serious delay." The blacksmith shop operated by the United Order Foundry had seven forges, all furnished with wind from a fan in the machine shop worked by waterpower. By 1881 the company employed sixteen men, including blacksmiths, expert machinists, molders, wagon and carriage makers, and apprentices. Among other things, they cast the twelve bronze oxen supporting the baptismal font of the Logan Temple. The company also made wagons and sold imported ones. The company works were destroyed by fire in 1886.[36]

Almost nothing is known of the United Order in Ogden. Apparently the Order there was organized by districts created for the purpose, rather than by wards, an unusual and perhaps promising innovation. On May 3, 1874, the first district was organized. The second and third districts were organized on May 17 and 18. Whether these efforts developed into enterprises of substance is not known, but the absence of recorded activities suggests that they did not.

On the whole the Saints in the north seemed wary of efforts to alter dramatically their accustomed economic and social patterns. The accomplishments of their cooperatives greatly complemented but did not supplant traditional economic forms. Perhaps their caution worked ultimately to their advantage. Where no fast lines could be drawn between those who worked in the Order and those who did not, occasions for intramural conflict over Order affairs were greatly reduced. In the southern Utah village of Kanab factions of Order advocates were strong and unyielding in their desire to make a living reality of the communal form favored by the prophet. Treading roughly upon the more reticent, they left a legacy that divided the community for many years thereafter.

CHAPTER 11

Kanab:
Many men,
many minds

HE UNITED ORDER rent the southern Utah village of Kanab into hostile factions and parties, each convinced that its particular vision of the Order represented the highest form of religious communal life. In one sense Kanab was unique among Mormon communities. Nowhere did feelings stirred by the Order run so high or leave such enduring scars. Yet the Kanab experience illuminates and clarifies forces that worked more subtly in other communities to undermine Brigham Young's great economic experiment before it had become viable. Thus Kanab may be seen as a caricature of the more disturbing and troublesome aspects of the United Order—a distortion of features attenuated elsewhere by unusual piety, by strong leadership, or in some cases, such as Orderville and Bunkerville, by the separating out of the otherminded into new settlements. Kanab is worthy of detailed study because the experience there illustrates with striking force and clarity the difficulties involved in making a success of the United Order.

Until 1876 Kanab was the extreme southern outpost of Mormon settlement in the Southwest. Initial colonization began in the late 1850s and early 1860s when a few stockmen began to drift into the area. Jacob Hamblin, preeminent Mormon Indian scout and missionary, frequently crossed through the region in the mid-1860s and made it the center of his operations in the south. At least a dozen of Hamblin's associates eventually settled in Kanab, including Brigham Young's nephew, John R. Young. Among the several other members of Hamblin's band of adventurers who became prominent residents of the town in the 1870s were Jehiel McConnell, Taylor Crosby, Andrew S. Gibbons, and Ira Hatch.[1]

When the Navajos organized an effort to push Mormon settlement back into the north in 1865, most of the early residents fled. The site retained strategic importance, however, as an early warning station and first line of defense against possible Indian attacks upon the more established settlements of St. George, Santa Clara, and Virgin City. By 1867 a crude fort enclosing several log cabins had been erected, serving as a trading post and a stopping place for scouts and missionaries, and offering a modicum of safety to those who might be called to resettle the area.[2]

By 1870 Brigham Young had decided that the time was right to recommence expansion into the south. On April 2 the Mormon leader and a delegation of church officials visited Hamblin's fort and declared the region fit for resettlement. One member of Young's company who was not a regular traveling companion of the church president was Levi Stewart. He apparently had been invited to accompany the expedition because President Young envisioned an important role for him to play in the development of southern Utah. Within a month Stewart was heading south from the Salt Lake Valley as leader of a colonizing party bound for Kanab.[3]

A native of Illinois, Levi Stewart was a mature fifty-eight in 1870. He had accompanied Brigham Young on another peregrination to the south in the early 1860s, but had made his Salt Lake Valley home in Big Cottonwood since his arrival in Utah in 1847. Through railroad contracting he had become a man of considerable means and influence. He had a respectably large family of two wives and at least fifteen children.[4]

Brigham Young's verbal instructions to Stewart during the trip north from Kanab in April must have been of the sketchiest nature. On May 2, shortly before setting out on the return trip, Stewart felt obliged to ask the president for an elaboration of the details of his mission.

Where and at what do you want me and those acompanying me to goe to work. Unto whome am I to look for Council. If from 10 to 15 men goes to Kanab in that event would it be wisdom to take a woman to that Fort of Bro Hamblins. Will there be a city layd out and directions given in time for to goe to building. . . . Shall there be a full and correct acount kept of all seed and tools furnished and work performed. By whome and when will we be instructed how and to what extent to cooperate.

Stewart then proceeded to list the nine men who had agreed to go from Big Cottonwood and from Salt Lake City, including John Rider, James L. Bunting, and two of his own sons. Four more men from Bountiful were on Stewart's list of prospective settlers: Allen Frost, Charles Dean, Edward Cooke, and Benjamin Peal. These men had attracted the church president's attention when on their own initiative they founded a cooperative family order in Bountiful. Others from Farmington, Goshen Valley, Pleasant Grove, Santaquin, and Nephi were listed, of whom David Udall and "Bro Noble" (probably Edward A. Nobles) were the only ones to settle in Kanab for a significant length of time. At least ten of the twenty-four men on Stewart's list responded to his call to help build a new settlement on cooperative principles at Kanab. As many as two families not on the initial list joined forces with the company, most notably that of Moses Farnsworth.[5]

James L. Bunting's account of his own calling at the age of thirty-seven was probably typical. While mourning the death of a son he received a notice from Stewart that he had been called on a mission to the south. Consulting with Brigham Young in the matter, Bunting was requested by the church president to undertake the mission if he could subscribe to two conditions— "cooperation in all things and treat the Indians kindly." Consenting to these conditions, Bunting, a shoemaker, sold his home in the Salt Lake City Eleventh Ward, outfitted his family, and on November 5 began the month-long journey to Kanab.[6]

That summer and fall the core of explorers, missionaries, and Piute Indians inhabiting the fort graciously crowded together to make room for the trickle of incoming settlers from the north. When James L. Bunting, his wife, Harriet Dye, and their four children arrived on December 2, after twice suffering the annoyance of a broken kingbolt on their wagon, they "found Bishop Levi Stewart & the rest of the brethren located in an old fort by the side of a small stream called the 'Kanab.' Most of the building consisted of logs very roughly put up. About twenty-five (25) families in all. . . . I obtained a small adobie building without door, window, or floor, which we fixed up & made very comfortable."[7] Kanab's unlikely amalgam of adventurers, ranchers, and dirt farmers would henceforth find it necessary to adjust differing life-styles and personal loyalties to the perquisites of church authority and the necessity of collective survival. It would not be an easy task.

Brigham Young visited the fledgling colony in September 1870 and chose Levi Stewart to be bishop. Thus Stewart became responsible for the secular as well as spiritual health of the new colony. Jacob Hamblin was freed to dedicate himself fully to the sensitive task of keeping relationships with the native inhabitants peacefully stable, and Hamblin's associates were henceforth obliged to subject themselves to the authority of the newly designated leader. Apparently Stewart found that the moral conduct of the settlers in the frontier outpost left much to be desired. That winter he stopped administration of the sacrament because he "thought it wisdom to suspend the partaking of that ordanence until the Saints could partake of it worthily." Not until the following September did the people advance sufficiently in worthiness to cause the bishop to recommence the ordinance.[8]

Though dogged by a calamitous fire, epidemics, and lean harvests, the community continued to grow in the succeeding years. Two prominent families were added as a result of another visit by Brigham Young in January 1871 when James A. Little and John R. Young, members of the visiting party, decided to settle in the area. The prophet's nephew, of course, had long been familiar with Kanab through his work as explorer and Indian missionary. Several families of Mormon converts from the deep South and the border states arrived during the next two years, adding yet another cultural dimension to the encampment on Kanab Creek.[9] Finally, in 1873, a few men returning from the initially unsuccessful Arizona colonization mission followed the advice of church leaders and settled in the growing community.[10] William H. Solomon, John H. Standifird, and Abel A. DeWitt were among the settlers from this group. With the addition of these families, the key groups that would comprise Kanab's population in subsequent years had settled into the community. Individual families would continue to drift in and out of the settlement, but the enduring community structure had been shaped and defined.

When the U.S. census marshal made a quick trip to the narrow valley on June 9, 1870, Levi Stewart's colonization had just begun. The census taker counted seventy-three persons huddled in the rustic fort, living in eleven households. As one might expect of a frontier outpost, there were significantly more men than women, very few elderly (only Stewart was over the age of fifty), and few children for a settlement of its size. Of the fourteen adult men at Kanab, seven were a part of Stewart's company and seven were associates of Hamblin, residing in the fort before the new colonists began to arrive. No one lived alone—outside of a household group.[11]

Four years later when a census was taken to help inaugurate the United Order, the influx of settlers had changed the nature of the community dramatically. Kanab had more than quintupled in population, totaling 416 persons. The predominance of males over females in the town had been diminished by the commencement of settled family life. Large numbers of children had been added to the population, bringing the median age to a very young 15.1, well below the territorial median of 17.5. The community had moved from the fort and begun to build permanent homes in a square-surveyed village sufficient to shelter eighty-one households. There were twenty-four plural wives in the village, 30 percent of all the married women, most of them living in the same household as their husbands' other wives and children. The families were comprised on the average of five persons, counting parents. Each married woman had on the average three living children. Eleven persons, including but one woman, were single and lived alone. Half of the entire population was under fifteen years of age, providing, together with the twenty-one persons over sixty, an abundance of hungry mouths for the working adults to feed. Each spring and summer there was a long period when grain had to be imported and carefully rationed to tide the inhabitants over until the fall harvests began.[12]

The geographic placement of the population had been altered dramatically as well. Abandonment of the fort had begun in 1871, and while most settlers moved to the new village site, one group of southerners and former associates of Hamblin moved about forty miles to the east and north, to the settlement of Pahreah. The family names of Smithson, Smith, and Hamblin were prominent in Pahreah. Another smaller group dominated by the Johnson family chose, quite appropriately, to call their new homesite Johnson; it was located just ten miles northeast of Kanab. About fifteen miles to the northwest refugees from the "Muddy Mission" to Nevada had settled nearby Long Valley, where they built two villages, Mt. Carmel and Glendale. One of their number and a few from Eagle Valley, Nevada, notably the Zadok K. Judd family, settled in Kanab.[13] The main route to the local capitals of Toquerville and St. George led south from Kanab over Pipe Springs in Arizona and then northwest, a good three days' drive to the closest centers of Mormon population.[14] Thus isolated, the villages of Kanab, Johnson, and Pahreah, though physically separated from one another, tended to form one community, with the Kanab Ward and its bishop as the central unifying force. Families from all the settlements com-

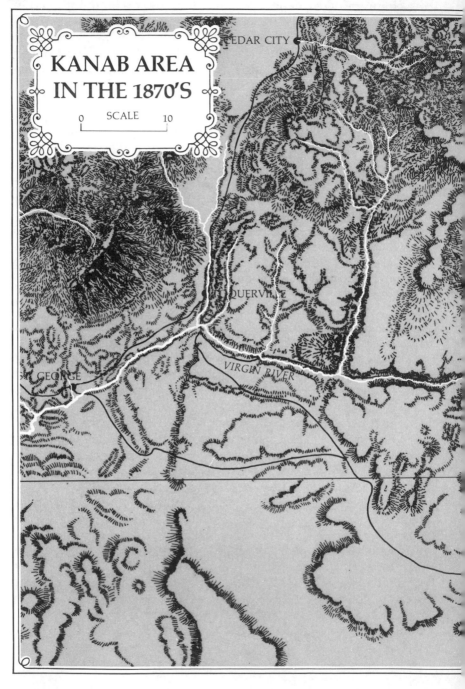

KANAB AREA
IN THE 1870'S

SCALE
0   10

CEDAR CITY

QUERVILLE

VIRGIN RIVER

ST. GEORGE

prised one congregation, paid tithes to one tithing house, inter-married their sons and daughters, and enjoyed a surprisingly high level of social contact. There was also much shuffling of popula-tion back and forth between Kanab and the Long Valley villages, but because Long Valley was a separate church unit, the contacts were not as frequent or close as those in the three Kanab-centered settlements.

Visually, the region was spectacular. The settlements were in narrow valleys where green patches of arable lands were edged by brilliantly variegated sandstone cliffs and buttes. Situated below the southern rim of the Great Basin, Kanab Creek and the neighboring waterways made their way southward through a twisted, broken terrain, emptying their scanty flow of water into the Colorado. The numerous small springs and creeks did not join into a single significant watershed, making the region more suitable for stock raising than for irrigated farming. Higher country to the north provided sites for sawmills and for dairy, cat-tle, and sheep ranches.

Since the bishop and a significant number of the early settlers had agreed that their endeavors should be accomplished through collective effort, one would suspect that the community would have been primed for the United Order when it was instituted in the spring of 1874. But there is evidence that from the beginning the colonists had difficulty cooperating as fully as Brigham Young had wished. Two days after the president visited Kanab in September 1870, Levi Stewart, the newly appointed bishop, called the adult male population of the colony to a council meeting. Explaining that the object of the meeting was "to consult on some points for our future guidance" and that he "wished all the brethren to feel free in all our councils," the bishop then proceeded to speak "upon the principle of cooperation and also in regard to our farming interests and how our farming land should be divided." After this introduction he asked the assem-bled men to discuss the question "How shall we manage our farming interests?" A lively debate ensued in which "several of the brethren expressed themselves pro and con upon cooperating together or having the land divided, when Bishop Stewart decided upon dividing the land and apportioning to each man."[15] Ap-parently the first effort at cooperation had fallen flat, the bishop choosing the course that he felt would provoke the least con-troversy.

The decision did not dampen enthusiasm for other attempts at cooperative endeavor. Early the next spring a Farmer's Association was organized at Kanab that empowered an elected board of directors to "dictate the putting in and cultivating of the land, to put a price upon all labor, grain, and produce of all kinds, also to price the clearing and breaking of all land, and price all other kinds of labor that may have been done that is used by said company." The board of directors was given the responsibility of distributing the harvest according to the following rules: A tithing was to be paid of the full harvest; one-third was then to be divided among the landowners according to the amount of land each held; the debts of the company would then be paid and any residue divided among company members as dividends. Thirty-four men, including the bishop, signed the agreement, representing virtually all the population of Kanab at the time.[16]

Though some fencing was accomplished and the telegraph line to Kanab completed through cooperative labor in 1871, the more formal farming association was apparently not successful. On February 10, 1872, another farming cooperative was organized, and still another on March 18, 1873.[17] The 1872 organization planned to open a farming area below the city. In 1873 the most recent organization was still attempting to complete fencing of the land. James L. Bunting was among those who by April had moved their fences from individual parcels to assigned positions in the fence that was to enclose the entire tract. Others, however, were not as diligent in the operation, leaving gaps through which loose stock could enter the fields. "I have moved my fence from around my field unto the line," Bunting complained in his diary, "and now the stock prayes upon my wheat." Bunting brought his objection to the bishop, who recommended that he attend a council meeting and voice his complaint. At the meeting the outspoken Bunting asserted that anyone would be a fool to remove the fence from his own crop until it was clear that the whole company would commit itself to an early completion of the main fence. Bunting wrote that brothers Lewis and Thomas Robertson "felt a little cross about the affair and on Monday 21st they wished me to state whether I was going to cooperate my land I had been cultivating the last year or not, to which I replied 'not until after I had raised and secured the crop already planted.'" Though the Saints, through their persistent efforts at cooperation, had successfully transformed the verb from intransitive to transitive, their efforts to cooperate their land that season bore bitter fruit. In October the field was not yet fenced. The issue was brought to a head when the horses of David Udall, Joseph G. Brown, and Zadok K. Judd, all members of the cooperative board of appraisers, entered the field on two separate occasions and destroyed more than ten bushels of Bunting's corn. Frustrated and angry, Bunting retaliated by refusing to turn his improvements in to the cooperative. The matter was eventually resolved, but not before the co-op secretary, James Lewis, had brought it before the ecclesiastical court of Bishop Stewart. Bunting was praised by Jehiel McConnell and others for his exceptional diligence and skill in fencing and farming the cooperative land, but the bishop asked him to acknowledge the error of his decision and to turn his improvements in to the common treasury. Mollified by the praise, he complied willingly with the bishop's request.[18]

The event illustrates perfectly the type of situation that put strains upon the cooperative desires of the settlers and militated against the success of their collective institutions. In retrospect the ten bushels of corn appear trivial. At the time, however, when an extra margin of foodstuffs might prevent hunger in one's household until the next harvest, even small matters stirred feelings and occasioned great controversy. The incident caused Bunting to believe that he could have done better alone than through the cooperative. Had others been as diligent in building their share of the fence as he, there would have been no cause for complaint. As it was, he had reason to suspect that his own efforts, and perhaps those of others, had been sabotaged rather than aided by the cooperative. Friendships were marred, mistrust created, party and faction increased, and the likelihood of further cooperation diminished through small incidents such as this.

In some settlements the cooperative movement seemed to prepare the people for the more comprehensive United Order that would follow. In Kanab the many efforts at cooperation may have exacerbated natural divisions already existing in the community, diminishing rather than increasing the chances that the United Order would be a success. A hint of possible future division was suggested in the recollection of William Thomas Stewart, the bishop's son, a young man of sixteen at the time Kanab was settled:

RULES

THAT SHOULD BE OBSERVED BY MEMBERS OF THE

UNITED ORDER.

RULE 1. We will not take the name of the Deity in vain, nor speak lightly of His character or of sacred things.

RULE 2. We will pray with our families morning and evening, and also attend to secret Prayer.

RULE 3. We will observe and keep the Word of Wisdom according to the Spirit and meaning thereof.

RULE 4. We will treat our families with due kindness and affection, and set before them an example worthy of imitation; in our families and intercourse with all persons, we will refrain from being contentious or quarrelsome, and we will cease to speak evil of each other, and will cultivate a spirit of charity towards all. We consider it our duty to keep from acting selfishly or from covetous motives, and will seek the interest of each other and the salvation of all mankind.

RULE 5. We will observe personal cleanliness, and preserve ourselves in all chastity by refraining from adultery, whoredom and lust. We will also discountenance and refrain from all vulgar and obscene language or conduct.

RULE 6. We will observe the Sabbath day to keep it holy, in accordance with the revelations.

RULE 7. That which is not committed to our care we will not appropriate to our own use.

RULE 8. That which we borrow we will return according to promise, and that which we find we will not appropriate to our own use, but seek to return it to its proper owner.

RULE 9. We will, as soon as possible, cancel all individual indebtedness contracted prior to our uniting with the Order, and when once fully identified with said Order, will contract no debts contrary to the wishes of the Board of Directors.

RULE 10. We will patronize our brethren who are in the Order.

RULE 11. In our apparel and deportment we will not pattern after nor encourage foolish and extravagant fashions, and cease to import or buy from abroad any article which can be reasonably dispensed with, or which can be produced by combination of home labor. We will foster and encourage the producing and manufacturing of all articles needful for our consumption as fast as our circumstances will permit.

RULE 12. We will be simple in our dress and manner of living, using proper economy and prudence in the management of all entrusted to our care.

RULE 13. We will combine our labor for mutual benefit, sustain with our faith, prayers and works, those whom we have elected to take the management of the different departments of the Order, and be subject to them in their official capacity, refraining from a spirit of fault-finding.

RULE 14. We will honestly and diligently labor, and devote ourselves and all we have to the Order and the building up of the Kingdom of God.

Printed at the Deseret News Steam Printing Establishment, Salt Lake City.

Rules of the United Order stressed a general code of ethical behavior as the foundation of successful cooperative living. (Broadside in Church Archives)

Everything in the new colony went well for a time but it appeared that some who came from the different settlements were of a class who does not sustain order. . . . there began to work up feelings of dissentions against the Bishop, but in the main things went well till 1874 when it was counselled to establish the United Order.[19]

There were heavy snows in southern Utah in early March 1874. Two feet were reported on the level in Long Valley and six feet on the passes leading from there to Panguitch. No doubt the settlers welcomed the unusually heavy spring snows as a promise of ample water and abundant harvests for the ensuing summer. A peculiar set of circumstances, however, was to transform that promise in Kanab into a harvest that all would wish to have avoided. Early in March Brigham Young began a journey from St. George to organize the United Order in settlements east of his winter capital. On March 6 he sent a telegram from Rockville to Salt Lake City announcing that he had successfully "organized the brethren of Rockville and Virgen wards which comprise all the settlements on the river east of Toker and below Long Valley into the United Order." Apparently he would have continued through Kanab and Long Valley except for a report of deep ground snow brought him by his nephew John R. Young. The president's party returned to St. George, having visited as far east as Shunesburg, about forty miles short of Kanab.

The president was reluctant to give up his wish to put his personal prestige and presence behind the organization of the new Order, however, and on March 17 he informed the authorities awaiting him in Salt Lake City that "we think of making a flying trip to Kanab" before starting north in early April. But the weather caused him to reconsider, and the next day he wrote further, "This cold storm is so severe that we have about given up the idea of going to Kanab."[20] He returned to Salt Lake City without making the proposed journey.

Responsibility for initiating the United Order in the southeastern settlements thus fell wholly upon John R. Young, who had been authorized to do this by his uncle when the two had met in Rockville the first week in March. John R. Young was thirty-six at the time, married to Albina Terry, Lydia Knight, and Tamar Black, and father of eight children. Much of his life had been spent in service to the church, as proselyting missionary to Hawaii on two occasions, as captain of immigrant companies from Omaha, as Indian scout, and as colonizer. He had fulfilled exploring and Indian missions with Jacob Hamblin and other Kanab residents. In 1874 he was dividing residence between Kanab and the upper Long Valley settlement of Glendale, about thirty miles from Kanab.[21] Bold and adventuresome in spirit and wholly devoted to carrying out the wishes of his uncle Brigham, he enthusiastically urged the Saints of the Kanab region to join the United Order organization.

By the time Brigham Young had given up the idea of visiting Kanab himself, his nephew had initiated the Order in Kanab, Pahreah, Johnson, Glendale, and Mt. Carmel. Moreover, in both Long Valley and Kanab he had acquiesced in and perhaps promoted the election of United Order presidents who were not bishops of the communities, permitting himself to be elected president in Kanab. By thus splitting off a large portion of the traditional responsibility of the bishop in a Mormon ward, he was creating a potential for division. On March 12, when the Kanab United Order was organized, he stressed to the people "that Bishop Stewart was still Bishop of the Ward the same as before the order was established," but in fact the bishop's authority was unavoidably diminished by the establishment of an alternative figure responsible for the settlement's economic activity. Levi Stewart indicated his support of the Order, however, by accepting the position of first vice-president. Probably neither John R. Young nor Stewart anticipated the full consequences of a division of labor at the very head of Kanab community life.

John R. Young was undoubtedly moved not so much by ambition as by the wish to be certain that United Order leaders gave unqualified support to its principles. Not pride but zealotry was his vice, a vice Brigham Young feared in United Order members and sought to forestall. "Be sure and not urge any one to join this holy order against their will," he instructed the Mormon apostles on March 12. "Such as do not wish to join treat them with all the kindness and fellowship as though they were in the order." Had the severe spring storms not prevented the church president from visiting Kanab, the importance of such tolerance would have been stressed in the village by the highest authority and one source of difficulty within the Order perhaps minimized.

Indian problems interrupted efforts toward completing organization of the Order, but on June 23 John Young and Stewart informed Brigham Young that substantial progress had been made.

All the men at Kanab but two have joined the Order and are working harmoniously. All our property is turned in. We are doing all we can to sustain ourselves, but greatly need supplies of leather, guns, saddle, and ammunition. Can we exchange beef cattle anywhere in the order for these things. A word from you would be cheering to the people. Our crops are good. With kind love.

Levi Stewart, John R. Young[22]

In the communities of Kanab, Pahreah, and Johnson, 416 persons representing eighty households had been enrolled in the Order. The Kanab officers were elected on March 12, the day the Order was initiated. John R. Young was chosen president; Levi Stewart, first vice-president; Thomas Robertson, second vice-president; James Lewis, secretary; John Rider, treasurer; and Taylor Crosby, foreman of farming. On March 18 a nurseryman and a foreman for the proposed dairy were appointed. In addition, wood haulers were chosen, butchers designated, and five appraisers appointed. In late May plans were made to acquire a ranch as a dairy and livestock center, and additional workers for farming, gardening, and building were chosen. Dairymen, brickmakers, blacksmiths, and wheelrights were appointed and a general freighting and woodhauling division was set up.[23]

This flurry of activity concealed a groundswell of anxiety and uncertainty that found expression not only in Kanab, but in other communities as well. Bishops became alarmed when they noted donations had fallen off because Order members thought they were exempt from tithing.[24] "Had we better turn into the Order our farms, houses and lots, teams, cattle, landed claims, and all our property at once, or shall we wait awhile?" the Kanab settlers asked. "When we build a house for a member of the Order, must we charge that house to the person occupying it? . . . Is it advisable to divide up our lots and thereby concentrate in our buildings, or retain them in their present size?" Brigham Young responded that possessions should be turned in at once. "The sooner we comply with the ordinances of the Gospel the easier it will be to yield obedience thereto." The Order should build houses for the members. Apparently, however, the church president did not want individual homes to be built upon separate lots. He advised the Saints "to build a house large enough to accommodate the organization at Kanab as soon as you can and devote your lots to vineyards, orchards, lucern, etc."[25] Again in July, Levi Stewart felt it necessary to ask the church president for advice. "Shall we have a board of Directors for each Branch of business or shall we have one Board to direct all the Branches of business we have," he asked.

Shall we organize to vote by shares or shall men be entitled to but one vote each. Shall labor be credited to men as capital stock—if so how often shall men be settled up with and receive their credits. . . . Would it be advisable to turn in saddle and carriage horses, light conveyances and carriages, books and stationary. Sewing machines. Pieces of music. Household furniture. . . . Will there be a dividend paid on property of this class the same as on live stock when turned into the Order.[26]

By this time similar questions from all parts of Utah were descending upon the church leaders in such numbers that answers could be given only through general epistles or through wide circulation of the questions of one community together with appropriate responses. Such letters ultimately suggested that communities should work out the details of the Order according to their own inclinations and needs. Nevertheless, it was clear that in spite of injunctions to tolerate non-Order members, the church president really wanted all to join, and in spite of suggestions that the Orders adapt themselves to local conditions and desires, the ideal order would be one in which the entire community lived as one family. Those of extreme and of temperate views could find apparent confirmation of their positions in the speeches and letters of church leaders.

Besides administrative and organizational questions there were everyday practical problems of managing efficiently the productive resources of the Order—both manpower and equipment. The experience of James L. Bunting on a torrid Monday morning, July 6, 1874, was probably typical. He reported for work to Charles H. Oliphant, gardening foreman, at the comfortably late hour of 10:30 A.M. and asked what he should do. Oliphant hemmed and hawed, ultimately admitting that he did not know where Bunting's services might be most needed. Bunting suggested that the potatoes might need attention, half of them having died for want of water. Oliphant concurred and Bunting went off to work by himself in the potato patch. A goodly portion of the hapless vines were beyond redemption, so Bunting decided it would be best to get a plow and turn them under. When he applied to the freighting division for mules, however, he found the animals were all being used. Forced to borrow a hoe from Thomas Robertson, he chopped at weeds and dying potato vines under the scorching Kanab sun until noon. By that time mules were available. He then requisitioned harnesses and a wagon and returned to foreman Oliphant for help in the plowing. Oliphant replied that "he could not go down. Said he was going to tend his lot. He had a good place and he should not let it go backwards." The United Order potato patch, unlike those in individual gardens, presumably was left unattended.[27]

It may be that the harmful effects of such experiences could have been overcome had the community been able to unite on the grander issues of what the legal form of the Order should be and how voting representation should be determined. But as the year drew on, unresolved aspects of these latter questions became a major preoccupation of Order leaders and members alike.

Levi Stewart had asked Brigham Young in his letter of July 9 if members were "to vote by shares" or if they should be entitled "to but one vote each," an issue obviously of concern to him. Apparently he received no definite reply. Later the same month James A. Little, a wealthy sheep rancher, reported at a Sunday meeting impressions he had received concerning the state of the Order generally, during a recent visit to St. George. Order members there "appeared to be waiting for something, some kind of an organization which they have not got." Little felt "we had gone a little too far in our zeal and must take a step backward and shield ourselves under the laws of the Territory." Noting that the recently passed Poland bill divested the Mormon-dominated probate courts of criminal jurisdiction, he pointed out that an apostate could take his case to the gentile courts and get a judgment against the Order of as much as $20,000 cash. Little's remarks, according to John L. Bunting, "had a tendency to destroy the faith and energy of the people who had gone into the order with good faith that the Lord would open the way for our safety and protect our interests." The negative impact of the report could only have been strengthened when Bishop Stewart endorsed Little's remarks, offering the unsettling information that a Brother Copeland of Beaver had sued the United Order there and gotten a judgment for $10,000 cash.[28]

During the time these events were taking place in Kanab, John R. Young was in Salt Lake City on a mission for the Order, bartering livestock for guns, ammunition, and leather. While taking care of this business he was seeking information pertaining to the same questions being raised in Kanab. He returned in mid-August with a copy of the model Articles of Association prepared by church authorities in Salt Lake City for general use throughout the commonwealth (see Appendix VI).

The new articles were the object of intense interest at a meeting of the board of directors held August 18 in the home of Bishop Stewart, but the document failed to settle the central issues. "A few thought it meant cooperation and property representation," William Solomon wrote in his diary, "but the majority was in for equality and individual representation or the United Order."[29] So pressing was the need for a resolution that John R. Young sent his uncle a letter the next day, reporting that

some of the brethren here are desirous of ascertaining whether you intended shares to vote or that it was optional with the Board of Directors in making the By-Laws of the Association. We have a small minority who are very strenuous regarding this point and wish your decision. The question is does shares vote, or each Stockholder have a vote Equal irrespective of the amount of property he may have put into the corporation or the amount of shares he may have. Your answer is solicited at your earliest convenience.[30]

No record has been preserved of what answer, if any, the Saints in Kanab were given. But either in consequence of instructions from above or as a result of agreement among themselves, the matter was at least temporarily settled.

On September 7, John R. Young announced that he "had been instructed to get together six men and subscribe their names and organize in the United Order and others could come in from time to time as they had opportunity." To this proposition the bishop offered his opinion that it would be "the best course to pursue," and the group agreed upon prices for shares and capital stock. Apparently it was expected that the proposed new order would absorb the membership of the community and become the successor to the 1874 Order. Public meetings the next weekend served to drum up support for the reorganization, influential members of the community expressing their devotion to the Order. If reservations or differences of opinion were held by members concerning the future shape of the Order, they were not revealed in the clerk's minutes of the meetings. In closing the Saturday (September 12) meeting, John R. Young expressed his gratitude that the time had come when some of the burden of directing the Order would be taken from him, apparently anticipating that a new election would bring a change in the executive officers.[31] Such was not to be the case.

On Tuesday, September 15, elections were held to choose a new board of directors. Voting was by shares, with thirty-two shareholders casting 11,848 votes. Only two of the thirteen directors elected were clearly Young's partisans, but in a subsequent meeting the board proceeded to reelect him to the office of president; Stewart, his old office of first vice-president; Taylor Crosby, second vice-president; James Lewis, secretary; and John Rider, treasurer.[32] There is no evidence permitting one to say with confidence why a board of directors that later proved loyal to Stewart would have chosen John R. Young president for a second term when it was clear that his continuation in the office divided authority at the head of the community. Conceivably Stewart was confident of his own control of the board of directors and felt that retaining Young in office would do the least possible injury to community solidarity. Or perhaps the board simply felt that Young was more competent to manage the far-flung economic enterprises of the village. Or perhaps he did indeed have a letter of authorization from his uncle Brigham. Whatever the reason, the Order was reorganized under the corporate form with little open controversy, and the reelected president began preparations to take Kanab peacefully into its second year of United Order life.

It will probably never be known precisely what happened during the ensuing months to shatter that prospect. Sometime in late September or October either Stewart or Young or both decided that they could not continue to work together as officers in the same United Order. "Quite a party spirit has sprang up in Kanab in the U.O.," James L. Bunting wrote on November 8. "Bp. Levi Stewart has taken a stand against J.R. Young and the people are divided. The Bishop takes a stand for property qualification and J.R. Young for the United Order in the Spirit thereof."[33] Obviously the accord of mid-September had fallen apart over the same issues that had troubled the Order earlier in the year. Since the voting in September had been by shares, it is possible that John R. Young began to have second thoughts about the procedure and returned to his insistence that all members have an equal vote regardless of the number of shares held. If this had happened, his motive in thus reopening the controversy is not immediately obvious. Clearly it was not simply prestige and power he was seeking, for he had already been granted that in his reelection to the presidency. The most persuasive explanation, when Young's convictions and personality are taken into account, must be that he did not feel Bishop Stewart was fully committed to the United Order in what Young believed to be the only divinely approved form.

Alternatively, it is not difficult to imagine that Levi Stewart, after the September elections, had reason to regret that the board had chosen Young. The minutes of the board of directors between September and December show Young to be vigorous and strong in his leadership, exerting a presence and influence upon the board far more evident than that of Stewart, who participated in but two of the eight meetings held between September 15 and December 15. It is not inconceivable that the bishop, observing Young's growing influence in the community, decided that the spiritual and economic affairs should be governed by one leader, the properly ordained bishop, and so began deliberate efforts, as Young charged on December 13, "to pull me from my position." One witness later asserted that Brigham Young advised the ward to meet and decide upon one person to be both bishop and president, but no contemporary evidence has been found to support his account.[34] Whatever the exact circumstances, by mid-December the parties agreed that for the health of the community the issue must be resolved once and for all. John R. Young, as president of the Order, called a general meeting to be held at Stewart's home on Monday, December 13. Fully aware that important things were afoot, the citizens crowded into the Stewart residence. There they were greeted by Young and by church leaders from Long Valley—Bishop Howard O. Spencer and Jonathan Heaton. The choir sang a song and a prayer was offered. Following what had by now become a common procedure in important village gatherings, the president explained that a purpose of the meeting was to permit the members to express their feelings with regard to the Order. Discourses should be kept short, but the brethren were asked "to speak with life and spirit and to the point. . . . We are divided in the order," Young said, "and are losing strength and confidence. I stand face to face with my brethren not as I did last spring. Then I was sent by authority. Today I stand free. This afternoon we will . . . vote who we will have for President of the Order."

This announcement promised a significant departure from the

election procedures of the previous September. In September John R. Young had been chosen president by the procedure Stewart favored—selection by a board of directors who had themselves been elected by shareholders voting according to the number of shares they owned. Now the procedure Young favored would be followed. The whole community would be permitted to vote in choosing a new president. Moreover Young was announcing, somewhat obliquely, that his authorization by Brigham Young to organize the Order the previous spring put the Saints under no present obligation to elect him president.

After a morning spent in reading instructions from Brigham Young and in hearing discourses on the importance of unity from the visiting Long Valley officials, the Saints took a break and reassembled at two o'clock for the main business of the gathering. Tempers flared at the very beginning of the meeting when David Udall bluntly stated his belief that John R. Young must have "extorted" his authorization from the church president—that it could have been obtained only by "misrepresentation." Responding to Udall's remarks, Young and Stewart exchanged words themselves over who was in fact presiding officer at the gathering. "I am willing to meet my acts," Young declared, "and am answerable for them to Pres't Young and G. A. Smith and I am willing to have my acts investigated." Stewart did not respond to Young's comments directly, but instead offered a moving sermon on the lamentable state of affairs in the village. "When we came here and organized," Stewart said,

I used my utmost to be organized as directed and it [is] with sorrow that I see so much division springing up among the people. Why? Because I feared the adversary would take advantage and delay the day of our becoming what we should be. . . . If we start out in different orders we shall have to divide the water and land and shall have difficulty.

When the bishop had finished, Young proposed that all the ward members vote on the question of whom they wanted for president of the United Order. Stewart's name was put in nomination. Someone in the group, probably hoping to embarrass the bishop, asked him "whether he was in favor of property representation." Stewart responded that "the law would bind us to vote by shares as it would draw the mantle of the law over our property, the property of the whole people. It is a matter of expediency to vote by shares." The clerk, who later identified himself with Young's cause, recorded the ensuing events as follows:

The people voted and quite a number voted, some who did not belong to the order and quite a number of children. The opposite vote was called and 14 voted in the negative, many not voting (expecting another nomination). J. R. Young said those who had voted for Levi Stewart should now rally around him and receive his instructions, to organize under him and let the Brethren follow the directions of Pres't Young. Cease all bickering and unkindness in each other and unite in the spirit of the gospel.[35]

Placing their own interpretation on Young's pious remarks, his friends left the meeting and two days later founded their own United Order, asking him to accept the presidency.[36] He concurred, and the community approached the Christmas holidays burdened with the mournful task of dividing its real assets between J. R. Young and Company and Levi Stewart and Company.

All efforts at reconciliation failing, the United Order officers spent the remainder of 1874 and the first months of 1875 closing the accounts of the 1874 Order and dividing its assets between the bishop's followers and those of John R. Young. Even the Kanab Agricultural Association, a company antedating the Order, was disbanded and its assets divided between the two groups. "It was proposed," the clerk recorded, in language that gave little indication of the human drama involved, "that J.R. Young and Company take the Dairy Ranch, and they pay to Levi Stewart and Company one cow and calf. And Bp. Stewart and company take the Dry Ranch. Each owning all the improvements made upon either ranch." By February 6, a special "committee on the division of land" had completed its report, "defining the division of land permanently by erecting stakes and upon said stakes was written the definition of said division."[37]

During the spring and summer delicate negotiations took place between the two groups over several matters of mutual concern. Consideration was given to the establishment of separate schools, and a building was referred to in United Order minutes as the John R. Young schoolhouse, though the record does not definitely confirm that a second functioning school was established. Social events were planned and funded separately. By June the Young group had decided to draw away from the old set-

tlement, asking Bishop Stewart if they could use "a block of land
north of the present field upon which to gather together." The
bishop replied that they "could have the land provided [they]
would dispose of [their] lots in the town as soon as possible."[38]

So hostile were the factions that Taylor Crosby, an officer in
the Stewart faction, believed "that the people could not partake of
the sacrament under the present state of feeling."[39] The observation was a telling one. The two communities could diverge
sharply in their social and economic affairs without necessary
affront to their common religion. But a new ecclesiastical unit
could be organized only by higher authority, and thus in religious
affairs all were under one bishopric and obliged to attend one
meeting. The reluctance of church leaders to authorize the founding of a separate ward forced intermingling at weekly meetings
and prolonged the agony of Kanab.

Years later, Levi Stewart's son, William Thomas Stewart, added his voice to a chorus that until the present had chosen to find
the source of Kanab's troubles in the personality of John R.
Young. The result of Young's service as president of the Order,
according to Stewart, had been "to produce confusion where
there had been comparative order before, the more so that John R.
Young felt that his office absorbed that of Bp."[40] William H.
Solomon, a participant in the December 13 meeting, alleged that
when Young accepted the presidency of the insurgent Order, he
was reneging on a prior promise to abide by the vote of the community. The consequence "was again a division of the people
there being two meetings held on the Sabbath day representing
two parties, one under the direction of Bp. Stewart, and one under
the direction of J. R. Young. Being satisfied that the Bp. was the
right authority I rendered myself subject to his direction."[41]

Certainly Young showed a remarkably creative talent for ra-
tionalizing his actions in some particulars, but it is difficult to
believe that were it not for him all would have been sweetness
and light. He was acutely aware that his actions required the le-
gitimizing assent of Brigham Young, and he was eager to com-
municate all he did to the church president. Because his purpose
in such explanations was to solicit support from his uncle, he
naturally presented a version of events of Kanab supporting his
own point of view.

Young was clearly the loser in the voting of December 13,
1874. In a community composed of no less than 80 households

and 416 persons, only 14 persons voted against Levi Stewart. James Lewis, who probably was one of those 14, explained in the minutes that many did not vote because they were waiting for another nomination. But he did not explain why no other nominations were made or why more of those awaiting another nomination did not express their dissatisfaction with the one candidate nominated by voting against him. Young's followers simply refused to accept the majority decision and decided to go their own way. They justified their actions to themselves and to church authorities as best they could.

William Solomon was wrong, however, in his assertion that Young had agreed earlier to support whoever was chosen in the election. Young's position was reiterated by the bishop himself on December 13. The Order president had agreed that if the people could unite behind one man, he would support that man fully. A substantial minority had refused to support the one man nominated, permitting Young to accept the presidency of the insurgent group without going back on his word. If the distinction does not seem as clear to the historian as it did to contemporaries, it nonetheless served the purposes of those who devoutly wished to build an ideal United Order community while preserving their personal honor and their loyalty to church authority. When these ideals came into conflict, the United Order was of paramount importance and they determined to pursue it even if compromises must be made in other areas.

The motives of the insurgent group were apparent in the letter of explanation they sent to Brigham Young on December 17, 1874. Moved by a desire to enter "into the Order in the Spirit thereof," they had rejected the leadership of the bishop in favor of that of John R. Young as the man most sympathetic to their desire "to carry out the instruction given by the Presidency last spring in uniting as a family, cultivating that unity and peace necessary for progress in the work of God." Young was the man, they felt, "who has the Spirit of the Order," and he had expressed willingness to serve as their president if the approval and blessing of the church leadership were granted. "We wait your answer with instructions directing our further movements," they concluded.[42]

By the year's end the Order was organized with John R. Young as president. There was ample time between the letter of December 17 and the organizing meeting of December 30 to receive a response from Brigham Young at St. George. If such a response were received—and the absence of a copy among his letterbooks suggests that Brigham Young did not reply with a written communication—it did not unequivocally direct Young not to accept the presidency of the insurgent group. It is highly unlikely that the Kanab leader would have dared openly disobey the commands of his uncle in the matter, since the telegraph lines to St. George were as open to Bishop Stewart as they were to John R. Young. Almost certainly he undertook the presidency with the tacit if not express approval from the church president.

There was but one hint of possible official dissatisfaction with the course of events in Kanab. Early in February there were apparently straws in the wind that John R. Young might be called elsewhere on a mission for the church, a means of easing uncomfortable situations that church leaders had employed in other instances. On February 7 he wrote his uncle that he was willing to serve in England, the Sandwich Islands, or in Kanab, wherever he might be needed, but if he were to be called from Kanab he would like to know as soon as possible. Perhaps hoping to assure Uncle Brigham that his remaining in Kanab could benefit the settlement, he wrote that "if I felt certain I was wanted at Kanab I would take an active part in building a flour mill."[43] The church president apparently decided his nephew should stay, for by the end of the month John R. Young was still president of the group and was completing plans to incorporate their Order under territorial law.

On March 1 Young sent his uncle a report on the activities of his group—a report that would seem to have been poorly designed to attract the sympathies of the church president to their cause. He began the letter by informing his uncle that his was the only Order in Kanab. "It is now over two months since the division of the people and still there is no other organization but our own," he wrote. "Our Bishop Brother Levi Stewart has not joined us but constitutes one of the outside element." In fact, another Order had been organized on January 5 with Levi Stewart as president and J. H. Standifird and Taylor Crosby as vice-presidents.[44] But no account books or minute books of Stewart's Order have survived, suggesting that its activities were minimal and perhaps not even evident to the zealous insurgent group. By the end of the year an outside observer was to recognize Young's group as the only functioning Order in Kanab. In all probability Stewart's Order operated primarily as a cooperative stock company—organizing community resources for specific enterprises, such as the herding of livestock, but not requiring members to put the whole of their possessions and labors under the direction of Order officers. There is no evidence of communalism in the Stewart company. In short, he did not organize an Order as J. R. Young understood the United Order to be.

Pointing out the obvious—"the interests of the United Order will of necessity sometimes clash with what [the others] suppose to be their interests"—Young hopefully asked his uncle, "How far is it the privilege of the Order to act independently for its own interests?" The "family order," as Young's group called themselves, had been holding meetings two evenings a week during times that would not conflict with other church meetings. But they felt that "some of the preaching in the Ward Meetings has been rather calculated to irritate than otherwise," and that they "no longer feel the spirit of brotherhood which alone can make an attendance on them pleasant and desireable." Noting that Bishop Stewart had not administered the sacrament in over three months, Young asked, "Is it our privilege to observe this ordinance in our Order meetings where there is union and harmony?" Members of the new Order were "united in our desires to carry out your counsels of last spring with regard to collecting together," Young added, asking "if it is not our privilege to select a piece of unoccupied ground where we may carry out this council." Hoping finally that the group might appoint teachers to visit among themselves, rather than relying on the bishop, who had not sent out teachers in nearly a year, Young closed by pleading that "our present position is without precedent in our past experience. Your advice on these points and any others on which you might feel that advice would be beneficial would be thankfully received."[45]

From one point of view the proposals seem an audacious attempt to undercut the bishop in the one realm where he retained undisputed authority in the community—that of ecclesiastical leader. But seen in another light Young was proposing nothing more than what Thomas Chamberlain and his group were planning upon advice of their bishop in nearby Mt. Carmel. Permission was granted and Orderville, the most famous and successful of the family orders, was launched on her famous career. (See Chapter 12.) In Kanab permission was denied and old animosities were permitted for a time to fester and grow.

John R. Young's March 1 letter to Brigham Young apparently brought a strong reply. Before the end of the month the nephew was admitting to the church president that he "may have had more zeal than wisdom" in directing the Order at Kanab. At the same time, however, he justified his actions by maintaining that he had acted only at the request of Brigham Young's son, John W. Young, president of what was then called the Southern Stake of Zion. According to the letter, it was his expectation that the stake president was planning to visit Kanab and organize a new ward, or, as he put it, to "arrange so that I would have the liberty to act according to my own judgment in directing the labor of the Brethren." Hurt by Brigham Young's apparent response, the nephew added the comment that he would "be more cautious hereafter in responding to calls of the Brethren who preside over me in a local capacity. I now submit to you that . . . I shall decline presiding over the Brethren working in the Order and refrain from taking part in any responsible position. Unless I am counseled by the Presidency of the Church to do otherwise." He further informed the president that a letter had been written and read at a general meeting of the Order, presumably explaining these intentions to Kanab's citizens, and that he "would be pleased to take your answer to the brethren." In effect, he was still hoping to get permission to continue as president of the Order.[46]

Nothing remains to tell us how church authorities responded to Young's letter. He had indicated his intention to resign as president of the Order and had told Brigham Young that he would not take a responsible position in the Order unless instructed by the presidency to do so. He did not attend Order meetings or preside in the Order between March 15 and April 14. On April 14, however, he reassumed his old position.[47] It strains one's credulity to believe that he lied to Brigham Young or went back on his word in a matter where he could so easily be caught in an act of bad faith. One can only conclude that after a hiatus, taken up partly at least by travels away from Kanab, he returned to his office in the Order with the understanding that he had received from the First Presidency, directly or indirectly, the needed authorization. Through the summer of 1875 he continued without further incident to serve as president of Kanab's United Order idealists.

It is misleading, however, to discuss the Kanab United Order as if it were simply an affair between John R. Young and Levi Stewart with Brigham Young as arbiter. Kanab's experience in the Order involved hundreds of people whose loyalties, prejudices, and private decisions were surely as important in determining the course of events as John R. Young and Levi Stewart were.[48] Particularly noteworthy were the 23 men and women who dared disregard the traditional lines of church authority, breaking away from the bishop's governance to unite in an order of their own. Altogether 167 persons were in the company Young was asked to lead, a following far more significant in numbers than that which was to follow Edward Bunker into the wastelands of southern Nevada for similar reasons the following year. About 24 percent of Kanab's households and 37 percent of its inhabitants entered the Order led by John R. Young.[49] These were substantial people, not the type who could have been duped by Young had he been a man of little character seeking power through misuse of name and family connections.

A number of factors entered into the individual decisions that moved families to join the Young Order. Former associations seem to have been of some importance. At least five heads of families in the group—John R. Young, Andrew S. Gibbons, Ira Hatch, Zadok K. Judd, and Jehiel McConnell—had worked with Jacob Hamblin, serving as explorers of the Southwest and as missionaries to the Indians. Of the 1870 Stewart migration to Kanab only Allen Frost and James L. Bunting joined Young's group, and neither of these was from Stewart's old community of Big Cottonwood. A unique type of former colonization experience may have been important as well. Six of the families were refugees from Nevada colonization attempts. These included the families of Gibbons, Hatch, and Judd and also those of Mary A. Leavitt Hamblin (widow of William H. Hamblin, who died in Clover Valley, Nevada); James A. Little, prominent and wealthy sheepman; and the family of Charles H. Oliphant, a son-in-law of Judd. The predominance of former Nevada colonists in the Orderville group at Long Valley has raised the possibility that a strong sense of common identity was built up during their ordeal

in Nevada that sharpened their desire and ability to make a success of communal life. Lorenzo Snow, leader of the Brigham City
cooperative, suggested the idea when he spoke to the Orderville
Saints in 1877. "If we could have our people in the North pass
through such a mission as you did on the Muddy, then have the
goods from other settlements come on to us, we could unite
ourselves as you have done."[50] In Kanab it would appear that
former Nevada colonists committed themselves to the more ideal
form of United Order in far greater numbers than their proportion of the whole population would indicate.

As the Judd-Oliphant connection suggests, family relationship was also significant. An important addition to the Young
group was William M. Black, an early settler of Long Valley and a
father-in-law of John R. Young. Joseph G. Brown's wife, Harriet,
was a sister of John R. Young. James Lewis and one of his sons,
James H. Lewis, joined the group together. There were probably
other family connections not readily discernible in the available
records. Continued research may make it possible to assess re-
liably how important these factors were as people in Kanab chose
to risk defying church authority in forming their own United
Order.[51]

In addition to sharing bonds of old friendships, relationships,
and common experience, the United Order group of Young was
different from the general population of Kanab in several other
respects. Their families tended to be larger. The average home in
the Young group housed over seven persons, compared with an
average of just over five in the population at large. The number of
living children for each husband and wife was nearly four, while
in the community at large there were less than three. There were
eighteen obvious plural wives among Young's following, just six
short of the total number of plural wives in the whole population.
Only one of the ten single persons living alone in the village
joined the Young group, Jared Young, son of Alfred D. Young
(possibly a relative of John R. Young).

The Young group was even more predominantly male than
the population at large, with a remarkable 135 males for every 100
females. In all of Kanab there were 112 males for every 100 females, a ratio close to that prevailing in rural areas of the western
United States in 1960. (In the territory in 1880 the figure was
107).[52] This did not mean, however, that there was a plenitude of
hardy farm hands in Young's following to feed the Order

members. Some 57 percent of the group were under the age of 15, compared with 50 percent in the whole community. The median age of the Young group was 13, while it was 15 for the whole of Kanab and 17.5 for the territory. Every 100 men and women of working age (15-65) in the Young group had to feed and clothe nearly 139 others—persons too old or too young to contribute substantially to the work force. In all of Kanab each 100 working persons had to support 111 who could not work; in the territory, 92. Kanab's age dependency ratio diminished the chances that clearly demonstrable economic progress could be made, yet any failure under the Order would certainly be charged to the Order and not to the demographic patterns that were key determinants of the economic success or failure of the community.[53]

The most striking difference between the population of the United Order and that of the whole village raises important questions about the motivations of those who committed themselves to the more idealistic communal form. It has generally been assumed that men of greater means tended to favor a form of the Order in which voting would be by shares rather than by membership in the company. In this way the wealthy would be assured that responsible persons with a greater stake in the organization would have the most important voice in determining policies affecting their investment. P. T. Reilly intimated that Levi Stewart's commitment to voting by shares sprang from precisely these motives—indeed, that the whole community was divided between the "haves" and the "have nots," with the latter group advocating voting by membership.[54]

The records of the Kanab Order offer the opportunity to examine this hypothesis further. In 1874 and 1875 evaluations for tax purposes were made of the real and personal property of each head of household in Kanab and the neighboring settlements. Only a portion of the 1874 evaluation remains, but the 1875 evaluation is intact, permitting a comparison of the wealth of those in John R. Young's Order with that of the rest of the community. The average per family wealth of the Young Order was $853, while that of the rest of the village was $486. In a group devoted to achieving economic equality and sharing income-producing capital, the average or mean may be the best measure of central tendency. But even if the median is used, the Young group's figure of $415 is well above the $330 median wealth for the rest of the community. The Young group, with their significantly larger proportion of children, was even slightly higher in per capita wealth than was the rest of the village. There was $107 of evaluated wealth for each man, woman, and child in Young's following, compared with $102 in the rest of the community. The hypothesis that poorer people generally favored the more ideal communal order does not hold true in Kanab, where the relatively wealthy tended to be more idealistic.[55]

In retrospect the observation James L. Bunting made in his diary in November 1874 seems significant: "Quite a party spirit has sprang up in Kanab in the U.O. . . . and the people are divided. The Bishop takes a stand for property qualification and J. R. Young for the United Order in the Spirit thereof."[56] The personality and offices of opposing leaders, the lingering effects of former associations and experiences, and the strength of family ties no doubt were among the complex forces leading people to identify themselves with one camp or the other. But if we were to choose a single most important determinant of the lines of division in Kanab, it would surely be religious ideology. John R. Young's group favored the Order in what they deemed to be "the spirit thereof." They called themselves "the family order," stressing their desire for communal life. Moreover they hoped to achieve economic equality within their community. Consistent with this desire was their conviction that each person, rich or poor, should have a vote in determining Order affairs. It is not surprising that members of the Order group had already demonstrated unusual piety in other aspects of their lives. Church leaders encouraged the practice of polygamy as a demonstration of the Saints' willingness to overcome the traditions of the world and fully embrace God's revealed truth. The great majority of polygamous wives in Kanab were in Young's family order. An obviously related, and equally important, value taught by church leaders was the Adamic injunction to multiply and replenish the earth. Strong sermons against artificial limitation on births were preached by church authorities on numerous occasions, and Mormons were constantly taught to place a high value on large families.[57] It seems possible that in their significantly larger families, the Young following evidenced a more unquestioning obedience to the teachings of church authorities than did their neighbors in the village. The word they used on several occasions to distinguish their gatherings was that used by Bunting. Their optimistic idealism—their persistent desire to effect a better earthly order—was seen in their minds as a manifestation of God's spirit. The members of the Young Order were religious idealists; some might have used the word "fanatics." With their hopes and ambitions fixed upon the high goal of building a better, more just and harmonious world, they became defensive and intolerant of anything that might interfere with that vision.

The sensitivity of the Young group was demonstrated in conflicts over the role of priesthood teachers in the community in 1875. The Mormon institution of home teaching, which continues in a modified form today, required male priesthood holders to visit all the families each month to offer spiritual and economic assistance to members where needed and to keep the bishop informed of the spiritual progress of the congregation. United Order affairs had so preoccupied the leadership of the ward that the bishop had not sent the teachers on their rounds for nearly a year when a meeting was called on May 19. Stewart had warned the dissidents the previous December that "if there are two orders I shall choose teachers out of both parties to go to the people."[58] Now, true to his word, he called upon all those in the village holding the rank of teacher in the priesthood to do their teaching. Perhaps remembering Stewart's earlier remarks, the Young group came to the meeting primed to take offense at any sign of partisanship on the issues dividing the village. Instructing the teachers on the delicate task of going among the people without exacerbating the tension in the community, the bishop told the group "to go forth among the people and cultivate the spirit of peace and try and heal up the breach that now exists in our midst, ignoring the fact of there being two orders entirely in our ministrations among them." A general discussion ensued, mainly supporting Stewart in his recommendations, all but one of the participants being his partisans.[59] Young's followers sat on their hands and left the meeting in a rage, convinced that the bishop had instructed the teachers not to teach the United Order as a gospel principle. Jehiel McConnell, after some hesitation, decided the matter was sufficiently serious to call to the attention of Brigham Young. "Bishop Stewart has at last started his teachers around (the first since the Order was first preached in Kanab)," he reported. Bishop Stewart had sent the teachers out

with a strict injunction not to teach the United Order. If they do he says they may stay at home for he does not wish them to go and teach. And as I was one who was chosen to teach I write to know whether the Lord has

gone back on what He told His servant Brigham for the people to
organize themselves under the law of the land and work in the United
Order. If there has been any change, or if it is unnecessary to teach the
Order I wish to know it. I shall await patiently your answer and continue
to teach according to the Bishop's instructions.[60]

Brigham Young's response was a masterful blend of support and
reprimand, carefully avoiding any possibility that either party
could interpret his remarks as favoring their position. "Yours of
23rd ult. is to hand," he wrote,

and again I learn from it a repetition of the old old story: "Many men,
many minds," right in the midst of gathered Israel at this late date,
proving that we have not all attained to a "unity of the faith."
    The duties of my office and calling require me to teach the people
the way of truth and life, but fortunately I am not obliged to compel
them to do so. We are all placed here to observe laws for saving
ourselves with as complete a salvation as may be possible, and to aid in
saving others so far as we may be able; and this work seems to require, in
addition to faith-fulness and diligence on our part, patience, forbearance,
and a kindly conduct and conversation toward all.
    Trusting you may all be abundantly blest in every good work and
words, and prosper as coworkers in hastening the time, in its season,
when the faithful will "see eye to eye in Zion." I remain as ever your
brother in the gospel. Brigham Young.[61]

Probably the church leader had already begun to act upon a
plan for healing the wounds Kanab had suffered. One month
later, on August 30, he wrote nearly identical letters to Bishop
Stewart and to John R. Young informing them that a new bishop
had been chosen for Kanab and asking them, "with a view to
unite the hearts and feelings of the brethern and consolidate and
strengthen the interests of the people," to resign their offices into
the hands of L. John Nuttall, lately of Provo.[62]

By September 5 rumors of Nuttall's appointment were being
circulated among the people and twelve days later a full retinue
of church officials arrived to preside over Nuttall's installation,
lending their authority to him in the transfer of power. Stewart
and Young resigned their offices and the stage was set for a new
era of United Order history in Kanab.[63]

A phrenologist had told Nuttall in 1867, "You are cautious in
your moves and actions and prudent in all your measures."[64]
Caution and prudent compromise were indeed the hallmarks of
Nuttall's initial policy as bishop. Though John R. Young had

resigned the presidency, he continued to serve on the board of directors. The Order ran its business as usual for the next three months with vice-president Thomas Robertson directing its affairs, clearly with the sanction of Bishop Nuttall. In the meantime the bishop was engaged in building support for the Order among other members of the community, rebaptizing those who expressed a desire to be organized under his leadership. By the end of the year he had completed his efforts and was ready to begin his reorganization. Recognizing Young's group as the legitimate and only functioning United Order of Kanab, he addressed a letter to the president and board of directors on January 3, asking that himself and a long list of citizens wishing to join the Order under his auspices be admitted to membership. This accomplished, the board of directors moved from its accustomed meeting place in the home of C. H. Oliphant to the schoolhouse—a significant gesture—where a public meeting was held to elect new officers. The directors asked the bishop to appoint a committee to select candidates for the new board. Two of the seven on the nominating committee were from Young's group. They nominated nine men, three of them from Young's group, and these were elected by acclamation. Young declined the office, however, and his brother-in-law, Joseph G. Brown, was elected in his place. Within three days the new Order had incorporated under the law and the directors proceeded to elect Nuttall president, Stewart vice-president, Thomas Robertson vice-president, James Lewis secretary, and John Rider treasurer, neatly dividing the officers between the Young faction and the Stewart faction, with the bishop carrying a swing vote. Sixty-three men brought their families into the reorganized Order, including the most important men from each faction, brightening the hopes that a full reconciliation might be accomplished and harmony brought to the village at last.[65]

The year 1876 thus began optimistically in Kanab. John R. Young worked unstintingly to expand Order holdings of ranch and grazing lands with an enthusiasm Kanab had not seen since the spring of 1874. Order members undertook the annual ritual of reappraising property, choosing brands, appointing directors of the various departments, and setting wage scales. Bishop Nuttall led efforts to concentrate the lands of Order members so they would not be broken up by holdings of the substantial minority not in the Order.[66]

The shot of energy given the Order by Nuttall's appointment was not, however, to last the year. Fully one-third of the village had chosen not to enter the Order at all. Among the rest, old differences as to the most desirable form of the Order had not been resolved. By including men of all parties as officers in his new organization, the bishop succeeded only in confining the battle to a smaller arena. Fragments of an undated meeting suggest the impassioned nature of board meetings that year. "I asked for your lives. I gave you mine," Nuttall pleaded with the officers of the Order. "If we have had any feelings . . . we will not have a Spirit. We will not have but one order in Kanab. I ask the brethren to join with me."[67] In an attempt to resolve such differences, the bishop asked Brigham Young that fall if a move toward the more individualistic stewardship system might not be desirable. The church president replied emphatically that it was not. "The system of stewardships which we have counseled the people here to enter upon is not so far advanced and does not approach so near to the Order of Enoch as that system which you have entered into in your bishopric," he wrote. "For you to change your method of doing business to that of stewardships would be to take a step backward, and would not be in accordance with our feelings. . . . What end can be accomplished by your turning back?"[68]

This strong advice and a disappointing harvest caused the bishop to call the Order members together for an important meeting in mid-September. Though ostensibly to provide "a general review of the past nine months and the want of our success the present season," the main purpose of the meeting was to tie the people more firmly to the position Brigham Young had recommended. After a full day of testimony and commentary on the Order, Bishop Nuttall asked members to sign a pledge "to put in all their property and time and be controlled in their labors by the Board of Directors that we may fully identify ourselves in the order with all we have, hold sacred our covenants, the rules of the order, live our Holy religion and seek to build up Zion." Allen Frost, after meditating on the matter for a whole day, signed the document. It is not known how many others followed his example.[69]

Adding to the bishop's troubles was a significant event that was changing the position of Kanab as southern outpost of the Mormon kingdom. "Arizona missionaries continue to arrive,"

Frost wrote in his diary early that year. "Looks as though we have ceased to be the frontier settlement."[70] The continuing trickle of settlers moving back and forth across the Colorado during the year kept the dissidents of Nuttall's flock constantly aware of the fact that new opportunities to shape the Order as they wished were theirs for the taking. In the founding of new settlements had always lain the promise of new and better beginnings. In addition, the unparalleled success of nearby Orderville kept the more zealous communitarians rigidly close to their ideals and offered them an escape should their wishes not be followed in Kanab.

Attracted by these alternatives, a number of families were contemplating moving when the bishop called a general meeting of Order members in December 1876.[71] The meeting became a series, reviving strong feeling and bitter animosities in what had become an annual village crisis. Weekly meetings of the Order membership had dwindled during the summer until only the bishop and one other attended. Members of the Order had withheld their labors from the collective effort. "Today we have not a bushel of wheat in the Treasury," Nuttall announced.

We have not sufficient wheat to pay our debts. . . . Some want to go into a Big House. No one in this town wants to go into a Big House more than I do. If the board of directors had sustained me as they should have done we should have been better off. . . . We have had as good a living as we have earned. . . . Express your feelings here at this meeting and [do] not caucus among yourselves. Come to me if you wish to know what is wanted. . . . My feelings are good for this people and I want to do them good.[72]

Meetings were then held for three successive evenings, giving everyone a chance to air his grievances. Defending his policies at the end of the last meeting, the bishop countered dissenting views. "Can you [give] any reason for the order to run either as Bro Stewart or J. R. Young had run the order?" he challenged.

The [way] they run the order carried the results with it. Dewitt [Abel A. Dewitt of Young's group] told us that he and his party was ignored. I fail to see the ignoring. We hear it said that the J. R. Young party was ignored from the start. . . . I have heard T. [Thomas] Robertson say that if the United Order did not run as it should he would go to Orderville where he believed it did run right. I would aid him or anybody else all I could. Either to go to Orderville or to Arizona.[73]

From the acerbic tone of both the bishop and the members it is not surprising that the December meetings did little to revive the Order. When board members met for the annual meeting of shareholders on January 1, 1877, a majority of those "claiming to belong to the order" were not present.[74] Since the clerk had not prepared a financial statement, the meeting was postponed until February. At the February meeting, the proportion of Order members in the community the previous year was reversed. Only thirty men joined the Order, representing about one-third of the families in the village.

The year 1877 would see a continuing dissolution of the Order. Bishop Nuttall asked advice of Brigham Young in another letter on March 19. "I find that the same men are now there, who have for the past three or four years been the cause of all the troubles, so far as dissensions are concerned," he complained.

Notwithstanding they have all agreed to bury the hatchet and have peace, and have renewed their covenants and been baptized as a witness, my experience has shown they did not bury the hatchet so deep, but what they knew where to find it when their own views were interfered with; hence with a few (say six or eight) they are now more radical than heretofore. We find at present four classes: One for the United Order on the consolidation or Big House principle, that or nothing—another on the cooperative principle, or business and dividends. . . . Another (the majority) who are willing that the Priesthood shall direct all things, whether it is Big House, Cooperation or to let each branch of industry make its own success. . . . Another class much mixed; some can see nothing but previous failures and are very fearful; others, when the Order is run as revealed through the Prophet Joseph they will take hold; others, give us our Stewardships; others, we do not want any Order, please let us alone to conduct our own affairs.

Young's reply seemed directed more toward the solution of detailed procedural matters than questions of overriding philosophy. "If they were all Latter-day Saints at Kanab," he wrote, "conduct the affairs on the Order on the Gospel plan. But when you are dealing with Mormons who are apostatizing or on the way to it, you should take a course to head them off." He then advised that members should work together, that accurate records of wages and withdrawals from Order supplies be kept, and that an annual accounting be completed. In this way dissidents could not injure the Order. This advice was already well-known, however, if not always practiced, and did not help Bishop Nuttall solve his fundamental problem of division in the community.[75]

During the summer the Order began to lease out its holdings for others to operate, and to liquidate its assets. At another crisis meeting in September members offered their opinion that "there was a weakness and debility about the Order, and it would be impossible to keep up and sustain the United Order under the present circumstances." Others added that it was "of little use for us to attempt to make any further progress, while the members of the Board were as divided in their feelings as they seem to be at present." John Rider observed, "We were becoming the laughing stock, not only of the town but of the county." On November 17 "the board of directors decided not to issue any more supplies except by way of settlement, as no further work was being done for the United Order."[76] For all practical purposes, the Kanab United Order was dead.

During the year church officials had been preparing the community for a final admission that the Order had failed. In April a delegation of apostles conducted a conference in the village, organizing the Kanab Stake of Zion and calling Bishop Nuttall from his position in the ward to become stake president. In his sermon that day, John Taylor, president of the Twelve Apostles, reduced the Order to its fundamental purposes—to "feed the hungry, clothe the naked, and build up Zion"—offering his opinion that some entered the Order to avoid rather than achieve these ends. Clearly he did not feel these were goals that could be achieved exclusively by those within the Order.[77] Bishop Howard O. Spencer of Orderville spoke at a church conference in August and advised "that if we in Kanab could not live unitedly in the Order," the members were "to go to work individually." In the same meeting Bishop William H. Seegmiller of Richfield offered his opinion "that a man may not be a member of the United Order and still be a good man, sustain his bishop, pay his tithing &ct. as any member of the church."

The continuing disunity prevailing in Kanab was embarrassingly apparent in the afternoon session of the same conference. During the conference bishops has been sustained for all the wards in the stake but Kanab. Before closing the meeting apostle Erastus Snow explained the omission. "The reason there was no Bishop appointed for Kanab was that the people were not united."[78] Four months later he again visited the settlement, explaining in a morning meeting that "if the people were ready to unite upon someone for Bishop that he would give us one in the afternoon." That afternoon he asked the community to choose a new bishop. William D. Johnson, Jr., a twenty-seven-year-old schoolteacher who had taught in Kanab since 1871, was nominated and sustained in the office. Shortly after the appointment Johnson wrote his reaction to the day's events: "How I felt and do feel no one but myself can ever tell. I feel as though the burden is more than I can carry unless I have the faith and prayer of the brethren and sisters. I pray God that I may remain faithfully true to the trust imposed upon me. . . . that I may prove a blessing to Kanab."[79]

Under the kindly, gentle guidance of Bishop Johnson the community began at last to grow together. The principals who had launched the Order on its thorny path were soon removed from the scene. Brigham Young, the guiding light for the Order in the church, had died in August. His successors seemed glad to let the Order die with him. Levi Stewart suffered a sudden heart attack in June 1878 and was buried amidst great mourning in Kanab.[80] John R. Young had in the meantime moved his families to Orderville, where a United Order was flourishing to the model he had hoped to achieve in Kanab. Several of his former colleagues in the Order followed his example. Many other dissidents applied their zeal to the founding of new colonies in Arizona.

The wounds were not fully healed for many months. Bishop Johnson, who had never been a firm advocate of the Order, nevertheless suffered his share of its bitter legacy. It is certainly no accident that after he was appointed, Kanab's troubled Orders were rarely mentioned in the minute books of ward meetings. The long travail was drawing to an end. A tide of devotion to individualism and capitalism was rising across America. Even the Mormon settlers of remote southern Utah would not be kept from catching its flood.

Undoubtedly many of Kanab's citizens had occasion in after years to ponder their experience in the Order and wonder why they had failed utterly to build the harmonious, united community envisioned by Brigham Young. Some took to their graves the conviction that if John R. Young had not imposed himself upon the village, Bishop Stewart would have gathered the people about him and built an Order that was united indeed. Others would remain equally convinced that had a man possessing the spirit of the Order been bishop rather than Stewart, they could have built a community to rival Orderville. It would be easy to forget that Kanab had been from the beginning a disunited settlement—the Indian scouts and missionaries possessing a different set of attitudes from those in the Stewart migration, ranchers accustomed to a different life from that of farmers, southerners from northerners, and Nevada colonists from others. The villagers barely had begun building a sense of common identity and community when the Order was imposed from above, laying ideological faction upon cultural faction, translating old sources of divisiveness into the new language of the Order.

Conflict was encouraged when Brigham Young posited an ideal form of the Order but encouraged local leaders to adapt and modify to whatever extent necessary for local compliance. Those adhering to the original vision found it easy to assume a self-righteous attitude when they saw others of more temperate bent counsel compromise to encourage the laggards. And it was no doubt true that many faithful Saints not committed to the Order found it easy to make the reluctance of some their own excuse. Finally, Kanab was poor and burdened with a heavy economic task of feeding many mouths with limited resources and but a few hands. It would be easy, when harvests were scant and food reserves dwindling each spring, for men to blame the Order—to believe they could better provide for their families on their own. At least then if a man failed he had no one to blame but himself.

But then, devotees of the Order in Kanab, if confronted with this argument, needed only point toward Orderville. "I visited Orderville some two weeks since," one Kanab resident wrote to Brigham Young in January 1877. "Found peace, plenty and harmony prevailing. Like fraternal brothers they were furnishing Bro. Lott Smith's camp with a large quantity of bread stuff. A united order indeed with purpose and effect against the day of want and famine."[81] The contrast with Kanab was striking, but there is reason to believe that the circumstances favoring Orderville's success were more exceptional among United Orders than were those leading to Kanab's failure.

CHAPTER 12

Orderville: A little family

HARLES NORDHOFF, in his classic 1875 account of communitarian societies in the United States, made the general observation that "a commune could not long continue whose members had not, in the first place, by adverse circumstances, oppression, or wrong, been made to feel very keenly the need of something better."[1] If ever a group of settlers had been tempered by adversity sufficient to evoke the need of something better, it was the small group of families who in 1875 separated themselves from the southern Utah village of Mt. Carmel and dedicated themselves to the task of making a reality of the United Order in its most ideal form.

Several aspects of the Orderville United Order make it stand out from others. Before Orderville was settled its people had developed the camaraderie that comes from the sharing of common hardships. They were part of a group that had been called by leaders of the Mormon Church in the 1860s to form colonies on the Muddy River in what was then thought to be southwestern Utah, and which later turned out to be southeastern Nevada. The Muddy colonies, located in an area now partly inundated by Lake Mead, were established for the purpose of raising cotton to supply a Mormon cotton factory at Washington, Utah, and also to maintain a stopping place for emigrants and freighters on the way to and from California. The colonization effort was not a success. The valley was hot and dry and subject to insect infestation, flash floods, and disease. The settlers eked out a living in a condition approaching outright destitution. Only the practice of mutual helpfulness and the patriarchal organization of the community made survival possible. When Brigham Young visited the Muddy settlements in 1870 and observed the condition of the settlers, he gave them permission to return to Utah. His advice was based partly on a survey that showed the settlements to be located in

Nevada Territory, whose officials had required the colonists to pay back taxes in gold, despite the fact that they had already paid taxes in Utah.

The colonists abandoned their Nevada homes and fields in 1870-71. The two hundred or more who had no homes to which they wished to return were advised to settle in Long Valley, where exploring parties had found 1,300 acres of tillable land and extensive ranges suitable for grazing. Timber abounded and the Virgin River would provide water for irrigation and power. Mt. Carmel, so-called because of its supposed resemblance to the Palestine town of the same name, was one of two Long Valley communities founded in this exodus. (The other was Glendale.) At first, the transplanted Saints experienced many difficulties raising crops, and once more cooperation and unselfish division of product facilitated survival. The experiences on the Muddy, and during the first year or two in Mt. Carmel, had trained the families to work and pray as a unit.

After their sojourn in Mt. Carmel, this Nevada group founded Orderville specifically for the purpose of making the more idealistic form of United Order a living reality, a fact that both favored and obstructed their progress. Certainly many major problems of setting up a communitarian order in other settlements were problems of transition. The co-ops, which Brigham Young hoped had prepared the people for a more advanced form of cooperation, were in reality benevolent corporations. With a few exceptions, most notably Brigham City, the local co-op was either a retail store or a factory paying day wages, neither establishment providing the basis of a full economic community held together by clear ties of common economic interest. In these communities the United Order was imposed upon an economy already functioning in essentially individualistic and capitalistic forms, though the harsher aspects of frontier society had been attenuated by the Mormons' sense of community and tradition of cooperative endeavor. Tradesmen, accustomed to established wages for their labors, were thrown in with farmers, who did not think in terms of dollars earned for hours spent. A means of fairly rewarding both had to be devised. Individual homes had been built, businesses established, lands parceled out, and water rights allotted. Brigham Young hoped that eventually, if not immediately, all of these private holdings would be voluntarily put into a common fund. Even he, however, recognizing that it was much to ask, did not require that all possessions be put into the Order. He emphasized that labor was the source of all wealth. If men would but cooperate intelligently in the use of land and water, he maintained, they could start barehanded and soon acquire an abundance of possessions. It was of little consequence whether men entering the United Order subscribed their property so long as they fully dedicated their time and talents to the development of the new system. When the material results of union became apparent, men would be fully convinced of the wisdom of putting their possessions into a common fund.[2] His hopes in this regard proved overly optimistic. Most United Orders failed before the thorny task of transition was fairly complete.

The group that founded Orderville was less encumbered by membership in an older, more established order. They built their community from the ground with labor, land and water, and very little else. Having little, they had little to lose. Starting new, they were less hesitant to forsake the old. Transition was much less a problem for these people. They did not have to change a settled community—only to build a new one.

Reinforcing this advantage was the fact that the settlers of Orderville had selected themselves from a larger community precisely because of their desire to make the United Order a success. It would not be surprising, in fact, if a desire to show their erstwhile doubting associates that they could make the Order work did not cause them to put exceptional effort into their enterprise. The others were on the outside, just two miles away, and no doubt looking carefully and hopefully for the first signs of failure.

These circumstances brought disadvantages as well. Brigham Young's expectations notwithstanding, a certain amount of capital was required in founding a new colony. Tools, equipment, housing, and stock were needed to make the community a success. Only strict curtailing of present consumption would permit the accumulation of capital needed to insure future growth. The people of Orderville began poor, and though their condition improved greatly, they remained poor, relative to more affluent outsiders, for the duration of their communal experience. Efficiency needed to assure a modicum of food and shelter for all the inhabitants imposed a drab uniformity upon the dress and activities of the people, contrasting unfavorably, in the eyes of the younger generation at least, with life on the outside. Even though the residents were adequately clothed and housed and were guaranteed security in old age or disablement, there were aspects of life in Orderville that imparted the appearance and, in the opinion of some, the substance of poverty. Such impressions were more illusory than real. The young Order member, looking outside, would envy the occasional store-bought dress or imported shoes without noticing that only a few could afford such amenities. The even distribution of wealth within the Order did not permit a few who were wealthy to enjoy pleasures denied to the whole community, as on the outside. Thus, though well provided for, some in the Order no doubt felt themselves deprived. Those on the outside who took occasional displays of fashion and variety as their measures of affluence agreed.

The circumstances surrounding the establishment of Orderville and the unusual nature of its population may account, in part, for other distinctive aspects of the Orderville experiment. It lasted as a functioning full cooperative longer than other United Orders. It accomplished this while hewing more closely to the "gospel plan" than did most of the others. After its dissolution its members looked back upon their communal experience as a time when they nearly realized the perfect Christian brotherhood envisioned by the Mormon prophets. Unlike the residents of Kanab or Brigham City, they retained fond memories of their Order.

The Order began in March 1874 when John R. Young met with the settlers in Mt. Carmel to organize a United Order among them. Ninety-four of 112 persons in the community over the age of fourteen expressed their willingness to join the Order.[3] Francis L. Porter, historian for the community, reported that shortly thereafter "the Order was possessor of everything appraisable, from real estate to chickens, featherbeds and Ladies Wardrobes." This original zeal was apparently not shared by all, and by midsummer a powerful member of the board of directors became disgruntled and withdrew, taking with him a small but significant following. Despite the withdrawal, "the Saints who came from the Muddy in Nevada were desirous of continuing to labor in the Order." Following the advice of Howard O. Spencer, who had been sent by Brigham Young to help resolve problems in the community, those favoring the Order decided to separate themselves from the dissidents. Two miles up the Virgin River they selected a townsite "at the mouth of a small canyon on the north side." Settlement began in March 1875 and continued "until the whole community who were desirous of laboring together were moved." They called their community Order City, which was later changed to Orderville.[4]

While some of the settlers cut a canal and planted 300 homesteaded acres to wheat, corn, oats, barley, potatoes, sugar cane, alfalfa, garden, and orchard, others surveyed the land and laid out a townsite, 30 rods square. In July 1875 the settlers incorporated as the United Order of Orderville. All of their economic property, both real and personal, valued at approximately $21,500 in 1875 prices, was deeded to the community corporation. This property included 335 acres of land, 18 houses, 19 oxen, 103 head of cattle, 43 horses and mules, 500 sheep, 30 hogs, 400 chickens, a threshing machine, reaper, mower, cane mill, 30,000 feet of lumber, and a variety of farming equipment, provisions, and supplies.[5] All of the property was clear of indebtedness.

In connection with the founding of the Order, a sacred religious ceremony was held at which each person was baptized by immersion and placed under a solemn covenant to obey certain rules suggested by Brigham Young as being essential to harmonious and successful Christian living. It was evident that the participants believed the Order was ordained of God.

The principles that motivated the establishment of the United Order of Orderville, according to their historian, were the same as those that motivated the establishment of the communitarian Law of Consecration among the Latter-day Saints during the first few years after the Mormon Church was organized. These principles were:

That all people are literally the sons and daughters of God, that the earth is His and all it contains, that He created it and its fulness, especially for the use and benefit of His children, that all, providing they keep His commandments, are equally entitled to the blessings of the earth; that with proper regulations there is enough and to spare for all, that every person is simply a steward and not an owner of property he has in charge, and that he is under obligations to use it, and his time, strength and talents for the good of all. They believe in living as a patriarchal family, and in common, according to their circumstances fare alike. All are required to be diligent in their labors, economical in their habits and temperate in their lives.[6]

There was to be no private property. "No man could say 'this is mine.'" The property was the Lord's and was to be used "for the advancement of the Order and the Church."[7] However, each person was made steward over such personal effects as clothing, books, and jewelry. Each family was to have (but not own) a separate home, and these were to consist principally of one- and two-room apartment house units or "shanties," joined together in a semi-fort arrangement around a town square. The typical shanty had a living room twelve feet square and an adjoining bedroom eight by twelve feet. Between the rows of shanties a community dining hall and other public buildings were to be constructed. Shops and factories were to be located outside the residence block.

A group of laborers was immediately assigned the task of building the homes and the dining hall. The latter, twenty-two by forty feet, was built of rough lumber, put together with wooden pegs, and lined with adobes. Large enough to seat all members of the Order, it was used for prayers, religious meetings, and social gatherings, as well as for eating. A kitchen and bakery were later attached. Members of the Order also built a large apartment house, United Order office with storeroom and shoe shop attached, blacksmith shop, carpenter shop, cooper shop, tannery, schoolhouse and telegraph office, woolen factory, garden house, and dairy barns and sheep sheds.

One visitor found "the settlement itself . . . grievously disappointing in appearance." He contrasted the external appearance of Orderville with that of "the charming little hamlet of Glendale," with its "sunny wealth of orchard and meadow and cornland." Orderville, the visitor said, "at first sight looks like factory. The wooden shedlike buildings built in continuous rows, the adjacent mills, the bare ugly patch of hillside beyond it, give the actual settlement an uninviting aspect." A closer examination, however, proved the initial impression to be misleading. "Within the settlement scene changes wonderfully for the better," the visitor wrote.

The houses are found, the most of them built facing inwards upon an open square, with a broad side-walk, edged with tamarisk and mulberry, boxelder and maple trees, in front of them. Outside the dwelling-house square are scattered about the schoolhouse, meetinghouse, blacksmith and carpenters' shops, tannery, woolen mill, and so forth, while a broad roadway separates the whole from the orchards, gardens, and farm lands generally. Specially noteworthy here are the mulberry orchard—laid out for the support of the silkworms, which the community are now rearing with much success—and the forcing ground and experimental garden, in which wild flowers as well as "tame" are being cultivated. Among the buildings the more interesting to me were the schoolhouse, well fitted up, and very fairly provided with educational apparatus; and the rudimentary museum, where the commencement of a collection of the natural curiosities of the neighborhood is displayed.[8]

The town, as a whole, bore more resemblance to a Christian military camp than to an individualistic society of free men and women. With periodic calls by the United Order bugler (or by the clanging of the dining hall bell) to arise, to attend prayers, to eat breakfast, to go to work, to eat dinner, to attend evening prayers, and to retire, life must, indeed, have had a military aspect.[9]

The first dinner in the community dining hall was served July 24, 1875, after which, for more than five years, an average of more than eighty families ate food prepared by a male supervisor and six women. The women in the Order were divided up into groups and each group took a week's turn of dining hall duty. The food was placed upon three rows of tables running the full length of the dining hall. The men were served at 7, 12, and 6 o'clock; the women and children ate later.[10] Teams of girls took turns serving as waitresses and dishwashers. The food was simple: molasses and bread, potatoes and gravy, assorted vegetables and dairy products, and meat at least once a day. A variety of fresh fruits was served in season. Milk, fruit juices, and water were the standard beverages. When a disastrous flood filled the bakery with sediment and caved in the brick ovens in August 1880, eating together was necessarily abandoned. Garden products and other foods were then apportioned to families according to numbers and ages.[11]

Foodstuffs were produced on an average of some 400 acres of land, which included, in addition to the Orderville farms, a special farm at Leeds, down the river, which grew early fruits and vegetables; a 20-acre garden and orchard plot near the center of Orderville; a so-called hennery, or poultry project; three dairies, with a combined total of 250 cows; and a sheep enterprise with several thousand head of sheep. The chief of the local Shivwits Indians granted the Order the perpetual right to graze its cattle on Buckskin (Kaibab) Mountain in exchange for a rifle and some ammunition.[12] At its height the Order occupied the best grazing areas in southern Utah. The grain was ground at a community gristmill purchased, at a price of $3,000, from Glendale residents. Sugar cane was pressed into molasses at a number of

Orderville

Orderville, Utah, 1880. The community dining hall is in the center of the town, left of flagpole. The long row of buildings on the left is quarters for individual families. Buildings on far right, front to back, are the United Order office, United Order store, and cabinet shop. The three-story

SKETCH BY EVERETT THORPE
from an old painting

out 1880

building to the right of center was called the "big house" and was the
social and recreational center of the community. (Sketch by Everett
Thorpe from an old painting)

Order molasses mills. Milk was put up in ten- and fifteen-gallon kegs, and part was churned into butter or made into cheese. The garden and orchard plot was fenced to prevent pilferage and contained a variety of fruit trees, vegetables, and a nursery for the growing of seed. A special watermelon plot was maintained at one of the dairies. For each of these and all other enterprises there was an overseer or foreman.

The group attained almost complete self-sufficiency.[13] Changing price levels had little effect on the citizens of Orderville. Members of the Order raised broom corn and made their own brooms; they made their own soap and lye of local materials; a nearby coal mine furnished fuel and energy; they obtained red cedar from the canyons and made their own wooden buckets, tubs, kegs, barrels, firkins, and churns; they conducted a silk enterprise, produced silk thread, and wove handkerchiefs and other articles; they obtained leather from a Salt Lake tannery and fashioned their own leather products, later erecting their own tannery and, using cowhides tanned with local barks, making their own boots, shoes, harnesses, and saddles.[14] A United Order cabinet shop made their furniture, spinning wheels, and shingles. Assigned workers cut and sawed timber for the community with a United Order steam sawmill. They produced an excess of wool and freighted it to Washington, Provo, and Salt Lake City, Utah; and with the store-pay received for the wool and some few other items, they purchased the supplies that they could not produce or do without. One member of the Order was specially designated to make these trips by wagon. Since Orderville was three hundred traveling miles from Salt Lake City, the two annual trips to that place required from six to eight weeks each. The Order also, on occasion, produced surplus furniture, leather goods, and other products and services, which were sold in other southern Utah communities to build up a capital fund with which to buy land. In buying goods from individuals and business houses in other wards and settlements the Orderville group used accumulated credits at the St. George Tithing Office and/or orders on the Washington Cotton Factory, Provo Woolen Mills, and the Salt Lake City ZCMI. On one or two occasions the group had balances in Salt Lake City banks.

Their clothing needs were met at the outset, in typical pioneering fashion, by the labor of individual family units. Mothers and daughters operated spinning wheels and hand looms, many of which were Order-made. Some standard needs, such as buckskin cloth and blankets, were obtained from the nearby Navajo Indians by trading horses. In 1876 the Order acquired a $2,000 interest in the Washington Cotton Factory and obtained cloth on exchange for wool. The next year a tract of one hundred acres of land was purchased and several members were "called" to raise cotton. Like other members of the Order, the families laboring in the Cotton Farm lived in houses built together in a long row and operated a community kitchen. The cotton was ginned at an Order cotton gin, was carded at a community carding machine, and, together with locally produced wool, was taken to the Washington Cotton Factory for manufacture into linsey cloth. Eight "companies" of workers thus supplied the town with cloth. In 1882, under the direction of its Department of Public Works, the Order erected a woolen factory. Some secondhand machinery was purchased from a factory in the East and was placed in the thirty by seventy foot two-story lumber building. Machinery and all, the factory cost $10,000.[15] The weaving looms were made by Order carpenters. As the most important enterprise yet undertaken by the Order, the factory, before it was put into operation, was dedicated to God in a special ceremony conducted by church apostle Francis M. Lyman. Six employees operated the two hundred spindles in the factory. The factory made yarn, batting, and cloth. All dyestuffs were made of local materials. Using the cloth, Order tailors made women's clothes of linsey and men's suits of "gray jeans," an all-wool cloth. All of this homespun was of a rather coarse texture, and all clothing worn by the members of the Order came from similar bolts. The hats were also made locally of straw gleaned from the fields by crews of women who braided and pressed them into desired shapes. Some of the women's hats were made of denim, percale, or quilted cotton.

The service occupations were also conducted under appointment by the Order. A school was maintained during the winter months and occasionally in the evenings during the remainder of the year. Apparently, only the younger children went to school. Although they worked the year round, the older children did receive some instruction in some of the church organizations. Medical care was provided by a number of women who were appointed as midwives to serve under the direction of a female chairman. Priddy Meeks, an herb doctor, joined the group in 1876 and remained to practice his art until his death ten years later at the age of ninety-one.[16] The Order also had its quota of blacksmiths, clerks, artists, musicians, telegraphers, and other skilled people. Every able-bodied person was given an assignment. Recreation, including regular dances, was an integral part of Order activities.[17]

The Order also played a role in general church projects and activities. It furnished lumber, tar, and labor for the construction of the St. George Temple; and after its completion in 1877, the Orderville organization appointed two members to help erect the temple at Manti. Orderville was credited with having done more for the Manti Temple than any other ward in the Kanab District, of which Orderville was a part. Orderville also supported, from time to time, gospel missionaries in the eastern states, England, and Europe. In addition, ten percent of the net increase of the Order was paid to the church each year for tithing. (Individual members were not asked to pay tithing.)

As a result of the labor of the community, the assets of the Order rose from $21,551 in 1875 to $69,562 in 1879 and $79,577 in 1883. While their circumstances were modest, their production was amazingly high, and in terms of present values averaged several hundred thousand dollars, worth of goods per year.[18] W. D. Johnson reported of the community in 1877 that "it forcibly reminds one of a hive of bees. They work in perfect harmony and they have a power 'to do' that cannot be found in any other place among the saints."[19]

In the beginning, while the ideal of the "one big family" held sway, it seemed unnecessary to keep individual accounts; accordingly, except for a record of appraisals of property turned in and credited to the respective subscribers as share capital, no books were kept. Nevertheless, Brigham Young had a different opinion; in a letter dispatched from St. George he advised the keeping of individual accounts, crediting in money wages for labor performed and charging for living costs. Wages and prices could be fixed arbitrarily, he said, and it mattered not how low, but everyone should agree in uniting to accept the rate as full compensation. Thus, it would be impossible for malcontents withdrawing from the Order to bring a cause of action for unreasonable amounts.[20] Following Brigham Young's instructions, members of the Order set up a standard scale for crediting all work done. Men were credited with $1.50 per day, while women were rated at 75 cents per day. These rates, low as they seem to-day, had been in effect less than a year when fear developed among officials that withdrawing members would seriously cripple the Order. By common consent, therefore, wage rates were cut in half and a wage-scale was established for three different age groups of males and females. Children under eleven years of age were credited at the rate of 12.5 cents per day; boys from thirteen to seventeen were allowed 75 cents per day. Girls from eleven to fifteen years of age were credited at 35 cents per day, and women over fifteen were granted 50 cents per day. There was no differentiation in the rate of return of any type of labor or occupation, be it skilled, unskilled, or managerial. Each assignment was considered the equal of every other assignment. No dividends were declared, so there were no property incomes.

After 1877, the Order operated on the price system. Values were given to all commodities, as well as to labor, and each department was charged for its use of labor, horses and wagon, oxen, lumber, furniture, blacksmith services, wool, feed, food, and so on. Families were charged a nominal room rent, depending upon the service afforded. The cost of two rooms, kitchen, and fuel for one representative family in 1877 was $21.00. Board for adults averaged $5.00 per month until 1878, after which it was $41.60 per year for men and $30.00 per year for children. When the boardinghouse was discontinued in 1880, men were charged 90 cents per week for rations, while women were charged 60 cents, adolescents 40 cents, and children under twelve 20 cents. Men were allowed $17.50 per year for clothing, while for women, it was a dollar less. Clothing allowances for children were from one-half to three-fourths these amounts. Similar allowances were made for shoes, blankets, and furniture. The services of a midwife could be had for $3.00.[21]

The agency of distribution for all goods, both local and imported, was the storehouse, which was initially under the charge of the bishop and first president of the Order, Howard O. Spencer. Beginning in 1877, every department of manufacture was ordered to do its business through the store. Each family and department was allowed to make withdrawals as needed. For the first two or three years supplies of consumer goods were so scarce that a committee of three women was appointed "to learn the necessities of the people and to decide who needed things most and issue orders on the store when things were to be given out."[22]

Store goods, thus apportioned, were carried to each family by boys and girls appointed for the purpose.

The group voted that, beginning in 1880, those who had had more credits than debits to their accounts at the beginning of each year were to consecrate to the Order "with their own free will and consent," for a nominal consideration, all surplus credit earned by them during the preceding year. At the same time, all individual overdrawals or debts were also to be cancelled. Thus, at the beginning of each year, all would "start out equal"; there would be no economic reason for any worker to prefer one department of labor to another. These changes were made on the recommendation of general authorities of the church and were attested by signed statements in order to forestall litigation.[23] The financial statements indicate that there was always a balance of credits over debits.

A strict accounting of all activities was insisted upon. One man and his wife were sent to Leeds to take care of the Order's fruit farm. The wife took advantage of the opportunity to wash and iron clothes for nearby miners and spent the income derived from this labor on her children. When the family returned to Orderville, complaint was made that she had privately spent money that should have been turned in to the Order treasury. But "as she had always been a faithful worker, she was forgiven and told to 'Go [to work] and sin no more.' "[24]

The society was governed by an annually elected board of management, consisting of a president, two vice-presidents, secretary, treasurer, and four directors. An election was held each year. These nine men (they were invariably men) supervised the appraisal of property turned in to the Order (or taken out of the Order in case of withdrawal), bought and sold properties in the name of the Order, directed the labor force, made investment decisions, drew up schedules of values, heard complaints, and, in general, regulated the affairs of the Order. All important matters were presented to the body of the Order at regular meetings, however, and all things were done by common consent. The president of the society was invariably the bishop, and the two vice-presidents were usually his two counselors. The secretary of the society was usually the ward clerk. Thus, there was almost an identity between spiritual and temporal leadership, as was no doubt intended.

The board of management met at the beginning of each year to plan work for the ensuing year and make assignments. These meetings usually lasted over a period of several days. Each department head or foreman made an annual oral report, and consideration was given to the need for improvement and the desirability of expanding or contracting a given field of activity. The board relied heavily on the judgment of the department head in such matters, and the principal task of the board in these meetings seems to have been the assignment of duties. Administratively, the Order consisted of thirty-three different departments, running alphabetically from the Blacksmith and Wagon Repair to the Woolen Cloth Manufacturing departments.[25] For each of these a department head or foreman was selected. Subforemen were appointed to have charge of the various enterprises conducted by the larger departments. The remaining members of the Order, male and female, were then assigned to be assistants in the various departments according to the number needed. A portion of the minutes of a meeting held February 14, 1880, at which some of these arrangements were worked out, illustrates the procedure by which Order members were assigned to their respective tasks:

On motion Henry W. Esplin was sustained as foreman of the farming department the present year and C. N. Carroll is sustained as foreman of our lucern farm. And Levi Hampton as foreman of the second farm. Alvin F. Heaton was sustained as foreman of the third farm, and Allen Cox was sustained as foreman of the fourth farm. Jonathan Heaton is sustained as foreman of the Enterprise or cotton farm. John J. Esplin was sustained as foreman of the Lake Farm.

Thomas Robertson was sustained as foreman of the Blacksmith shop. On motion F. L. Porter was released as foreman in the kitchen and boarding house. On motion Persis A. Spencer to take charge of the boarding house, with Susana Fackrell and Elizabeth Brown as assisting house [department]. On motion Carie W. Porter is appointed to labor in the kitchen under the direction of Persis A. Spencer. On motion Elizabeth Brown is released from assisting in the cloth department. On motion Albina Young was sustained as foreman of the cloth department, with Marinda and Maria Black as assistants.

On motion D. M. Cox was sustained as foreman of the carpenter and wagon shop. On motion Warriner A. Porter was sustained as foreman of the cabinet shop. On motion John C. White was sustained as foreman of the garden. On motion Lydia E. Young is sustained as foreman of the millinery department with sister Johannah Covington, Salley Palmer, and Hannah Glispy as assistants. On motion Isaac Assay is sustained as foreman of the sawmill. On motion William M. Black was sustained as foreman miller. On motion Thomas Blackburn was sustained as foreman of the shoe shop.

On motion Edward M. Webb was sustained head school teacher, with Francis L. Porter, Mary Fackrell, and Ann Cox as assistants. On motion John R. Young was sustained foreman of the sheep-herd department. On motion Sarah Ann Robertson was sustained as foreman of the sewing department, with Clarissa Hoyt and Susan B. Heaton as assistants. On motion Edson P. Porter is sustained as foreman of the tannery. On motion Israel Hoyt is sustained as foreman of the feed department. On motion Harriet Bowers is sustained as foreman of miscellaneous work. On motion Thomas Stolworthy is sustained as foreman of odd jobs. On motion Matilda Stolworthy is sustained as foreman of the knitting department, with Nuna A. Spencer and Priscilla Porter as assistants. On motion I. V. Carling is sustained as foreman of the tin shop.[26]

After all the foremen and their assistants had been selected, the minutes of these meetings were then read to the entire Order, assembled in the dining room, and prayers were said for the success of the Order throughout the ensuing year.

For the religious and economic health of the community, it was necessary that the Order adopt rules limiting membership, in addition to the provision in the by-laws requiring a two-thirds favorable vote. Otherwise, disharmonious elements might disrupt the organization and the population would quickly press upon the limited resources. The rules governing admission were, in general, moral and religious in nature rather than economic.[27] Applicants were asked their purpose in seeking to unite with the Order, whether their families were trained in the fear of the Lord, whether they were willing to put up with the inconveniences "without murmuring or fault finding," and whether they were willing to practice economy, give up the use of tobacco, tea, coffee, and intoxicating liquors, forsake swearing and cursing, cease quarreling, and refrain from abusing dumb animals. Each must agree to forgive his brethren and "do as you are told cheerfully and not sullenly." Each prospective member was also asked to signify willingness to "try to the best of your ability to maintain the peace and prosperity of this Order and as much as lies in your power, deal honestly, impartially and justly in all transactions you may be called upon to perform from time to time."[28]

Although prospective members were asked their "present situation in regard to food and clothing, and the nature and amount of their property, encumbrances, and debts," none of these financial criteria seem to have counted for as much as moral factors in deciding whether to accept a given family into the Order. In some instances the Order provided transportation for the families of prospective members too poor to pay their own way to Orderville. This liberality in accepting newcomers is illustrated by an experience recorded by Samuel Claridge, a vice-president of the Order, who was absent for two years serving as a missionary to England. Upon his return to Utah, in 1878, he called at the office of John Taylor, successor to Brigham Young as head of the church. "Bro. Taylor," wrote Claridge, "had been to Orderville and knew we took Everybody in that came along and He gave me some good advice. . . . He said Brother Claridge whatever you do dont overload the boat for there is Danger when there was too many in [the boat] of being Capsized." When Claridge reached Orderville a short time later, he attended a meeting of the board of management at which a number of applications to join the Order were considered.

I told them [wrote Claridge] what Brother Taylor had said and I said I thought it was wisdom to try and make those we had more comfortable; but they thought the Lord had given a Command to join the Order and it would be as wrong to deny them [as] it would be for the Repentant believer to be denied of baptism. So they came and altho poor they became some of the most useful mechanics and faithful workers we had in the Order.[29]

Thus, despite Brigham Young's repeated advice against "allowing those who might become parasites on the body from becoming members" and despite the similar advice of President Taylor, the condition occurred and, in the words of Henry Esplin, who was bishop of Orderville from 1884 to 1911, it "became a menace by breeding discontent and throwing the responsibility for the support of their families on those who must assume it." Continued the bishop:

If all had accepted responsibility and had worked for the good of the whole, all would have been well, but with a leak here and a leak there, inroads were made. Too much responsibility reverted to a few and could not be distributed. It would eventually resolve itself into injustice to the posterity of those who carried little or no responsibility.

President Taylor repeated the caution of Brigham Young to be careful and not allow themselves to become overburdened with a class that would not work, but avoidance seemed impossible and through it, largely, selfishness and jealousy crept in, elements destructive in any community.[30]

With other Orders not functioning in the late 1870s and early 1880s, and with a serious problem of poverty and underemployment in southern Utah until 1880, it was manifestly impossible for this small, though successful, organization to provide a living for all those who wished to join, no matter how pious their resolves.

It is also quite probable that members withdrawing from the society took with them a disproportionate share of the property of the Order. Withdrawing members were paid the equivalent of the capital stock they had invested, plus their accumulated credits during the year of the withdrawal, less 10 percent for tithing. These payments were usually made in teams, wagons, livestock, and other moveable property. In addition, the debts of those who withdrew were usually cancelled "for the sake of the children." The following document, one of many like it in the Orderville records, reveals this charitable tendency of the Order:

Whereas .... has seen fit to sever his connection with the United Order, and upon settlement it is found that he is in debt to the Order the sum of $665.93, and whereas for several months past he has been unfaithful in his labors, loitering and trifling his time away and otherwise breaking his covenants he made when he united with us. Therefore be it resolved that it is right and just in every respect, to hold him to the full and complete payment of the above named indebtedness. Nevertheless, as he has a large family to support and his best days are gone, be it further resolved as an act of charity to his little children, that the above indebtedness be canceled by the entry of this resolution, on the Ledger.[31]

Such leniency not only increased the burdens on faithful workers, but also created a certain amount of discontent among those who were prone to criticize and complain.

Beginning in 1880 a number of changes, external and internal, began to transform the Order into a less collectively organized society and eventually brought about the dissolution of the Orderville United Order in 1885. The most important external change to affect the Order was, paradoxically, the improvement in the economic climate of southern Utah, which began with the end of the Panic of 1873 and was abetted by the completion of the Utah Southern Railroad to Milford, Utah, in 1880. Orderville had been founded in an atmosphere of poverty. The hope that unified action might alleviate dire want was regarded, by Brigham Young at least, as justification, along with supposed spiritual benefits, for the adoption of this unique system of social and economic solidarity. Orderville was an immediate success in the sense that its citizens came to eat and dress better than they had done for years—better, in fact, than many residents in surrounding settlements who had not successfully combined their efforts in a United Order. In the late 1870s some non-Mormons discovered extensive silver deposits at Silver Reef, less than fifty miles from Orderville. When the Utah Southern extension brought railroad facilities within one hundred miles of Silver Reef in 1880, these mines were fully exploited. Within five years, more than ten million dollars worth of silver was extracted. Southern Utah farmers found in the mining town a lucrative market for their produce; employment rose sharply; cash income became more commonplace. Orderville's neighbors suddenly found themselves able to buy imported clothing and other store commodities. The Saints in Orderville thus became "old fashioned." Their floppy straw hats, their "gray jeans," their "valley tan" shoes, and their crowded shanties suddenly became objects of ridicule and derision. Orderville adolescents began to envy the young people in other communities, and their discontent spread to the older members of the Order. And it must be admitted that the future of Orderville children was not exactly propitious, though they might never know unemployment. The Order was clearly a short-run solution to a pressing economic problem. It would have been virtually impossible for a young man growing up in the Order, without special provision, to acquire capital stock. While some of the older members of the Order compared their position with the days of poverty on the Muddy, Orderville youth compared its opportunities with those of young people in other communities.

As the result of the friction produced by this new external relationship, and the discontent of some with existing institutions, two important changes were made. The first was the cessation of communal dining, which occurred, as previously mentioned, in 1880.[32] This caused the families to become less group conscious than formerly. Three years later, the wage system was modified to permit discrimination in credits given for different types of labor.

At the same time, families were also given special "Order money" with which to do their own purchasing. These changes pushed the communal elements farther in the background, heightened the latent tendencies toward individualism, and set the stage for final dissolution.

It was customary, of course, for all decisions affecting the structure and function of the Order to be referred to superior ecclesiastical authorities for their advice and counsel before definite action was taken. Orderville leaders maintained contact with the officers of Kanab Stake, apostle Erastus Snow in St. George, visiting general authorities of the church, and the church's First Presidency in Salt Lake City. When church policy had been ascertained, suggested changes were then debated in a public meeting of the Order. After a majority ruling from that group was obtained, those in disagreement either complied or completely withdrew from the Order.

In general, the advice of directing church officials followed three lines of thought: (a) the institutions, rules, and regulations of the society were not as important as harmony and unity, within whatever framework; (b) the Orderville group should not disband, whatever their problems, but should attempt if at all possible to perfect a system that might be applied in other villages, for Orderville was a useful social experiment that should be given full opportunity to justify itself; and (c) all business procedures and transactions should be executed and recorded in such a manner that the Order would be amply protected from suit in any gentile court.

When his opinion with regard to communal dining facilities was asked, in 1877, Erastus Snow was recorded as having made the following comment:

He said he had been exercised much with regard to the method adopted by the people of Orderville; he did not think the Lord was particular how we made the garments with which we are clothed or as to the manner in which we prepared our food. Neither did he think the Lord cared much about whether we sat down to one or many tables.[33]

Later he stated:

I am just as sanguine now as I have been in time past, that the Lord wishes His people to be united as the Nephites [a people described in the Book of Mormon] were, when there will be no more poor among them; when all will be faithful in their labors. The people of Orderville or those that are organized in the United Order deserved credit for what they have done, but that they are exactly on the line, I cannot say. I can see some defects in their organizations that will show themselves at some time, and will cause some to feel disaffected.[34]

The issue of abolishing the community dining hall did not split the group, however, as did the decision to shift to an unequal wage and partial stewardship system in 1883. Some thought that the original provision that the labor of all should be subject to common direction and entitled to equal credit (except for the age and sex groups previously mentioned) had led to inefficiency, sluggardliness, and loss of personal freedom. Others thought the original system was the Word of God as relayed to Brigham Young, and that any change would be blasphemous. Viewing the procedural disagreement with alarm, Erastus Snow, as resident general church authority in southern Utah, began to emphasize the experimental nature of the Order. He argued that the various enterprises and departments of the Order were not significantly different from ordinary Mormon cooperative stores; that the system of giving equal credit for unequal labor had been unsound; and that the United Order, as practiced, was not a commandment of God but a financial experiment initiated by Brigham Young. He thought resort to simple cooperation might be the better course.[35]

Although based undoubtedly on a realistic appraisal of the new external situation caused by the working of the Silver Reef mines, Snow's advice seems to have produced, if anything, even more discontent than had previously existed, and partially alienated some of the most valiant supporters of the Order. When an appeal was made to the First Presidency in Salt Lake City, their advice was of a general character, calculated to encourage unity behind any plan that the Order could agree upon. This was quite different from saying, as many thought Brigham Young had said before, that the system was a commandment of God, to be preserved and continued at all costs. As the result of this counsel, the group voted to adopt something approaching a piece-rate wage system, with six-month stewardships for many enterprises of the Order. A portion of a letter written by one of the directors of the Order on August 18, 1883, shortly after the change was made, gives a particularly revealing comment on the dilemma that faced Order leaders:

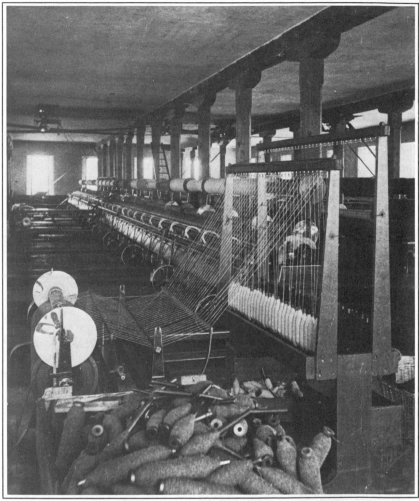

Textile mills were built in several locations as United Order enterprises.
This photograph of the Provo Woolen Mills shows a typical
manufacturing establishment of the period. (C. W. Carter photo,
Church Archives)

Accumulating wealth was not our object, that was farthest from our minds, our aim was to establish a principle of equality as near that spoken of in the Revelations, as our fallen natures would admit of, striving always to grade upwards towards the mark. . . .

Now this command from God, as we supposed, was our cement; this is what brought us together, what held us together, what comforted us in all our sorrows, what cheered us up when cast down, and in our vicissitudes we felt to rejoice and put on new determinations to endeavor to surmount every obstacle and make every sacrifice necessary to and consequent upon establishing a new order of things. . . . We verily believed we were in the line of our duty endeavoring to work out a problem and felt that we were sustained by the General Church Authorities until our last quarterly conference, when we were told by Apostle Erastus Snow that our organization was no more (not much more) than Canaan Co-op, Z.C.M.I. or any other co-operative company in the territory, that it was not a commandment of God and never has been, that it was a financial experiment of Brigham Young and that there was nothin[g] binding on the people in that respect. . . . So you see we are thrown entirely on our own responsibility. . . . The consequence was many have "drawn out" and have gone and strange to say that no one of our industries have failed as yet; but all are moving along as formerly and some of them even more prosperous than formerly.[36]

Finally the Order came to substitute, albeit with considerable hesitancy, a system of limited individual stewardships for the strict common-stock property arrangement under which they had lived for eight years. Beginning in July 1883, the town lot was enlarged and divided into half-acre home and garden lots. Each lot was given a number and a price, and a drawing was held to determine which families received which lots. Each family was permitted to use its capital stock and/or labor credit to buy one lot, the best of which were appraised at $70. Families were also allowed to purchase a shanty, presumably the one in which they were living, for five or ten dollars, depending on the accommodations, and move it on the lot. Each family was also entitled to buy one cow, typically priced at $30, and some chickens.[37]

At the same time, the various farming enterprises were placed on a semiprofit basis. A record was kept of the expenses and receipts, and the profit was awarded as book credit to the various persons working on the enterprise. The actual proceeds, however, "were cast into the Order for the benefit of all."[38]

Other community enterprises were leased, usually to the foremen, for a certain percent of the yearly income, or for a fixed sum. The following signed agreements illustrate the method by which stewardship was introduced:

"Isaac Losee agrees to herd sheep for $40 a month and board himself and make what improvements he can on the ranches and pay 10c a day for the use of a cow. One person will assist in herding."

Henry Blackburn: "I agree to freight for three-fifths of what I make and bear three-fifths of the expense of teams and wagons. I am to have two teams and two wagons."

Isaiah Bowers: "I agree to run the Orderville United Order sawmill and bear two-thirds losses and expense and furnish everything but the mill, one truck, the cart and the team. I also agree to pay $10 per thousand for the logs already cut and for this I am to have a credit at $10 per thousand feet. I also agree to pay 5¢ a day for the use of each cow. I have to take five pigs valued at $20 and keep them during the summer, have them valued in the fall and get credit for the difference in price."[39]

These lease arrangements, of course, left many in the position of working for the few who had stewardships, and caused many divergences in earned income. Those who, through lack of ability, willpower, good fortune, or opportunity, earned little, were so much the poorer. And there was no longer any provision for wiping the slate clean at the end of the year.

These new arrangements were admittedly provisional and experimental. Church leaders hoped they would result in a happier and more efficient arrangement. The company continued to hold the economic property, the mills and machinery, farming land, and most of the livestock, but the changes made stewards of the members, provided a reason for increased initiative among foremen, and gave them more individual responsibility for the functioning of the departments. Tithing and other church donations were now to be paid individually. Each transaction was accompanied by a corresponding payment of Order money. Nothing could be obtained from the commissary without the Order tickets or currency.[40] Many were thus forced to search for profitable employment, and a wage system was introduced.

As a result of the change, several families withdrew,[41] but even those remaining were not happy under the revised system. Once the group departed from its simple original system—once tampering with its fundamental institutions had begun—every member began to develop his own individual concept of the best course to pursue. Some thought the Order should be disbanded; others preferred an extension of the stewardship system; still others advocated a return to the "revealed system" of Brigham Young.[42] When the First Presidency and other general authorities visited southern Utah in April and May 1884, they considered the Orderville problem at some length. L. John Nuttall, ex-president of Kanab Stake, now private secretary of church president John Taylor, reported the interview as follows:

> At 7:30, Presidents Taylor and [George Q.] Cannon and Elder Nuttall met with Bp. Thomas Chamberlain and Elder Thomas Robertson [of Orderville]. . . . The affairs of the United Order of Orderville was considered, it having been said that it was the design to break up the Order next September [1884]. Prest. Taylor said he did not want the people to thus break up, but to continue their labors in the United Order. [He] referred to other institutions wherein, when the capital stock is put in, it becomes the company property, and cannot be drawn out without the consent of the company. Bro. Chamberlain explained the circumstances and condition of the people of their ward. After consideration Prest. Taylor promised to write a letter to the people of Orderville giving his mind as to how they shall continue their labors.[43]

Nuttall added in his entry for the next day that Orderville representatives "left for home much encouraged" as the result of their "conversation with the Presidency and myself."

The letter promised by President Taylor was written under his direction by George Q. Cannon, also a member of the First Presidency, and was as follows:

> Salt Lake City, June 2, 1884.
> Bishop Thomas Chamberlain, Orderville, Kanab, Utah
>
> Dear Brother:
> We promised you when we were at Toquerville, when we departed from you and Brother Robertson, that we would write you our views upon the question you propounded to us. It is in compliance with that promise that we now address you.
> When you changed your system from that of equal labor credits and disbursements to that of giving men credit according to their skill etc., just as is done in society elsewhere, you opened the door for selfishness and other feelings to enter, which such society has to contend with. By this change you dropped back to the old level. With such a change it cannot be reasonably expected that your organization can hold together for any length of time. Therefore, we said to you in our conversation at Toquerville, that it was our counsel to return to your old system of giving the people equal credit for labor. We feel that this is the better course for you to pursue.

You informed us that some of the people at Orderville desired the organization broken up and division of the property to be had in September next. We said to you that we did not think it advisable. This is still our counsel to you. If a majority of the people still have a desire to keep together and labor as they had done, we think they had better do so, and maintain your organization.

We understand the young people of Orderville have not felt entirely satisfied with their position in the organization. Steps should be taken to form a reserve fund out of your dividends. From this reserve fund you should make arrangements to give the young people, when they attain their majority, such shares and stock as your circumstances and wisdom would permit. In this way you will show to the rising generation that you have their interest at heart; and it will be the means of binding them more closely to your organization.

Another feature might be added to your system, we think, with good results. The most of families have a taste of some kind, which is a pleasure to them, when they have the means to gratify it. We understand that under your system this has not always been possible, as all your funds have been concentrated. Would it not be possible, to so arrange your affairs that a small amount could be given each individual and family for them to have to spend as they please for gratification of some personal want or taste?

In reply to your question as to what are the objects to be sought after and obtained by continuing in your organization: We say one great object should be, to reach a better order of social life, and more in accordance with the higher teaching of the Gospel in which men and women can carry out more perfectly the commandments of the Savior, to love our neighbors as we do ourselves.

Hoping these views and suggestions will be accepted by yourself and the Saints in the spirit in which they are given.

> We remain your brethren,
>
> (signed) George Q. Cannon,
> In behalf of the First Presidency.[44]

Clearly, church officials wanted the Order kept alive as an inspiration to the rest of the church and as an experiment in Christian living. Their letter also indicates dissatisfaction with the recently adopted stewardship plan.

As the result of these instructions and encouragement, agitation for discontinuance of the Order stopped temporarily. However, the stewardship plan was retained, and was even extended in 1884. Thus, each producer was given credit for his production and others were placed on a piece-rate commission or wage. By that time most of the families were established on their own plots of ground and were growing their own gardens and owning their own livestock and poultry. Nearby farming lands were also divided into five- and ten-acre lots, and these were sold by allowing each member of the Order to submit a bid, with each lot going to the highest bidder, although none was sold for less than the appraised value. Thus, an important part of the life of the Order became subject to private ownership and operation.

During the period of these internal changes, as previously, the Order was continuing to grow and prosper. New farms were purchased, new enterprises were initiated, and new investments were undertaken. General church authorities were so impressed with the Order members' sense of responsibility and enterprise that the Order was given charge of the large church cattle ranch at Pipe Springs, Arizona. The community was even giving serious consideration to the purchase of the Washington Cotton Factory. Many people in southern Utah began to wonder if it would not be long before the Orderville company would own the whole region.[45]

Despite the external and internal problems confronting the Order, it is not unlikely that the Orderville experiment would have been continued in one form or another for many years had not national legislation interfered. Adoption of the suggestions of the First Presidency, a clarification of individual responsibility, provision for young people, and careful choosing of new members would have made the Order workable, if not ideally efficient. But the enforcement of the Edmunds Act, beginning in February 1885, dealt the Order the *coup de grace.* Passed in 1882, the Edmunds Act provided fines and punishment for the practice of plural marriage and "unlawful cohabitation." When federal deputies began circulating through the territory early in 1885, many Orderville leaders, most of whom had entered into plural marriage, went into hiding to avoid arrest. Some of these men, including the president, Thomas Chamberlain, were eventually apprehended, convicted, and sent to the Utah Penitentiary.

In consideration, therefore, of the internal stresses and strains that had rent the basic institutions of the Order; the changing economic climate of southern Utah, which had stigmatized the Order as "unprogressive"; and now, under the prospect of being completely deprived of a functioning leadership by the enforcement of the Edmunds Act, the general authorities of the church counseled the dissolution of the Order in 1885. After listening to the advice of apostles Brigham Young, Jr., and Heber J. Grant, who had gone to Orderville to represent the church, the members voted—somewhat reluctantly, according to diaries and reminiscences—to disband.

It was easier to vote to dissolve than to work out a plan of equitably dividing the more than one hundred thousand dollars' worth of property owned by the Order among eighty-odd families belonging to the Order. E. D. Woolley, who had succeeded L. John Nuttall as president of Kanab Stake, and who was left in authority, suggested the dissolution plan finally adopted, describing the process as follows:

We were a week laboring and counseling, talking and praying with the people as a whole and with the leaders separately. Finally they voted unanimously to discontinue their operations in Utopia. As soon as that was done the apostles skipped back home and left me to the reconstruction. . . . it was a pretty job for that time and for my abilities. . . .

After exercising all the faith we could and calling for Divine aid, we evolved the following plan. We had the Secretary to go over the capital stock, and list everything that had been put in at inventory price. After that was done, teams, land, etc., being named so that we knew what and where it was, we held an auction sale of all the community belongings. . . .

The Secretary would read off the article by name and the inventory price. No one could bid below the inventory price, so as to protect the corporation, but as high as they desired so long as the bid came within their credits. . . . At the end of the week we had the community paid off and satisfied. I have never heard a criticism or complaint since.[46]

Three properties of the Order remained in the hands of the incorporated company—the tannery, the woolen factory, and the sheep enterprise (including both sheep and the ranch).[47] These were leased to private contractors, however, and community cooperation was completely eliminated. The board of management continued to preside over these three enterprises until 1889, at which time the remaining stockholders bought the sheep and ranches and formed the Orderville Sheep Association, later called the Orderville Co-op. The tannery was also sold to one of the stockholders. The woolen factory was operated until 1897 and eventually was given to Thomas Chamberlain, who used it for a hay barn. The incorporated Order was finally allowed to lapse in 1900. A silver-jubilee anniversary celebration was held at the time.[48]

Studies of the Amish, Doukhobors, Mennonites, Hutterites, and Pueblo Indians, whose societies resemble those of Orderville, Kingston, Sunset, Bunkerville, and kindred United Orders, indicate that it is possible to live successfully under such institutions as those which prevailed in Orderville. And, indeed, survivors later recalled their United Order experience as having been a happy one. When a flash flood destroyed several thousand dollars' worth of property in August 1885, the local correspondent to the *Deseret News* wrote: "Hitherto we have sustained more or less damage each year by floods, but the loss was on all and not so much felt. Now [because the property was privately owned] we are brought to realize individually what a loss means."[49] As the struggle for a living heightened the conflict between man and nature and between man and man, the memories of cooperation under the Order became sweeter and sweeter. Almost every published reminiscence of life under the Order mentions it as the closest approximation to a well-ordered, supremely happy Christian life that it was possible to achieve in human society. Andrew Jenson, who visited Orderville in 1892 to write its history, concluded:

The good Saints of Orderville gained an experience that will never be forgotten by those who passed through it and I was assured by several of the brethren who stuck to it till the last that they never felt happier in their lives than they did when the Order was in complete running order and they were devoting their entire time, talent and strength for the common good. Good feelings, brotherly love and unselfish motives characterized most of those who were members until the last.[50]

Henry Fowler, an Orderville veteran, substantiated this view: "We were happy in the Order. A spirit of true brotherhood prevailed as long as we obeyed counsel and lived up to our instructions."[51] Another wrote:

I have lived in Utah, Arizona, California, Idaho and in many different towns and I never was so much attached to a people, I never experienced greater joy nor had better times than during the period of time I was connected with the United Order in Orderville. . . . The United Order is a grand institution. . . .[52]

It is a fact worth noting that when a number of Orderville families moved to Cave Valley, Chihuahua, Mexico, during the 1890s, they formed themselves into a United Order organization that closely resembled that under which they had lived in Orderville in the early 1880s.[53]

One must discount to some extent the nostalgia of the participants in this interesting economic and social experiment. Contemporary letters and diaries indicate that they chafed more than they later cared to admit under the many necessary regulations and restrictions of the Order. Their neighbors, envious of their success, accused them of assuming an attitude of superiority, and ridiculed some of their customs. Some discontent is further evidenced by the fact that several important families withdrew from the Order before its dissolution.

Nevertheless, it is undeniable that the Orderville United Order improved the economic fortunes of its members, which had reached rock-bottom as the result of the failure of the Muddy colonies and the Panic of 1873, and induced a form of mutual cooperation and assistance that contributed to short-run, if not to long-run, advantage. Its members exhibited a remarkable willingness to subordinate self and labor for the public good.

Today Orderville, a farming and cattle-raising community of four hundred people, is hardly distinguishable from dozens of other southern Utah villages except for the ruins of its "factories" and its memories of "the Order."

CHAPTER 13

Extending the borders of Zion:
Arizona's Little Colorado settlements;
Bunkerville, Nevada; and Cave Valley, Mexico

N APRIL 1873 apostle Orson Pratt spoke on equality among the Saints to those assembled at a general conference of the church in Salt Lake City. Reviewing the history of their cooperative endeavors since 1831, he chided members for failing to live the Law of Consecration—and even the lesser law of tithing:

I do not see, for my part how we can begin to approximate to that law of oneness in regard to our property unless we commence in some new place, where the Church and the settlers might be gathered together and set a pattern for all the rest. I do not know but we might accomplish it in that way.[1]

In all probability his reference to a "new place" was not just a rhetorical invention. The previous winter Brigham Young and Colonel Thomas L. Kane, longtime Mormon friend and advocate, had met in St. George to plan their own particular version of Manifest Destiny—envisioning a chain of settlements extending southward to a possible second axis of Mormon dominion in the Mexican state of Sonora.[2] At the time Pratt spoke of new settlements, plans were being laid for establishment of the first outposts on the road south to Mexico. That same month a party of colonizing missionaries crossed the Colorado and headed into the tortured landscape of northern Arizona. Within two months they were in full flight toward Utah, beaten by what one of their party described as "the moste desert lukking plase that I ever saw, Amen."[3]

When Mormons ventured a second time to settle in Arizona, two and one-half years later, they did so with specific instructions from church leaders as to the nature and purpose of their colonizing effort—instructions that would seem to have been the natural product of the Pratt sermon of 1873. The settlers were called to a dual mission. They were to establish model communities, demonstrating to wayward Utah Saints that a more perfect society could be achieved under Brigham Young's United Order. The church president wrote to one of the leaders, Lot Smith, that the company had been "carefully selected . . . for the express purpose of . . . building and improving after the Order of Enoch." The disappointing experience in Utah had led him to conclude that "it was far better and easier to introduce the principles of the United Order at the beginning of new settlements, than to bring people into them after their individual interests were more firmly established."[4] The more remote and untouched the landscape—the fewer the alternative social forms in the new area—the better would be the chances for perfecting the Order. The Mormon villages on the Little Colorado River were founded specifically for the purpose of providing a model of the good society for Utah and for the world.[5]

Their mission, however, included more than this. The Church leaders' vision of Mormon destinies in the West remained imperial in scope. The Arizona pioneers were to establish stable, viable colonies that would serve as a base from which to press further into the Southwest. In a sense the sites were selected more for their strategic value than for their promise as habitations for the Saints. As one of the early missionaries into Arizona observed, "I do not know that it makes any difference whether a country is barren or fruitful if the Lord has a work to do in it."[6] Brigham Young affirmed that the Lord did have a work to do in Arizona, and those who began settling there in the spring of 1876 rarely questioned his word on the matter.

It was expected, of course, that the dual purposes of the Arizona mission would be complementary. The United Order would provide the discipline, organization, and spareness of lifestyle needed to build and sustain communities in so hostile an environment. At the same time, the harsh desert country would make close cooperation a condition of survival, maximizing the possibilities of building a more perfectly united people. There was implicit in this circularity of expectations the idea that the United Order was most viable not only in a new settlement, but in a settlement where the hostility of the natural environment made individual survival unlikely. God was deliberately sending the Saints into the wilderness to make of them a better people— an ancient Judeo-Christian theme. The corollary to this, which Brigham Young and other leaders did not discuss, would be that success in the one task might eventually diminish success in the other. Once the communitarian endeavor had tamed the environment, what would hold the Saints together? Could the United Order survive the absence of adversity? That, apparently, was a bridge to be crossed when it was reached.

The pioneers established four settlements in the lower valley of the Little Colorado in the spring of 1876, Lot Smith, William C. Allen, George Lake, and Jesse O. Ballinger each heading a group. Within two years one of the settlements, Obed, had been abandoned, leaving Joseph City (first called Allen's Camp, then St. Joseph) under Allen, Sunset under Smith, and Brigham City under Ballinger. The colonists set themselves at once to the task of building at each site a square enclosure or fort, in which all of the homes were located. Only Joseph City was to survive long enough to permit the building of a village outside the enclosure. Brigham City was abandoned in 1882 and Sunset in 1885.[7]

While the stockades were being built, detachments were sent out to set up sawmill operations in Pleasant Valley, forty miles from the nearest of the settlements, and to begin the surveying and building of dams and irrigation systems. In these, as in all other enterprises, the members apparently took the instructions of church leaders in Utah seriously. "It is all the United Order here and no beating around the bush," John Slythe wrote shortly after the settlements were founded. "It is the intention to go into it to the full meaning of the term."[8] In three of the four communities the United Order arrangement included a common table. All the major tasks of pioneering the new country were accomplished under the supervision of United Order officers and through the division of labor that Brigham Young saw as a chief advantage of the Order. The communities even pooled their resources in "conjoint" major undertakings, such as the operation of the sawmill or the management of herds of range cattle, a practice unusual among the United Orders in Utah.

The United Order at Sunset was in many respects the most idealistic of all those on the Little Colorado. There was no regular accounting of hours worked or credits earned. The entire community (numbering in 1878 some 136 persons) sat at a single "family" table presided over by Lot Smith. Smith, who had gained a formidable reputation harassing government supply lines during the Utah War of 1857-58, imposed an iron will upon the entire settlement. His firm rule ensured the economic success of the colony. So successful were the farming enterprises in the first years at Sunset that food was exported to subsidize the other settlements, earning for the community the nickname of the "Egypt of Arizona."[9] Mormon church leader Wilford Woodruff concluded, after a stay of several months in Sunset, that "these settlements in connection with Orderville were living in the United Order as near as any people could, in mortality, until a better way shall be revealed."[10]

There were, however, divisive forces at work beneath the harmonious exterior. In many respects Smith was autocratic; his high-handed tactics were resented by many who left the community and no doubt by many who stayed. He insisted upon plowing a major portion of the profits back into investment at a time when members felt they lacked the bare necessities of life. He moved the community from the ideal of a balanced, self-sufficient economy toward that of an increasingly specialized livestock ranch. Finally, in 1886 pressures from within and without led to the appointment by high church authorities of a special committee to attempt a reconstruction of the financial history of the Sunset United Order and to settle its affairs. After a study of several months the committee found that total assets, not counting sums already distributed to those leaving the Order, amounted to more than $85,000. Of this amount $51,000 was awarded to Smith and his sons and the remaining $34,000 divided among the forty-seven families who had claims against the Order, many of whom, unlike Smith, had already received allotments in a previous settlement. Probably most were better off than they had been when they entered the Order and perhaps better off than they would have been without Smith's strong leadership. But a legacy of resentment and distrust had marred the unity that was to have characterized the community.[11] Though the Order was a financial success, its social ideals had been compromised by Smith's excessive zeal and by the unpleasantness surrounding the final settlement.

Men of different temperament and more democratic inclination governed the Order at Joseph City. One suspects that to an observer from the outside, their community would have appeared less united and less orderly than that of Sunset. They departed quickly from the communal living arrangement Brigham Young had recommended. A desire to preserve a small place for individuality is evident in the motion of April 4, 1878, by John Bushman "that we have every Saturday afternoon for any purpose of our own that we wish to do." Unanimous consent was given to the motion.[12] Careful accounts were kept of hours worked, each individual receiving the amount of credit per hour. Frequently members raised questions and made suggestions as to the best system of reporting hours. In 1879 it was decided that tools be assigned to specific workers and marked with the name of the individual to whom they were assigned. This stewardship arrangement with regard to tools was extended in 1883 to embrace the whole communal endeavor when, after a protracted debate and discussion, the members voted to divide up the Order's assets and proceed under a stewardship arrangement.[13] From the beginning the community was small (seventy-six persons in 1878), apparently incapable of attracting new settlers to add to its numbers. Also from the beginning there was a discernible trend toward individualism. Most remarkable is the fact that apparent good will and harmony prevailed throughout the life of the Order. When in 1886 the Order was dissolved, division of the remaining assets was accomplished with none of the acrimony that crept into the Sunset settlement. Though not prosperous and not holding strictly to the form of the United Order recommended by Brigham Young, it would seem that the highest ideals of the Order came closer to realization in Joseph City than in most United Order communities.

The history of the Arizona experiments is a valuable study in the dynamics of social design. Two experimental communities, far from Mormon centers and building upon a vague, general set of guidelines, were forced to look inward, working out the details of the United Order as best fit their temperament and their interpretation of what was necessary and fundamental to the successful completion of their mission. They chose strikingly different forms for the social orders they sought to build. Bold leadership was asserted in the one instance, resulting in an autocratic and strictly communitarian Order. The other was democratic and seemed troubled from the beginning by outbreaks of individuality that compromised the communitarian ideal. Each had its successes and its failings. The Arizona experience makes it clear that there was place for variety and improvisation in the Order as the Saints sought to apply general principles to specific human situations.

What was left in 1886 of Orson Pratt's hope that the United Order would best succeed in new settlements? By that time the Arizona missionaries had lived in cooperative communities far longer than most Saints elsewhere. Pursuit of wealth had in some instances broken the spirit of love that was to prevail. A rigid adherence to the form of the Order caused some to lose sight of its greater objectives. Nevertheless, most remaining accounts of the Arizona Orders are warm and mellow. Only in Orderville did the Saints demonstrate a greater commitment to communal life. Like the Little Colorado settlements, Orderville had been founded as a United Order community. But its people were a select group, hardened by their experience on the Muddy and determined to show their erstwhile neighbors in nearby Mt. Carmel that they at least could make a success of the Order. Equally important, the pleasant, well-watered landscape of Long Valley provided a striking contrast to the barren desert of the Little Colorado. In Arizona the building and rebuilding of dams destroyed by the treacherous river was a constant necessity, diminishing community reserves of capital and of will. It is likely that those who became discouraged and left the communities were as disheartened by the hostility of the landscape as they were by the difficulties of attempting to live the United Order. Many of them settled in more attractive sites, such as Woodruff, Holbrook, and Snowflake, establishing United Orders and cooperative stores that endured for a time at the new locations. The Order helped the Arizona missionaries to eke out an existence in a hostile environment and to establish a permanent center of Mormon activity and influence in the Southwest. Dissenters and new settlers who opposed the Order began to expand into neighboring localities, providing more individualistic alternatives to the communal forms under which settlement had been launched. Pioneers of the Little Colorado moved south into the Salt River Valley, the Gila Valley, and finally into Mexico, the last more in flight than in conquest but nonetheless greatly extending the borders of the western Zion.

The Arizona settlements fell short of the most optimistic hopes of Brigham Young and his advisers. Far from being a model for the Utah Saints, they were admired but not emulated. Expansion into the south was more a guided drifting than a disciplined march of planned communitarian orders. Yet one suspects that Brigham Young and Orson Pratt, were they to see the continuing presence and influence of Mormons in the Southwest, would be pleased with the enduring accomplishment of the Arizona mission.

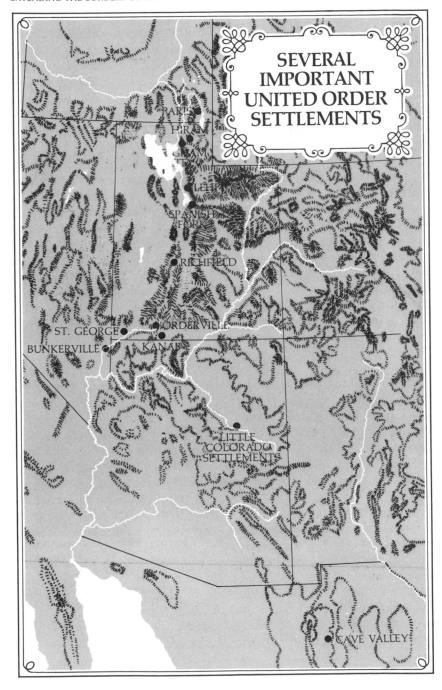

SEVERAL IMPORTANT UNITED ORDER SETTLEMENTS

Bunkerville, Nevada

Bunkerville, Nevada, like Orderville and the Little Colorado settlements, was founded specifically for the purpose of making the United Order a practical success. In 1862 Brigham Young had called Edward Bunker, native of Maine and member of the Mormon Battalion, to be bishop of the Santa Clara Ward, located in a small Utah valley a few miles northwest of St. George. When church leaders introduced the Order in 1874 Bunker accepted its principles unreservedly. "I put in all I possessed," he recalled, "the labor of myself and two boys and two teams," in addition to a "nice crop of grain growing, said by the appraisers to be the best in the field." Within a year, however, the enthusiasm of the ward members for the Order had waned. When a settlement of the Order's affairs was made, the bishop received back his teams and wagons but "not . . . a pound of hay, grain, flour or cotton with twenty in family. Be assured this was a dark day for myself and family." Though obviously hurt and disappointed by the experience, Bunker did not lay his ill-fortune to the principles of the Order. Concluding that "the Lord knows we obeyed that principle with a pure motive and he will not let us suffer," he supported his family until the next harvest by doing occasional hauling work.[14]

Edward Bunker did not elaborate on why the United Order had failed at Santa Clara or how he might hope to improve upon it. But he had "seen by the Spirit of the Lord, the necessity and blessings of the United Order." Compelled by this vision, he succeeded over the next two years in convincing a few close friends and family to help him organize a new community fully committed to its principles. Consulting with Brigham Young, he was advised that he could "go any place in the South, but . . . not to go North." Finally, in January 1877 eight families, including those of Bunker and his son Edward, Jr., met at Santa Clara and organized themselves into a company for "carrying out the United Order elsewhere." Moving southward, they finally settled on a stretch of land along the Virgin River previously known as Mesquite Flat, fifty miles southwest of St. George. Settlement commenced with an impressive ceremonial blessing of the land, reminiscent of ancient Israelitish ritual. Standing in the center of a circle of seventeen men, Edward Bunker "dedicated the land known as Bunkerville, to the Lord. During the prayer, . . . [he] let wheat fall through the fingers of one hand and soil from the land through the other."[15]

The Bunker party, like most who sought unoccupied land, was soon to find that there were reasons why others had not settled there. A tenacious overgrowth of mesquite had to be grubbed out, yard by yard, before crops could be planted. It was necessary to level the rolling landscape before successful irrigation could be undertaken. The Virgin River, as Bunkerville's illustrious daughter, Juanita Brooks, later observed, was cruelly misnamed. "Not only was it muddy," she wrote, "but it was full of deceit and treachery."[16] In August of the first year a flash flood partially washed out the newly completed dam, an event that occurred regularly in Bunkerville for three-quarters of a century. One is wearied by the mere reading in early diaries of the countless hours spent repairing dams and ditches. The drinking water came from the river, a foul-tasting, highly mineralized solution that earned for itself the nickname of "Virgin Bloat." Strong hot winds from the south periodically blasted the settlement, hampering work projects, damaging partially built homes, warping young trees, and enveloping every object, animate and inanimate, in a fine layer of desert dust.

Moreover, the town was remote—remote in a manner quite different from the Arizona settlements. It did not fill a strategic place as the end point of an advancing line of settlement. Parties traveling between southern California and Utah did occasionally stop by the village, but even these visits seem to have been infrequent. Bunkerville was a product of one man's desire to find a place where he and a few like-minded Saints could practice the United Order. The initiative came from Edward Bunker, his family, and friends, not Brigham Young or other church leaders. The settlement had no part to play in the imperial visions of the Mormon hierarchy. The Bunker party found a place that permitted them the solitude to shape their own society as they wished. A century later Bunkerville was still remote and isolated, barely larger than it was during the first years of settlement. The settlers, as it turned out, were not pioneers leading the way for others— they sought to build a secluded oasis.

Initially, the Bunkerville community was organized according to the family arrangement practiced in Orderville and the Arizona settlements. The group prepared meals in a common kitchen and ate in one large dining room. The women shared cooking, laundry, and dairy tasks, rotating the duties on a weekly basis. The men were organized into crews for clearing and leveling the land, building ditches and dams, and planting, tending, and harvesting crops. Residents of Bunkerville credit the organization achieved under the Order with having brought their colony successfully through the initial settling period. "The United Order . . . was a great blessing to the colony," one member wrote, "because there was order and system with Grandpa Edward Bunker at the head."[17] In terms of productivity, the early Order was a phenomenal success. The community reportedly harvested at the end of the first year nearly 400 bushels of wheat, 700 gallons of molasses, 9,000 pounds of cotton, and a large variety of garden vegetables. By the end of the second year a molasses mill, flour mill, and cotton gin were all in operation, powered by water from canals the community had built. When it is considered that this was accomplished by perhaps a dozen families, one begins to feel that there was real justification for the respect old residents of Bunkerville seemed to share for the usefulness of the United Order in the settling of a new community.

Beneath the placid surface, however, there were divisive undercurrents. The family-living arrangement was dropped at the end of the first year. Nothing is known of the precise nature of the discussions and debates that led to abandonment of common dining. Beginning their communal life as a family, Bunkerville residents, like the members of any close-knit dynasty, have preferred not to remember intramural squabbles. Some said the earlier system was dropped because the growing community simply became too large to efficiently maintain the common table. A hint of other problems is suggested in one recollection that "we young people liked it, but don't know so much about the older ones."[18] Apparently central management and cooperative labor on nonhousehold tasks continued until August 1879. At that time "some of the members having become dissatisfied . . . the stewardship plan was now more fully introduced and every man became responsible for his own labor."[19]

Something of the nature of the new stewardship system can be gleaned from the "By Laws of the Bunkerville United Order." Administrative officers consisted of a president and two counselors, following the traditional Mormon pattern of church organization. They were assisted by a secretary and a treasurer, all to be elected by members of the company. Membership was restricted to those willing to "put in themselves and all that they possess, that there may be no conflicting interest outside the order." Perhaps here is a clue to the nature of Edward Bunker's dissatisfaction with the Santa Clara Order. Certainly the Bunkerville group went beyond the instructions of Brigham Young, who permitted property to be retained outside the Order on the expectation that those who entered even half-heartedly would eventually be drawn in with all their possessions. Even in Orderville members were permitted (though not without grumbling from those who had given their all) to own property outside. It may be that some Santa Clara residents, unlike Bunker, had not consecrated everything, and had possessions outside the Order to fall back on when the Santa Clara accounts were closed. The 1879 stewardship system was carefully designed to eliminate such a possibility. Following the Law of Consecration as in Joseph Smith's 1831 revelation, all property of new members was to be appraised, entered upon company books as capital stock, and then "turned over to the members as in joint stewardship, or otherwise, as may be for the best interest of the company." The stewards were to bring "the increase of their stewardship" to the storehouse "and after making the property of the company good (which they have handled)" receive credit and draw supplies as needed. Company property was to be reappraised annually, with depreciation and appreciation of the stewardship properties to be balanced off and the balance entered into the company books. A committee of four or more was assigned to this task, and also to "say how much each member or stewardship shall have to use and to say whether they shall have all, or what portion, of the increase of said property placed to their credit." A fund was to be retained from any increase of general property owned by the company to balance off any company losses. Members could withdraw if they wished, and would be given back their capital stock and a part of the profits proportionate to the amount of their labors while in the organization. However, they could not claim real estate or improvements thereon and would have to be content with payment in "stock and produce in prices as specified by the appraisers." The by-laws ended with a covenant to "individually and unitedly . . . agree to sustain and abide by the above rules in the spirit and meaning thereof. Praying for the assistance of our Father in Heaven to help us so to do."[20]

So far as is known, this was the first time the Bunkerville settlers had put the terms of their United Order into a formal document. The enterprise was, even in the altered stewardship form, a highly idealistic system. The "increase of their stewardship," presumably grain, cane, vegetables, eggs, or livestock—whatever was produced—was brought into the storehouse. This entitled the stewards to draw supplies "according to their necessities." So long as cooperative labor had prevailed, the incidences of mismanagement and sloth were kept to a minimum or concealed within the collective achievement of each labor crew. But under the stewardship system individual vices of the less industrious and the less competent were given opportunity to emerge. When accounts began to be kept of the production and consumption of each family, it became glaringly obvious to the company that some were not carrying their weight. As recorded in the records of the St. George Stake with which Bunkerville was affiliated,

some stewardships through their economy and industry were gathering and laying up in abundance, while others, through carelessness and bad management, were wasting the means of the Company, each year being increasing in debt. This was very unsatisfactory to those whose ambition was to accumulate, at least, the necessaries of life.[21]

While the harvests of the 1880 season were being gathered, the issue came to a head. Bishop Bunker was becoming increasingly dissatisfied with the state of company affairs. On September 26, Myron Abbott noted in his diary that at a council meeting the previous night "there was a bad spirit manifested by the Bishop. He felt like cursing everybody but his own family. At meeting today he felt the same though gave some good instruction on the Word of Wisdom." Two days later the bishop and S. O. Crosby privately proposed to Abbott that a change in the rules of the Order be made. Abbott opposed the suggested changes, but on October 2 the bishop apparently raised the question in a council meeting, causing the group "much confusion and a division of opinion," without leading to any definite conclusions. Two days later the entire company was assembled to consider the proposed amendments. "We had a company meeting," Abbott wrote in his diary that day, "and the Bishop introduced a rule that split the company."[22] The new rule proposed by the bishop was undoubtedly that which was described in the St. George Stake Historical Record. According to that account, at a general meeting of the company in October it was voted that each steward would have the right to draw only 80 percent of the proceeds of his labor. The remaining 20 percent was to be retained in the treasury "as a fund to keep the capital stock good." In other words, each family's consumption was to be reduced to a level below its production, whereas earlier it could apparently draw up to and even beyond that amount. Dissent against so drastic an effort to prevent the less productive from draining away company assets destroyed the Order. In the carefully neutral phraseology of the St. George Stake clerk, the new rules "proved unacceptable to some and they gave notice of withdrawal. This caused a settlement to be made of the whole business. Dissatisfaction increased, and it was decided 'to disorganize the Bunkerville United Order. The company paid off all the Capital Stock and 17 percent of the labor performed.' "[23] Each family or member received back the possessions they had brought to the Order three and one-half years earlier and a payment of goods and land equivalent to 17 percent of the book value of the labor they had performed during the period. By United Order standards this was not a bad settlement.

The process of settling accounts was painful and protracted. A committee appointed to settle the company affairs met frequently through the fall of 1880 and into the summer of 1881 before final settlement was made. Oblique passages in the diary of Myron Abbott suggest the nature of some of the difficulties that arose. In November 1880, Abbott "and Edward Bunker, Jr., S. O. Crosby, Edward Leavitt had a quarel. It being Sunday morning I would not go to meeting nor Sunday School." The next day he wrote that "we commenced our appraising," indicating that disagreement over apportionment of property, especially land, was the cause of the recent dispute. The measurement of land continued through the winter. In February 1881 a surveyor was commissioned to set property bounds. On February 2, 1881, Abbott wrote, "The Surveyors sectionised our land. . . . At night Dudley Leavitt and I went to E. Bunkers and finished our settlement." In April a meeting was held at the home of Lemuel Leavitt. "S.A. Sprague and Samuel Crosby and E. Bunker, Jr. had some words tonight. We will look over the accounts and finish our settlement." On April 6: "The Committy are still trying to settle."[24]

Except for the hints in these few brief passages, all evidence of issues and faction in the problems that plagued the Bunkerville

United Order at its end has been discreetly withheld from the historical record. Apparently all parties regretted whatever feelings were aroused during the settlement, and in the interest of village harmony the dispute was not mentioned again. The historian who would like to know more precisely what troubled the Bunkerville United Order and what comprised the substance of its successes and failures regrets that the circumspection of Bunkervillians has barred him forever from detailed insights into the demise of a social experiment that had been the sole reason for the community's existence. One wonders why the Bunkerville settlers, with their *raison d'etre* at an end, bothered to stay and fight the treacherous Virgin River for a life so impecunious and remote from urban comforts. It could be that from the perspective of the villagers their purposes in keeping mute about the unhappy end of the Order are more justifiable than those of the scholar who would like to gain greater understanding of practical experiments in social and economic reform by peering into their lives. The Order had built a community that possessed a sure instinct for self-preservation. Perhaps the settlers of Bunkerville rightly chose to sacrifice their United Order and forget the troubles associated with it so the community would be assured of survival.

Some, however, held stubbornly to the dream of "unity and order." On July 10, 1881, a meeting was called at the mill to consider reinstituting the Order. Several in attendance were willing to join, including Abbott, Dudley Leavitt, and Thomas Leavitt. Thomas Leavitt later backed out, and the attempt came to nothing. The "Rules of the United Order by Myron Abbott," which appear at the end of the first volume of his diary, were probably written for that occasion. They bespeak an earnest desire to go back to the Bunkerville of 1877—to revoke all the subsequent changes in the Order, which Abbott apparently felt had led to its demise:

Rule 1: We will have a president and two vise-presidents and will work under superintendants and we will have a business agent.

Rule 2: All business of importance shall be done by the coman consent of the president and the agent and the superintendants.

Rule 3: As fast as posible we will establish the big tabel among us So that all may share Equal. All of our grain shall be stact in one yard. All our hay shall be stack in one yard. All our teams shall be fed by one man. All our miling shall be done by one man—the treasurer or some one that may be apointed.

Rule 4: Any man failing to do his duty shall be delt with and if he will not do his duty he shall be expelled from the company.[25]

The document is an eloquent and poignant testament of Bunkerville's United Order.

The Cave Valley Commonwealth: Chihuahua, Mexico

The southernmost point of Mormon colonization in the American West provided the setting for the last known church-authorized attempt to realize the United Order. This occurred at Cave Valley, a branch of the Pacheco Ward, in what later became the Juarez Stake, Mexico. The majority of the little colony had lived in the United Order at Orderville, and it occurred to apostle George Teasdale, who was presiding over the Mexican colonies at the time, to suggest that a community be organized after the pattern of the earlier experiments. The colonists readily accepted the suggestion, and following a meeting on January 9, 1893, at which the plan was discussed, they adopted the following articles of agreement, comprising, almost, a summary of the whole United Order experience.

We the undersigned covenant to unite our temporal interests for the common benefit.

We will be known as the Cave Valley Commonwealth. Our organization can only be dissolved by the counsel of the Presidency of this Mexican Mission of the Church of Jesus Christ of Latter-day Saints and a three-fourths majority vote of the organization.

We will adopt for our guidance the rules known as Rules that should be observed by members of the United Order.

This shall be a stewardship system. Its officers shall be a president, two counselors, a secretary, and a treasurer and a board of directors.

Property shall be appraised and credited to those contributing the same as capital stock, which capital stock shall not be added to by dividend, nor diminished by assessment during the time of our continuing in an organized capacity.

Members desiring to withdraw shall not have power to compel the company to deliver up their capital stock till the end of three years, but the company may do so if the board so decides, which decision must be presented and sustained by three-fourths vote of the company.

There shall be no shares of capital stock, but each shall receive credit in dollars and cents for the amount turned in.

We will have a scrip or circulating medium, good only to members of our commonwealth, and MEMBERS WILL BE PAID IN THIS SCRIP PRO RATA FOR THEIR SUPPORT.

Membership in the Church and commonwealth constitutes eligibility to vote for the election of officers, which voting shall be done by uplifted hands. . . .

Members shall be received by the common consent and vote of the commonwealth and membership withdrawn in the same way.

Members shall not receive any advantage one above another by the system of credits.[26]

The articles of agreement suggest that economic equality was a principal object of the commonwealth. Those who subscribed to the agreement were for the most part members of four families, of whom John R. Young's father-in-law, William M. Black, Christopher B. Heaton, Marriner A. Porter, and William Carroll were the heads. The various families had their own homes, but put all their capital into a common fund and worked together on a basis of complete equality. No scrip was ever issued. The commonwealth dissolved and redistributed its capital following the death of Christopher B. Heaton in November 1895.[27]

CHAPTER 14

Zion's Central Board of Trade
and the decline
of the United Order

ITHIN FIVE YEARS of the death of Brigham Young, the church had changed significantly its position in regard to the United Order and other forms of cooperative enterprise. Except for the institution of Zion's Board of Trade in 1879, the church increasingly gave its sanction to economic individualism restrained only by a proper respect for the rights and the welfare of others. Business practices opposed by the church president in the early 1860s were not only tolerated but approved by his successors two decades later, evidence of changes in circumstances as well as differences of opinion. Conceivably, Brigham Young himself, had he lived a few years longer, would have been compelled to adopt the policy later approved by his successor in office. Nevertheless, it was common knowledge that John Taylor and other leaders did not agree in some respects with Brigham Young's economic program. The emergence of new opinions and circumstances after his death forms an important epilogue to the United Order experience.

President Young had committed the church first to a program of cooperative merchandising and cooperative industry and then to the United Order, a system into which he expected the co-ops to be absorbed. The major difference between the two systems was succinctly stated by George Q. Cannon. Cooperation, as organized by the church, was a union of capital; the United Order was a union of capital and labor. A wholehearted supporter of the cooperative program, John Taylor had been one of those to recommend the Hooper plan for wholesale merchandising in 1860, a plan that Brigham Young vetoed then but accepted later as the fundamental principle in the establishment of ZCMI. But John Taylor was never enthusiastic about the United Order. As he was not present at St. George when President Young inaugurated the movement, he received first notice of the president's intentions in a communication dispatched to the brethren in Salt Lake City. His reactions were not entirely favorable:

We like freedom, God has put it in our bosoms; and as I said to President George A. [Smith], the other day, in talking about this matter, in organizing the Order of Enoch, as it may be called, we want on the one hand the most perfect union; and on the other hand the most extended personal liberty that it is possible for men to enjoy consonant with carrying out the principles of unity. Not the liberty to take from people that which belongs to them; not the liberty to infringe upon public interests or the public benefit, but personal liberty so far as we can enjoy it.[1]

With others of his brethren Taylor journeyed to Nephi to meet President Young's party and participate in the public discussions of the new Order before the Saints of the region. His misgivings about the practicability of the Order are apparent in his remarks at that time.

We have heard a good deal since we have assembled, in relation to what is called the Order of Enoch, the New Order, the United Order, or whatever name we may give to it. It is new and then it is old, for it is everlasting as I understand it. I am sometimes asked—"Do you understand it?" Yes, I do, no, I do not, yes, I do, no, I don't, and both are true; we know that such an order must be introduced, but are not informed in relation to the details, and I guess it is about the same with most of you. . . . When President Young communicated with us a little before starting from the south, about this new order, I really did not know what shape it would assume or how it would be introduced, but it has got to come; and then, on the other hand, I do not know that we need have very much anxiety in relation to the matter, for if it be of God, it must be right, and its introduction is only a question of time. . . . The greatest embarrassment that we have to contend with at the present time is not in knowing what to do, but knowing how to do it.[2]

Despite reservations, however, John Taylor was prompt to assert his readiness to support the church president's plan.

But I will tell you how I have always felt, both in Joseph's day and since then, whenever the Lord has wrought upon the man who stands at the head of his people to introduce anything for the welfare of his kingdom, it is time to look out, and to carry out the counsels that are given; and yesterday, after I arrived here, and had seen President Young and conversed with him, and then heard him and others speak on these principles, I said to him, "The old fiddle is in tune, the sacred fire is glowing and burning;" and I think so still. The old fiddle is in tune, the right feeling, spirit and influence are operating, and we all feel them.[3]

The difficulties impeding the progress of cooperation and the United Order became more and more apparent as time passed. In Salt Lake City, where President Taylor resided, the Order had been thwarted at the outset. Men of property were unwilling to relinquish their control, and finally the decision was reached that each should be steward over his own means. Thus far in accord with Joseph Smith's plan, the Salt Lake City program lacked the necessary redistribution of property under the direction of the bishops. Speaking for the plan in the fall of 1875, John Taylor said the avails of the system after families were supplied would be subject to the will of the board of directors. Each ward had been organized early in 1874, but only one Salt Lake City ward filed articles of incorporation. Otherwise, little record of activity has been found, and it is a safe conclusion that by the fall of 1877, when John Taylor succeeded Brigham Young, the United Order was still an unrealized hope in Salt Lake City, except for projects of limited scope in four of the twenty city wards.

Orders of the St. George-Richfield type, where homes and garden lots were held as family stewardships while farming, the production of livestock, and handicrafts were managed by a central board, were definitely on the wane. Many had suspended at the end of the first year and most at the end of the second. In 1877 the St. George United Order disincorporated, and it was actively being liquidated when John Taylor became head of the church. Immediately prior to his death President Young had approved the withdrawal of the capital of the Joseph A. Young estate from the Richfield United Order, making the latter's continuance impossible.

The family type of United Order maintained considerable vigor in some localities. Still in its ascendancy, the Orderville society displayed little evidence of the internal strains that would later lead to its demise. True, apostle Erastus Snow had recently questioned in public the wisdom of the communal practices at Orderville, but with little immediate effect on the attitude of the members. Other family associations on the Orderville pattern were scarcely out of the bud, among them the Bunkerville Order and those in the Arizona settlements. John Taylor did not approve of the "big family" orders, as they greatly restricted the individual freedom that he so strongly advocated.

Although showing every outward appearance of success, the industrial and mercantile cooperative system at Brigham City was causing concern to its president and principal stockholder. In an undated letter to Brigham Young, allegedly written a few months before the president's death, Lorenzo Snow unburdened himself of the causes of his anxiety.

In working up to the principles we call the United Order we have shouldered very serious responsibilities. Over one thousand persons, little and big are depending entirely upon the Institution for all their supplies, for their food, their clothing, and all their comforts and conveniences. . . .

This . . . is a responsibility that I should never dared to have assumed. In fact I never anticipated such a result, though I have felt it gradually approaching, but yet could not see how to escape and be justified.[4]

Similar in its essentials to ZCMI, yet broader in its scope, the Brigham City cooperative system antedated the Order and acquired the name by common consent without changing its form or its corporate title.

In general, the cooperative institutions were holding their own in 1877. Some of the retail co-ops had disappeared in the hard times of 1873-77; others, though they retained original names, were slowly assuming a change of character from community undertakings to closed corporations with stock held by fewer and fewer stockholders. By eliminating dividends from 1874 to 1877, ZCMI had emerged from the depression in a strong financial position so that it was able to pay an obligation of $100,000 to the estate of Brigham Young and declare a dividend in 1878.

Despite the growth of the cooperative system, there was much to disappoint church leaders. In the first place, gentile merchants still flourished; they had not succumbed as a result of the withdrawal of Mormon trade. Of the twenty-three firms that subscribed to the offer to withdraw from the territory in 1866 if Mormons would buy them out, several were still in business ten years later, advertising in the *Deseret News* for Mormon patronage. The co-ops were meeting competition not only from non-Mormon merchants, but also from enterprising church members who were entering into trade on their own account. In 1875 the retail departments of the ZCMI were closed and the trade taken over by William Jennings, David Day, and others. Privately owned stores, sometimes using the term co-op in the title, sprang up to compete for the trade of the local cooperative associations. Here and there measures were taken to suppress these institutions, as at Brigham City in 1880, when those undertaking to open stores in competition with the co-op were threatened with excommunication.

In the midst of such difficulties regarding cooperation and the United Order, John Taylor succeeded to the presidency of the church. Soon afterward he made a public statement that implied that the United Order under Brigham Young had been but one aspect of a general church program to unite the people, and not vital to the broader objective.

I wish to make a few remarks in relation to what we term the United Order. We are united today with God and with the Holy Priesthood that existed before us. . . . They in their different spheres and callings are operating with us and we with them and the whole thing is a grand, cooperative system, and everything we do here should be with the view of uniting our earthly interests that we may be one in things temporal and one in things spiritual, one on the earth and one with those in the heavens, helping with our united efforts to roll on the Kingdom of God according to his purposes and not according to our erratic notions.[5]

In agreement with President Taylor, another church leader who spoke at the April conference in 1878 pronounced a benediction upon the United Order. Notwithstanding the many errors and failures, he explained, much had been accomplished in making the Saints familiar with the cooperative principle, so that whenever a feasible plan could be devised the people would be ready to carry it out. The speaker informed his audience that leaders from all over the territory had been brought together to confer with church leaders on cooperative methods, and that suggestions had been formulated into a plan for a board of trade made up of the best businessmen to maintain fair-trade practices and promote manufactures.[6]

As time passed it became more and more apparent that although John Taylor was unwilling to lend the weight of his authority to sustain the orders based on "visionary and impractical schemes," he was heartily in favor of cooperation. The United Order, he taught, was the ultimate goal; cooperation was the road by which it might be approached.

In many places cooperation and the United Order have been started under various forms. In some they have succeeded very well and in other places people have voted foolishly and covetously, seeking their own personal, individual interests under the pretense of serving God and carrying out his designs. Others have been visionary and have undertaken things which were impracticable while others have not acted in good faith at all. There has been every kind of feeling among us as a people that is possible to exist anywhere, and I have thought sometimes in regard to our cooperative institutions that some of those who are engaged in them and sustained by them are as much opposed to cooperation and the United Order as any other class of people we have.[7]

In the address from which the above is quoted, President Taylor fully defined his own position. He indicated that the development of cooperative methods and the United Order was a definite responsibility of the Latter-day Saints and that efforts to make cooperation effective were not to be abandoned because of apparent difficulties. There had been abuses; men had in practice distorted the principles and controlled institutions for their own selfish ends. Joseph Smith, in attempting to apply the same principles, had been thwarted by the "great covetousness, selfishness, and wickedness of the people." Conditions had changed very little. Individual enterprises contrary to the cooperative principle were springing up in every part of the territory. Many of these were laudable because they increased employment, but all unions and partnerships of Latter-day Saints in any line of manufacture should be formed with the understanding that when the proper time came they could be merged into cooperation or the United Order.

On another occasion President Taylor praised the accomplishments of Lorenzo Snow at Brigham City, but he emphasized the point that the organization there was not the United Order. Nevertheless, he commended the plan as a pattern for Saints in other communities to follow.

We have had enough talk about these things; the only thing left is to contrive in all our various settlements, to introduce such things, gradually and according to circumstances, as will subserve the interests of the people and make them self-sustaining. And then let the people throughout the Territory do the same thing, and we shall be progressing in the march of improvement, and get, by and by, to what is called the United Order. But I will tell you one thing you can never do—unless you can get the United Order in the hearts of the people, you can never plant it anywhere else; articles and constitutions amount to very little; we must have this law of God written in our hearts.[8]

John Taylor retained his faith in cooperation, partly because he was reluctant to permit the church to lose the initiative in shaping the regional economy. In an attempt to maintain church influence in temporal affairs and to salvage some of the goals of the United Order, he organized Zion's Central Board of Trade in 1878. This institution lasted a full five years and achieved significant results in promoting the economic welfare of Mormon communities throughout the Great Basin.

As with each of the programs instituted by church leaders for the attainment of economic unity, welfare, and independence, Zion's Board of Trade, and the philosophy it represented, demonstrates the flexibility of Mormon thinking in meeting new economic problems on a group level. Although at times this flexibility did not produce successful and enduring institutions, it illustrates the social inventiveness of early Mormon leaders. Whereas the building of the Kingdom has been an absolute ideal in Mormon philosophy, the means adopted by the church to establish it have been pragmatic. The refusal of early church leaders to insist upon the retention of static programs, or rather, the readiness to abandon programs when they proved unworkable in practice, is evidence that, while idealists in theory, these leaders were instrumentalists in administration. If they attempted to establish "ideal" economic orders, they were willing to discontinue them when such programs threatened to impede progress.

The United Orders established by Brigham Young in 1874 differed from community to community, but common to all was the pooling of resources of members in an attempt to achieve local self-sufficiency and economic independence. While not abandoning the goal of instituting the Law of Consecration and Stewardship, John Taylor did not identify the ideal economic system of Mormon thought with the particular Orders that had been established by his predecessor. Zion's Board of Trade, he felt, was a means of assuring practical and effective group cooperation while encouraging the continued growth of an expanding regional economy. It represented a type of mild economic planning and social experimentation consistent with prevailing capitalistic tendencies.

President Taylor decided to establish Zion's Central Board of Trade after a visit to Cache Valley in the summer of 1878. His first public mention of the new scheme was on September 5, 1878, in a brief talk to Mormon bishops in the Salt Lake City area. He "spoke of the unanimity prevailing in Cache Valley in the sale of products, no middlemen being employed, but the highest prices being obtained for the producers." "It was high time," he said, "for the Saints to fall into line. Every revelation given Joseph Smith would have to be carried out. . . . We must turn round as a people and become united, both in temporal and spiritual things. Many things had been started here in the name of God in the way of cooperation, but the covetousness of men had stepped in and destroyed the confidence of the people. If we would put away our selfishness and blend together our interests, God would pour out his blessings on Israel and make us the richest people on the face of the earth."[9]

The Cache Valley plan of cooperation referred to by President Taylor had begun in March 1872. At that time the presidents and managers of the cooperative stores in Cache Valley met to work out a way of improving the marketing facilities in the valley. Middlemen, usually non-Mormons, had been buying up all available marketable products and hauling them to railway centers, where they were sold to commission merchants who shipped them to California, Nevada, Montana, and other consuming areas. This was especially true of eggs, butter, and grain, bought at low prices in Cache Valley and sold at elevated prices in mining camps. The middlemen were said to be "waxing rich." It is probable that local cooperatives felt they could perform this marketing function themselves and save "to the people" profits that were going to outside middlemen. The meeting of cooperative officials resulted in agreements to: (1) offer uniform prices for the farm products brought to them for marketing; (2) use their influence in improving the quality of products brought to their particular stores; (3) find markets for the exportable products of the valley; (4) form an organization, the Board of Trade, for carrying out the above aims.[10]

The Cache Valley Board of Trade had functioned briefly prior to the organization of the Cache Valley United Order in 1874, and it was revived in March 1876. Moses Thatcher was a prime mover in the later organization. He was president of the Cache Valley Stake and also manager of the Cache Valley Cooperative in Logan, a branch of ZCMI. The purpose of the Cache Valley Board of Trade, he said, was to "regulate the commerce of producers and consumers and introduce a more healthy and stable condition of supply and demand."[11] Non-Mormons must have viewed the movement as an unconscionable attempt to fix prices—as means of tightening the monopoly powers of the church-sponsored cooperatives. But the system apparently improved incomes of

John Taylor, Brigham Young's successor as leader of the Mormons,
moved his people into less communal forms of economic organization.
(Church Archives)

producing farmers and soon spread to other settlements. In June 1878 the Saints in Bear Lake Valley organized a board of trade to engage in buying and selling produce.[12]

President Taylor, as previously indicated, foresaw immense possibilities in this type of organization as a form of collective control and cooperative endeavor. A churchwide board of trade would provide cooperation on a greater scale than was provided by ZCMI and its branches, and the many local cooperative organizations. In addition, regional or churchwide integration and direction of economic activities could be more effectively accomplished. The scheme would diminish growing criticism directed against ZCMI, local cooperatives, and local United Orders, and replace the failing United Orders with a less communal, more regional, form of collective control.

The church was the obvious institution to perform the organizational tasks required in establishing such a system. The contemplated board of trade could meet in connection with the general conference of Saints in April and October of each year. President Taylor could preside at meetings of the board of trade as well as at the religious conferences, and thus an identity of interests would be maintained. The board of trade could solve short-run problems such as those involved in cooperative marketing, cooperative buying, development of manufacturing industries, arbitration, and the regulation of trade in the interests of the group as a whole. It would also, in its long-run aspect, prepare the way for a more completely cooperative society such as that contemplated in the Order of Enoch.

Prior to the general conference of the church held in October 1878, President Taylor talked the matter over with his counselors, the executives of ZCMI, and other leading Mormon businessmen. According to his counselor, George Q. Cannon, the organization that President Taylor envisioned would have rather broad functions. The church needed to have "a permanent organization of her best businessmen, and the most practical men from all parts of [Utah] Territory, acting in the capacity of a board of trade, whose duty [would] be to look after . . . manufacturing, mercantile and other interests; and should there at any time be anything wrong in [their] systems of doing business, tending in the least to prevent perfect union, . . . the necessary measures [must] be devised to remedy these things and bring about a concert of action upon all hands."[13]

President Taylor appointed a committee—variously called an "Investigating Committee," a "Committee on the Manufacturing and Mercantile Interests of the Territory," and a "Committee on Cooperation, Home Manufactures, and Industries"—with H. S. Eldredge, manager of ZCMI, as chairman. According to the church president, the committee was "organized for the purpose of introducing measures to promote the interests of that institution [ZCMI] as well as the general interests of the people throughout the Territory." This committee was to form the basis upon which a permanent committee or board of trade would be organized, "according to the order of this Church and Kingdom of God."[14]

Under President Taylor's instructions, this churchwide board of trade was to maintain close relations with ZCMI. After ZCMI's close call with bankruptcy in 1873, Brigham Young had tended to emphasize financial soundness in its operation, but John Taylor, as the new ZCMI president, took the attitude that it had broader social functions to fulfill. "We are striving," he said in the October 1878 church conference,

to adjust matters relative to our cooperative institutions, and to place them on a basis more in consonance with the revelations given to us on that subject. Zion's Mercantile Institution has been established as a stepping stone to the introduction of the United Order, and it is proper that in all of our moves of a temporal nature we should have this great object in view. The Institution is emphatically called Zion's Cooperative Mercantile Institution, and ought to operate, as the name indicates, in the interests of Zion; and all the various Stakes, being what are termed "Stakes of Zion," ought to do their business through that institution, and sustain it in all of their mercantile operations; on the other hand, that institution should act in behalf of, and in the interest of all the people in the several Stakes, and while it is being sustained and helped by all, ought to shield, protect and help all, that a mutual reciprocity of feeling and action may exist as between the people and that institution.[15]

President Taylor thought that the merchandising cooperatives in 1869 and afterward were only a preliminary step, and that it was now necessary to establish industrial cooperation on a wide scale. The cooperative mercantile movement had been essential, to be sure. The editor of the *Deseret News* wrote:

It has been the means, as a distributor of imported goods, of furnishing merchandise at remarkably low prices, thus bringing them within the reach of the masses; it has been a regulator of trade; it has prevented "corners" in any article in general demand; it has kept large supplies at a convenient point for dealers in the various parts of the Territory, by which the people could obtain comforts at all seasons of the year without difficulty; it has also been a repository for many articles of home manufacture, by which they have been brought to the attention and patronage of the public. . . . It is eminently a commercial success. But no matter how cheaply and easily we can obtain imports by means of Z.C.M.I., it is conceded that our true policy is to make, as far as possible, at least what we need for home consumption, with an eye to future exports of those articles which we can sell abroad at a profit. To determine what can be produced and manufactured to the best advantage, on sound business principles, in this Territory, and to devise measures by which those articles can be produced for the benefit of the community and the advantage of all engaged in the enterprises, . . . are the purposes which will be served by the organization of Zion's Board of Trade.[16]

It was now necessary to work out the details of the "new cooperation" under a churchwide board of trade. The investigating comittee appointed by President Taylor was divided into five subcommittees, which made suggestions on dry goods, groceries, produce, wool, and wagons, as well as on the proper objectives of cooperation as a whole. The reports of these subcommittees were read to the semiannual conference of the church on October 8, 1878, by President Cannon. These reports are interesting documents because they reflect the thinking of the business leadership of the church. They also carried the approval of the First Presidency. Unfortunately, they are too lengthy for reproduction here. Among the observations and recommendations contained in these reports, however, are the following:

1. During the preceding year (i.e., 1877-1878) Z.C.M.I. purchased, for sale, over $125,000 worth of "home-made" articles. This encouragement to home industry should be continued. Preference should be given home manufactures. The various branches of home manufacturing should work out a plan by which each would specialize in its outstanding product, thus improving the over-all quality and efficiency of Utah production. (This was done with the woolen industry.)

2. Z.C.M.I. was not only in the position of being able to import products from the States under the best possible circumstances but was also able to export the market "valley" produce to the best advantage of Utah farmers and dealers. Z.C.M.I. should operate on a "near-cost" basis to avoid profiteering on its patrons, on both buying and selling ends, as "outside" middlemen had done in the past.

3. The Church's cooperative system—that is, Z.C.M.I. as the Parent, with branches strategically located, and with local cooperative stores as patrons—could unite the Mormon people temporally if all cooperative institutions dealt fairly with the people and demonstrated their economic soundness.

4. The best method of assuring enlightened trade practices, as well as cooperation between local producers and dealers and the central agency (Z.C.M.I.), would be the establishment of a local Board of Trade in each Stake.

After these reports were read to the assembled Saints, they "unanimously sustained" the plans of the First Presidency in "adjusting matters relative to [the] temporal interests" of the Mormon people. President Taylor then followed with a sermon on temporal unity. He said, " . . . if mistakes and blunders had been made in trying to establish the United Order, that should not prevent us from carrying out the revelation of God, to be united together in our temporal and spiritual affairs; for unless 'we were one,' we were not the Lord's. . . . All who felt to endorse and carry out *the principles of union,* as dictated by the Presidency and the Twelve would say amen." A "hearty and universal response" was given.[17] In short, attempts to revive the United Orders were to be abandoned, but control over economic life by the First Presidency to achieve "temporal unity" was not to be relaxed. The objectives were the same, but the means of achieving those objectives would be altered.

In spelling out the meaning of "the principles of union," President Taylor stated that he would begin with Zion's Board of Trade, which was to protect both the people and the parent institution. Stake organizations would then be set up, with a representative—or representatives—from each stake on the general or central board.

And when we get things into a proper fix we will pull with a long pull and a strong pull and a pull all together. We will strive to be one; . . . we will begin with this, and then cooperate in all the different Stakes, not only in . . . merchandising, but in . . . manufacturing affairs and in . . . producing affairs; and in everything it will be the duty of this general Board of Trade to regulate the interests of the whole community, honestly and faithfully, at least we will do it according to the best ability we have; and if there should be any mistakes arise, we will try to correct them; if they are on the part of the people, we will talk to them about it, if on the part of the institution, we will talk to its management about it.

And we will keep working and operating until we succeed in introducing and establishing these things that God has desired, and until Zion shall be a united people and the glory of all the earth.[18]

The day following these conference transactions (October 9, 1878) a meeting was held in Salt Lake City to effect a preliminary organization of Zion's Board of Trade. A further meeting of the group was held ten days later at which the organization was completed. John Taylor was elected president, William Jennings and Edward Hunter, vice-presidents, and T. G. Webber, secretary and treasurer. A board of directors was chosen, plans were made to establish stake organizations, and a committee was appointed to draft articles of association.[19]

The drive to organize stake boards of trade was carried out under the leadership of Moses Thatcher, who was called on a special mission for this purpose. He organized associations in Utah, Juab, Sanpete, and Sevier counties and laid the groundwork for similar organizations in other stakes. Soon, practically every stake in Zion was organized. President Taylor aided in this drive by writing to some, if not all, of the stake presidents. For example, he wrote to apostle Erastus Snow at St. George under date of April 29, 1879, in relation "to organizing Stake Boards of Trade and encouraging cooperation among the people, preparatory to more fully entering into the United Order."[20] This letter indicates the lofty ideals used in advocating support of the board of trade movement. It also demonstrated that President Taylor clearly distinguished, in his own mind, the United Order movement, which was a permanent part of the church heritage, from the particular United Order organizations that had been established from 1874 to 1879.

The stake board of trade organizations were patterned after the Cache Valley board. Although we cannot be entirely sure that all of the local leaders accepted his ideas, Moses Thatcher was the most vocal of the advocates of the "new cooperation," and it is to him that we must look for an interpretation of the function of the stake boards.[21] A lengthy letter published by him in the *Deseret News* and read at various stake conferences listed the following objectives of the stake boards:

1. To seek remunerative markets for the produce of the brethren and help to bring to them as cheaply as possible what they have to buy.

2. To aid in organizing and sustaining such home industries as will tend to the independence and self-sustenance of the people.

3. To attempt to prevent the Saints from introducing and sustaining among themselves hurtful competition.

4. To recognize, and, as far as possible, become familiar with the law of supply and demand, and aid the central and local boards of trade in keeping the supply offered not greatly in excess of the demand made.

5. To bring home producer and manufacturer into close business relations with the consumer, preventing intermediate parties from exacting margins for transacting business which, with a little forethought and care, the people, through the Board of Trade, can do as well for themselves.

6. To help the producer fix living prices on the fruits of his own toil.

7. To prevent friends from overstocking the market, and thereby selling two loaves for less than one costs them.

8. Where the supply is greater than the demand, they will use all honorable means to increase the latter, rather than decrease the former.

9. The watchword will be "organization," having in view always that "Union is strength, division weakness."

If a local board of trade had fully exercised the function Thatcher recommended, it would have resembled a combination of chamber of commerce, price control board, produce broker, industrial development corporation, and trade practice conference. But it is clear that the list was to serve primarily as an outline of excesses of free competitive enterprise that might be avoided or curbed by the stake boards of trade.[22]

Of greater importance to the region was the Central Board of Trade. This board was formally approved and organized in connection with the general conference April 8, 1879, at which time the officers were sustained and the articles of association approved. The officially declared purposes of Zion's Central Board of Trade are found in the Preamble to its Articles of Association:

1. To maintain a Commercial Exchange.

2. To promote uniformity in the customs and usages of producers, manufacturers and merchants.

3. To inculcate principles of justice and equity in trade.

4. To facilitate the speedy adjustment of business disputes.

5. To arrange for transportation.

6. To seek renumerative markets for home products.

7. To foster capital and protect labor, uniting them as friends rather than dividing them as enemies.

8. To encourage manufacturing.

9. To aid in placing imported goods in the hands of the consumers as cheaply as possible.

10. To acquire and to disseminate valuable agricultural, manufacturing, commercial and economic information.

11. Generally, to secure to its members the benefits of cooperation in the furtherance of their legitimate pursuits, and to unite and harmonize the business relations of the Stake Boards of Trade.

Thus was launched what the historian Tullidge heralds as "the greatest industrial event that has occurred in the settling and growth of [Utah] Territory."[23] The details of the administrative organization of Zion's Central Board of Trade do not concern us here. The board was composed of fifty members chosen from the various stakes, the number from each stake varying from one to seventeen depending upon the stake population. The over-all organizational pattern conformed rather closely to the church model. While a part of its leadership consisted of General Authorities of the sponsoring church, Zion's Board of Trade had one significant innovation: it made extensive use of Mormon businessmen and specialists in both making and carrying out its policies. It provided businesslike direction to the initiation and operation of programs aimed at developing the region. In contrast with the 1874 United Orders, in which local planning was done by ward leaders, often with little business experience or expertise, the scope of planning by Zion's Board of Trade was regional, or at least as regional as Mormon interests extended. The success of many board of trade activities probably can be attributed to the energy and sound direction of Mormon business leaders.

Labor, as such, was given no representation on Zion's Board of Trade. This might imply that the organization was potentially anti-labor in its structure and function. In fact, however, there were no important unions in Utah during the 1879-1884 period except miners' unions. Few Mormons were miners and consequently few Mormons belonged to unions. Moreover, Utah was not yet sufficiently industrialized to have an industrial laboring class. Almost every Mormon was a property owner or a potential property owner. His property included, in most cases, a home and a city lot on which he could raise much of his food. If he happened to be a clerk for a business establishment, or a mechanic or artisan, he was still tied to the land in economic interest as well as in philosophy. He did not depend upon his wages for all his living. He did not regard himself as being in the working class.

Board of trade representation for laborers would have been superfluous: each industry and region was already represented.

Nor should it be inferred that the establishment of boards of trade as regulating devices was something entirely novel. Boards of trade had been organized in preceding decades at Chicago, Kansas City, Omaha, New Orleans, and other trading centers. According to one writer, "The general purpose of all these exchanges, as expressed in their charters, was to provide an organized market place for buyers and sellers; to collect and disseminate useful market information; to adjust controversies among members; to provide uniform rules, regulations, and standards; and to establish just and equitable principles of trading."[24] Although it is entirely possible that such regulated exchanges suggested the idea, President Taylor and other Latter-day Saint leaders gave the institution a scope much wider than that of other American boards of trade.

Of greatest interest in retrospect are the accomplishments of the board of trade, i.e., the influence of that organization upon the development of the intermountain economy. Perhaps the outstanding event in the history of Zion's Central Board of Trade was the sponsorship of a four-day conference in Salt Lake City from May 17 to May 20, 1881. Present at this conference were all the members of the Central Board of Trade and almost complete representation from the stake boards of trade. This group attempted a comprehensive review of the resources of the territory. In preparation for the conference, a circular signed by John Taylor, president, had been distributed in which nineteen subjects were listed for discussion. These included iron, lead, glass, wool, clothing, silk, wagons, agricultural machinery, paper, leather, dairy products, flour, soap, sugar, matches, salt, glue, hats, horticulture, and animal husbandry. The circular stated the purpose of the conference was that of "arriving at a better understanding of what is needed to more thoroughly develop and assist home industries: to establish them on a better and firmer footing, and to utilize the natural resources of the Territory." It concluded with the following note signed by John Taylor: "By counseling together we hope to be able to see the way clearer for establishing some of the industries referred to; of devising methods for assisting those already started and utilizing for the benefit of all, some, at least, of the many natural resources of our rich and growing Territory."[25]

The emphasis of this conference, both in intent and in practical result, was on the development of regional manufacturing industries. For each of nineteen industry groups and fields of interest, a permanent committee of leading men was appointed to study ways and means of developing the industry in question. The committee was also to take such action as might seem desirable, such as organizing a company, calling a special convention to further the industry, or publishing information with regard to proper practices.[26]

Obviously, the interchange of ideas and the kindling of enthusiasm are two results of conferences of this nature. In almost every one of the nineteen fields discussed, however, active steps were taken to develop new manufacturing in the area. Given the scope of the proposals, it is no surprise that efforts to establish these new industries were stopped short of success at many points. Activity in the important fields of iron manufacture, sugar manufacture, and the manufacture of wagons and agricultural implements indicates some of the far-reaching results of the board of trade conference.

In May 1881 the board of trade convention appointed a committee to organize a company for the manufacture of iron and coke. In August the Utah Iron Manufacturing Company, with a capitalization of $1,000,000, was organized. This company acquired coal and iron lands and was prepared to experiment with iron manufacture when some of its claims were allegedly "jumped" by a wealthy non-Mormon, and the case remained in the courts until 1884. When the litigation was nearing completion, the First Presidency of the Church, with the assistance of the Board of Trade committee, organized a new company called the Iron Manufacturing Company of Utah, with $250,000 capital stock. The church subscribed a considerable amount of money for the patenting of iron and coal land claims, as well as for the support of laborers engaged in developmental activities. The Iron Manufacturing Company hired an experienced ironmonger, built a furnace, factory, and storehouse. Some twenty men were employed during the winter of 1883-84. A small railroad, twenty miles in length—the Nevada Central Railway—was purchased and rails, cars, and equipment were transported to southern Utah for use in carrying coal to the iron furnace. Another railroad was laid out, running from Iron City to the Utah Southern (now Union Pacific) line at Milford, Utah.

In spite of the enthusiasm of all this preparatory work, there were some who doubted the wisdom of spending half a million dollars to develop an industry of such questionable profitability. A special Central Board of Trade committee was selected to make an exhaustive study and recommendation. Apostle Moses Thatcher, the leading spirit in this investigation, appears to have made an unfavorable report. That report, plus the anti-polygamy crusade that began late in 1884 in Utah, put a stop to all efforts to develop the iron and coal resources in southern Utah for over ten years. These efforts of the Board of Trade, however, were ultimately vindicated with the establishment of the Columbia Steel Company and the Geneva Steel Division of the United States Steel Corporation.[27]

The Central Board of Trade also gave a great deal of attention to the development of local beet sugar industry. A committee was appointed to study the relative advantages of sugar cane, grain sorghums, and sugar beets. The territorial legislature was persuaded to offer a substantial bounty for the development of locally produced marketable sugar. A considerable amount of experimentation resulted. A small company was organized in 1886 to manufacture cane sugar. Later, in 1889, the Utah Sugar Company, which eventually grew into the Utah-Idaho Sugar Company and Amalgamated Sugar Company, was organized to develop the beet sugar industry.[28]

Of special interest to an agrarian society was the provision of cheap farm wagons and machinery. A particularly distinguished committee of the Central Board of Trade gave serious attention to this industry. After the failure of at least two attempts to manufacture these items in Utah, the committee decided to organize a cooperative company to import wagons, carriages, implements, and tools.[29] In 1883 the Cooperative Wagon and Machine Company was organized with a capital of $100,000. This company later merged with the Consolidated Implement Company to form the Consolidated Wagon and Machine Company, with a capital of $2,500,000. The latter company occupied a strategic position in this field in the intermountain area for almost four decades.

Zion's Central Board of Trade had other successes. The three industries mentioned—iron, sugar, and agriculture implements— do not exhaust the efforts of the Central Board of Trade to stimulate home industry. In wool, silk, paper, leather, dairy products, soap, and salt manufacture, Board of Trade committees took active steps to establish profitable enterprises within the territory. Where new companies were organized, they were usually cooperative ventures. Some success met the Board of Trade efforts in stimulating the manufacture of wool, paper, leather, dairy products, and salt. Progress was also made in silk and soap manufacture, but in these two industries the territorial firms soon succumbed to outside competition.

Nor should it be assumed that the function of the Central Board was restricted to efforts to establish and stimulate home industry. The organization succeeded in reducing freight rates on agricultural exports from Utah and in finding markets for surplus grain during the severe depression in 1884.[30] It also sponsored an outstanding Territorial Fair in 1881.

The activities of local (i.e., stake) boards of trade were even more extensive, but can only be summarized here. These boards, being arms of the church as well as local representatives of the Central Board of Trade, were, in a sense, business agents of the stake presidencies of their respective stakes. In at least three instances stake boards of trade served as mediums through which contracts were acquired for the construction of railroads.[31] "Mormon" work on the Utah Northern, Southern Pacific, and Denver and Rio Grande Western railroads was handled in this way. These contracts provided lucrative employment to hundreds of men, especially during winter months, and at the same time insured cooperative division of contracting profits.

At least two stake boards of trade established a centralized marketing agency for the disposal of farm produce. For years the Cache Valley Stake Board of Trade marketed almost all the butter, eggs, and grain that were shipped out of Cache Valley to San Francisco, Montana, and other buying centers. The Salt Lake Board of Trade established a central wool-marketing agency that is reported to have increased wool prices to farmers and stockmen by a considerable margin. Before the organization of the Cooperative Wagon and Machine Company, the Cache, Weber, and Bear Lake stakes, among others, had also established agencies for the importation and retailing, under cooperative principles, of agricultural implements, wagons, and buggies.[32]

In some instances a local board of trade actually set up agencies for the regulation of the prices of local farm products. The Snowflake, Arizona, board, for example, set hay and grain prices. There were cases in which local trade competition was effectively regulated by the industry-group concerned, under the direction of a board of trade, to prevent excessive price and product competition. An example of these activities was the regulation of the Cache Valley lumber industry by the Cache Stake Board of Trade.[33]

Several boards of trade made strenuous, and at times successful, efforts to reduce freight rates for local produce for export from the producing area, and also on products imported into the local area.[34] In the minds of some board of trade leaders, their outstanding accomplishment was countering the so-called monopoly and discriminatory tactics of the Union Pacific Railroad Company during this period.

It cannot be too strongly emphasized that though Zion's Board of Trade was a creature of the First Presidency of the Mormon Church—John Taylor, George Q. Cannon, and Joseph F. Smith—it did not strive to build up the church and its business interests at the expense of the people. Its planning was devoted to increasing private production and employment in the region by a comprehensive plan of resource development, and by a calculated policy of regulated competition. Unlike many chambers of commerce at the time, its purpose appears to have been whole-group economic welfare rather than business-group welfare. It was established as a temporal organization for a spiritual purpose. The philosophy behind the institution is reminiscent of the medieval "just price" and "just wage" concepts, in which municipal authorities worked together with the guilds to enforce the regulations by which justice was to be secured. Fortunately, perhaps, the board of trade program was not carried to that extreme in Utah—nor was it intended to do so.

For obvious reasons the board of trade movement was initiated and made greatest headway in the more heavily populated, more industrialized northern counties of Utah, such as Cache, Weber, Davis, and Salt Lake. It had little influence in the more self-sufficient southern counties. The success of the movement in the north no doubt reflects the growing commercialization of agriculture in that part of the territory. Zion's Board of Trade also reflects the improved facilities for transportation and communication in the north, which made feasible the establishment of regional manufactories to replace village industries, the economic justification for many of which would seem to have been removed by 1879. The United Order that Zion's Board of Trade replaced, while of undoubted temporary advantage in counteracting the effects of the 1873 depression, was, in its practical effect, a rejection of the exchange economy and an affirmation of the self-sufficing household and village economy of the frontier. Perhaps this is why it was doomed to failure when prosperity was restored after the depression of the early 1870s. Zion's Board of Trade was consistent with the trend of economic events, for it represented a growing belief in the advantages of commercial agriculture and specialized industry and attempted to cope with the problems that arose under the expansion of market activities. It represented acceptance of a regional exchange economy in which businessmen played a prominent part in the planning and execution of programs; its predecessor had proposed, in a sense, a return to a village-oriented pre-capitalism.

Looking back, it seems strange that in the very year that Zion's Board of Trade seemed to be making greatest headway in the accomplishment of its aims—1884—it died. Mormon leaders proffered an explanation that was summarized in an editorial in the *Deseret News* ten years later:

It seems inseparable from history, that whenever any beneficial project was afoot for the benefit of the people of Zion, all the malignity of the opposition has been evoked to frustrate and prevent success, and instances in great number could be given as evidences of this fact. In this special instance [that is, from 1879 to 1884 under the boards of trade] when unanimity was growing, when prices of produce were being held up, and the masses were prospering exceedingly, and promise was beyond all past experience, that infamous raid was commenced which compelled almost every leading citizen into exile or into privacy, the organization meanwhile struggling along in a decapitated condition, until finally, they succumbed to compulsory inaction.[35]

Whether our sympathies lie with congressional efforts to stamp out polygamy, with the efforts of Latter-day Saint leaders to preserve their culture, or with competing non-Mormon businessmen, the conclusion stated so succinctly above is inescapable: the enforcement of the Edmunds Anti-polygamy Act in 1884 and thereafter destroyed Zion's Board of Trade. There is no alternative explanation. Board of trade activities were not declining, but gaining momentum when "the raid" started. Yet, after 1884 there is no mention whatever of any activities by any board of trade except for the retail institution in Logan and for local organizations on the fringe that were untouched by "the raid," as in Mormon colonies located in Arizona and Mexico. The Juarez Board of Trade, functioning as late as 1896, and the Snowflake (Arizona) Board, operating as late as 1897, were the last remnants of the movement.[36]

Until Utah became a state in 1896, the great mass of Mormon businessmen remained outside the Salt Lake City Chamber of Commerce. That chamber had been sponsored by non-Mormons to take the place of the now-defunct Central Board of Trade, and there was suspicion that it was (or had been) devoted, ultimately, to the destruction of Mormonism. But that was changed with the Manifesto of 1890 and statehood in 1896. Church authorities no longer held out the hope of a Mormon commonwealth, but appeared to encourage cooperation with non-Mormons in such organizations as the Chamber of Commerce.[37] After 1896 chambers of commerce in the intermountain region operated seemingly without friction between Mormons and non-Mormons. This did not mean that the church had given up the hope of eventually establishing the Order of Enoch and regulating economic affairs thereby. The twentieth-century Church Welfare Plan (Chapter 15) would seem to be a continuation of the steps in that direction.

Unlike the United Order movement of 1874, the boards of trade did not require the participation of all, or even most, of the people in each community. They coordinated the leadership and channeled the activities of the strategic few in ways that, it was hoped, would result in the economic expansion of Mormondom. In this, they represented a partial fulfillment of Brigham Young's expectations in founding his United Order Number One in 1875. Certainly his successor, John Taylor, considered the formation of Zion's Board of Trade an outstanding feature of his administration. In his mind, it was a realistic and dynamic approach to the problems of economic unity and Mormon economic welfare. Zion's Board of Trade was inaugurated and administered in the same flexible spirit that characterized the earlier Mormon experiments with consecration and stewardship, cooperative production and marketing, and self-sufficient United Order communities. Having been conceived in the same spirit and with the same objectives—though different methods—as the United Order, Zion's Board of Trade might be described, not too inaccurately, as a "Third United Order."

Zion's Board of Trade ultimately failed to check the decline of the cooperative principle. Private enterprise was eager to enter actively into the field of trade, either openly or under the guise of the cooperative insignia. Entertaining misgivings that church efforts to influence economic affairs too greatly restricted individual freedom, President Taylor, as head of the church, withdrew his support for the continuance of such activities. When he perceived, after much effort, that he could not preserve the spirit of cooperation within the institutions that had assumed the name, he decided to remove existing obstacles to individual trade and in May 1882 issued an epistle that marks the end of an epoch in the economic history of the Mormon people.

Cooperation had been talked about considerably from time to time as being a stepping stone to something that would yet be more fully developed among the people of God, namely, the United Order. We had no example of the United Order strictly in accordance with the word of God on the subject. Our cooperation was simply an operation to unite us together in our secular affairs, tending to make us one in temporal things as we were one in spiritual things. A feeling had been manifested by some of our brethren to branch out in the mercantile business on their own account, and [President Taylor's] idea as to that was if people would be governed by correct principles, laying aside covetousness and eschewing chicanery and fraud, dealing honestly and conscientiously with others as they would like others to deal with them, that there would be no objection on our part for our brethren to do these things; that it was certainly much better for them to embark in such enterprises than our enemies. . . .

Under existing circumstances it had been thought best to throw open the field of trade, under proper restrictions, but that we should do all we could to confine it as much as possible in the hands of our people. . . . All should be subject to the principle of cooperation and not recede a particle from it; but we should put our own business people in the place of outsiders and sustain them inasmuch as they sustain the principle of cooperation themselves by acting honorably in their dealing. . . . There was no going back on the principles of cooperation. It was not standing still, but moving on, and it would continue to move on.

Our relations with the world and our own imperfections prevent the establishment of this system at the present time and therefore, as was stated by Joseph in an early day, it cannot yet be carried out; but cooperation and the United Order are a step in the right direction and are leading our brethren to reflect upon the necessity of union as one of the fundamental principles of success in temporal things as well as in spiritual things and indeed as one of the essentials pertaining to permanent prosperity, for the Lord hath said, "If ye are not one, ye are not mine."[38]

Thus was brought to a close a fifteen-year struggle to realize a unity of interests in trade and industry. Nominally there were still many cooperatives. The community of Orderville, still ascendant, dissolved within three years, and one by one the ward co-ops failed or took on new life under other names.

CHAPTER 15

Taking care of their own:
The Mormon welfare system,
1936-1975

HE NINETEENTH CENTURY closed with The Church of Jesus Christ of Latter-day Saints abandoning many of its long-held temporal roles and struggling to redefine itself in a way more acceptable to the nation. The major Mormon economic drive of the early twentieth century was aimed not at social welfare but at institutional survival and expansion. The difficulties of the closing years of the last century had left the church heavily in debt. The total church debt in 1898 amounted to more than $1,250,000 while tithing income to the church was around $600,000—scarcely enough to meet the day-to-day cost of church administration. To reduce the staggering debt, church president Lorenzo Snow called for two bond issues of $500,000 each, which were then paid back over a period of several years of increased tithing revenues brought in by his charismatic pleas that the Saints obey the commandment of tithing. He and his successors moved the church in a new economic direction, away from participation in cooperative enterprises and into direct ownership of hotels, hospitals, industries, and other income-producing ventures. By the mid-twenties, the church was in strong financial position and was able to undertake a widespread building and education program, but the unifying cooperative ethic of the previous century was rapidly disappearing. It would take a new crisis to rekindle the cooperative spirit in the twentieth century.

The Great Depression did not hit Utah with the sudden crash it produced in other areas. No stockbrokers were seen leaping from Salt Lake City windows. The parrot seen walking New York's streets crying "more margin, more margin" had no seagull counterpart. The depression came to the Mormon domain instead as a final demoralizing climax to a decade of difficulty for most of the state's residents. Brigham Young's dream, as we have seen, had been to establish Deseret as a self-sufficient agricultural and industrial commonwealth, largely independent of outside economic activity. His cooperatives and United Order were intended, among other things, to counteract the harmful effects of the railroad—to forestall a destructive integration of the Great Basin economy into the national pattern. After his death, however, church leaders came increasingly to accept the inevitability of such an integration, abdicating responsibility for economic development of the region and permitting Mormon Country to merge fully into the commercialized, interdependent economic structure emerging in America. In the twentieth century the region would concentrate its energies on the production of minerals, livestock, and farm products for a nation that generally found these commodities abundant and available at less cost elsewhere.[1]

Between 1920 and 1930 Utah farmers saw the purchasing power of their annual production slip by as much as 20 percent. The end of the war, technological advances, a large labor supply, and other factors had increased production in advance of demand well before the depression cycle beginning in 1929 cut purchasing power and further aggravated the farmers' plight. When the crash of October 1929 occurred, most Utah farmers had already marketed their summer's produce and thus felt few immediate effects unless they had lost savings in the early bank failures that were epidemic in agricultural areas in the late twenties. National farm income slipped by some 15 to 20 percent in the first plunge between 1929 and 1930, but farmers had already experienced an even greater decline in 1920 and 1921 and thus probably had little inkling of what was to come. The real crisis came in 1931 and 1932, when farm income dropped another 20 percent and then again to less than half the 1929 total. In 1932, farmers in the nation as a whole received only 46 percent of the income they had received just four years earlier. The combined effects on farmers of lowered income and a depressed currency were catastrophic. In 1932, pre-1929 debts required farmers to triple their production to repay the same amount. By 1933, 49 percent of all farm mortgages in the Mountain States were delinquent.[2]

Utah's economy was agriculture-centered, and the effects of the depression on that sector indicate the trend in other sectors of the state's economy. Agriculture-related industries such as supply, processing, and transportation were soon forced to reduce their working forces. Despite economy measures, many went bankrupt. Government services such as education and public works construction were faced with drastically reduced revenues from the agricultural and related sectors that paid the bulk of the region's taxes. Soon teachers were laid off, given reduced salaries, or paid in scrip redeemable for only a portion of the recipient's actual salary if cashed immediately. Private construction fell off precipitously in response to both local conditions and the unavailability of credit. Bank runs and failures became even more common than during the 1920s.

The real tragedy of the depression in Utah, as elsewhere, was in the disrupted lives and suffering of the individuals who lost their jobs, their incomes, and often their self-respect as the depression spread in widening circles to every corner of life. National unemployment mounted to more than 25 percent in 1932. Of those who retained their jobs, many worked reduced hours at reduced wages or, like farmers, found that the more they worked, the more harm they did themselves. In the Mormon-dominated areas of the nation, joblessness often seemed particularly shameful. One hundred years before, Joseph Smith had admonished the Saints,

> Cease to be idle; cease to be unclean; cease to find fault one with another; cease to sleep longer than is needful; retire to thy bed early, that ye may not be weary; arise early that your bodies and minds may be invigorated.[3]

The jobless Mormon, a superfluous person in Caroline Bird's term, found in the excess time on his hands a source of guilt. "Like prisoners in solitary confinement," writes Bird, "the superfluous people got up every morning as late as they could and fought time as if it were an enemy."[4] The vigor of the Mormon scripture, "This life is the time for men to prepare to meet God; yea, behold the day of this life is the day for men to perform their labors,"[5] rankled in the unemployed or underemployed Mormon as he made his daily rounds of possible employers only to be turned down time and time again.

The tragedy of unemployment and underemployment was, of course, not purely or even primarily psychological. In Utah, as elsewhere, hunger, cold, and postponed dreams were the prices exacted by the depression. The responsibility to stem the outright suffering and more subtle anomie produced by the depression fell first upon local and state governments and charitable institutions.

In Utah, local government units delegated the task of relief to local Mormon church units as early as 1931. Persons were asked to report to the bishops vacant lots that might hold gardens for the use of needy families. Scout troops and Relief Societies collected clothing and food supplies and transported them to central receiving storehouses from which bishops disbursed the goods to those in need. Throughout the state, similar efforts were made with varying degrees of success. Despite the best efforts of local government and church authorities, the situation became steadily worse through 1933.

Late in the presidential term of Herbert Hoover, the first influx of federal aid came to Utah. Hoover's Reconstruction Finance Corporation made large loans to the Bankers' Livestock Loan Company of Utah, which in turn loaned money to local individuals and associations. During Franklin D. Roosevelt's term a succession of depression agencies provided relief and employment. The Civilian Conservation Corps, the Emergency Relief Administration, the Civil Works Administration, and a number of relief agencies set up by the states with federal aid made frontal attacks on the conditions of the depression and significantly reduced its effects on the people. But Latter-day Saints were not wholly satisfied with the efforts of the federal government. Not only were such federal relief and recovery measures often inadequate and late in coming, but Mormon leaders also felt a religious obligation to care for their own members, to reduce dependence on outside aid, and to administer relief (i.e., to share) in a manner consistent with their historical and doctrinal peculiarities.

While LDS leaders seemed not to doubt their obligations in acting to secure the property and bolster the income of their people, it was only after several years that their anti-depression efforts were coordinated on a churchwide level. At first, church officials contented themselves with supplying advice and guidance to local church units and individuals in their efforts to supplement federal and stake relief efforts. A *Deseret News* editorial of 1931 contended that while it was not subject to argument that the poor must be fed, clothed, and sheltered, relief money could best be spent in providing work. The paper further suggested road construction and irrigation work as two projects worthy of attention.[6] A year later Elder George F. Richards of the Council of the Twelve outlined the Mormon response to the conditions then prevailing. He told the Saints to look to tithes and offerings as the proper source of aid for the poor, and promised the Mormons that if they would faithfully pay one-tenth of their income to the church and turn over the full cost of the meals missed during their monthly fasts, all the church's poor would be cared for without resort to outside aid. In 1933 the First Presidency ordered a survey to be taken of the economic status of the church membership and cautioned the Relief Society to expect "a considerable burden" to be placed on its shoulders in the relief activities of the church. Along with its exhortations to local church leaders to use the existing apparatus of the church to provide relief, the high church leadership offered a caution: employable members should not become dependent on "the dole," that is, on money given without requirement that the recipient work.

Implementation of such general policies was generally left to local church bodies. In Cache Valley, ward bishops and Relief Societies established storehouses where surplus produce and clothing could be collected and distributed to needy members. In Salt Lake City, hard hit by the depression, stakes and stake presidencies bore the brunt of the effort. Between September 30, 1931, and June 20, 1932, ten Salt Lake stakes distributed $177,438 for relief. Of the total, $34,027 came from fast offerings and other donations, $28,471 from Relief Society funds, and $105,114 from tithing funds. During the same period the church as a whole expended $361,243 for relief.[7]

The leader in providing relief assistance to its members was the Pioneer Stake of Salt Lake City with its young stake presidency composed of Harold B. Lee, Charles S. Hyde, and Paul C. Childs. More than half the men of the stake were unemployed in 1932. The stake presidency first set about finding employment for the men through contacts with the larger industries and businesses of the valley. When that indirect source of relief was exhausted, the stake requested that they be allowed to keep all their tithing revenues within the stake rather than sending them on to the central church offices. Granted this additional source of funds, stake leaders were able to organize an exchange of stake labor for food grown on local farms, then to buy a farm to be run by the stake itself. At first the farm was planted in sugar beets; later other crops became more important. Pioneer Stake soon purchased warehouses and a canning factory, thus enabling the members to ship produce not needed by stake residents to distant points where cash was available for produce. Using cash and canned goods, the stake welfare project was then expanded to include the purchase and renovation of unsalable clothing articles produced at the Logan (Utah) Knitting Mills. By 1935 the Pioneer Stake project had become a near self-sustaining venture that provided for the sustenance of poverty-stricken stake members by supplying them with goods produced by labor on the stake farm or obtained from other church and private sources through the trade of farm products.[8]

The singular successes of church-sponsored welfare in the Pioneer Stake did not go unnoticed. On April 20, 1935, the stake president, Harold B. Lee, was invited to meet with the First Presidency of the church. Later he remembered that experience:

> It was a Saturday morning; there were no calls on their calendar, and for hours in that forenoon they talked with me and told me that they wanted . . . to . . . release me from being stake president; that they wished me now to head up the welfare movement to turn the tide from government relief, direct relief, and help put the church in a position where it could take care of its own needy.[9]

From the beginning, two interpretations were given to his task. On the one hand, the Mormon effort was held to be simply a response to the need of the church membership for aid to supplement the government projects available. This need became especially critical later in 1935 when the Roosevelt administration announced its intention of ending all direct federal relief activities and shifting the burden to the state and local governments. Aware that Utah and Idaho state finances were in no condition to bear any added burdens, Mormon leaders viewed the imminent shifting of relief burdens as a serious challenge: "Where preparation is being made to meet this problem there will be but little difficulty. But where no preparation has been made, suffering, difficulties, and bloodshed are not remote possibilities."[10] There was an obvious need for a program to help carry the burden of poor relief when the government began curtailing its activities.

Many Mormons, however, held the view that the proposed program must be more than a supplement to the federal program—it must supplant federal efforts, which many regarded as based on false premises. Thus, when Roosevelt announced in 1935 that he would ask Congress to eliminate all direct relief in favor of work relief programs, he was applauded by Mormon leaders. Most Latter-day Saints agreed with his assessment that the direct dole was contributing to spiritual and moral disintegration. [11] When plans to eliminate direct relief bogged down, the *Deseret News* was quick to lament the continuation of the dole but added that considerations of humanity stood in the way of doing away with it as winter approached. [12] Harold B. Lee's own recollection of the beginning of the Church Welfare Plan states that one objective was to "turn the tide" against the dole. J. Reuben Clark, Jr., a member of the First Presidency and a widely respected statesman, issued perhaps the most direct condemnation of relief when he stated that "no man is politically free who depends upon the state for his sustenance."[13]

Actually, there were several underlying objectives of the Church Welfare Plan. The economic well-being of the Saints was to be provided for, their dependence on outside influences diminished, their self-reliance increased, and all this was to be done in a manner consistent with traditional church principles. Church President Heber J. Grant's statement in 1936 summed up their multiplicity of goals, both moral and practical:

Our primary purpose in organizing the Church Security Plan [renamed Church Welfare Plan after passage of the Social Security Act] was to set up a system under which the curse of idleness would be done away with, the evils of a dole abolished, and independence, industry, thrift and self-respect be once more established amongst our people. The aim of the Church is to help the people to help themselves. Work is to be re-enthroned as the ruling principle of the lives of our Church membership.[14]

Harold B. Lee's task of initiating the system on a churchwide scale was monumental. His first step was to survey the needs of the church membership. An inquiry conducted in September 1935 found that 88,460 persons, representing 17.9 percent of the total membership, were receiving some sort of relief. About 16.3 percent of the members were dependent on public sources, while 1.6 percent received church assistance. Some 13,455 of those receiving relief were unemployed, while the others were working on government-sponsored programs. The report also stated that between 11,500 and 16,500 "did not need such assistance."[15]

During the April 1936 general conference a special meeting for bishops and stake presidents was held in which they were instructed that the church would shortly take a more active role in promoting the financial independence and social security of church members. A detailed plan for accomplishing this, promised at the meeting, was sent out to local leaders two weeks later and announced to the general membership in the *Church News* of April 25. The Church Security Program, as it was officially titled, was designed to assist worthy members of the church by providing employment in church-operated agricultural and farming enterprises, which would in turn produce goods to be used in assisting other poverty-stricken members. A chain of storehouses was to be established as an integral part of the plan. Mormon bishops or authorized members would be able to make withdrawals from these storehouses to fill the needs of the poor. Three groups already in existence—the ward bishoprics, the male priesthood quorums, and the female Relief Societies—were to fill the primary role in determining need, establishing enterprises, managing them, and distributing produce to the poor. The rank and file of church membership was expected to donate both labor and goods to assist in the program. A proportion of tithes and all the fast offerings collected in each area were also apportioned to the Church Security Program. Overproduction of one commodity in one region was to be balanced by trade with other welfare regions. Those receiving assistance from the plan were to be paid chiefly in commodities and would receive amounts proportionate to their needs; that is, the size of an individual's family and the availability of other resources, not the strict value of labor, would determine the compensation returned for work under the system. "One gives what one has and gets what one needs," explained an official description of the plan published in 1941.

While the Security System was being established church leaders seldom spoke of the obvious parallels between it and the United Orders established in Mormon communities within the living memory of many of the older Saints. The members, however, were quick to notice similarities and to ask authorities if the two systems were related. When Harold B. Lee helped set up the program with apostle Melvin J. Ballard during the summer of 1936, he noted that the apostle "was asked everywhere: 'Is this the beginning of the United Order?' " Invariably Ballard responded that the program "is not the beginning of the United Order, but it may be that in this movement the Lord may be giving His people an examination to see how far they have come toward a condition where they might live as one."[16] President Heber J. Grant opened the October 1936 conference with an official statement on the early operations of the plan. But though the new welfare system became a dominant theme of the three-day conference, neither President Grant nor other speakers made an explicit connection between it and the United Order. The Security System was not introduced as a resumption of the traditional Mormon compulsion to build the city of God on earth, but rather as an inspired response to calamitous contemporary circumstances. There was almost no suggestion that innovators of the new program had been guided by their understanding of the Law of Consecration and Stewardship taught by Joseph Smith or the United Order of Enoch preached by Brigham Young.[17]

Nevertheless, there is evidence that such considerations were in the minds of top church leaders. Describing his initial meeting with President Grant and David O. McKay of the First Presidency to plan the Welfare Program, Harold B. Lee remembered his astonishment to learn "that for years there had been before them, as a result of their thinking and planning and as the result of the inspiration of Almighty God, the genius of the very plan that is being carried out and was in waiting and in preparation for a time when in their judgment the faith of the Latter-day Saints was such that they were willing to follow the counsel of the men who lead and preside in this church."[18] Apostle and church historian Joseph Fielding Smith told the Saints during the October 1936 conference that he looked upon the plan, not as something new, but as "a return to that which is old."[19] J. Reuben Clark, Jr., of the First Presidency added his testimony that the plan "goes back to the principles which were given the Church over a hundred years ago, puts us once more on the road leading to the establishment of a Christian rule."[20]

Under the plan needs of members who had accepted, or would be forced to accept, direct relief were to be met by the Church Security Program. Aged persons who were not covered by old age and survivor's insurance and who had no other means of support would contribute funds and labor to the Security Program in their productive years and then draw it out after retirement or when they became incapacitated. Under the church plan many old persons could also earn their assistance by doing vicarious work for the dead in one of the church's temples.

The idea of work-relief was essential to the church relief program. The exact number of persons to be helped was not known, but it was thought that it might run as high as 15,000. The plan intended that "those now on WPA projects shall continue on these projects making sure to give a full day's work for value received but they are expected to contribute of their time when not so employed to the carrying out of the Plan."[21]

In contrast with statements later made about it, the Church Security Program was not ultraconservative. In many ways it actually supplemented parts of the New Deal. For example, both the New Deal and the church instigated resettlement programs in order to make better use of productive land. In western Canada members were transported from unproductive land to fertile areas where they could become self-sustaining. In some areas land was opened up for purchase. Young men who wanted to farm, but who lacked the funds with which to purchase farms, were assisted by the program. Aid was also given in obtaining implements and seed—a plan not unlike the New Deal long-term low interest loan and seed loan plans. Another feature of the program was the vocational education provided for unskilled workers.[22]

Under the federal Social Security Act, as originally passed, the farmers were not covered and often had little to look forward to in old age. The LDS farm population—especially in Idaho and Utah—was included in the Church Security Program by laboring on church projects during the farmers' productive years. Later, in old age, they were entitled to receive welfare assistance. While the church encouraged elderly persons to retain title to their homes and sufficient ground for a garden and facilities for keeping livestock for milk and meat purposes, these persons were expected to give the state a lien against their home or property in order to secure government pensions.[23]

Governor Henry H. Blood of Utah, a Democrat, said while visiting California that the church program was an aid to the "already sound financial status of Utah." He called the church plan a "progressive step" and added that the program was a large undertaking, but had a fine goal and would give a big lift to Utah's relief problem. Similarly, Salt Lake City Mayor J. Will Erwin, also a Democrat, said that big cities and counties were crippled financially and could not stand for a heavy cut in federal relief. That Salt Lake City was now in better shape from an employment standpoint than other first-class American cities, said the mayor, was due to the Church Security Program.[24]

When church leaders stated that "any activity or project which tends in the direction of 'helping the people to help themselves' to a position of security is in harmony with the great objectives of the plan,"[25] it was not illogical for Latter-day Saints to conclude that the PWA and WPA were such harmonious projects.

It is also clear that contemporary New Deal officials did not feel that the church was opposing federal relief efforts. Details of the church's program were put into the *Congressional Record,* May 25, 1936, and in late May and early June, Elder Melvin J. Ballard of the Council of the Twelve, who was also first manager of the program, met with President Roosevelt and Utah's liberal New Deal senator, Elbert D. Thomas, in Washington to explain the church plan. He reported that the President gave his personal commendation of the Security Program and promised "full cooperation" on the part of the federal government. Elder Ballard went out of his way to assure Roosevelt that the church was "anxious to be in full cooperation with the government." The motives behind the church program, he said, were pride in caring for church members and sympathy for the unfortunate. According to the report, not only did Roosevelt endorse the program, but he also expressed hope for its ultimate success. He hoped, he said, that the program might inspire other groups to do something of a similar nature.[26]

While those actually involved in administering the Church Security Program and the New Deal saw little conflict between the Mormon plan and the federal recovery program, as soon as the Mormons announced their plan, the conservative press lauded the church for its proposal "to transfer all Church members from government relief to Church relief." Conservative magazines and journals, such as the *American Banker, Cosmopolitan, Saturday Evening Post,* and the *Reader's Digest,* saw the program to be an anti-New Dealer's dream come true.

A year and a half ago [stated the *Reader's Digest*] 84,460 Mormons, about one-sxith of the entire church membership, were on direct relief. Today none of them are. The Church is taking care of its own. . . . Within a year every one of the 84,460 Mormons was removed from the government relief rolls all over the country.[27]

The article was inaccurate, for not all of the 84,460 were on government relief. Nor did the church at any time succeed in removing all of its members from government relief, and at the outset the church did not even attempt to do so.

This interpretation of the Security Program, *cum* Welfare Plan, as a gesture of defiance against the New Deal was also reiterated in the "liberal" press. "Although it ridicules federal work projects," wrote Martha Emery in *Nation*, "the church attempted to solve the unemployment problem among Mormons by creating projects of its own." The Welfare Plan, she asserted, "was an ultra-conservative gesture of withdrawal into the old isolation which in the past was a major source of the Church's strength." Mormon leaders, wrote a Utah political scientist, generally opposed federal social security and relief measures. "Angered and alarmed by . . . the flocking of its members to federal relief and public works payrolls, it [the church] issued an open announcement . . . endorsing the presidential candidacy of Republican Alf Landon," and simultaneously established its own welfare program.[28]

The reaction of both conservative and liberal theorists to the Mormon welfare system was understandable. Conservatives were desperately in need of a practical alternative to Roosevelt's New Deal, while liberals were prone to be strident in defense of "that man" and his policies against all real or imagined attackers. Both groups missed the heart of the Mormon plan, which was, essentially, a reaching back into the Mormon heritage of cooperation and shared burdens to find a solution to pressing modern problems.

Experience during the months after the announcement of the Church Security Program may not have merited the exaggerated compliments paid by certain national magazines, but were nevertheless encouraging to the church. In 1935 church appropriations for the care of the poor, hospitalization, and other charities had amounted to $183,810. Fast offerings, tithes, and Relief Society contributions amounted to $402,939, so that the total cash value of church welfare in 1935 was $586,759.[29] One year later, after little more than six months of the Church Security Program, charity for the care of the poor amounted to $234,019; fast offerings, charitable contributions, and Relief Society assistance totaled $554,350. (Fast offerings had risen 107 percent in the period.) Total church assistance to the poor was $788,369. In addition, $24,450 was appropriated for the Primary Children's Hospital and $50,350 was collected from cash donations. The total cash value of the Church

Welfare Plan in 1936 was $1,097,188. In addition to cash assistance, 2,292 persons were provided with temporary or permanent employment in private industry during 1936. A total of 3,865 needy persons and 13,712 who did not need relief were given work in farming, canning, or sewing for the church. Moreover, the erection and improvement of church buildings, stimulated by larger contributions, amounted to $769,473 appropriated by the general church and $513,000 raised by the localities, for a total of $1,282,473 in 1936.[30]

In the October 1937 general conference, after eighteen months of the church plan, Presiding Bishop Sylvester Cannon reported that tithes were increasing, fast offerings were up 53 percent over the six-month period from April to October, and the amount dispersed to the needy through the Church Security Program was up 97 percent. The number of persons assisted by direct relief was 16,163 and those helped on work relief was 8,110. This was an increase of 51 percent over the previous year. It was reported that a nonprofit financial organization, the Cooperative Security Corporation, had been incorporated in April 1937 to handle the legal and financial transactions of the Church Security Program. In 1938, as the program began to establish more permanent features, the name was changed to the Church Welfare Plan. By then, annual welfare expenditures had increased to $1,827,000, a considerable part of which was cash, and there was left on hand at the end of 1938 some $127,450 worth of preserved foodstuffs, clothing, and fuel.[31]

In 1938 the Deseret Industries was instituted. Using discarded goods and reprocessing them at church-owned and operated plants and factories, the church-owned Deseret Industries stores marketed the goods in the more populated areas at less than normal retail prices for such items. Deseret Industries also provided employment for the unskilled and handicapped.

A continuation of traditional church policy toward the problem of involuntary unemployment and economic disaster, adapted to the new needs and demands created by the depression of the 1930s, the Church Welfare Plan was not in essence a political move. Church leaders joined with national leaders in proposing the abolition of the dole—i.e., relief unaccompanied by a program of work. At a time when the nation began to suspend direct relief in favor of a program of work-relief, the church proposed to mitigate suffering among its own members by instituting its own program of work-relief. Such action was welcomed by the administration in Washington and followed with intense interest. The Security Program progressed satisfactorily and helped to ease the relief burden of local units of government as the federal government abandoned direct relief.

It was perhaps too much to hope that in the heat of political campaigning the Mormon program would not be involved. Conservative magazines continued to praise it as a welcome alternative to the New Deal, while liberal journals continued to condemn it as politically inspired reactionism. It was a disservice to the church as well as to the government to misrepresent the plan in this way, for many rejected the plan for political reasons at a time when, with proper support, it might have rendered yeoman service to families, municipalities, and state governments. Those who belittled the program because of its failure to remove all church members from federal relief rolls did not perceive that its primary object was simply to assist its members in a time of dire emergency.[32]

More detached historical judgment of the LDS response to the Great Depression nevertheless preserves something of the reactionary label applied to the Welfare Plan, even while lauding the church for its sense of responsibility. Dixon Wecter's comment is perhaps typical:

> The Catholics kept more successfully in touch with their unemployed than did most Protestant denominations, but the Mormons in Utah achieved a conspicuous record. Proudly refusing federal aid and not a little wary of New Deal financing, they made each "ward" of Latter Day Saints responsible for its needy, and higher units came to the rescue when local capacity was overtaxed. The chief aim was to make the family self-sustaining through such means as cooperatives, colonization schemes, home canning and handicrafts and the vigilance of church employment agencies.[33]

Another comment, that of Marriner Eccles, the Utah Mormon banker and financier who held high posts in the Treasury Department during the Depression and later served as chairman of the board of governors of the Federal Reserve System, better explained the forced cooperation that existed between federal and church programs:

> Within Utah and throughout the country the impression has been fostered that the Mormon Church "took care of its own" during the

depression of the thirties. Yet the facts do not square with this impression. It wasn't that the church didn't want to take care of its own; it was more than diligent in this respect. But within an economy that was prostrate no organization or group could be expected to provide care for its adherents. . . . it is impossible for any organization other than the federal government to carry the massive relief burden imposed by a severe and sustained depression.[34]

After the short but sharp "Roosevelt Recession" of 1938, Utah and the nation made rapid recovery from the conditions that had prevailed for nearly a decade. Employment rose, especially after the nation made the decision to rearm in the face of the growing European crisis. While the Church Welfare Plan had been created to deal with a sharp economic crisis, it soon became apparent that church leaders had little intention of abandoning the system once prosperity was restored. Records for 1939 show that rising general prosperity, and perhaps the increasing success of the program's leaders in explaining and popularizing the plan, had greatly increased the income of the program. In 1938, 184,755 Mormons paid fast offerings and welfare contributions to the church. The following year this figure had risen by more than 30 percent to 251,436. The average offering, another indicator of both prosperity and enthusiasm, had grown from 73 cents to 82 cents. The welfare canning operation, which had really just begun full operation in 1938, grew by 34 percent the following year. Total commodities produced by the system rose by 58 percent in 1939 while employment in church projects rose 65 percent. As employment in war industries absorbed all available workers in the early 'forties, full-time employment by the welfare system dropped. This, of course, was a goal of the program. More and more of the work during the war years came to be done by volunteers.[35]

A formal statement as to the future of the Welfare Program was issued in the fall of 1940. "I do not hesitate," wrote Presiding Bishop Joseph L. Wirthlin, "that the future will hold a greater need for [church welfare] than there has been in the past." He predicted that relief would become more and more a responsibility of local government units and churches and called for members to make preparation for the day when welfare will be left entirely to them.[36]

Once it became clear that the system was to endure beyond the depression crisis and become a regular part of the church organization, church leaders began explicitly to describe the Welfare Plan as a revival of the most fundamental aspects of the United Order in preparation for its eventual full restoration. Disturbed by a tendency among a few church members to confuse doctrines of socialism and communism with those of the Order, J. Reuben Clark, Jr., in 1942, discoursed at length on the United Order, affirming its importance to the modern church and discussing its relationship to the Welfare Program. Strongly conservative in his own political leanings, he described the Order of Enoch in terms drawn more from the Law of Consecration and Stewardship as taught by Joseph Smith than from the more communal United Orders organized under Brigham Young's leadership. "The Welfare Plan," he maintained, "is not the United Order and was not intended to be. However . . . when the Welfare Plan gets thoroughly into operation . . . we shall not be so far from carrying out the great fundamentals of the United Order." He characterized the Order as primarily a means of caring for the "abjectly poor" and encouraging the idle to work. He noted further that reinstitution under the Welfare Plan of the bishop's storehouse and the providing by wards of church-owned lands or industries as working places for the poor closely paralleled the earlier operations of the Order. "In its great essentials," he concluded, "we have, as the Welfare Plan has now developed, the broad essentials of the United Order."[37]

During the war years the church's welfare programs and policies coalesced around what can be identified as three primary goals that encompassed the major welfare activities of the church over the next three decades. The first of these goals was to act as a catalyst in ordering and unifying the economic life of the church and its members and in educating the members to the value of thrift, hard work, honesty, and charity. From its inception the program was meant to instill these values in those who participated in it. Members were expected to fast one day a month and donate the money saved to the program. They were also expected to donate time and labor to do the welfare projects of each stake. Some hauled hay on farms; others canned fruit or made clothes. As members worked on welfare projects and made donations to the program, the economic policy of the church was continually stressed. Growing directly out of the depression experience and the stress on the welfare program were a number of peripheral but highly significant programs. Members were cautioned to maintain a reserve food supply sufficient to last them and their families for up to two years. Mormon leaders also constantly stressed the importance of avoiding debt for all but the most essential of purposes. Security, solvency, and preparedness were the keynotes of church economic counseling.

The second goal of the church Welfare Program involved an expansion of the depression era activities of making timely disbursements of aid to those needing it. Each local bishop was charged with the primary responsibility of keeping a close watch for the onset of economic problems among the members of his ward. When such a case appeared, the bishop was expected to meet with other church leaders, such as the Relief Society president, and determine a program suited to meet the family's or individual's specific needs. While the infirm, the aged, and the widowed were perhaps the most common recipients of welfare, those passing through momentary crises of illness, unemployment, and financial overextension and mismanagement could also apply for aid. During a recent year cases were reported of students who were aided in finishing school, of ward members who tended a sick member's cattle, of families who were advised on how to reduce their debts, and of a number of families who were aided in recovering from fires, the expenses of catastrophic illnesses, and natural disasters.

The overall scope of the program and its remarkable growth can be seen in a chart summarizing Welfare Program activities from 1946 to 1960.

Church Welfare Plan Assets
and Disbursements 1946-1960

	1946	1950	1955	1960
Value of commodities in bishops storehouses	$385,836	1,218,270	1,537,442	2,420,770
Total assets of Church Welfare Plan	4,248,126	12,606,964	25,719,026	44,294,227
Number of families assisted by the church	8,509	ap. 8,500	ap. 17,449	ap. 27,080
Dollar value of commodities distributed from storehouses	435,054	935,980	1,435,570	2,557,752
Percent of disbursements produced by church-owned projects	78	90	92	n.a.

Source: Annual Reports of the LDS Church Welfare Plan, 1946-1960

The third goal of the Church Welfare Plan has been to assist in times of large-scale natural disaster and crisis. At no time was this better illustrated than immediately following World War II, when much of Europe lay prostrate and starving. Even before railway shipping could be arranged for the bulk of the Mormon aid to war-torn Europe, Latter-day Saints began sending parcel-post packages to Belgium, Czechoslovakia, Denmark, Finland, France, the Netherlands, Norway, and Great Britain. Between October 29, 1945, and December 31, 1946, some 8,198 bundles of clothing and 6,726 bundles of bedding reached Latter-day Saints in those countries. In 1946, between February 15 and the end of the year, the church collected and dispatched to Europe $166,949 worth of canned food, filling 27 freight cars, and $212,229 worth of clothing and bedding, filling another 12 cars.[38] Subsequent donations brought the total to 85 carloads. Emergency aid has been sent in recent years to victims of earthquakes, tornados, floods, and other natural disasters in many parts of the world.

A complete picture of welfare activities for one year, 1971, perhaps gives the best summary of the importance of the welfare program. In that year, the Welfare Plan provided direct assistance in the amount of $17,722,800. The seventeen million dollars disbursed came from $8,635,000 in fast offerings, $5,487,800 in grants from church funds, and $3,600,000 in commodities donated. Church members also donated 3,990,515 hours to welfare work. The Relief Society gave assistance at more than 15,000 funerals. Work opportunities totaling 1,480,000 hours were made available to handicapped persons unable to find work in the commercial sector. Local stakes owned and operated 478 welfare projects that year; 255 produced agricultural crops—26 in the dairy field, 24 supplying fruits, 79 livestock, and 71 grain. Eleven projects packaged and processed agricultural produce, while 4 manufactured bakery goods, brooms, soap, and cheese. Several dozen tons of church welfare goods were donated that year to victims of the floods in Rapid City, South Dakota.[39]

The Church Welfare Program has played a vital role in twentieth-century Mormon history. The Mormon welfare system has become a churchwide network of producers' cooperatives, sustained, for the most part, by the volunteer labor of church members with other livelihoods and by paid labor of the handicapped, disabled, and temporarily unemployed. A surplus of community labor and financial resources is transformed through welfare projects into foodstuffs and basic household commodities and distributed to the poor through regional and local bishops storehouses. The church attempts to meet fully the welfare needs of the poorer members, asking them not to seek assistance from government programs. Those applying for church assistance who are already on government programs are told that they must report what they receive from the church to those administering government programs and that their government assistance may be reduced accordingly.

Official policy is that church welfare assistance should be restricted to the "worthy poor"—those who are active and faithful church members and are willing to work for the program in exchange for what they receive. Those unable to work are expected to have contributed to the program in the past. This policy has caused casual observers to see the program as essentially conservative and harshly restrictive—an expression of American individualism and self-help rather than the communitarian, egalitarian principles at the heart of the United Order.[40]

The actual practice seems in most cases to depart significantly from the policy. Perhaps taking their clue from the sermon of a Book of Mormon king, bishops have tended to provide assistance to the needy of all classes, whether or not they qualify as "worthy poor" under officially stated guidelines. The ancient prophet Benjamin had commanded that

ye . . . will succor those . . . in need of . . . succor; ye will administer
of your substance unto him that standeth in need. . . .
        Perhaps thou shalt say: The man has brought upon himself his
misery; therefore I will stay my hand, and will not give unto him. . . . But
I say unto you, O man, whosoever doeth this the same hath great cause
to repent. . . . For behold, are we not all beggars? Do we not all depend
upon the same being, even God, for all the substance which we have?[41]

Certainly many close observers of the program would agree that bishops for the most part have administered church welfare in a manner wholly consistent with the spirit of the scriptural injunction. The present welfare system has a near-negligible effect upon the functioning of the whole economy in Mormon-dominated areas. It does not provide the central direction for regional economic development, which was an essential part of the economic orders preached by both Joseph Smith and Brigham Young. But it does provide an effective means of drawing a surplus from the community to provide for the poor, also an essential part of the systems taught by the earlier Mormon prophets. In the scale of its activities it is unquestionably the most successful of all the Mormon cooperative experiments.

Besides benefiting many thousands of poor each year, the Welfare Program has less tangible but important effects upon those whose volunteer labor sustains it. One example, from recent experience in a Salt Lake City ward, may illustrate. Members of the Ivins Ward are given assignments perhaps once a month to work on a fruit orchard owned and managed by the Wells Stake. Twenty-five people responded to such a call one evening, traveling in carloads to the farm, about forty miles from the ward meetinghouse.

There, a paid full-time manager assigned the volunteers to their various tasks. One young man in his mid-thirties worked elbow-to-elbow at an apple-sorting table with a seventy-year-old grandmother. Assisting at the table was a child of two years, obviously convinced that his tossing of an occasional apple to the juicer pile contributed significantly to the collective effort. Teenagers brought boxes of apples from the cooler and dumped them into a hopper, which sorted them according to size and distributed them among the sorting tables. A young woman in an advanced state of pregnancy stood at the hopper picking out obviously rotten apples before they were conveyed to the sorting department. Men trucked the sorted cartons to cold storage areas or to vehicles waiting to transport them to the Church Welfare Center in Salt Lake City. Small boys amused themselves by sailing flat basket lids up to the loft of a barn for storage. In two and one-half hours nearly three hundred bushels of rich, red, top-quality apples were ready for consumption. Those contributing to the effort were permitted to purchase apples for home use at a price below that prevailing in the market. Most of the fruit was sent to central warehouses in Salt Lake City, where it would be redistributed to bishops storehouses either canned, in juice, or as eating apples. The rest was sold on the market to raise cash needed to pay full-time help and maintain and purchase machinery and equipment for the farm.

There seemed something wholesome about an event that put urbanites—factory workers, truck drivers, college professors, and mailmen—in touch with processes that bring forth the sustenance of human life. Another season, pruning or transplanting might

Weeding beans on a modern Church welfare farm. All wards are given a welfare assignment to be completed each year through volunteer labor. (Courtesy LDS Church)

have been the task; on another project, the production of soap or sugar beets. Participants that night experienced the warm feeling that must have characterized old-time quilting bees or barn-raisings. An intangible spirit of community solidarity mingled in the sorting shed with the restrained, aristocratic scent of Delicious apples.

Coming to give, the participants left feeling they had taken more than they had brought. In those moments, one suspects, they came close to realizing in a small way the elusive hope of their great-grandfathers, that the spirit of the United Order might be one day instilled in the hearts of Latter-day Saints. If the account seems overly romanticized, it should be noted that it was not the sugar-coated observation of a pious apologist, but that of a rigorously trained social scientist, bitten rather strongly by the bug of cynicism to which his training had exposed him. He had come to the occasion more out of obligation than dedication. But it did seem that many fruits were produced that night that could not be carried away in bushel baskets. This was one product of 150 years of effort to efface human selfishness and build a harmonious, equitable society. It did not seem modest when we reflected that here, at least, the visions of 1831 still intruded upon the meanness of men's lives, keeping alive the promise that a city of God just might one day be built on earth.

CHAPTER 16

*Reflections on
the Mormon United Order
movement*

IGHT YEARS AFTER POVERTY had forced him to leave his ancestral village of Topsfield, Massachusetts, and start life anew in rural Vermont, Asael Smith, grandfather of Joseph Smith, Jr., summarized the wisdom of his years in a letter to his children. "Bear yourselves dutifully and conscionably towards the authority under which you live," he wrote, "and hold union and order as a precious jewel." The family patriarch hoped that his children would have no part of "any party or faction, or novelty."[1] The staid New Englander would no doubt have been shocked had he lived to see the spectacular fashion in which one of his descendants, Joseph Smith, Jr., sought to carry out his wishes.

Anxiety over the future of a people who had boldly defied authority and embraced republican rule was not uncommon in early nineteenth-century America.[2] The general fear that an excess of liberty in the new world might lead to revolution was heightened in the Smith family by two generations of decline in family fortunes and by a succession of moves to less populated areas where settled village life was built and maintained by conscious effort. Moreover, the Smiths finally settled in an area where the character of rural villages recently won from the wilderness was newly threatened by a dramatic increase in population and unstable growth in economic activity. A dream of social order was dissolving under the impact of libertarian ideologies and unprecedented economic opportunity.

It has been suggested that these developments prepared the people of upstate New York for the waves of religious revival that began to sweep the region in the early 1820s.[3] In the Smith home religious enthusiasm occasioned still further stress, as the father remained steadfastly Universalist despite the conversion of his wife and most of his family to Presbyterianism. It was in this set-

ting that young Joseph Smith received his first vision and subsequent revelations condemning pluralism in many aspects of life
and promising a restoration of religious truths that would assure
order and harmony in a chaotic world. Doing more honor to his
grandfather's admonition than he perhaps realized, he launched a
movement that in spite of crushing vicissitudes would hold te-
naciously to "union and order as a precious jewel."[4]

"If ye are not one ye are not mine," God warned Joseph Smith
and his followers in a revelation of January 1831 at an early
conference of the church.[4] During the succeeding century the
scripture would serve Latter-day Saint leaders as a rallying cry in
their efforts to urge compliance of the general church membership to three grand designs for building greater economic
cooperation among the Saints. The first of these was the Law of
Consecration and Stewardship, initiated by the Prophet himself in
Ohio and Missouri in 1831. The second began under the direction
of Brigham Young with his launching of the cooperative movement in 1869 and its transformation into the United Order of the
1870s. The most recent was the Welfare Plan, begun in 1936 as a
response to the Great Depression. In the latter two movements
there was a conscious hearkening back to Joseph Smith's original
laws and revelations as authoritative vindication of the correct-
ness of new directions being undertaken. Both occurred at critical
junctures in the history of the Mormon people—when outside
forces threatened the perpetuation of their distinctive way of life.
In fact, the move toward cooperation was called forth each time
by a set of circumstances similar in the anxieties they raised to
those which prompted Joseph Smith to question existing religions
in his own day. The desire of church leaders to maintain authority
over their people—to preserve unity and harmony in the face of
disintegrating forces from the outside—promoted renewed efforts
to make the people one in all things.

Cooperative and communitarian experiments among the Latter-day Saints were not just defensive responses to external
threats, however. It is important to remember that Mormonism
began as a millennial religion, and remains so to a surprising
degree today. The Law of Consecration and Stewardship was to
lay the groundwork for the whole economic and social structure
of God's earthly kingdom. Mormons, living under the revealed
order, would be a perfected and holy people, worthy to build in

Missouri the City of Zion. From this people Christ would choose officials and administrators for the millennial reign. A continuing concern of Mormon church leaders since the time of Joseph Smith has been to create a people sufficiently selfless, dedicated, and disciplined to take up the reigns of world government in the wake of an expected collapse of earthly authority—an objective that has indeed led Latter-day Saints to seek refuge and withdrawal, but as a short-term, tactical maneuver. For nearly a century and a half faithful Mormons have confidently expected to see the day when the people of the earth shall come to them for instruction and leadership and "the law shall go forth [from] Zion."[6]

Church leaders have continued to affirm both publicly and privately the belief that faithful Mormons would one day be called upon to live the United Order in connection with the redemption of Zion and the return of Christ to the earth. In an interview in 1973, Marion G. Romney, counselor in the First Presidency, explained that "from the very beginning" of the Welfare Program he felt it would "eventually move into the Law of Consecration." The Welfare Program was

the trial pattern. Until I can pay my tithing and make liberal contributions of my money and labor to the Welfare Program, including fast offerings and so forth, I will not be prepared to go into the United Order, which will require me to consecrate everything I have and thereafter give all my surplus for the benefit of the kingdom. I think the United Order will be the last principle of the gospel we will learn to live and that doing so will bring in the millennium.

The importance of the United Order as a model for present-day church welfare programs was emphasized publicly by several speakers in a welfare conference held in October 1975. On that occasion church leaders were told by President Romney:

The procedural method for teaching Church Welfare has now changed, but the objectives of the program remain the same. Its principles are eternal. It is the gospel in its perfection—the united order, toward which we move.[7]

Sermons on the United Order do not often appear, however, in local ward meetings during the 1970s. Certainly the majority of the church membership is not preoccupied with the possibility of an imminent call to move to Missouri and live the United Order in preparation for the Second Coming. Yet that prospect remains as official doctrine, at least in the hymnody that is an integral part of weekly worship service.[8] Discussions among Mormons of world events, especially in the Middle East, and their significance as possible signs of an approaching Armageddon, are not uncommon. The continuing advice of church leaders that Mormon families be prepared to sustain themselves for one year is taken by many as an intimation that prophetic visions of worldwide calamity have been received. Church leaders deny that their advice justifies this interpretation, but the fact that such beliefs persist in spite of official disclaimers is evidence of the continuing strength of millennial expectations among the Mormon folk. An eloquent expression of the force of such expectations occurred in 1969 when a migration of Samoans to Independence, Missouri, began, contrary to the advice of many church leaders. By 1973 more than three hundred Samoans had sold their possessions and migrated to what they believed to be the future center of the Mormon Zion. Members of the group are active in the Independence First and Second Wards of the established church, and they fully believe that their migration was an inspired preliminary step in the preparation for Christ's return.

More significant, however, is the fact that so long as millennialism remains a part of official doctrine, the potential for a sudden renewal of Mormon communitarianism remains. This may at first glance seem unlikely; the church hierarchy is predominantly composed of businessmen and lawyers—men who, for the most part, are firmly devoted to conservative principles. It should be remembered, however, that in the past Latter-day Saints have been quite willing to accept demands made upon them by the church that they would have found intolerable if imposed by the government. Moreover, the most devout Mormons still promise in solemn ceremonies to consecrate all they have to the church if called upon to do so. Willing obedience to church authority is a cardinal virtue among the faithful and has been a cause of wonder by nonmembers.

If a future national or world catastrophe were to threaten, it is possible to imagine that Mormon prophets, as in the past, might issue a call for the Saints to pool their resources and cooperate to insure group survival. Were this to happen, the response could be dramatic. The ordered hierarchical structure of the Mormon lay priesthood organization could turn itself quickly to the task of

A Latter-day Saint town. The social ideals of unity and order continue to knit the social fabric of settlements such as this. (Photo by Michael Clane Graves, Deseret Book Co.)

building upon the economic superstructure of the Welfare Plan and undertaking direction of economic as well as religious and political affairs among the Saints. The force of such a people, willingly responsive to church authority and fired by the assurance that they were being granted the inestimable privilege of bringing Joseph Smith's plan to fruition in preparation for ultimate cosmic events, could be staggering. It would be a curious twist of history if Mormon communitarianism and cooperation in the past had indeed prepared a people capable of preserving an enclave of order in the face of spreading chaos. Holding union and order "as a precious jewel," the Latter-day Saints, no doubt, would stride boldly forth to put the finishing touches on their city of God.

Deeds of consecration
and of stewardship in Missouri

There are several problems with these documents that make it difficult to assess their importance in clarifying the actual functioning of the Law of Consecration and Stewardship in Missouri. First, with one exception (that of Joseph Knight, Jr.) those which have survived were never dated or given legal status through proper witnessing and signing. It is likely that they were trial drafts for transactions later completed on another form. They were apparently saved only because the frugal Bishop Partridge subsequently penned letters and notes on the blank back side. It is surprising that of the several hundred Latter-day Saints who consecrated their properties and received inheritances only one (Joseph Knight, Jr.) is known to have retained his deeds into the Utah period. Certainly the 1833 persecutions were abrupt and brutal, but an inheritance in Zion was of great religious as well as economic significance. One suspects that the Missouri Mormons would have kept the deeds among their most valued possessions, especially in light of the fact that for a long period they hoped to repossess Zion at some future time. The fact that only one has survived causes one to wonder how generally the deeds were used.

Second, it is not known who prepared the forms and whether Joseph Smith approved them before their use. Scholars have generally assumed that they represent a unilateral attempt on the part of Edward Partridge to put the more general concepts of the Prophet's revelations into a practical, working format. It should be noted, however, that Partridge had already attempted to organize a community under the Law of Consecration and Stewardship in Ohio at a time when he could have consulted the Prophet with problems as they arose. Moreover Partridge was one of the few persons selected by Joseph Smith to travel in his company the entire distance from Ohio to Jackson County, Missouri, on the occasion of the Prophet's first visit there. During this trip the site for the city of Zion was selected and Partridge was commissioned to stay and supervise the temporal aspects of building up the new kingdom. Certainly he would have had a clear reading of the Prophet's intentions and incorporated them into the document. It is even possible that the two drafted the forms together before Joseph Smith returned to Ohio. Given Partridge's pious, obedient character, it is unlikely that he would have acted in so important a matter without being assured that his policies reflected the Prophet's will. However widely the consecration and stewardship forms were used, they undoubtedly represented Joseph Smith's mind, or at least Edward Partridge's best reading of his mind on how the new order was to be established.

Obviously, the forms were written to provide legal protection for the

Mormon communitarian experiment, and they accordingly reflect the spirit and intent of both leaders and members only insofar as this could be translated into the language of civil law. The verb "give" did not adequately convey the meaning to Mormons of the verb "consecrate." The words "lease" and "loan" did not fully capture the meaning of the words "inheritance" and "stewardship." In effect the forms represent only the dry bones of a system animated by high sentiment and religious fervor. The essence of the system does not translate readily into legal forms.

It has been proposed alternatively that the documents should best be read as an in-house agreement between bishop and communicant intended to represent the "real" terms of a sacred covenant, whatever form civil law might require. By this view, for example, it would have been understood by both parties that land tenure was only during the continued faithfulness of the member, even though the land might be legally deeded to the member in fee simple. The document was to underline the important terms of the religious agreement, whatever civil law might require in the matter.

Three observations argue strongly against this point of view. First, the document itself reads clearly as an effort to draft the Law of Consecration and Stewardship into the language of civil law. This would not have been necessary had parallel civil transactions been intended. Second, there is evidence that Joseph Smith's letter of May 2, 1833, to Edward Partridge (see text of Chapter 2) was a response to requests by church members that land be given them in fee simple rather than leased, representing an about-face in official stewardship policy. Third, to date no evidence has been found to show that individual Mormons other than Bishop Partridge held title to lands in Jackson County, or at least to lands granted as an inheritance. It is possible that such evidence, had it existed, was destroyed by Missourians who altered records to conceal their illegal seizure of Mormon lands. But Partridge in 1839 still claimed title to 2,136 acres of land in Jackson County, an extent of land probably made up for the most part of parcels already granted as inheritances to individual members. (See the *Evening and the Morning Star* 2 (July 1833): 110; DePillis, "Mormon Communitarianism," pp. 191-95, 200-4 and passim; Joseph Smith, Jr., *History of the Church of Jesus Christ of Latter-day Saints*, ed. B. H. Roberts, 7 vols., 2nd ed. rev. [Salt Lake City, 1964], 1:297-99, 340-41, 365; Edward Partridge statement of losses in Missouri, May 15, 1839, Church Archives, Salt Lake City, Utah.)

BE IT KNOWN, THAT I, *James Lee*

Of Jackson county, and state of Missouri, having become a member of the church of Christ, organized according to law, and established by the revelations of the Lord, on the sixth day of April, 1830, do, of my own free will and accord, having first paid my just debts, grant and hereby give unto EDWARD PARTRIDGE of Jackson county, and state of Missouri, bishop of said church, the following described property, viz:— *a number of saddlers tools, one candlestick & one wash bowl valued seven dollars twenty five cents,— also saddlers stock, trunks and harness work valued twenty four dollars,— also extra clothing valued three dollars*

in Jackson county Mo,

For the purpose of purchasing lands, and building up the New Jerusalem, even Zion, and for relieving the wants of the poor and needy. For which I the said *James Lee* do covenant and bind myself and my heirs forever, to release all my right and interest to the above described property, unto him the said EDWARD PARTRIDGE, bishop of said church. And I the said EDWARD PARTRIDGE, bishop of said church, having received the above described property, of the said *James Lee* do bind myself, that I will cause the same to be expended for the above mentioned purposes of the said *James Lee* to the satisfaction of said church; and in case I should be removed from the office of bishop of said church, by death or otherwise, I hereby bind myself and my heirs forever, to make over to my successor in office, for the benefit of said church, all the above described property, which may then be in my possession.

In testimony whereof, WE have hereunto set our hands and seals this day of in the year of our Lord, one thousand eight hundred and thirty

IN PRESENCE OF

[SEAL.]

[SEAL.]

[SEAL.]

Deed of Stewardship or Lease and Loan Agreement
of Joseph Knight, Jr. (handwriting is in italics)

Be it known, that I, *Edward Partridge* of Jackson county, and state of Missouri, bishop of the Church of Christ, organized according to law, and established by the revelations of the Lord, on the 16th day of April, 1830, have leased, and by these presents do lease unto *Joseph Knight, jun.* of Jackson county, and state of Missouri, a member of said church, the following described piece or parcel of land, being a part of section No. Thirty *three,* township No. *forty nine* range No. *thirty three,* situated in Jackson county, and state of Missouri, and is bounded as follows, viz: *Beginning forty two rods E. from the N.W. corner of sd Sec. thence E. on the N. line of sd. Sec. ten rods, thence S. 5½° W. thirty six rods twenty one S. thence W. six rods to land leased to N. Knight, thence N. thirty six rods to the place of beginning, containing one acre and eighty one hundreths be the same more or less.*
And also have loaned the following described property, viz:—*sundry articles of crockery, tinware, knives, forks and spoons, valued nine dollars forty three cents. Sundry articles of iron ware and household furniture valued twelve dollars ninety two cents,—one bed and bedding valued nineteen dollars,—sundry articles of clothing valued twenty two dollars thirteen cents,—Grain valued seven dollars,— sundry articles of joiner tools valued twenty dollars forty four cents,—one cow valued twelve dollars.*

TO HAVE AND TO HOLD the above described property by him the said *Joseph Knight, jun.* to be used and occupied as to him shall seem meet and proper. And as a consideration for the use of the above described property, I the said *Joseph Knight, jun.* do bind myself to pay the taxes, and also to pay yearly unto the said *Edward Partridge* bishop of said church, or his successor in office, for the benefit of said church, all that I shall make or accumulate more than is needful for the support and comfort of myself and family. And it is agreed by the parties, that this lease and loan shall be binding during the life of the said *Joseph Knight, jun.* unless he transgress, and is not deemed worthy by the authority of the church, according to its laws, to belong to the church. And in that case I the said *Joseph Knight, jun.* do acknowledge that I forfeit all claim to the above described leased and loan property, and hereby bind myself to give back the leased, and also pay an equivalent for the loaned, for the benefit of said church, unto the said *Edward Partridge* bishop of said church, or his successor in office. And further, in case of said *Joseph Knight, jun.* or family's inability in consequence of infirmity or old age, to provide for themselves while members of this church, I the said *Edward Partridge* bishop of said church, do bind myself to administer to their necessities out of any funds in my hands appropriated for that purpose, not otherwise disposed of, to the satisfaction of the church. And further, in case of the death of the said *Joseph Knight, jun.* his wife or widow, being at the time a member of said church, has claim upon the above described leased and loaned property, upon precisely the same conditions that her said husband had them, as above described; and the children of the said *Joseph Knight, jun.* in case of the death of both their parents, also have claim upon the above described property, for their support, until they shall become of age, and no longer: subject to the same conditions yearly that their parents were; provided however, should the parents not be members of said church, and in possession of the above described property at the time of their deaths, the claim of the children as above described, is null and void. In testimony whereof, We have hereunto set our hands and seals this twelfth day of October in the year of our Lord, one thousand eight hundred and thirty two.

In presence of

John Corrill
Newel Knight
Edward Partridge [Seal]
Joseph Knight jun? [Seal]
Betsy Knight

12th October 1832

BEIT KNOWN, THAT I, *Benjamin Eames*

Of Jackson county, and state of Missouri, having become a member of the church of Christ, organized according to law, and established by the revelations of the Lord, on the sixth day of April, 1830, do, of my own free will and accord, having first paid my just debts, grant and hereby give unto EDWARD PARTRIDGE of Jackson county, and state of Missouri, bishop of said church, the following described property, viz:— *sundry articles of furniture valued fourteen dollars twenty five cents, also two beds, bedding and extra clothing valued thirty two dollars seventy five cents, also sundry farming utensils valued ten dollars seventy five cents, also one yoke of cattle and one cow valued thirty eight dollars*

in Jackson county Mo,

For the purpose of purchasing lands, and building up the New Jerusalem, even Zion, and for relieving the wants of the poor and needy. For which I the said *Benjamin Eames* do covenant and bind myself and my heirs forever, to release all my right and interest to the above described property, unto him the said EDWARD PARTRIDGE, bishop of said church. And I the said EDWARD PARTRIDGE, bishop of said church, having received the above described property, of the said *Benjamin Eames* do bind myself, that I will cause the same to be expended for the above mentioned purposes of the said *Benjamin Eames* to the satisfaction of said church; and in case I should be removed from the office of bishop of said church, by death or otherwise, I hereby bind myself and my heirs forever, to make over to my successor in office, for the benefit of said church, all the above described property, which may then be in my possession.

In testimony whereof, WE have hereunto set our hands and seals this

day of   in the year of our Lord, one thousand eight hundred and thirty

IN PRESENCE OF

                                                                        [SEAL.]

                                                                        [SEAL.]

                                                                        [SEAL.]

BE IT KNOWN, THAT I, EDWARD PARTRIDGE, of Jackson county, and state of Missouri, bishop of the church of Christ, organized according to law, and established by the revelations of the Lord, on the sixth day of April, 1830, have leased, and by these presents do lease unto *Benjamin Eames* of Jackson county, and state of Missouri, a member of said church, the following described piece or parcel of land, being a part of section No.

township No.   range No.

situated in Jackson county, and state of Missouri, and is bounded as follows, viz:

And also have loaned the following described property, viz:— *sundry articles of furniture valued fourteen dollars twenty five cents,— also two beds, bedding and clothing valued thirty two dollars seventy five cents,— also sundry farming utensils valued ten dollars seventy five cents,— also one yoke of cattle and one cow valued thirty eight dollars*

TO HAVE AND TO HOLD the above described property, by *him* the said *Benjamin Eames* to be used and occupied as *he* shall seem meet and proper, during *his* life, unless *he* transgress and is not deemed worthy, by the authority of the church according to its laws, to belong to the church; and in that case I the said *Benjamin Eames* do acknowledge that I forfeit all claim to the above described property, and hereby bind myself to quit the said leased premises, and also to pay an equivalent for the loaned, for the benefit of said church, unto the said EDWARD PARTRIDGE, bishop of said church, or his successor in office. And as a consideration for the use of the above described property, I the said *Benjamin Eames* do bind myself to pay the taxes, and also to pay yearly unto the said EDWARD PARTRIDGE, bishop of said church, or his successor in office, for the benefit of said church, all that I shall make or accumulate more than is needful for the support and comfort of myself and family. And in case of the said *Benjamin Eames* and family's inability to provide for themselves while members of said church, I the said EDWARD PARTRIDGE bishop of said church, do bind myself to administer to their necessities out of any funds in my hands appropriated for that purpose, not otherwise disposed of, to the satisfaction of said church. And in case of the death of the said *Benjamin Eames* his wife or widow, being at the same time a member of said church, has claim upon the above described leased and loaned property, upon precisely the same conditions that her said husband had them, as above described; and the children of the said *Benjamin Eames* in case of the death of both their parents, also have claim upon the above described property for their support, until they shall become of age; subject to the same conditions yearly that their parents were: Provided however, should the parents be found transgressors of the law of said church, and be expelled from the same, before their death, the claim of their children is null and void. But after said children become of age, if members of said church, they have claim upon the Lord's storehouse for inheritances.

In testimony whereof, we have hereunto set our hands and seals this   day of in the year of our Lord, one thousand eight hundred and thirty

IN PRESENCE OF

[SEAL]

[SEAL

*Deeds of Consecration and of Stewardship in the Archives
of The Church of Jesus Christ of Latter-day Saints (1975)*

Name	Both Deeds in Collection	Consecration Only	Stewardship Only
Titus Billings	X		
Stephen Chase*	X		
Benjamin Eames*	X		
George W. Pitkin*	X		
James Lee		X	
Sanford Porter†			X
Joseph Knight, Jr.			X
Levi Jackman	X		

*Deed contains no land description or only partial land description.
†Deed contains no personal property description.

The stewardship agreement of Joseph Knight, Jr., was copied in 1862 by Thomas Bullock from an original then in possession of Joseph Knight. The original is not in the Church Archives. The copy in the Church Archives has question marks behind the signature of Joseph Knight, apparently because the signature was not sufficiently legible to be certain that it was his or because he used a signatorial flourish that appeared to the copyist to be a question mark.

These documents are all in the Edward Partridge papers, Church Archives, Salt Lake City, Utah. It is entirely likely that more such documents will be found as inventorying of materials in the Church Archives continues. Also, it is possible that the archives of the Reorganized Church of Jesus Christ of Latter Day Saints in Independence, Missouri, contains Deeds of Consecration and Stewardship not included in the tabulation.

Schedule of Personal Property Evaluations in Extant Deeds of Consecration

Name	Value of Income-Producing Property (Livestock, tools, etc.)	Value of Household Furnishings and Personal Effects	Total
James Lee	$ 31.25	$ 3.00	$ 34.25
George W. Pitkin	192.50	115.37	307.87
Benjamin Eames	48.75	47.00	95.75
Stephen Chase	175.02	86.17	261.19
Titus Billings	188.00	128.52	316.52
Levi Jackman	11.25	81.50	75.99
Total	$646.77	$389.56	$1,091.57
Mean	$107.80	$64.93	$181.92
Plus Schedules in Extant Deeds of Stewardship			
Joseph Knight, Jr.	32.24	70.40	102.64
Total	$679.01	$531.96	$1,210.97
Mean	$ 97.72	$75.99	$173.00

The aggregation of property schedules into income-producing and household furnishings-personal effects categories was done by the authors. The evaluation of property consecrated was done by the bishop in consultation with the grantor. The schedule of Knight was added separately because of the possibility that his Deed of Stewardship might have been exceptional in showing property of less value than that consecrated because a surplus had been taken into the Lord's storehouse. His Deed of Consecration has not survived.

The data are only a very rough indicator of values involved because of the very few cases for which records have survived. A rough conversion to present values could be made by multiplying 1832 values by a factor of three or four. These figures are based from conversion of wholesale price index tables in U.S. Bureau of the Census, *Historical Statistics of the United States, Colonial Times to 1975* (Washington, D.C.), and U.S. Bureau of the Census, *Statistical Abstract of the United States: 1972,* 93rd edition (Washington, D.C., 1972). A pound of butter costing $.15 in the 1830s costs about $.80 in 1974. Average annual wages for laborers ranged from $200 to $900 in 1890. Though aggregative data for earlier periods are not available, literary evidence suggests that a $150 annual wage was not uncommon in the 1830s. By 1974 $10,000 was a common figure. See *Statistical Abstract*, 93rd editions, table #379 and subsequent editions; and *Historical Statistics*, pp. 293-94.

Brigham Young's Deed of Consecration
April 11, 1855, Book A, page 249[1]

BE IT KNOWN BY THESE PRESENTS That I, Brigham Young of Great Salt Lake City in the County of Great Salt Lake, and Territory of Utah; for and in consideration of the good will which I have to the Church of Jesus Christ of Latter-day Saints, give and convey unto Brigham Young, Trustee in Trust for said Church, his successors in office and assigns, all my claim to, and ownership of the following described property, to wit:

Block 89 in Great Salt Lake City Survey, with all the buildings and improvements thereon, consisting of "White House," Barn, one Row of Log Houses, one small adoby house, one milk house, one smoke house, one corn house and garden, entire value $25,000.

Lots 1 & 2 south quarter of lots 7 and 8 in block 88, one large house, garden, and a small Doby Shoe Shop and log house, value $60,000.

Lots 1, 2, 3, 4, 5, 6, 7 in Block 5, Plat B, and debts due value $14,000.

Half of lot 2 in block 74 value $500.

Lot 4 in block 17, with log and doby house, and all improvements thereon, value $300.

Lots 6 and 7 in block 14, value $100.

Lot 2, block 4, value $150.

One Doby house & garden north adjoining Block 89, value $2,000 including little Saw Mill.

Lot 2 in block 14, in B. Young's new survey, and one doby house thereon, value $1,000.

114 Lots in said new survey, value $11,400. All of which is within Great Salt Lake City survey.

One old garden farm, situated east of Great Salt Lake City survey, but within the limits of Great Salt Lake City incorporation, $2,000.

The undivided share of Chases Mill, and farm of 100 acres, value $40,000.

One half of Kanyon Creek Flouring Mill, and farm of 200 acres, value $14,000.

Three Lots of 5 acres each, No. 10 Block 15, No. 11 Block 15, No. 3 Block 7, Value $300.

One Farm over Jordan value $2,000.

40 acres of mowing land at the mouth of South Willow Creek, value $400.

Improvements on Antelope Island $500.

House and farm in San Pete County, the house of rough stone, in Manti City, the farm immediately north, value $5,000.

Three hundred and fifty head of Cattle, value $7,000, and ten horses,

---

[1] *Pioneer Records,* Salt Lake County Recorder's Office.

value $500 on Antelope Island. Nine Horses value $1,350.
  Nine mules, value $1,350.
  Eight wagons, value $400.
  One Coach $400.
  Three carriages, value $450.
  One Omnibus value $300.
  Two Buggies, value $250.
  One Sleigh value $150.
  One Fanning Mill value $50.
  One Threshing Machine $800.
  Three good sets of Harness, value $125.
  Nine common sets of harness, value $135.
  Twenty ploughs value $300.
  One Harrow value $10.
  Fifteen Cows in the G. S. L. City value $525.
  Five pigs value $50.
  Seven head of Cattle at Church pasture value $200.
  One gold watch and chain $750.
  One gold watch value $100.
  Four gold watches at $65 each value $260.
  Three silver watches at $50 each value $150.
  Six clocks at $20 each value $120.
  Silver plate value $250.
  Six cooking stoves at $50 each value $300.
  Twenty-one beds and bedding at $100 each, value $2,100.
  Four small beds value $100.
  Crockery and table ware value $500.
  Other household furniture value $1000.
  The Butterfield lot No. 4 in Block 84 in G. S. L. Survey $1,000.

RECAPITULATION

$25,000	$ 300	$250	$ 260
60,000	2,000	150	150
14,000	400	50	120
500	500	800	250
300	5,000	125	300
100	7,000	135	2,100
150	500	300	100
2,000	1,350	10	500
1,000	1,350	525	1,000
11,400	400	50	1,000
2,000	400	200	
40,000	450	750	
14,000	300	100	
		Total:	$199,625

Together with all the rights, and privileges, and appurtenances thereunto belonging or appertaining. I also covenant and agree that I am the lawful claimant and owner of said property, and will warrant and forever defend the same, unto the said Trustee in Trust, his successors in office and assigns, against the claims of my heirs, assigns, or any person whomsoever.

Brigham Young

Witnesses: Daniel H. Wells
             Joseph Cain
             Albert Carrington

Territory of Utah
County of Great Salt Lake

I, Elias Smith, judge of the Probate Court, for Great Salt Lake County, certify that the signer of the above transfer, personally known to me, appeared this Eleventh day of April, A.D. 1855, and acknowledged that he of his own choice, executed the foregoing transfer.

E. Smith

Constitution and by-laws of the Zion's Co-operative Mercantile Institution

PREAMBLE

The inhabitants of Utah, convinced of the impolicy of leaving the trade and commerce of their Territory to be conducted by strangers, have resolved, in public meeting assembled, to unite in a system of co-operation for the transaction of their own business, and for better accomplishment of this purpose have adopted the following:

CONSTITUTION

"Holiness to the Lord." Zion's Co-operative Mercantile Institution

Sec. 1. This Association shall be known by the name and style of "Zion's Co-operative Mercantile Institution," and shall have perpetual succession.

Sec. 2. The objects of this Institution are to establish and carry on in Salt Lake City and such other places as may be determined by the Board, the business of General Merchandising.

Sec. 3. The Capital stock of this Institution shall be three millions of dollars ($3,000,000) and may be increased to five millions ($5,000,000) and be divided into shares of one hundred dollars ($100) each.

Sec. 4. The officers of this Institution shall consist of a President, Vice-President, Board of Directors, Secretary and Treasurer, each and every one of whom shall be stockholders in this Institution.

Sec. 5. The Board of Directors shall consist of not less than five (5), nor more than nine (9) persons, including the President and Vice-President, who shall be ex-officio members of the Board.

Sec. 6. It shall be the duty of the President to preside at all meetings of the Institution and of the Board and to sign all documents, as are, or may be, prescribed by the Constitution and By-Laws, except certificates of dividends to stockholders. In case of absence or disability of the President, the Vice-President shall perform the duties of the President, and in all meetings of the stockholders the President shall have the power to adjourn the meetings from time to time to accomplish the transaction of the business.

Sec. 7. It shall be the duty of the Board to enact By-Laws for the general management and direction of the business of this institution and to procure suitable places for the transaction of the business by lease, purchase or construction, also so far as may be necessary, to employ and appoint committees, delegates, agents, attorneys and clerks to assist in carrying on the business and promoting the welfare of the Institution, and to discharge the same at pleasure.

Sec. 8. They shall also have full power to bargain, sell, convey and deliver under seal or otherwise any and all species of property belonging to this Institution, which may not be needed for the business thereof, on such terms and conditions as they may deem for the best interest of the same; provided, that the sale of shares and merchandise shall be for cash only.

Sec. 9. It shall be the further duty of the Directors to furnish quarterly statements of the business and balance sheets of the books for the inspection of the sharcholders, the first to be furnished on the fifth day of July, 1869, and quarterly thereafter, said statements and balance sheets shall remain open in the office of the Secretary for not less than thirty days.

Sec. 10. There shall also be furnished by the Directors, a semiannual statement in detail of the business of the Institution, to be read before the general meeting of the stockholders to be holden at 2 p.m., on the fifth days of October and April in each year, at such places as the Directors may designate, also declaration of dividend, the first semiannual meeting to be held on the fifth day of October, 1869: Provided that if any of said days shall fall on Sunday, said reports shall be furnished and meetings held on the day preceding.

Sec. 11. The Directors shall have further power to call general meetings at such other times and places as in their judgment may be required, reasonable notice being given thereof.

Sec. 12. The Board of Directors shall have power by a two-thirds vote of their number, to remove any Director or other officer from his office for conduct prejudicial to the interests of the Institution; if the officer sought to be removed be a Director he shall not vote on any matter connected with such removal.

Sec. 13. All business brought before the Board for consideration shall be determined by a majority of the whole number, each member being entitled to one vote and one only, irrespective of shares held by said Director.

Sec. 14. The Directors shall convene for the transaction of the business of the Institution at the call of the President, and as they shall adjourn from time to time.

Sec. 15. All officers of the Institution shall be elected by a majority of votes given at the general meeting, holden on the fifth day of October in each year, provided, that whenever a vacancy shall occur from any cause, the Board may fill such vacancy by appointment, till the next general meeting; all officers shall hold their office until their successors are elected and qualified.

Sec. 16. In all matters transacted in general meetings each stockholder shall have one vote, and one only for each and every share owned by him.

Sec. 17. The Secretary shall record the minutes of all meetings, and conduct all correspondence under the direction of the Board, he shall hold the common seal and attend to all other duties, whether prescribed by this constitution or the by-laws or required by the President.

Sec. 18. The Treasurer shall have charge of all funds belonging to the Institution, and shall employ or disburse the same, as required by the provisions of the Constitution, and shall furnish statements of account when required by the Board.

Sec. 19. The funds of the Institution shall be subject to appropriation by the Board only, and disbursed by the Treasurer on order signed by the President or Vice-President, and countersigned by the Secretary.

Sec. 20. No person or persons shall be eligible for membership, except they be of good moral character and have paid their tithing according to the rules of the Church of Jesus Christ of Latter-day Saints.

Sec. 21. The Directors of this Institution shall tithe its net profits prior to any declaration of dividend, according to the rules of the Church mentioned in the preceding section.

Sec. 22. The President, Vice-President, Board of Directors, Secretary and Treasurer, before entering upon the duties of their several offices, shall take oath or affirmation for the faithful performance of all duties required by this Constitution.

Sec. 23. The Treasurer shall give bonds with approved securities to the Institution, in such sums as may be deemed necessary by the Board, subject to increase, as circumstances may render advisable.

Sec. 24. The Secretary and Treasurer shall be the only paid officers of the Institution, and their remuneration shall be as determined by the Board of Directors.

Sec. 25. All certificates of stock issued by the Institution shall be for one share, or multiple thereof: they shall be signed by the President or Vice-President and Secretary, under the common seal, they shall be registered in the office of the Secretary, and shall be deemed personal property and as such, subject to sale and transfer. The form of certificate, registration and mode of transfer shall be prescribed by the Board.

Sec. 26. All dividends shall be paid if required, within thirty days after the same shall have been declared.

Sec. 27. The private property of shareholders shall not be held subject to the liabilities of the Institution.

Sec. 28. The seal of this Institution shall bear the inscription "Holiness to the Lord" "Zion's Co-operative Mercantile Institution, 1869," with beehive and bees in center.

Sec. 29. This Constitution may be amended or altered at any general meeting of the shareholders, by a two-thirds vote of the shares represented, provided that thirty days notice shall have been given in some public newspaper published in this Territory, of such contemplated amendment or alteration.

BY-LAWS

1. All houses wherein the business of this Institution may be transacted shall have placed over the main entrance the following inscription: "Holiness to the Lord" "Zion's Co-operative Mercantile Institution."

2. The number of Directors may be increased when deemed necessary, by a two-thirds vote of the shares represented at any general or special meeting of the Institution.

3. The number of Directors may be diminished by a two-thirds vote of the shares represented at any semi-annual meeting held on the fifth day of October.

4. The capital stock of this Institution may be increased to its constitutional limit by a majority vote of shares represented at any general meeting.

5. All business transactions of this Institution shall be done by its authority and under its name and title.

6. All documents authorized by the Board requiring an acknowledgment and seal shall be signed and acknowledged by the President, attested by the Secretary and seal of the Institution.

7. All certificates of stock issued by this Institution shall bear date of the first legal day of the month succeeding the day of purchase.

8. Registration of stock certificates shall consist of an entry in the Stock Ledger of the Institution, of the name of the person to whom the certificate is issued, the number of shares for which it is issued and the number and date of the certificate. Such registration shall be deemed prima facie evidence of ownership.

9. The following shall be the form of the certificate of stock issued by this Institution. It shall be nine inches in length, exclusive of the stub, (which shall be two and a half by five inches) by five inches in width, and shall be an engraving on steel or copper plate.

10. There shall be kept a Transfer Book in the Secretary's office, in which shall be recorded the transfer of all stock and shall be in the following form: (Form given)

11. The Secretary shall be paid by the person making a transfer of stock, the sum of fifty cents for every transfer recorded by him.

12. All dividends after the same shall have been declared shall be deemed individual property, and shall be paid by the Treasurer, on the certificate of the Secretary, under the seal of the Institution, stating the sum due to the stockholder.

13. Shareholders requiring more than one certificate for stock purchased at any one time, shall pay the Government tax on all such certificates in excess of one.

14. The Secretary shall have the general oversight of the Books of the Institution, under the direction of the Board to whom they shall be at

all times open for inspection.

15. There shall be preserved in the Secretary's office a copy of all correspondence, and on file, copies of all contracts, powers of attorney, leases and letters of instruction executed by the Institution, and all original bonds and conveyances to the Institution; also a duplicate copy of all original invoices of merchandise purchased by the Institution.

Name and location of the cooperative stores organized and those in operation in Utah 1868-1880

City	Name of Store
Box Elder County	
Brigham City	Brigham City Co-op. Merc. & Mfg. Association.
Bear River City	Bear River City Co-operative Institution.
Honeyville	Honeyville Co-operative Mercantile Institution.
Mantua	Mantua Co-operative Mercantile Institution.
Portage	Portage Co-operative Mercantile Institution.
Willard City	Willard City Co-operative Mercantile Institution.
Deweyville	Deweyville Co-operative Mercantile Institution.
Cache County	
Logan	Logan Branch of Zion's Co-operative Merc. Inst.
Logan	Fourth Ward Co-operative Mercantile Institution.
Logan	United Order Store.
Clarkston	Clarkston Co-operative Mercantile Institution.
Hyde Park	Hyde Park Co-operative Mercantile Institution.
Lewiston	Lewiston Co-operative Mercantile Institution.
Hyrum	Hyrum Co-operative Mercantile Institution.
Mendon	Mendon Co-operative Mercantile Institution.
Newton	Newton Co-operative Mercantile Institution.
Paradise	Paradise Co-operative Store and Saw Mill.
Millville	Millville Co-operative Mercantile Institution.
Providence	Providence Co-operative Store and Saw Mill.
Richmond	Richmond Co-operative Mercantile Institution.
Smithfield	Smithfield Manufacturing & Mercantile Institution.
Wellsville	Wellsville Co-operative Store, Saw Mill, and Butcher Shop.
Rich County	
Lake Town	Lake Town Co-operative Mercantile Institution.
Randolph	Zion's Co-operative Mercantile Institution.
Weber County	
Ogden	Ogden Branch, Zion's Co-operative Mercantile Inst.
Ogden	Second Ward Co-operative Mercantile Institution.
Plain City	Plain City Co-operative Mercantile Institution.
Morgan County	
Morgan	ZCMI Incorporated.
Croydon	Croydon Co-operative Mercantile Institution.

Table compiled by Olsen from the following: Edward L. Sloan, *Gazetteer of Utah and Salt Lake City 1874*; H.L.A. Culmer, *Utah Directory and Gazetteer 1879-80*; reprinted from Olsen, *The History of Mormon Mercantile Cooperation in Utah.*

City	Name of Store

Summit County

City	Name of Store
Kamas	Kamas Co-operative Mercantile Institution.
Coalville	Coalville Co-operative Mercantile Institution.
Peoa	Peoa Co-operative Mercantile Institution.
Wanship	Wanship Co-operative Mercantile Institution.
Oakley	Oakley Co-operative Mercantile Institution.

Davis County

City	Name of Store
Centerville	Centerville Co-operative Mercantile Institution.
Bountiful	Bountiful Co-operative Mercantile Institution.
Bountiful	West Bountiful Co-operative Mercantile Institution.
Farmington	Farmington Co-operative Store.
Kaysville	Farmer's Co-operative Store.

Tooele County

City	Name of Store
Tooele	Tooele Co-operative Manufacturing & Mercantile Inst.
Grantsville	Grantsville Co-operative Mfg. & Merc. Institution.
St. John	Rush Valley Cooperative Mercantile Institution.

Salt Lake County

City	Name of Store
Salt Lake City	Zion's Co-operative Mercantile Institution.
Salt Lake City	First Ward Co-operative Mercantile Institution.
Salt Lake City	Second Ward Co-operative Mercantile Institution.
Salt Lake City	Third Ward Co-operative Mercantile Institution.
Salt Lake City	Fourth Ward Co-operative Mercantile Institution.
Salt Lake City	Fifth Ward Co-operative Mercantile Institution.
Salt Lake City	Sixth Ward Co-operative Mercantile Institution.
Salt Lake City	Tenth Ward Co-operative Mercantile Institution.
Salt Lake City	Eleventh Ward Co-operative Mercantile Institution.
Salt Lake City	Twelfth Ward Co-operative Mercantile Institution.
Salt Lake City	Thirteenth Ward Co-operative Mercantile Institution.
Salt Lake City	Fourteenth Ward Co-operative Mercantile Institution.
Salt Lake City	Fifteenth Ward Co-operative Mercantile Institution.
Salt Lake City	Sixteenth Ward Co-operative Mercantile Institution.
Salt Lake City	Twentieth Ward Co-operative Mercantile Institution.
Salt Lake City	Twenty-first Ward Co-operative Mercantile Institution.
Sandy	Sandy Co-operative Mercantile and Manufacturing Co.
Murray	People's Co-operative Mercantile Institution.
Draper	Draper Co-operative Mercantile Institution.
Taylorsville	Taylorsville Co-operative Mercantile Institution.
South Jordan	South Jordan Co-operative Mercantile Institution.
West Jordan	West Jordan Co-operative Mercantile Institution.
Mill Creek	Mill Creek Co-operative Mercantile Institution.

City	Name of Store
Utah County	
Provo	Provo Branch ZCMI
Provo	Provo Co-operative Mercantile Institution.
Provo	West Branch Provo Co-operative Institution.
Alpine	Alpine Co-operative Mercantile Institution.
Spanish Fork	Spanish Fork Co-operative Institution.
Lehi	The Lehi Union Exchange.
Lehi	The People's Co-operative Institution.
Springville	Springville Co-operative Mercantile Institution.
American Fork	American Fork Co-operative Mercantile Institution.
Payson	Payson Co-operative Institution.
Pleasant Grove	Pleasant Grove Co-operative Institution.
Santaquin	Santaquin Co-operative Institution.
Salem	Salem Co-operative Mercantile Institution.
Goshen	Goshen Co-operative Store.
Benjamin	Benjamin Co-operative Mercantile Institution.
Fairfield	Fairfield Co-operative Mercantile Institution.
Cedar Fort	Cedar Fort Co-operative Mercantile Institution.
Wasatch County	
Heber	Heber Co-operative Store.
Charlston	Charlston Co-operative Store.
Midway	Midway Co-operative Mercantile Institution.
Wallsburg	Wallsburg Co-operative Mercantile Institution.
Uintah County	
Vernal	Ashley Co-operative Mercantile Institution.
Juab County	
Nephi	Nephi Co-operative Mercantile Institution.
Mona	Mona Co-operative Mercantile Institution.
Juab	Juab Co-operative Mercantile Institution.
Levan	Levan Co-operative Mercantile Institution.
Chicken Creek	Levan Branch Co-operative Mercantile Institution.
Sanpete County	
Manti	Manti Co-operative Mercantile Institution.
Ephraim	Ephraim United Order Mercantile Institution.
Mt. Pleasant	Mt. Pleasant Co-operative Mercantile Association.
Fairview	Fairview Co-operative Mercantile Institution.
Fountain Green	Fountain Green Co-operative Mercantile Institution.
Moroni	Moroni Co-operative Mercantile Institution.
Spring City	Spring City Co-operative Mercantile Institution.
Wales	Wales Co-operative Mercantile Institution.
Chester	Chester Co-operative Mercantile Institution.

City	Name of Store
Gunnison	Gunnison Co-operative Mercantile Institution.
Fayette	Fayette Co-operative Mercantile Institution.
Mayfield	Mayfield Co-operative Mercantile Institution.
Indianola	Indianola Co-operative Mercantile Institution.
Pettyville	Pettyville Co-operative Mercantile Institution.

Carbon County

Price	Price Co-operative Mercantile Institution.

Emery County

Castle Dale	Castle Dale Co-operative Mercantile Institution.
Huntington	Huntington Co-operative Mercantile Institution.
Emery	Farmers Co-operative Store.
Cleveland	Cleveland Co-operative Mercantile Institution.

Sevier County

Richfield	Richfield Co-operative Mercantile Institution.
Salina	Salina People's Co-operative Store.
Salina	Salina Co-operative Mercantile Institution.
Monroe	Monroe Co-operative Mercantile Institution.
Monroe	People's Co-operative Institution.
Red'mond	Redmond Co-operative Mercantile Institution.
Elsinore	Elsinore Co-operative Mercantile Institution.
Joseph	Joseph Co-operative Mercantile Institution.
Glenwood	Glenwood Co-operative Mercantile Institution.

Millard County

Fillmore	Fillmore Co-operative Mercantile Institution.
Scipio	Scipio Co-operative Mercantile Institution.
Kanosh	Zion's Co-operative Mercantile Institution.
Meadow	Meadow Co-operative Mercantile Institution.
Oak City	Oak City Co-operative Mercantile Institution.
Holden	Holden Co-operative Mercantile Institution.
Hamblin	Hamblin Co-operative Mercantile Institution.

Beaver County

Beaver City	Beaver Co-operative Mercantile Institution.
Beaver City	Equality Co-operative Store.
Minersville	Minersville Co-operative Mercantile Institution.

Piute County

Marysvale	ZCMI Incorporated.

Iron County

Cedar City	Cedar City Co-operative Merc. & Mfg. Institution.
Paragoonah	Paragoonah Co-operative Mercantile Institution.
Kanarrah	Kanarrah Co-operative Mercantile Institution.

City	Name of Store
Garfield County	
Panguitch	Panguitch Co-operative Mercantile Institution.
Washington County	
St. George	St. George Co-operative Mercantile Institution.
St. George	Ladies Co-operative Store.
Hebron	Hebron Co-operative Mercantile Institution.
Leeds	Leeds Co-operative Mercantile Institution.
Rockville	Rockville Co-operative Mercantile Institution.
Virgin City	Virgin City Co-operative Mercantile Institution.
Pinto	Pinto Co-operative Mercantile Institution.
Sant Clara	Sant Clara Co-operative Mercantile Institution.
Toquerville	Toquerville Co-operative Mercantile Institution.
Kane County	
Orderville	United Order of Orderville.
New Harmony	Harmony Co-operative Mercantile Institution.
Glendale	Glendale Co-operative Mercantile Association.
Kanab	Kanab Co-operative Merc. and Mfg. Institution.

Preamble and Articles of Agreement
of the United Order of the City of St. George

[Ed. note: Erastus Snow referred to the association created by the following articles of agreement as the gospel plan. This plan was superseded by the legal plan, which throws greater safeguards about property.]

The following has been matured and adopted without dissent, by the United Order of St. George. It is the result of much deliberation aided by the invaluable counsels and suggestions of President Brigham Young:

Realizing by the spirit and signs of the times and from the results of our past experience, the necessity of a closer union and combination of our labor for the promotion of our common welfare.

And, Whereas, we have learned of the struggle between Capital and Labor, resulting in strikes of the workmen, with their consequent distress; and also, the oppression of monied monopolies;

And, Whereas, there is a growing distrust and faithfulness among men in the political and business relations of life, as well as a spirit for extravagant speculation and over-reaching the legitimate bounds of the credit system resulting in financial panics and bankruptcy; paralyzing industry, thereby making many of the necessities and conveniences of life precarious and uncertain;

And, Whereas, our past experience has proven that, to be the friends of God, we must become the friends and helpers of each other, in a common bond of brotherhood;

And, Whereas, to accomplish such a desirable end and become truly prosperous we must be self-sustaining, encouraging home manufacture, producing cotton, wool and other raw materials; and not only supply our own wants with manufactured goods, but also have some to spare for exportation, and by these means, create a Fund for a sure basis upon which to do all our business;

And, Whereas, we believe that by a proper classification of our labors and energies, with a due regard to the laws of life and health, we will not only increase in earthly possessions at a more rapid rate, but will also have more leisure time to devote to the cultivation and training of our minds, and those of our children, in the arts and sciences.

And, Whereas, at the present time, we rely too much upon importation for a large share of our clothing and other necessaries; and also bring from abroad many articles of luxury and of but little value, for which we pay our money, most of which articles could be dispensed with;

And, Whereas, we believe that the beauty of our garments should be the workmanship of our own hands and that we should practice more diligently, economy, temperance, frugality and the simple grandeur of manners that belong to the pure in heart;

And, Whereas, we are desirous of avoiding the difficulties above alluded to and feel the necessity of becoming a self-sustaining community; fully realizing that we live in perilous times, socially, morally, politically and commercially;

Therefore: Be it Resolved that we, the undersigned, being residents of the places set opposite our respective names, do hereby, of our own free will and choice and without mental reservation, or purpose of evasion, and also without any undue influence, constraint or coercion having been used by any party whatever, to direct and guide us in this action, mutually agree, each with the others and with our associates, and successors, to enter into and form a co-partnership for the purposes and subject to the provisions as herein set forth, viz:

Article 1. The name and style of this co-partnership shall be the United Order of the City of St. George.

Article 2. The objects of this Order are to carry on a general business of farming, manufacturing, merchandizing, fruit-growing, stock-raising, dairying and as many other pursuits as will tend to the material prosperity of the Order.

Article 3. The principal place of business shall be at the City of St. George, but other places may be selected by the Board of Management, for carrying on the different branches of the business of the Order.

Article 4. The Officers of this Order shall consist of a President, two Vice-Presidents, a Secretary, two assistant Secretaries, one Treasurer and three Directors, who shall form a Board of Management, to do business for the Order. They shall be members of the Order and be elected by vote of two-thirds of the whole number of members; they shall hold their office during good behavior, or at the pleasure of the members of the Order.

Article 5. It shall be the duty of the President, to preside at all meetings of the members and of the Board. In case of absence or disability of the President, either of the Vice-Presidents may perform the duties of the President. The President shall call meetings of the Board or of the members whenever the business of the Order may require it.

Article 6. It shall be the duty of the Secretary to make a faithful record of the meetings of the members and of the Board; to keep the Account Book of the Order, and make a Financial Report of the business of the Order to the Board as often as required. In all these duties, the Secretary shall be assisted by the Assistant Secretaries. The Board may also appoint a corresponding Secretary if the business of the Order requires it.

Article 7. It shall be the duty of the Treasurer to receive, and safely keep all property belonging to the Order committed to his charge. He shall employ or disburse the same on Orders from the Secretary, or, as the Board may direct. He shall also furnish a true and correct statement of all money and other property received, disbursed and on hand to the Board of Management, whenever required.

Article 8. The Board of Managements shall have power to call to their assistance such help as may be required, for carrying on successfully the business of the Order.

Article 9. All property offered for investment in the Order shall be appraised by a committee elected by the members of the Order; who shall report their labors to the Secretary, whose duty it shall be to credit as Capital Stock the property invested by each individual as valued by the committee. Said Committee shall also fix upon the price of labor and all individual services rendered.

Article 10. There shall be a foreman elected for each branch of business; whose duty it shall be to superintend and manage the business entrusted to his care; he shall give credit for all labor performed by each member of his Department, and charge said members with all they may draw. Said foreman shall report their accounts to the secretary as often as may be deemed necessary by him; or required by the Board.

Article 11. There shall be a meeting held of the members of the Order in the City of St. George, on the first Monday of February in each year, at which time the Board of Management shall furnish an Annual Report of the business of the Order. At such meetings the Officers of the Order shall be presented for approval or disapproval by the members and shall be continued in office if sustained by a two-thirds vote of all the members of the Order Provided: That, if through disability, any member is unable to attend, he may have the right to state by letter whom he wishes to vote for, or vote by proxy. The Board shall have power to enact By-laws for the general management and direction of the business of the Order, which By-laws shall be presented to the members at the Annual meeting; and when approved by a two-thirds vote of all the members of the Order, shall become as binding upon them as these Articles of Agreement. The Board shall also have full power to buy real estate and to buy and sell personal property and products and do all other business consistent with the interest of the Order.

Article 12. We hereby agree to place in this Order, fully and entirely subject to these Articles of Agreement and all By-laws approved by the members, as above specified, all our time, labor, energy, and ability, and such property as we may feel disposed to transfer to the Order, to be controlled in the interest of the Order, as may be deemed best by the Board of Management.

Article 13. At the end of five years after the Organization of this Order, the Board of Management shall cause an Inventory to be taken of all the properties of the Order, and make a general settlement of the business during the said five years and compute a dividend of gains on the capital stock of the Order. Which dividend shall be credited to each individual member in proportion to the capital stock invested by him, or her and the time of such investment. At the end of every subsequent five years, a similar settlement of accounts shall be made and dividends credited to individuals as above provided for. Should any of us who are subscribers to this Instrument, choose to entirely withdraw from the Order at, or before the end of the fifth year from the organization of this Order, we hereby agree to accept at the end of said five years one-half of the Capital and one-half of the dividend, credited us, as above provided, as a full compensation, for all our claims of whatsoever nature or kind and for all services rendered. Should any of us choose to withdraw during any subsequent term of five years, we will accept the above mentioned rate of percentage in full of all our claims. And we hereby declare it to be our full belief, that, by uniting our labor and energies we shall receive such an increased profit beyond what we would be able to obtain by individual exertion, that we are willing to take the above named fifty per cent of the capital and dividend placed to our credit, as a just and equitable proportion of all our claims against the Order, in the event of our desiring to separate ourselves from said Order.

Article 14. We will not assume the payment of any individual's debts, contracted previous to his or her uniting with the Order, unless property be furnished the Order to enable the Board to cancel such indebtedness; and we will not become responsible for the payment of any debt that will be contracted hereafter by any individual member, unless said debt be contracted with consent of the Board.

Article 15. We further agree to encourage home manufacture to the fullest extent of our ability; to produce cotton, wool and other raw materials and to cease the importing and using of any foreign merchandise which can be reasonably dispensed with. And that we will make every effort to develop new branches of home industry, until we have become self-sustaining in every particular. To this end we will not patronize in our business relations, those who are not members of the Order, unless absolutely compelled by our necessities.

Article 16. We also agree to be temperate, economical and frugal in our food and drink, avoiding as much as possible, the use of imported luxuries.

Article 17. In our dress, we desire to be plain and neat and as much as possible, wish to be clothed in the workmanship of our own hands. We deprecate foolish and extravagant fashions; and while we have a due appreciation of neatness and beauty, we believe it ruinous to our interests to copy after extravagance and to be forever changing in style of apparel at a great and unnecessary expense.

Article 18. We further agree to be energetic, industrious and faithful in the management of all business entrusted to us and to abstain from all selfish motives and actions, as much as lies in our power. We desire to seek the interest and welfare of each other, and to promote the especial good of the Order, and the general welfare of all mankind.

The following circular letter was issued to the United Orders of St. George Stake by Presidents Brigham Young and George A. Smith.

Dearly Beloved Brethren:

Ever mindful of the true interests of those who belong to the Redeemer's Kingdom, and realizing that the time of His coming draweth near and that a great work of preparation remains yet to be done to fit those who have taken upon themselves His name and have covenanted at the waters of baptism, and oft times since then, to keep His command-ments with full purpose of heart, serving God with all their might, mind and strength and feeling that the time has come and now is, when the Latter-day Saints should truly manifest to themselves, to their fellows and to their God, by actual works, that they verily believe the declaration of the Lord Jesus, given to the Church in 1831, through the Prophet Jo-seph: "I say unto you be one and if ye are not one, ye are not mine," we deem it expedient to pen a few thoughts and suggestions to aid in secur-ing a more complete unity in earthly things, that, in these as well as in heavenly things we may be more completely one.

More than forty-two years ago, the Lord said to the Church, through Joseph: "Verily I say unto you the time has come and is now at hand; and behold and lo it must needs be that there be an organization of my people, in regulating and establishing the affairs of the storehouse for the poor of my people, both in this place and in the land of Zion, or in other words the City of Enoch, for a permanent and everlasting establishment and Order unto my Church to advance the cause which ye have espoused, to the salvation of man and the glory of your Father who is in heaven, that you may be equal in the bands of heavenly things; yea, and earthly things also, for the obtaining of heavenly things; for if ye are not equal in earthly things, ye cannot be equal in obtaining heavenly things; for if you will that I give unto you a place in the celestial world, you must prepare yourselves by doing the things which I have commanded you and required of you." This law and commandment given in March, 1832, together with other revelations on the same subject given before and since, have been before the Church, in the Book of Doctrine and Covenants these many years. And further, as a Church, we have had before us the express declaration of the Lord in the Revelation given on Fishing River, Missouri, in 1834. After finding fault with those who were not united according to the union required by the law of the celestial Kingdom; that "Zion cannot be built up unless it is by the principles of the law of the celestial kingdom, otherwise I cannot receive her unto myself; and my people must needs be chastened until they learn

obedience, if it must needs be, by the things which they suffer." Because
of the lack of experience in the ways of God, and that His people might
know more perfectly what He requires at their hands, obedience to this
Celestial Law has not been exacted from them. But now, after increased
experience and that we may prepare ourselves to live more completely in
accordance with the Spirit of the Gospel, we have commenced to give organizations of the United Order, or Order of Enoch, to the settlements
and shall continue to do so, until every settlement of the Saints shall
share this privilege and blessing.

To secure a greater amount of benefit from our combinations under
this Order, we offer the following suggestions. In the Management of our
affairs, family and otherwise, it will be well to adopt a spirit of proper
economy in the use of all committed to our care.

Fruit: Carefully gather the fruit, and under the most intelligent and
practical direction, have it canned, or dried, and put up in such a manner,
that it will be fit for any market.

Wine: Have this made in but few places, say, three or four for this
southern country. At these points obtain the best available skill to manufacture the wine, and have it properly graded in quality. Then store it in
oak barrels as far as possible and preserve it for exportation, rather than
for home consumption.

Forage: Put up lucern as carefully as possible and protect by movable
cheap roofs, called barracks in the East. At threshing time, also, have the
wheat straw and other straw and the chaff carefully husbanded and
protected by the same kind of roof.

Farming: Freely sow and plant, so that surplus of grain and other
products may be raised. Particular attention should be paid to increasing
the amount of cotton produced. Corn should be freely planted; and
where the prospect for water is good corn may be planted on wheat lands
after the wheat is harvested. For this season, it will be well for such
mechanics as can be spared, to apply their labor in farming, that as much
grain as possible, may be produced to sustain the people and avoid the
necessity of bringing bread from the North. It would be advisable to use
more of the labor of oxen on farms instead of using so many horses and
mules.

Improve Stock: Improve horses, cattle, sheep and other stock. To aid
in doing this, scrub horses should be got out of the way, by killing them,
or by otherwise getting them entirely out of the country. If they be killed,
their hides should be tanned. All the oil that can be obtained from the
carcass, should be properly taken care of; and the bones should be saved
for making buttons. In improving cattle it is suggested that long horned
Devons make the best draught oxen for farm work and general freighting.

Home Manufactures: We wish to produce, as much as possible what we need for our own consumption. Hides should be carefully taken off and properly cared for and tanned into good leather. In obtaining material with which to tan, small bushes of oak should be pounded up for tanning purposes and after peeling bark see that what poles may be stripped are hauled away for use and not left to waste.

We recommend for health purposes to say nothing of economy, which will also be served, that wooden bottomed shoes be used. We advise also for women and children and for the lighter wear of men that strong cloth be used for uppers, instead of leathers; particularly, while leather is scarce.

Make hats out of native material as far as possible.

Trading in the North: To attend to this business in the most economical manner and for the best good of all, one reliable agent will be used for this Southern Country and teams under the control of the Order, will be used to freight what may be needed. Members of the United Order are not expected to go trading to the North on their individual responsibility.

In Conclusion: Let every member of the United Order so live that each may have the Spirit of the Lord to be with them all the time.

Brigham Young
George A. Smith

Uniform articles of incorporation for branches
of the United Order, general instructions, and rules

Uniform articles of incorporation prepared in Salt Lake City, and presented to the branches of the United Order by presiding authorities of the Church who were themselves officers and directors of the United Order of Zion. It will be seen from Appendix VIII that only a few of the branches of the Order were incorporated.

Territory of Utah)

)ss.

County of   )

WHEREAS, We the undersigned, being desirous of forming a corporation for purposes hereinafter mentioned, do adopt the following:

ARTICLES OF ASSOCIATION

ARTICLE I

The name of this corporation shall be the United Order of

ARTICLE II

This corporation shall continue in existence for a period of twenty-five years.

ARTICLE III

The objects of this corporation are for Mining, Manufacturing, Commercial, and other industrial pursuits, and the construction and operation of wagonroads, irrigation ditches, and the colonization and improvement of lands, and for establishing and maintaining colleges, seminaries, churches, libraries and benevolent, charitable, or scientific associations, and for any other rightful object consistent with the Constitution of the United States and the Laws of this Territory. Also to take, receive, and execute trusts, either passive or active; and for these purposes shall have the right and power to receive, take, and hold, either by gift, purchase, or devise, the right, title, interest and possession of real or personal property; and may bargain, sell, and alienate the same and thereby pass such title thereto as it may hold therein.

But it is expressly understood and agreed that when property is held by this corporation as a trustee, the beneficiary of the trust shall not, in consideration of such trust, be entitled to stock in said company; and it is further understood and agreed that if the beneficiary holds and keeps possession of the trust property, this company shall not be accountable or liable, nor in any way responsible for the rents, issues, or profits thereof. But the trust, duty, power, interest, and authority of this company to such property shall be as expressed in the Deed of Conveyance thereto, of real property, or in the agreement between the parties, if personal.

ARTICLE IV

The general place of business of this corporation shall be in the Territory of Utah, with the right, privilege, and power to establish one or more branch places of business in each or any of the counties of the Territory.

ARTICLE V

The capital stock of this corporation shall be   dollars, which shall be divided into   shares of one hundred dollars each.

ARTICLE VI

The officers of this corporation shall consist of a Board of   Directors, a President, two Vice Presidents, a Secretary and a Treasurer (in number), whose qualifications shall be to own and hold in said corporation at least   shares of stock; and whose term of office shall be one year and until their successors shall be elected and qualified.

ARTICLE VII

There shall be an annual meeting of the Stockholders of this company, held at its general place of business in the county of   Territory of Utah, at   on the   in   of each year, for the purpose of electing Directors to serve for the ensuing year; notice of which shall be given as prescribed by the by-laws.

The Directors, when so elected, shall be notified of that fact by the secretary of the meeting at which such election is made, and thereupon they shall within twenty days thereafter, meet and organize as a Board, and shall elect from their number a President, two Vice Presidents, a Secretary and Treasurer.

ARTICLE VIII

All elections, whether by the stockholders or by the Board, shall be by ballot, unless at the meeting at which the election is to be made, it is decided by a majority of those present and entitled to vote, to make the election viva voce. The person receiving a majority of the votes cast shall be deemed and declared duly elected.

ARTICLE IX

The Board of Directors shall have power to make all by-laws for the management of the property of the company, the regulation of its affairs, the transfer of its stock, for prescribing the duties of its officers, agents and employees, and such other by-laws, rules and regulations as may be necessary for fully carrying out the objects of this corporation. They shall have power to appoint from the members of said Board or from the stockholders, an executive committee not to exceed five in number, whose part in the management of the affairs of the corporation shall be as prescribed by the by-laws, and shall also have power to appoint or provide for the appointment of all appraisers of property agents, assistants, and employees, whose services in this corporation may be necessary. And no contract shall be binding on this corporation except when made by the Board or its duly authorized agents.

ARTICLE X

Any officer of this corporation may be removed for conduct prejudicial to the interests of the same, by a two-thirds vote of the Directors.

ARTICLE XI

Any vacancy occuring in the Board of Directors or other office of the corporation, may be filled by the Directors until the next regular election.

ARTICLE XII

Any officer of this corporation may resign his office by giving the Board thirty (30) day's notice in writing, before the same is to take effect, but the same may be accepted on shorter notice.

ARTICLE XIII

The individual or private property of the stockholders shall not be liable for the debts or obligations of the company.

ARTICLE XIV

The subscribers hereto have each fully paid   of the capital stock subscribed by transferring, paying and conveying to said corporation the following real and personal property, the value of which has been ascertained by competent parties, duly appointed for that purpose, a description and kind of which are given in the schedule hereunto attached and which is hereby declared to be a part and portion of these articles.

ARTICLE XV

The Directors shall have the right and power to declare dividends on said stock whenever, in their judgment, there are funds for that purpose due and payable. But when so declared, the same may be paid to the stockholders in proportion as they may be entitled, or credited to them in the books of the company, and stock issued at them in payment therefor, at the option and in the discretion of the Directors.

ARTICLE XVI

The names, places of residence, and number of shares taken by each subscriber hereto are as follows:

	I		I No. of
Name	I	Place of residence	I Shares.

In witness whereof we have hereunto set our hands this   day of A.D. 187 .

Territory of Utah)
County of   )ss.
Precinct of   )
City of   )

On this   day of   A.D. 187__   personally appeared before me   , Probate Judge in and for the county of   , Territory of Utah, whose names are subscribed to the foregoing instrument, as parties thereto, and who on their part executed the same, and the said parties duly acknowledged to me each for himself and for the other parties to the agreement that they each respectively executed the same freely and voluntarily and for the uses and purposes therein mentioned.

In witness whereof I have hereunto set my hand and affixed my official seal, in the city of   , County of   , this   day of   , A. D. 187__.

PROBATE JUDGE.

Territory of Utah,
County of

We,
being the same persons whose names are in, and who subscribed the foregoing agreement, being first duly sworn according to law, on our several oaths to say that it is bona fide the intention of the persons named in said agreement to commence and carry on the business as therein mentioned, and that said officials and each of them verily believe that the parties thereto are able and willing to pay for the shares of stock subscribed by them in said company, and that   has been paid.

BY-LAWS OF THE UNITED ORDER OF

Section 1.

The fiscal or business year of this Company shall commence on the first day of   in each year, and shall terminate on the day of

Section 2.

All meetings of the stockholders of this company, whether regular or special, shall be held in the company's office in   , unless some other place be designated by the Directors; notice of which, stating the time, place and object thereof, shall be given by the Secretary of the Company, by publishing the same for at least ten days prior to such meeting.

Section 3.

The stockholders owning not less than one-third of the capital stock, may at any time call meetings, notice of which shall be given as prescribed in the foregoing section. If at any such meeting so called a majority of the stock is not represented, either in person or by written proxy, such meeting shall be adjourned from day to day, not exceeding three days, without transacting any business; and if within said three days, stockholders having at least a majority of the stock do not attend, and participate in such meeting, then the same shall be dissolved.

Section 4.

A regular meeting of the Board of Directors shall be held at o'clock on the   in each month, at such place as the Directors shall from time to time prescribe, which may be continued or adjourned at the discretion of the Board, a majority of whom shall be a quorum to do business.

Section 5.

The President or any three Directors may at any time call special meetings of the Board, due notice of which shall be given, of time and place, to the Directors personally, or by publishing the same for at least three days prior to the holding thereof.

Section 6.

It shall be the duty of the President to sign all deeds, bonds, notes, and other writing obligatory, to which the company is a party, when such writings shall have been approved by the Board or Executive Committee. He shall preside at all meetings of the Board of Directors and of Stockholders, and in cases of a tie, shall have the casting vote. In the absence of the President, or when, for any cause, he is unable to discharge his duties in person, one of the Vice Presidents shall exercise all the powers and perform all of the duties of the President; the Vice President shall have precedence in the order in which they are respectively designated in the order of their election. When the President and both the Vice Presidents are absent from any meeting of the Board or the Stockholders, a President pro tem. shall be elected by and from among the members thereof.

Section 7.

The Secretary shall, unless by the Board otherwise ordered, make out a statement at the end of each year, showing the financial condition of the company and lay the same before the Board at their next regular meeting. He shall have a general supervision of the accounts of the company, and shall have sole custody of the corporate seal, and affix the same to all instruments required to be sealed, and perform such other duties as shall be required of him, by the Board of Directors.

Section 8.

It shall be the duty of the Treasurer of this Corporation to receive and safely keep all moneys, valuables, evidences of value, and other property deposited or entrusted with him by the Board, and to disburse the same on warrants issued by the Secretary, countersigned by the President. He shall preserve the vouchers in support of all disbursements by him made and shall keep accurate and complete account of all money or other property received and paid out, and of all transactions appropriately belonging to the duties of his office, in books prepared for that purpose; which shall at all times be open to the inspection of any member of the Board. He shall render, at the end of each fiscal year, or oftener if required by the Directors, a statement of the receipts and disbursements during the preceding year, and present the same to the Board at its next general meeting thereafter, and shall do and perform such other duties as shall be required of him by the Board of Directors.

Section 9.

The Board of Directors shall elect from their number an executive committee of three, whose duty it shall be to attend to the business of the company, subject always to the control and direction of the Board. They shall appoint, either from their own number or from among the stockholders, two or more appraisers, whose duty it shall be to assess the value of all property to be bought by or turned into the corporation, provided, in case of dissatisfaction with such appraisal, an appeal may be had to the Board of Directors, or other appraisers may be added for that case.

Section 10.

The Secretary of the company shall keep, in a book provided for that purpose, a correct copy of the proceedings of each meeting of the stockholders, as well as of the Board of Directors. Such record shall show the name of each Director present at such meeting of the Board and the name of any Director voting against any proposition, whenever such Director shall desire the same placed upon record. He shall also keep a book, labelled "Book of Stockholders," containing the names of all persons alphabetically arranged, who are or shall be stockholders in this company, showing their place of residence if known, the number of shares of stock held by them respectively, the time when they became owners of such shares, as also the time when they have ceased to be stockholders, which books, during office hours of the company, shall be open for the inspection of stockholders.

Section 11.

A certificate of stock shall be issued for fully paid up shares, and shall be signed by the President, and countersigned by the Secretary, and shall express upon its face its number and date of issuance, the number of shares for which and the name of the person to whom it is issued. No transfer of stock shall be made when a certificate thereof has been issued, until such certificate is properly endorsed and returned to the company. In case of the loss or destruction of a certificate of stock a duplicate thereof may be issued, provided a sufficient indemnity bond against loss or damage to the company, by reason of the finding such lost certificate, be first approved by and filed with the Secretary.

Section 12.

This company will not be the recipient of a trusteeship for personal property, unless it has an active duty to perform in connection therewith, and full right, power, and authority to exercise and carry out such trust, as in its judgment, it may deem for the best use and benefit of the beneficiary thereof; nor will it be a mere passive trustee for real property, except the grantor thereof make provision for just compensation for all labor and duties by it performed in carrying out the object and design of such trust; and it is distinctly understood and agreed by this company and the party or parties making such deeds, his or their heirs or assigns, and this clause in effect shall be incorporated into every deed of trust to this company, that all expenses and costs incurred in protecting the legal title thereto, or other labor connected therewith, including the labor of making and executing the deeds of the same, shall be paid by the beneficiary of the trust; and that for such expenses, this company shall have a lien on such property for the security thereof.

Section 13.

When this company is called upon or required to exercise an active power, connected with the duty of trusteeship, and this provision shall be in substance incorporated into every such deed of trust, it shall not be liable, accountable, or in any way responsible for the rents, issues, profits or losses of such property so long as it allows the beneficiary of such trust to have and hold control over the same; but in consideration of its agreeing to have and exercise such trustship, it shall have the right, power, and authority to, at any time, take possession of such property, and out of the rents, issues, and profits thereof, apply the same, in its discretion, to the maintainance of the beneficiary of such trust, his heirs or assigns; but in case the beneficiary of such trust shall wish to sell his interest in connection with, or separate from the legal title, he shall first get the written consent of this company; and in case he fails to do so, and sells or attempts to sell his interest in such property, or in case of his insolvency or legal judgments against him or them, then said company shall have the right and power, at its option, to sell and dispose of such property on such terms, and in such manner as it may deem expedient, and out of the proceeds of such sale, apply the means arising therefrom, to the maintainance and support of the beneficiary of said trust, his heirs or assigns, or it may, in its discretion, pay the whole of said proceeds to said beneficiary, in which event its liability ceases. And it is distinctly understood that the said trustee shall, in all trust property, have the option to purchase the same at the lowest market value, whenever the beneficiary thereof is desirous of selling his interest therein.

Section 14.

This company will not be the recipient of any trusteeship, unless the property so to be conveyed is free from all incumbrances; nor will it accept the trustship unless the beneficiary of such trust or the grantor will sign and endorse those by-laws.

Section 15.

These by-laws may be amended, altered, or repealed at any general meeting of the Board by a two-thirds vote thereof.

INSTRUCTIONS FOR MEMBERS OF THE UNITED ORDER

For numerous reasons, obvious to the reflecting, it has been deemed best to organize the various branches of the United Order in accordance with the laws of our Territory, as they afford us ample scope for carrying out plans for our more prosperous temporal welfare in learning and practising the best methods for living, and letting live, and helping to live, until we can become self-sustaining, and all enjoy the necessaries and comforts of life; also that we may be better able to sustain our operations against aggressions, whether internal or external.

The brethren were instructed that the first "articles" were only for the time being, and that we should proceed under them until we had time to prepare others in accordance with our laws. They are now prepared as briefly and plainly as possible, with a hope that they will be satisfactory, as we feel assured they will be when understood.

In our farming operations, cleanly and thorough tillage and the best variety of seeds are specially recommended for producing the most satisfactory results.

The use of oxen on farms and in most of our team work is advised, because we deem it the most economical.

Plowing, planting, sowing, irrigating, haying and harvesting can be most profitably conducted under as extensive a combination as each locality will permit, and under the direction of the most competent persons. The most improved implements of husbandry should be provided as speedily and extensively as possible; and whenever combining our field operations leaves a surplus of mowers, reapers, threshers, wagons, plows, etc., they should be properly taken care of until they are needed or can be disposed of.

Good and sufficient storehouses should be prepared for grain, and sufficient hay properly stacked and otherwise secured and shelters made for humanely caring for stock during winter, so that none be lost.

When surplus grain or other products are to be disposed of, let it be done by or through committees appointed for that purpose, which committees will correspond with and be advised by the committee or secretary of the Central Branch of the United Order in Salt Lake City, so that the sales may not conflict in different branches of the Order. The proceeds of such sales should be deposited with the Treasurer of the Association to which they belong, and be safely kept by him until otherwise directed by the Board.

When surplus potatoes cannot be profitable fed to stock or marketed, they should be made into starch.

The best varieties of white corn should be raised in suitable localities, and mills constructed for making it into samp.

Mustard, broom corn, hops, and sorghum should be raised in sufficient quantities to supply home demand.

Inasmuch as some continue the use of tobacco, and as it is good for sick cattle, and when planted in orchards is said to be a preventative against coddling moth, it is recommended that enough be raised to at least supply our own wants.

All fruits should be carefully gathered at maturity, and each cared for in the method best suited to its kind, that all may be most healthful in their use, the surplus be in the best possible condition for market, and no inferior or badly conditioned fruits offered for sale, as such fruits are injurious to health, damage the repute of our excellent varieties, and consequently militate against the extensive and rapidly increasing interests of fruit raisers.

When hay and straw are stacked the work should be well done, and the stacks, so far as practicable, either thatched or covered with cheap moveable roofs; and all straw and chaff should be carefully saved.

Our situation renders it advisable, so far as we may be able, to keep on hand a supply of bread stuff sufficient for from three to seven years.

As rapidly as possible the finest varieties of grapes for raisins should be added to those already in our southern settlements, and all our markets supplied with the best of raisins. So far as wine and brandy are produced, pain should be taken that they be of the purest and best qualities, and vessels and storage cellars should be prepared for keeping the wines in the best condition.

In raising stock it is well to keep in mind that those most adapted to the locations and purposes of the producers afford the most satisfaction and profit; and that inferior varieties, particularly scrub horses, are to be got rid of as fast as practical, in favor of better breeds.

It is also well to keep in mind that both humanity and profit require that all stock be properly cared for in winter as well as summer, that such as cannot be so cared for be disposed of, and that young and surplus stock be summered as fully and invariably as possible, on ranges inaccessible in winter. Among the different breeds of cattle the Devons are reputed to make the best work oxen, and are also said to make good milch cows and beef cattle.

To attain a self-sustaining position, to the fullest extent our resources and climate will permit, it is requisite that more attention be paid to manufacturing as extensively and variedly as our wants may require. Much cloth of excellent quality is now made in our Territory, but the quantity comes short of supplying the people, though wool continues to be sent abroad. Such sale is obviously very unwise, for it curtails an essential branch of manufacture in the extent it could and would aid trade and agriculture, sustaining outside labor to the detriment of our own. So also is leather; our hides are exported, while we import leather and the articles manufactured from it, throwing idle or into other employments our tanners and many of our shoemakers. So far as tannic acid should fail to be supplied from our red pine bark and oak and sumac shrubs, it would be cheaper to import the deficiency in a concentrated form than to sell our hides to distant markets and import leather. In short, our financial comfort and prosperity require that we give our agricultural and trading interests the powerful aid of manufactures as rapidly and fully as possible, until we can produce a full home supply of all required classes of fabric made from wool and leather, all our furniture, farming machines, and implements, and wood work and wooden ware of every description, hats, caps, bonnets, brooms, buttons, molasses, and everything within our capability, from time to time, for advantageously producing all we can consistently desire.

So far as we may lack timber suitable for our purposes, it is much wiser to import such timber than the manufactured articles; and in the meantime, as fast and extensively as possible, take steps for raising the black walnut, ash, and other valuable timber trees adapted to our several localities.

Due attention should be given to saving all rags suitable for making paper, that we may be able to print our school and all other books on home made paper.

One important key to our success is dispensing with all vain and other unwise expenditures, restricting our expenses within our means, and using those means in the most judicious manner.

In wet weather and where minerals keep the soil damp and cold, wooden bottomed shoes, iron shod or leather soled for durability are recommended both for health and economy. And while it continues scarce, it is advisable to use strong cloth, so far as practicable, for uppers for leather-soled shoes, especially for women and children and the light wear of men.

Wisdom dictates that we do not receive into the Order property what we can not properly care for.

It behooves all to at times cultivate and practice frankness and fairness in all our business, conduct and conversation, that the fullest confidence may exist that each is diligently laboring to promote the welfare of all, and by so wise a course the more speedily attain the beneficial results we have in view. Let every member so live as to all times enjoy the Spirit of the Lord for guidance in all labors and duties.

RULES THAT SHOULD BE OBSERVED
BY MEMBERS OF THE UNITED ORDER
(see also photograph on p. 232.)

Rule 1. We will not take the name of the Deity in vain, nor speak lightly of His character or of sacred things.

Rule 2. We will pray with our families morning and evening, and also attend to secret prayer.

Rule 3. We will observe and keep the Word of Wisdom according to the Spirit and meaning thereof.

Rule 4. We will treat our families with due kindness and affection, and set before them an example worthy of imitation; in our families and intercourse with all persons, we will refrain from being contentious or quarrelsome, and we will cease to speak evil of each other and will cultivate a spirit of charity towards all. We consider it our duty to keep from acting selfishly or from covetous motives, and will seek the interest of each other and the salvation of mankind.[1]

Rule 5. We will observe personal cleanliness, and preserve ourselves in all chastity by refraining from adultery, whoredom and lust. We will also discountenance and refrain from all vulgar and obscene language or conduct.

Rule 6. We will observe the Sabbath day and keep it holy in accordance with the revelations.

Rule 7. That which is not committed to our care we will not appropriate to our own use.

Rule 8. That which we borrow we will return according to promise, and that which we find we will not appropriate to our own use but seek to return to its proper owner.

Rule 9. We will as soon as possible cancel all individual indebtedness contracted prior to our uniting with the Order, and when once fully identified with said Order will contract no debts contrary to the wishes of the Board of Directors.

---

[1]The last clause of the original draft prepared at St. George was, and will seek the interest of each other and of the Order.

Rule 10. We will patronize our brethren who are in the Order.[2]

Rule 11. In our apparel and deportment we will not pattern after nor encourage foolish and extravagant fashions, and cease to import or buy from abroad any article which can be reasonably dispensed with, or which can be produced by combination of home labor. We will foster and encourage the producing and manufacturing of all articles needful for our consumption as fast as our circumstances will permit.

Rule 12. We will be simple in our dress and manner of living, using proper economy and prudence in the management of all entrusted to our care.

Rule 13. We will combine our labor for mutual benefit, sustain with our faith, prayers and works, those whom we have elected to take the management of the different departments of the Order and be subject to them in their official capacity, refraining from a spirit of faultfinding.

Rule 14. We will honestly and diligently labor, and devote ourselves and all we have to the Order, and the building up of the kingdom of God.

QUESTIONS AND ANSWERS

Q. Can a person owning real and personal property and having members of his family in two or more Branches of an organization put all of his property in whichever of those Branches he may prefer?

A. As a general thing property had better be placed in the Branch where it is located.

Q. What is to be done about mortgaged property?

A. Let the Board of Directors exercise their discretion in regard to accepting property that has any encumbrance.

Q. Shall there be a Board of Directors for each Branch of business within an association, or shall one board direct all the branches?

A. Let there be a Superintendent for each branch of business in each association, who will be under the direction of the Board of Directors.

Q. Will voting be done by shares, or will each member be entitled to one vote?

A. The legal way of voting is by shares.

Q. Will labor be credited as capital stock, if so, how often is it to be credited up?

A. If labor is in excess of consumption, the overplus will be credited to the persons as capital stock.

Houses and city lots can be deeded to the Order on its appraisal and subject to its disposal, or in trust and remain in the possession and control of the owners, as persons may prefer.

There will be no stock issued nor dividend allowed for property retained in the private use of a member.

---

[2]The St. George draft of Rule 10 was: We will not knowingly patronize any person engaged in any business who is not a member of the Order, unless our vicinities absolutely require us to do so.

Original organization
of the United Order of Zion

Organized May 9, 1874, at Salt Lake City. The following officers were presented at a general conference session, a continuation of the April annual conference, which after the opening meeting April 6, 1874, had been adjourned for one month:

President, Brigham Young

First Vice-President, George A. Smith

Second Vice-President, Daniel H. Wells

Assistant Vice-Presidents, Orson Hyde, Orson Pratt, Sr., John Taylor, Wilford Woodruff, Charles C. Rich, Lorenzo Snow, Erastus Snow, Franklin D. Richards, George Q. Cannon, Brigham Young, Jr., Joseph F. Smith, Albert Carrington

Secretary, David McKenzie

Assistant Secretaries, George Goddard, David O. Calder, Paul A. Schettler, James Jack, John T. Caine

General Bookkeeper, Thomas W. Ellerbeck

Treasurer, George A. Smith

Assistant Treasurer, Edward Hunter

Board of Directors, Horace S. Eldredge, John Sharp, Feramorz Little, Moses Thatcher, John Van Cott, James P. Freeze, Henry Dinwoodey, Thomas Taylor, Elijah F. Sheets

List of United Orders
prepared by Feramorz Young Fox

Alphabetical by Stake or Locality and Within Stakes by Date of Organization. See also the More Complete Alphabetical Listing in Appendix IX

An attempt has been made to compile from newspaper items and ward and stake histories a partial list of the stake (county or district) and local branches of the United Order, which would include date of organization and the name of the president of each branch. The main designations are in many cases localities and embryonic stakes that were not fully organized until 1877. In all but a few instances, the bishop of the ward became president of the local branch of the Order. Exceptions are noted. The * indicates that the bishop is named, but information concerning the organization of a branch of the Order is either incomplete or unavailable.

District: County or Stake	Date of Organization	By Whom Organized	President
BEAR LAKE	May 17, 1874		Charles C. Rich
Paris	May 17, 1874		*Henry James Horne
Montpelier	May 18, 1874	Wilford Woodruff Charles C. Rich	Charles E. Robinson
Bennington	May 19, 1874	Wilford Woodruff Charles C. Rich	Joseph W. Moore
Liberty	May 22, 1874	Wilford Woodruff Charles C. Rich	Edwin Nelson Austin
Meadowville			*Josiah Tufte
Ovid	May 22, 1874	Wilford Woodruff Charles C. Rich	Peter Jensen
Bloomington	May 23, 1874	Wilford Woodruff Charles C. Rich	George Osmond
St. Charles	May 24, 1874	Wilford Woodruff Charles C. Rich	*John Alexander Hunt
Georgetown			*Henry Arundel Lewis
Fish Haven	May 26, 1874	Wilford Woodruff Charles C. Rich	Hyrum S. Rich
Preston			*Henry H. Dalrymple
Woodruff	May 28, 1874	Wilford Woodruff Charles C. Rich	William H. Lee
Laketown	May 27, 1874	Wilford Woodruff Charles C. Rich	Ira Nebeker
Alma†	May 28, 1874	Wilford Woodruff Charles C. Rich	Randolph W. Stewart

†In 1974 the co-authors could find no evidence that a settlement named Alma existed in 1874 in the Bear Lake area.

District: County or Stake	Date of Organization	By Whom Organized	President
Randolph	May 28, 1874	Wilford Woodruff Charles C. Rich	Randolph W. Stewart
Almy, Wyoming	June 3, 1874	Wilford Woodruff	Samuel Pike
BEAVER	Apr. 12, 1874	Brigham Young	John R. Murdock
Beaver	Apr. 12, 1874	Brigham Young	John R. Murdock
Greenville	Apr. 12, 1874		R. Easton
Adamsville	Apr. 12, 1874		Joseph H. Joseph
Minersville	Apr. 12, 1874		James McKnight
BOX ELDER			
Willard City	May 24, 1874		George Welton Ward
Washakie			
Mantua	June 3, 1874	Erastus Snow Lorenzo Snow	J. Jensen
Brigham City	June 27, 1874	Brigham Young	Lorenzo Snow†
CACHE	May 2, 1874		Brigham Young, Jr.
Paradise	May 16, 1874	Brigham Young, Jr.	David James
Logan			William B. Preston
Logan 1st Ward			
Logan 2nd Ward			
Clarkston	May 31, 1874	Erastus Snow Lorenzo Snow	Simon Smith
Mendon			*Henry Hughes
Hyrum	Inc. Mar. 15, 1875		Ole N. Liljenquist
Hyde Park			*Robert Daines
Lewiston			*William H. Lewis
Wellsville	Mar. 1, 1875		*William H. Maughen
Millville			*G. O. Pitkin
Newton			*William F. Littlewood
Providence			*Milton D. Hammond
Richmond			*M. W. Merrill
Smithfield			*Samuel Roskelley
DAVIS			
Farmington	May 13, 1874	Brigham Young	John W. Hess
Bountiful	June 4, 1874		
North Kanyon	June 4, 1874	George A. Smith Orson Pratt John Taylor	Anson Call
Kaysville			*Christopher Layton
Centerville	June 23, 1874	Brigham Young	William R. Smith

†In a few instances the president of the United Order was someone other than the bishop. Alvin Nichols was bishop of Brigham City Ward but not president of the United Order.

District: County or Stake	Date of Organization	By Whom Organized	President
IRON	Apr. 10, 1874	Brigham Young George A. Smith Erastus Snow	
Kanarra	Apr. 7, 1874	Brigham Young	Lorenzo W. Roundy
Cedar City	Apr. 8, 1874		John H. Higbee†
Parowan	Apr. 10, 1874		William H. Dame
Paragoonah	Apr. 10, 1874	Brigham Young George A. Smith Erastus Snow	Silas S. Smith
Panguitch	June 27, 1874		*George W. Sevy
JUAB			
Nephi	Apr. 19, 1874	Brigham Young	*Joel Grover
Levan	Apr. 21, 1874		
KANAB			
Kanab	Mar. 12, 1874	John R. Young	John R. Young ‡
Johnson Settlement	Mar. 13, 1874	John R. Young	Sextus E. Johnson
Pahreah	Mar. 15, 1874	John R. Young	Allen F. Smith
Mount Carmel	Mar. 20, 1874 Inc. July 23, 1875	John R. Young	Israel Hoyt
Glendale	Mar. 22, 1874	John R. Young	James Leithead
Orderville	Early in 1875 Inc. July 22, 1875		Howard O. Spencer
MILLARD			
Millard	Apr. 15, 1874	Brigham Young	*Thomas Callister
Scipio	Apr. 16, 1874		
MORGAN			
Morgan			*Willard G. Smith
Porterville	1874-75		
Weber City			*Charles S. Peterson
ONEIDA			
Malad City	May 28, 1874	Erastus Snow Lorenzo Snow	Daniel Daniels
Samaria	May 28, 1874	Erastus Snow Lorenzo Snow	Samuel Williams
Clifton			*William Pratt
Franklin			*Lorenzo H. Hatch
Mound Valley			*Robert H. Williams
Oxford			*George Lake
Weston			*John Maughan
Soda Springs			*J. G. Faulkman

†Henry Lunt was bishop of Cedar City but not president of the United Order.
‡Levi Stewart was bishop of Kanab but not president of the United Order.

District: County or Stake	Date of Organization	By Whom Organized	President
ST. GEORGE	Mar. 15, 1874	Brigham Young Erastus Snow was resident apostle; John W. Young was president of the Southern Mission	
St. George	Feb. 9, 1874 Inc. Oct. 1, 1874	Brigham Young	Robert Gardner†
Price City (Branch of St. George United Order)	Feb. 17, 1874 Inc. Oct.	Brigham Young	
Washington	Feb. 21, 1874	Erastus Snow John W. Young	John W. Freeman Niels Sorenson, Supt.
Santa Clara	Feb. 21, 1874 Inc. Oct. 14, 1874		Edward Bunker
Rockville	Mar. 6, 1874	Brigham Young George A. Smith John W. Young	Charles N. Smith
Virgen City	Mar. 5, 1874 Inc. Dec. 12, 1874	Brigham Young George A. Smith John W. Young	John Parker
Toquerville	Mar. 8, 1874	Brigham Young George A. Smith John W. Young	Wm. A. Bringhurst
Pine Valley	Mar. 15, 1874	Erastus Snow Milo Andrus Angus M. Cannon	William Snow
Pinto Ward	Mar. 17, 1874	Erastus Snow Milo Andrus Angus M. Cannon	Richard S. Robinson
Morristown	Mar. 18, 1874	Brigham Young	Richard Morris
Shunesburg	Mar. 5, 1874		Oliver Demill
Panaca	Mar. 22, 1874	Erastus Snow Milo Andrus Angus M. Cannon	Thomas J. Jones
Hebron	Mar. 24, 1874	Erastus Snow Milo Andrus Angus M. Cannon	George H. Crosby
Belleview	Apr. 6, 1874		Davis Neilsen
St. George 1st			Wilson D. Pace
Harmony	Apr. 7, 1874	Erastus Snow	Wylis O. Fuller
Leeds and Harrisburg	Mar. 19, 1874	Robert Gardner	
SALT LAKE			
SLC 1st Ward	May 23, 1874		Joseph Warburton

†Daniel D. McArthur was bishop of St. George but not president of the United Order.

District: County or Stake	Date of Organization	By Whom Organized	President
SLC 2nd Ward	May 28, 1874		James Leach
SLC 3rd Ward	May 26, 1874 (Organized as branch of the 8th Ward)		
SLC 4th Ward			*Thomas Jenkins
SLC 5th and 6th wards (Combined)	May 22, 1874		William Hickenlooper
SLC 7th Ward	May 15, 1874		William Thorne
SLC 8th Ward	May 18, 1874		E. F. Sheets
SLC 9th Ward	May 27, 1874		Samuel A. Woolley
SLC 10th Ward	May 28, 1874		Adams Speirs
SLC 11th Ward	May 21, 1874	Brigham Young	Alexander McRae
SLC 12th Ward	May 22, 1874		Bishop Leonard W. Hardy
SLC 13th Ward	June 3, 1874	Daniel H. Wells	Edwin D. Woolley
SLC 14th Ward	May 13, 1874		Thomas Taylor
SLC 15th Ward	May 22, 1874		Robert T. Burton
SLC 16th Ward	May 20, 1874		Frederick Kesler
SLC 17th Ward	May 27, 1874		Nathan Davis
SLC 18th Ward†			
SLC 19th Ward	May 24, 1874	Daniel H. Wells	A. H. Raleigh
SLC 20th Ward	Apr. 29, 1874	Brigham Young	John Sharp
West Jordan	May 3, 1874	Angus M. Cannon A. M. Musser	Archibald Gardner
Sugar House			*W. C. A. Smoot
Mill Creek Ward	June 1, 1874		*Reuben Miller
Big Cottonwood			*W. G. Young
South Cottonwood	June 7, 1874		Joseph S. Rawlins
South Willow Creek	June 7, 1874		Isaac M. Stewart
Brighton	June 14, 1874		A. H. Raleigh
SANPETE	May 28, 1874	Orson Pratt John Taylor	Orson Hyde
Gunnison	Apr. 30, 1874	Joseph A. Young	Joseph S. Horne
Fayette	May 1, 1874	Joseph A. Young	John Bartholomew
Manti	May 26, 1874 Inc. 1876	Orson Pratt John Taylor	Andrew J. Moffitt
Ephraim	May 27, 1874	Orson Pratt John Taylor	Canute Peterson
Mayfield	Sept. 14, 1874		*Hans N. Toft
Spring City	May 27, 1874	Orson Pratt John Taylor	Frederick Olsen
Wales			*John E. Rees

†Brigham Young and family made up a large part of the membership of the 18th Ward. No record has been found of the organization of the United Order in this ward.

District: County or Stake	Date of Organization	By Whom Organized	President
Mount Pleasant	May 28, 1874	Orson Pratt John Taylor Orson Hyde	William S. Seely
New London			*Ola C. Olsen
Fairview	May 28, 1874	Orson Pratt John Taylor Orson Hyde	Amasa Tucker
Moroni	May 29, 1874	Orson Pratt John Taylor	*George W. Bradley
Fountain Green	May 29, 1874	Orson Pratt John Taylor	Robert L. Johnson
SEVIER	May 24, 1874		Joseph A. Young
Richfield	Apr. 19, 1874 Inc. Nov. 9, 1874	Joseph A. Young	Joseph A. Young
Glenwood	Apr. 22, 1874 Inc. Oct. 2, 1874	Joseph A. Young	Henry Zuphelt†
Prattville	Apr. 23, 1874 Inc. Sept. 26, 1874	Joseph A. Young	Helaman Pratt
Annabella	Apr. 24, 1874	Joseph A. Young	
Monroe	Apr. 26, 1874 Inc. Oct. 8, 1874	Joseph A. Young	James R. Lisonbee
Joseph City	Apr. 29, 1874	Joseph A. Young	
Salina	Apr. 28, 1874 Inc. Sep. 28, 1874	Joseph A. Young	Peter Rasmussen
Axtel (Branch of Salina)			
Elsinore	Inc. Nov. 9, 1874		
SUMMIT			
Henneferville	July 6, 1874	John Taylor	
North Summit			*William W. Cluff
Kamas			*Samuel F. Atwood
TOOELE			
Tooele			*John Rowberry
Grantsville			*John Rowberry
UTAH	Apr. 26, 1874	Wilford Woodruff Erastus Snow	Abraham O. Smoot
Provo	Apr. 26, 1874	Wilford Woodruff Erastus Snow	Abraham O. Smoot
Pleasant Grove	Apr. 27, 1874		Thomas Wooley†
American Fork and Alpine	Apr. 27, 1874		Leonard E. Harrington

†A. T. Oldroyd was bishop of Glenwood but not president of the United Order.
†John Brown was bishop of Pleasant Grove but not president of the United Order.

District: County or Stake	Date of Organization	By Whom Organized	President
Lehi and Cedar Valley	Apr. 28, 1874	Wilford Woodruff Erastus Snow Abraham O. Smoot	David Evans
Santaquin			*George Halliday
Goshen			*William Price
Payson	May 1, 1874		*Joseph S. Tanner
Spanish Fork	May 2, 1874		George D. Snell
Springville	May 3, 1874		Wm. Bringhurst
Cedar Fort and Fairfield	May 3, 1874	Leonard E. Harrington	Henry F. Cook
WASATCH			*Abram Hatch
WEBER	May 3, 1874 (temporary organization)		Franklin D. Richards
Ogden	May 3, 1874		
First District			
Second District	May 17, 1874		Walter Thomas
Third District	May 18, 1874		
West Weber	May 19, 1874		Joseph Parry
Eden	May 20, 1874		
Huntsville	May 20, 1874		
Weber Ward			*Lester J. Herrick
Marriott's Settlement	May 22, 1874		
Lynne	May 22, 1874		
Plain City	May 23, 1874		Lewis W. Shurtliff
Slaterville	May 24, 1874		Thomas Richardson

*Alphabetical list of all known
United Order organizations†*

†Compiled from lists prepared by Feramorz Y. Fox, Leonard J. Arrington, and L. Dwight Israelsen. The dates refer to date of organization unless otherwise specified. Branches marked with an asterisk do not appear in the chart prepared by Feramorz Y. Fox for Appendix VIII. Those for which Fox listed no date of organization or organizers have been omitted from this list unless we have been able to verify independently that an order was organized at that locality. This list is as comprehensive as present knowledge permits, but researchers will undoubtedly continue to unearth information on additional United Orders. All localities are in Utah unless otherwise indicated.

Adamsville, Beaver Co. . . . . April 12, 1874
Almy, Uinta Co., Wyoming . . . . June 7, 1874
Alpine, Utah Co. . . . . April 27, 1874
American Fork, Utah Co. . . . . April 27, 1874
Annabella, Sevier Co. . . . . April 24, 1874
*Axtell, San Pete Co.
Bear Lake Stake, Rich Co., Utah; Bear Lake Co., Idaho . . . . May 17, 1874
*Bear River City, Box Elder Co.
Beaver, Beaver Co. . . . . April 12, 1874
*Beaver Stake
*Beaver Dams, Arizona (Littlefield Ward)
Belleview (Bellevue), Washington Co. . . . . April 6, 1874
Bennington, Bear Lake Co., Idaho . . . . May 19, 1874
Big Cottonwood, Salt Lake Co.
Bloomington, Bear Lake Co., Idaho . . . . May 23, 1874
Bountiful, Davis Co. . . . . June 4, 1874
*Box Elder County
Brigham City, Box Elder Co. . . . . June 28, 1874
*Brigham City (Ballenger), Navajo Co., Arizona 1876
Brighton, Salt Lake Co. . . . . June 14, 1874
*Bunkerville, Clark Co., Nevada . . . . Jan. 1877
Cache Valley Central, Cache Co., Utah; Franklin Co., Idaho   May 2, 1874
*Cave Valley, Chihuahua, Mexico . . . . Jan. 1893
*Cedar, Emery Co.
Cedar City, Iron Co. . . . . April 8, 1874
Cedar Fort (Cedar Valley), Utah Co. . . . . May 3, 1874
*Centerfield, Sanpete Co. 1874
Centerville, Davis Co. . . . . June 23, 1874
*Center Stake, Salt Lake Co.
*Circleville, Piute Co.
Clarkston, Cache Co. . . . . May 31, 1874
*Coalville, Summit Co. (Cluff Ward)
*Cooper Bottom, Washington Co.

*Davis Co. .... Inc. March 15, 1876
*Eden, Weber Co.
Elsinore, Sevier Co.
Ephraim, Sanpete Co. .... May 27, 1874
Fairfield, Utah Co. .... May 3, 1871
Fairview, Sanpete Co. .... May 28, 1874
*Farmers and Horticulturists, Salt Lake Co.
Farmington, Davis Co. .... May 12, 1874
Fayette, Sanpete Co. .... May 1, 1874
*Fillmore, Millard Co. .... April 15, 1874
Fish Haven, Bear Lake Co., Idaho .... May 26, 1874
Fountain Green, Sanpete Co. .... May 29, 1874
Franklin, Franklin Co., Idaho .... Org., but did not function
Glendale, Kane Co. .... March 22, 1874
Glenwood, Sevier Co. .... April 22, 1874
Goshen, Utah Co.
*Graham, Graham Co., Arizona
Greenville, Beaver Co. .... April 12, 1874
Gunnison, Sanpete Co. .... April 30, 1874
Harmony (New Harmony), Washington Co. .... April 7, 1874
Harrisburg, Washington Co. .... March 19, 1874
*Harrisville, Weber Co.
*Hayden's Ferry (Hayden), Gila Co., Arizona
*Heber, Wasatch Co.
*Heberville Bottoms, Washington Co. .... Feb. 17, 1874
Hebron, Washington Co. .... March 24, 1874
Henneferville, Summit Co. .... July 6, 1874
*Holden, Millard Co.
Huntsville, Weber Co. .... May 20, 1874
Hyrum, Cache Co. .... Inc. March 15, 1875
Hyde Park, Cache Co.
*Iron County
*Jericho, Juab Co.
Johnson, Kane Co. .... March 13, 1874
Joseph, Sevier Co. .... April 29, 1874
*Joseph City (Allen's Camp), Navajo Co., Arizona 1876
*Juab Stake
Kamas, Summit Co.
Kanab, Kane Co. .... March 12, 1874
(Kannara) Kanarraville, Iron Co. .... April 7, 1874
*Kanosh, Millard Co.
Kaysville, Davis Co.
*Kingston, Piute Co. .... May 1, 1877
Laketown, Rich Co. .... May 27, 1874

Leeds, Washington Co. . . . . March 19, 1874
Lehi, Utah Co. . . . . April 28, 1874
Levan, Juab Co. . . . . April 21, 1874
Lewiston, Cache Co.
Liberty, Bear Lake, Idaho . . . . May 22, 1874
*Liberty, Weber Co., Utah
Logan, Cache Co.
Logan 1st, Cache Co.
Logan 2nd, Cache Co.
*Logan 3rd, Cache Co.
Lynne, Weber Co. . . . . May 22, 1874
Malad (Malad City), Oneida Co., Idaho . . . . May 28, 1874
*Mammoth, Juab Co.
Manti, Sanpete Co. . . . . May 26, 1874
Mantua, Box Elder Co. . . . . June 3, 1874
Marriott's Settlement . . . . May 22, 1874
Mayfield, Sanpete Co. . . . . Sept. 14, 1874
*Meadow, Millard Co.
Mendon, Cache Co.
*Mesa, Maricopa Co., Arizona
Millard, Millard Co. . . . . April 15, 1874
*Millard Stake
Mill Creek, Salt Lake Co. . . . . June 1, 1874
Millville, Cache Co. 1874
*Mill Point, Arizona
Minersville, Beaver Co. . . . . April 12, 1874
Monroe, Sevier Co. . . . . April 26, 1874
Montpelier, Bear Lake Co., Idaho . . . . May 18, 1874
Morgan, Morgan Co.,
Moroni, Sanpete Co. . . . . May 29, 1874
Morristown, Washington Co. . . . . March 18, 1874
Mt. Carmel, Kane Co. . . . . March 20, 1874
Mt. Pleasant, Sanpete . . . . May 28, 1874
*Mt. Trumbull, Mojave Co., Arizona . . . . May 14, 1874
Nephi, Juab Co. . . . . April 19, 1874
North Kanyon, Davis Co. . . . . June 4, 1874
*Oak Creek, Millard Co.
Obed (Obid), Navajo Co., Arizona
Ogden Central, Weber Co.
Ogden 1st District, Weber Co. . . . . May 3, 1874
Ogden 2nd District, Weber Co. . . . . May 17, 1874
Ogden 3rd District, Weber Co. . . . . May 18, 1874
Orderville, Kane Co. 1875-1900
*Overton, Clark Co., Nevada

Ovid, Bear Lake Co., Idaho .... May 22, 1874
Pahreah, Kane Co. (Presently Paria) .... March 15, 1874
Panaca, Lincoln Co., Nevada .... March 22, 1874 (Failed 1875)
Panguitch, Garfield Co. .... June 27, 1874
Paradise, Cache Co. .... May 16, 1874
Paragonah (Paragoonah), Iron Co. .... April 10, 1874
Paris, Bear Lake Co., Idaho .... May 17, 1874
Paris, Kane Co. .... March 15, 1874
Parowan, Iron Co. .... April 10, 1874
Payson, Utah Co. .... May 1, 1874
*Peoa, Summit Co.
Pine Valley, Washington Co. .... March 15, 1874 (Failed 1875)
Pinto, Washington Co. .... March 17, 1874 (Failed 1874)
*Pintura, Washington Co.
Plain City, Weber Co. .... May 23, 1874
Pleasant Grove, Utah Co. .... April 27, 1874
*Portage, Box Elder Co.
*Porterville, Morgan Co.
Prattville, Sevier Co. .... April 23, 1874
Price, Washington Co. (same as Heberville Bottoms) ..... Feb. 17, 1874
*Price, Carbon Co.
*Provo Central, Utah Co. .... April 26, 1874
Provo, Utah Co. .... April 26, 1874
*Provo Central, Utah Co.
Randolph, Rich Co. .... May 28, 1874
Richmond, Cache Co.
*Rockport, Summit Co.
Rockville, Washington Co. .... March 6, 1874 (Failed 1875)
*Salem, Utah Co. (part of Payson)
Salina, Sevier .... April 28, 1874
*Salt Creek, Arizona
Salt Lake Central Branch, Salt Lake Co. .... May 9, 1874
Salt Lake City 1, Salt Lake Co. .... August 4, 1875
Salt Lake City 1st, Salt Lake Co. .... May 23, 1874
    2nd, Salt Lake Co. .... May 28, 1874
    3rd, Salt Lake Co. (Organized as a branch of the 8th Ward) May 26,
        1874
    4th, Salt Lake Co.
    5th and 6th, Salt Lake Co. (Combined) .... May 22, 1874
    7th, Salt Lake Co. .... May 15, 1874
    8th, Salt Lake Co. .... May 19, 1874
    9th, Salt Lake Co. .... May 27, 1874
    10th, Salt Lake Co. .... May 28, 1874
    11th, Salt Lake Co. .... May 21, 1874

12th, Salt Lake Co. .... May 22, 1874
13th, Salt Lake Co. .... June 3, 1874
14th, Salt Lake Co. .... May 13, 1874'
15th, Salt Lake Co. .... May 22, 1874
16th, Salt Lake Co. .... May 20, 1874
17th, Salt Lake Co. .... May 27, 1874
18th, Salt Lake Co.
19th, Salt Lake Co. .... May 24, 1874 (Reorg. Sep. 9)
20th, Salt Lake Co. .... April 29, 1874
Samaria, Oneida Co., Idaho .... May 28, 1874
*Sanpete Stake
*Sanpete South Stake
Santa Clara, Washington Co. .... Feb. 21, 1874
Santaquin, Utah Co. (part of Payson)
Sevier Stake, Sevier Co. .... May 24, 1874
Scipio, Millard Co. .... April 16, 1874
Shunesburg (Shonesburg), Washington Co. .... March 5, 1874
*Simonsville, Arizona
Slaterville, Weber Co. .... May 24, 1874
Smithfield, Cache Co.
*Snowflake, Navajo Co., Arizona
Soda Springs, Oneida Co., Idaho
South Cottonwood, Salt Lake Co. .... June 7, 1874
South Willow Creek (Draper), Salt Lake Co. .... June 7, 1874
*Southern Utah Mission
Spanish Fork, Utah Co. .... May 2, 1874
Spring City, Sanpete Co. .... May 27, 1874
*Springdale, Washington Co.
*Springlake, Utah Co. (part of Payson)
Springville, Utah .... May 3, 1874
St. Charles, Bear Lake Co., Idaho
St. George, Washington Co. .... Feb. 15, 1974
St. George, 1st Ward, Washington Co. .... February 28, 1874
St. George Stake .... February 15, 1874
*St. Joseph, Clark Co., Nevada
Sugar House, Salt Lake Co. .... April 10, 1874
*Summit Stake, Iron Co.
Summit, Iron Co.
*Sunset, Navajo Co., Arizona
*Tailors, Salt Lake Co.
*Tanners, Salt Lake Co.
*Taylor, Navajo Co., Arizona
(Tocquerville) Toquerville, Washington Co. March 8, 1874 (Failed 1875)
Tooele, Tooele Co.
Utah County Central, Utah Co. .... April 26, 1874

*Vermillion (Sigurd), Sevier Co.
Virgin City (Virgen), Washington Co. . . . . March 5, 1874
Virgin Field, Washington Co.
*Wanship, Summit Co.
Washington, Washington Co. . . . . Feb. 21, 1874
Wellsville, Cache Co. . . . . March 1, 1875
*West Jordan, Salt Lake Co. . . . . May 3, 1874
West Weber, Weber Co. . . . . May 19, 1874
Willard, Box Elder Co. . . . . May 24, 1874
*Willow Creek (Draper), Salt Lake Co. . . . . June 7, 1874
Woodruff, Rich Co. . . . . May 28, 1874
*Woodruff, Navajo Co., Arizona

Sources and Notes

Archival Collections

The most extensive collection of manuscript and printed sources for the history of the Latter-day Saints and their social and economic organization is the Church Archives of The Church of Jesus Christ of Latter-day Saints, Salt Lake City, Utah. The manuscript materials found there can be divided into five categories:

1. The "Journal History of the Church," comprising approximately 1,200 volumes of chronologically arranged documents. A day-by-day account of happenings in the Mormon Church from 1830 to the present, it includes typescripts from diaries, letters, reports, office journals, and newspaper clippings. A principal inclusion for the Brigham Young period, 1844-77, is the Manuscript History of the Church, a journal kept by Brigham Young's clerks, comprising 47 thick volumes, nearly all of which is copied verbatim into the "Journal History."

2. The historical record of each early settlement and mission kept by contemporary historians and clerks, and the manuscript history of each stake and mission of the church, one or more volumes for each stake and mission. The latter are chronologically arranged documentary histories of the various settlements and ecclesiastical units of the Latter-day Saints, including clippings, reports, letters, and excerpts from diaries.

3. Original journals, account books, minute books, and other records of ecclesiastical organizations, cooperative associations, corporations, and other enterprises with which the church and its officers have been associated.

4. Diaries of Latter-day Saint pioneers and church officials.

5. Minute books and other records of United Orders. The Church Archives hold records from the United Orders of the following wards or settlements (there may be others that have not yet been found): Brigham City, Cache Stake, Cedar City, Circleville, Fairview, Franklin, Gunnison, Joseph City, Kanab, Kingston, Mammoth, Monroe, Mt. Carmel, Mt. Pleasant, Orderville, Panguitch, Pahreah, Parowan, Payson, Pleasant Grove, Prattville, Price, Richfield, Salt Lake City, Santa Clara, Sevier, Southern Utah Mission, Spanish Fork, Sunset, St. George, Washington.

The Utah State Historical Society, Salt Lake City, also has much source material on Mormon and local history, as do the western and special collections at the libraries of University of Utah, Utah State University, and Brigham Young University. Other important collections used by the writers include Henry E. Huntington Library and Art Gallery, San Marino, California; Bancroft Library, University of California, Berkeley, California; and collections at Yale and Harvard University libraries, and the Library of Congress and National Archives,

Washington, D.C. There are presumably other important United Order materials in the extensive collection at the Daughters of the Utah Pioneers Memorial Building in Salt Lake City, but this collection is not open to scholars.

General Works on the Mormons and Mormon Country

An excellent one-volume history of the Mormon Church is James B. Allen and Glen M. Leonard, *The Story of the Latter-day Saints* (Salt Lake City: Deseret Book Company, in Collaboration with the Historical Department of the Church, 1976). An authoritative official history is B. H. Roberts, *A Comprehensive History of the Church of Jesus Christ of Latter-day Saints: Century I*, 6 vols. (Salt Lake City: Published by the Church, 1930). Two texts used at Brigham Young University and elsewhere that cover Mormon history from its beginning to the present are Ivan J. Barrett, *Joseph Smith and the Restoration: A History of the Church to 1846* (Provo, Utah: Brigham Young University Press, 1973), and Russell R. Rich, *Ensign to the Nations: A History of the Church from 1846 to the Present* (Provo, Utah: Brigham Young University Press, 1972). An economic history is Leonard J. Arrington, *Great Basin Kingdom: An Economic History of the Latter-day Saints, 1830-1900* (Cambridge, Mass.: Harvard University Press, 1958). Thomas F. O'Dea, *The Mormons* (Chicago: University of Chicago Press, 1957), is a book by a noted Catholic sociologist. A fine collection of professional articles is found in Marvin S. Hill and James B. Allen, eds., *Mormonism and American Culture* (New York: Harper & Row, 1972). The standard documentary source on early Mormon history is *The History of the Church of Jesus Christ of Latter-day Saints; Period I, History of Joseph Smith, by Himself*, with an introduction and notes by B. H. Roberts, 6 vols. (Salt Lake City: Published by the Church, 1902). The original manuscripts from which this was compiled are also in Church Archives.

Mormon doctrine, the knowledge of which is basic to an understanding of Mormon economic idealism, is expounded in the so-called standard works—the Bible, the Book of Mormon, the Pearl of Great Price, and the Doctrine and Covenants of The Church of Jesus Christ of Latter-day Saints, and in the compiled sermons and writings of Joseph Smith, Brigham Young, and others. All are available in many editions. Complete texts of the sermons of nineteenth-century Mormon leaders were published periodically in the *Journal of Discourses*, 26 vols. (Liverpool, 1854-86). A general biographical source is Andrew Jenson, *Latter-day Saints Biographical Encyclopedia*, 4 vols. (Salt Lake City: Andrew Jenson History Co., 1901-36).

General histories of Utah include: H. H. Bancroft, *History of Utah, 1540-1886* (San Francisco, 1889); Edward Tullidge, *History of Salt Lake City and Its Founders* (Salt Lake City, 1886); Edward W. Tullidge, *History of Northern Utah and Southern Idaho* (Salt Lake City, 1889); Orson F.

Whitney, *History of Utah*, 4 vols. (Salt Lake City, 1892-1904); Milton R. Hunter, *Utah and Her Western Setting* (Salt Lake City: Deseret News Press, 1943); and S. George Ellsworth, *Utah's Heritage* (Santa Barbara and Salt Lake City: Peregrine Smith, 1972).

The most important contemporary newspaper in pioneer Utah was the *Deseret News* (Salt Lake City, 1850—), published by the Latter-day Saint Church. Founded in 1850, it had a weekly edition until 1922 and a daily edition from 1867 to date. The *Salt Lake Tribune*, a non-Mormon paper, has been published daily from 1871 to the present. The *Utah Historical Quarterly*, published by the Utah State Historical Society since 1932, has published many articles of importance, as have *Brigham Young University Studies* (1959—); *Dialogue: A Journal of Mormon Thought* (1966—); and *Journal of Mormon History*, the journal of the Mormon History Association (1974—).

More closely related to Mormon history, as sources, are the *Latter-day Saints' Millennial Star*, published in Manchester, England, monthly from 1840 to 1842; published in Liverpool monthly, 1842-1845 and 1943-1970; semimonthly, 1845-1851; and weekly, 1852-1943. Also valuable is the *Improvement Era* (Salt Lake City), published monthly from 1897 to 1970; and the *Ensign* (Salt Lake City, 1971—).

The first published treatise on Mormon mercantile cooperation was by the Utah historian Edward W. Tullidge in *Tullidge's Quarterly Magazine* (Salt Lake City) 1 (1880-81): 353-432. This was followed by [Dyer D. Lum], *Social Problems of Today; or, the Mormon Question in its Economic Aspects* (Port Jervis, N.Y., 1886). In the same year Professor Amos G. Warner made a similar study of "Cooperation among the Mormons," which was published by the American Economic Association in 1887 as part of a larger monograph entitled *Three Phases of Cooperation in the West*. A German historical school appraisal is Albert Edgar Wilson, "Gemeinwirtschaft und Unternehmungsformen im Mormonenstaat," published in Gustav Schmoller's *Jahrbuch für Gesetzgebung, Veruraltung und Volkswirtschaft in Deutschen Reich*, 39 vols. (Leipzig, 1877-1915), 31 (1901): 1003-56. Hamilton Gardner contributed brilliant insight in "Cooperation among the Mormons," *Quarterly Journal of Economics* 31 (1917): 461-99; and "Communism Among the Mormons," *Quarterly Journal of Economics* 37 (1923): 134-74. These were followed by Joseph A. Geddes, *The United Order among the Mormons (Missouri Phase)* (Salt Lake City: Deseret News Press, 1924). Drawing on his own background in southern Utah and scholarly detachment, Professor Angus M. Woodbury of the University of Utah wrote a paper on "The United Order" in 1933, which was widely circulated, typescript in possession of Leonard Arrington.

Arden Beal Olsen prepared "The History of Mormon Mercantile Cooperation in Utah" (Ph.D. diss., University of California, Berkeley, 1935), only brief parts of which were published. There followed Edward

J. Allen, *The Second United Order among the Mormons* (New York: Columbia University Press, 1936); J. Reuben Clark, Jr., *The One Mighty and Strong* and *The United Order and Law of Consecration as Set Out in the Revelations of The Lord* (Salt Lake City: Published by the Church, 1939), by a leading theologian and member of the First Presidency of the Church. William J. McNiff, *Heaven On Earth: A Planned Mormon Society* (Oxford, Ohio: Mississippi Valley Press, 1940), is more a cultural history and discusses the United Order only superficially. William R. Palmer, "United Order in Utah," *Improvement Era* 45 and 46 (1942, 1943) is a primary source on many aspects. Gustive O. Larson, *Prelude to the Kingdom: Mormon Desert Conquest—A Chapter in American Cooperative Experience* (Francestown, N.H.: Marshall Jones Co., 1947), based on a 1926 master's thesis, is an early study of the immigration experience and its ramifications. The recent study by Mario S. DePillis, "The Development of Mormon Communitarianism, 1826-1846" (Ph.D., Yale University, 1960), is provocative and stimulating. Our study was too early to profit from reading Gordon E. Wagner, "Consecration and Stewardship: A Socially Efficient System of Justice" (Ph.D. diss., Cornell University, 1976). In this work Wagner argues that the Law of Consecration and Stewardship provides the theological and institutional framework (property system, allocation system, locus system of decision-making) supportive of the principles of "justice" and "social efficiency." Wagner identifies the law with the pure theory of labor-management as outlined by Jaroslav Vanek, ed., *Self-Management: Economic Liberation of Man* (Middlesex, England, 1975).

Notes

In referring to the publications and archives, described above, the following abbreviations or symbols are used:

Church Archives	The archives maintained in the Historical Department of The Church of Jesus Christ of Latter-day Saints, Salt Lake City, Utah.
D&C	Doctrine and Covenants of The Church of Jesus Christ of Latter-day Saints (Salt Lake City), many editions.
HC	Joseph Smith, *History of the Church of Jesus Christ of Latter-day Saints: Period I*, B. H. Roberts, ed., 2nd ed., 6 vols. (Salt Lake City, 1946-50), and a seventh volume under the same title, published in 1932 for the "Apostolic Interregnum (1844-1847)" period, with notes and introduction by B. H. Roberts.
JD	*Journal of Discourses*, 26 vols. (Liverpool, 1854-86).
JH	Journal History of The Church of Jesus Christ of Latter-day Saints, available in the Historical Department of The Church of Jesus Christ of Latter-day Saints, Salt Lake City, Utah.

CHAPTER 1
*Mormonism
and the
American dream*

[1]Felix Gilbert, *The Beginnings of American Foreign Policy: To the Farewell Address* (New York: Harper & Row, 1961), p. 3.

[2]Frank E. Manuel, "Pansophia, A Seventeenth Century Dream of Science," reprinted in *Freedom from History and Other Untimely Essays* (New York: New York University Press, 1971), pp. 89-113, esp. p. 92.

[3]Perry Miller and Thomas H. Johnson, eds., *The Puritans: A Sourcebook of Their Writings* (New York: Harper & Row, 1963), vol. 1, pp. 198-99.

[4]Dean C. Jessee discusses the various versions of Joseph Smith's account of his first vision in "The Early Accounts of Joseph Smith's First Vision," *Brigham Young University Studies* 9 (1969): 275-94.

[5]D&C 132:8.

[6]D&C 42. See also an earlier version of the revelation collected by Mario S. DePillis in "The Development of Mormon Communitarianism, 1826-1846" (Ph.D. diss., Yale University, 1960), pp. 297-312.

[7]Several of Parley P. Pratt's relatives were Shakers. Sidney Rigdon was a prominent Campbellite minister before his contact with Joseph Smith. Several of the Kirtland, Ohio, converts were already participating in a communal "family" before their conversion to Mormonism. David Brion Davis discusses the varieties of religious doctrines from which Joseph Smith might have drawn in "The New England Origins of Mormonism," *New England Quarterly* 26 (June 1953): 148-62. See also Marvin S. Hill, "The Role of Christian Primitivism in the Origin and Development of the Mormon Kingdom, 1830-1844" (Ph. D. diss., University of Chicago, 1968).

[8]Arthur E. Bestor, Jr., has dealt admirably with the influence of Owen on American communitarianism in *Backwoods Utopias: The Sectarian Origins and the Owenite Phase of Communitarian Socialism in America: 1663-1829* (Philadelphia: University of Pennsylvania Press, 1950).

[9]Martin Buber, *Paths in Utopia,* trans. R.F.C. Hull, with an introduction by Ephraim Fischoff (Boston: Beacon Press, Inc., 1966), p. 23.

[10]"The Morning Breaks; the Shadows Flee," *Hymns, The Church of Jesus Christ of Latter-day Saints* (Salt Lake City: Published by the Church, 1968), no. 269.

[11]Bestor, *Backwoods Utopias,* uses this expression.

[12]See Klaus Hansen's penetrating study, *Quest for Empire: The Political Kingdom of God and the Council of Fifty in Mormon History* (East Lansing, Mich.: Michigan State University Press, 1967); also Manuel, "Pansophia,

Dream of Science"; G. H. Williams, *The Radical Reformation* (Philadelphia: Westminster Press, 1962); and DePillis, "Mormon Communitarianism" pp. 211-14.

[13]Buber, *Paths in Utopia,* p. 73. A stimulating essay emphasizing this point is by Klaus J. Hansen, "Mormonism and American Culture: Some Tentative Hypotheses," in F. Mark McKiernan, Alma R. Blair, and Paul M. Edwards, eds., *The Restoration Movement: Essays in Mormon History* (Lawrence, Kans.: Coronado Press, 1973), pp. 1-25.

[14]In a study of income inequality by state for 1949, 1959, and 1969, Utah had the lowest Gini ratio (a measure of income inequality) of the continental United States at the first two decade intervals and was well below the median in 1969. Income was consistently more evenly distributed in Utah than in the five western states most like Utah in economic and social structure. It is conceivable that a further analysis of this data would support a hypothesis that Mormon Church programs and economic policies have the effect of redistributing income in favor of the less affluent. See Tom S. Sale III, "Interstate Analysis of the Size Distribution of Family Income," *Southern Economic Journal* 40 (January 1974): 434-41.

[15]A musical play, *The Order Is Love,* by Carol Lynn Pearson and Lex de Azevedo (Provo, Utah: Trilogy Arts, 1971), demonstrates the continuing importance of this tradition. The musical, produced several times since its opening at Brigham Young University in March 1971, evokes with gentle humor the mingling of warm idealism and human frailty that characterized the Orderville, Utah, experiment. The play emphasizes the twin themes of Mormon folk memory of the United Order: that it failed because the people were not yet sufficiently prepared and that one day faithful Mormons will be required to live under it again.

[16]Robert Houriet, *Getting Back Together* (New York: Avon Books, 1971), p. xiii. See also Ron E. Roberts, *The New Communes* (Englewood Cliffs, N.J.: Prentice Hall, Inc., 1971). Roberts' interest in modern communes had its origins in his doctoral dissertation on the Utopian ideology of Latter-day Saints, "Dilemmas of Utopian Commitment in a Contemporary Religious Sect" (Ph.D. diss., Louisiana State University, 1969).

[17]Useful insights into the relationship of contemporary communal life to that of the nineteenth century can be found in Rosebeth Moss Kanter, *Commitment and Community: Communes and Utopias in Sociological Perspective* (Cambridge, Mass.: Harvard University Press, 1972), esp. pp. 166-67.

[18]D&C 88:119.

[19]Richard T. Ely, "Economic Aspects of Mormonism," *Harper's Monthly Magazine* 56 (April 1903): 667-68.

CHAPTER 2
Communitarianism under Joseph Smith:
The Law of Consecration and Stewardship

[1]The first publication of the revelation occurred when a copy came into the hands of a non-Mormon newspaper editor and was printed without authorization in at least two newspapers during the summer of 1831. Excerpts were first published by the Mormon Church in *The Evening and the Morning Star* (Independence, Mo.) 1 (July 1832): [1] (hereafter cited as the *Star*), under the title "Extract from the Laws for the Government of the Church of Christ." It was later reproduced more completely in *A Book of Commandments for the Government of the Church of Christ* (Zion [Independence, Mo.], 1833), chap. 44. Somewhat expanded, the law was again reproduced in a reprint of the *Star* issued at Kirtland, Ohio, beginning in January 1835. In this form, the law was incorporated, with other revelations, in the first edition of the *Doctrine and Covenants of the Church of Jesus Christ of Latter-day Saints* (Kirtland, Ohio, 1835), section 13. All subsequent editions of the *Doctrine and Covenants* have carried the law in the 1835 version, but the law is now found in section 42 of that work. Other revelations, published in the *Star,* the Book of Commandments, and the Doctrine and Covenants, explain and elaborate upon the system as first announced in February 1831.

Three manuscript versions have survived in the Church Archives. The first of these is dated February 9, 1831, and is in the handwriting of Newel K. Whitney. The second is dated May 23, 1831, and was written by someone not in regular service to Joseph Smith as a scribe. The third is undated and in the hand of Orson Hyde. The three manuscripts vary in the wording of some passages and in the arrangement of verses. The presently printed verses 76-93 are not in the February 9, 1831, manuscript and the presently printed verses 1-11 are not in the Orson Hyde manuscript. The May 23, 1831, version is most like the presently printed version in the structure and arrangement of its verses, though significant changes in wording were made for the 1835 publication. This is also apparently the version upon which the nonauthorized 1831 newspaper publication was based, although the editors omitted nearly forty verses at the end of the manuscript.

It should be noted that early church members, eager to possess their own copies of Joseph Smith's revelations, often made copies for themselves and for friends, some written hastily and inaccurately. The survival of many such copies makes it extremely difficult to identify the original documents with complete confidence. Also, it was not uncommon for the Prophet to elaborate on revelations at a later date, changing

428 NOTES TO PAGES 15-17

the text and adding entire new sections. It has been the position of The Church of Jesus Christ of Latter-day Saints that revelation is a continuing process adapted to the needs and capacities of persons at any given point in time. Changes in revelations would, by this reasoning, be made under the same inspiration as the earlier versions and therefore those versions which contain the fullest development of the Prophet's thought (i.e. the latest changes made by him in his lifetime) most fully represent the word of God to that point.

The manuscripts referred to above are in the Church Archives, Salt Lake City. The newspaper version is reprinted by DePillis in "Mormon Communitarianism," pp. 299-309, from the *Western Reserve Chronicle,* September 22, 1831, which in turn was reprinted from the *Western Courier.* DePillis maintained (p. 19) that this text is "more accurate than the version subsequently accepted by the Mormons as standard," but gave no indication which text he himself accepted as the standard against which to compare the newspaper text.

[2]Or use the properties (which might include money) to purchase real estate and other goods to be assigned as stewardships.

[3]"Laws for the Government of the Church." See also the Book of Commandments, chap. 44, v. 26. The 1835 (and present) version of this part of the law is as follows: "And behold, thou wilt remember the poor, and consecrate of thy properties for their support that which thou hast to impart unto them, with a covenant and a deed which cannot be broken. And inasmuch as ye impart of your substance unto the poor, ye will do it unto me; and they shall be laid before the bishop of my church and his counselors. . . . after they are laid before the bishop of my church . . . every man shall be made accountable unto me, a steward over his own property, or that which he has received . . . , as much as is sufficient for himself and his family." D&C 42:30-32.

[4]D&C 49:20. The revelation was announced at Kirtland, Ohio, in March 1831.

[5]"Laws for the Government of the Church"; also Book of Commandments, chap. 44, vv. 28-29. The 1835 and the present version read as follows: "And again, if there shall be properties in the hands of the church, or any individuals of it, more than is necessary for their support after this first consecration, which is a residue to be consecrated unto the bishop, it shall be kept to administer to those who have not, from time to time, that every man who has need may be amply supplied and receive according to his wants. Therefore, the residue shall be kept in my storehouse, to administer to the poor and the needy, . . . and for the purpose of purchasing lands for the public benefit of the church, and building houses of worship, and building up of the New Jerusalem. . . . " D&C 42:33-35.

[6]In regard to this phase of the law a non-Mormon writer has made

the following suggestive comparison: "To outsiders it would appear that the Mormons have evolved an extreme system of income taxation by the church, the revenue from which they would use in establishing church farm loans, church rural credits, church home aid associations, church student loan funds, mothers' pensions, and old aid pensions, as well as a general scheme for church social and industrial insurance." Dean D. Mc-Brien, "The Economic Content of Early Mormon Doctrine," *Southwestern Political and Social Science Quarterly* 6 (September 1925): 190. It is also interesting to note that the late Brigham H. Roberts, a leading Mormon official and historian (and an ardent Democrat), saw a parallel between the Law of Consecration and Stewardship and the early New Deal under Franklin D. Roosevelt, particularly in the latter's capture of the social surplus to be used for the poor and for worthwhile community projects such as public works. *Discourses of B. H. Roberts* (Salt Lake City: Deseret Book Co., 1948), pp. 116ff.

Several young Mormon scholars have recently begun an important reassessment of Consecration and Stewardship, seeing it not as a historical curiosity, but as a viable program promising a more just and socially more efficient economic system than exists among the world's major populations today. See especially Gordon E. Wagner, "Consecration and Stewardship: A Socially Efficient System of Justice" (paper presented at a Brigham Young University Conference on Economics and Mormon Culture, October 5-7, 1975).

[7]"Laws for the Government of the Church," D&C 42:45, 54.

[8]Book of Commandments, chap. 40, v. 22, announced at Fayette, New York, January 1831.

[9]John Corrill, *A Brief History of the Church of Christ of Latter-day Saints* . . . (St. Louis, 1839), p. 45. Corrill added: "Yet their law gives every man the privilege of managing his own concerns, and provides against taking each others property without paying for it; and if a man gives for the benefit of the Church, it is considered a voluntary offering. Yet the law requires or enjoins a consecration of the overplus, after reserving for himself and family, and to carry on his business."

[10]Orson Pratt, "The Equality and Oneness of the Saints," *The Seer* (Washington, D.C.) 2 (July 1854): 294. *The Seer* was later repudiated by the church but this repudiation seems not to have applied to the article cited.

[11]Orson Pratt sermon, September 10, 1854, JD 2:100.

[12]"Laws for the Government of the Church."

[13]"Laws for the Government of the Church." The 1835 version of this passage reads: "He that sinneth and repenteth not shall be cast out of the church, and shall not receive again that which he has consecrated unto the poor and the needy of my church, or in other words, unto me." D&C 42:37. This reading seems to imply that an apostate could retain his

stewardship but had no right to request the return of any consecrations he had made over and above what was returned to him in the form of a stewardship. A revelation given at Thompson, Ohio, in May 1831, and not published until 1835, stated: "If he shall transgress and is not accounted worthy to belong to the church, he shall not have power to claim that portion which he has consecrated unto the bishop for the poor and needy of my church; . . . but shall only have claim on that portion that is deeded unto him. And thus all things shall be made sure, according to the laws of the land." In other words, anyone leaving the Order had no claim on the surplus he had consecrated, but he could retain his inheritance. D&C 51:5-6. This revelation also may have read differently in its original form consistent with that cited above.

[14]HC 1:146-47. According to the firsthand report of John Whitmer, the family was "going to destruction very fast as to temporal things" because "they would take each other's clothes and other property and use it without leave, which brought on confusion and disappointment, for they did not understand the scriptures." "Book of John Whitmer," chap. 2, MS in library of the Reorganized Church of Jesus Christ of Latter Day Saints, Independence, Missouri.

[15]Joseph Smith's opinion of the Kirtland Family, as he saw it in 1831, is reflected in the following notation in his journal in 1843: "I attended a second lecture on Socialism, by Mr. Finch; and after he got through, I made a few remarks, alluding to Sidney Rigdon and Alexander Campbell getting up a community at Kirtland, and of the big fish there eating up all the little fish. I said I did not believe the doctrine." HC 6:33.

[16]In the 1835 edition of the consecration revelation, the wording gave clear indication that the immediate purpose of "the law" was to provide the means of caring for the poor. D&C 42:30. An 1834 revelation pertaining to "the law" was specifically entitled "the order of the Church for the benefit of the poor." D&C 104.

[17]The Pearl of Great Price (Salt Lake City, 1935), Moses 7:18. According to the Prophet, the perfection of Enoch's city was such that he and all his people were taken into heaven, as related in Genesis 5:24. See also The Book of Mormon, trans. Joseph Smith, Jr., rev. ed. (Salt Lake City, Utah: The Church of Jesus Christ of Latter-day Saints, 1968), 4 Nephi 1:3.

[18]The literature on these societies includes Charles Nordhoff, The Communistic Societies of the United States (New York, 1875); William A. Hinds, American Communities and Cooperative Colonies, 2nd ed. (Chicago, 1908); Alice Felt Tyler, Freedom's Ferment: Phases of American Social History to 1860 (Minneapolis: University of Minnesota Press, 1944); V. F. Calverton, Where Angels Dared to Tread (Indianapolis: Bobbs-Merrill Co., 1941); Bestor, Backwoods Utopias; and Socialism and American Life, ed. Donald Drew Egbert and Stow Persons, 2 vols. (Princeton: Princeton

University Press, 1952).

[19]Cited in Phillips Russell, *Emerson, the Wisest American* (New York: Brentano's, 1929), 193-94.

[20]The strength of the individualistic elements in the plan as well as its short duration may explain why the Mormon experiment has received little attention in the literature concerning communistic and communitarian societies in the United States.

[21]The noted Mormon historian B. H. Roberts wrote: "I found in my early visitations to the cradles of the church, the branches in Colesville, Harmony, Fayette, and Palmyra, a tradition among the people of those localities that when the Mormons moved from their first locations, 'the rich shared with the poor.' And it was wonderment with them that they [the Mormons] took all their poor with them." *Discourses of B. H. Roberts*, p. 68.

[22]The "Plat of the City of Zion" is reproduced with an analysis in Lowry Nelson, *The Mormon Village: A Pattern and Technique of Land Settlement* (Salt Lake City: University of Utah Press, 1952), p. 39, et passim. The explanations of Joseph Smith concerning the plat are published in HC 1:357-62.

[23]Book of Commandments, Chap. 59 and 64, August 1831. To ensure that those coming to receive inheritances were faithful members of the Church, rather than opportunists, each newcomer was to bear a letter from the bishop in Kirtland or from three elders in the conference or branch from which he came.

[24]The functioning of the storehouse and other institutions is described more fully in Joseph A. Geddes, *The United Order among the Mormons (Missouri Phase): An Unfinished Experiment in Economic Organization* (Salt Lake City: Deseret News Press, 1924), pp. 68-75. Geddes' analysis was based exclusively on the 1835 wording of the consecration revelations.

[25]In November 1831, a literary firm was organized as a joint stewardship of six persons to handle the publication and sale of the sacred writings of the church.

[26]"The Elders Stationed in Zion to the Church Abroad, in Love, Greeting," *Star* 2 (July 1833): 110.

[27]These phrases are from a communication from the elders in Zion to the church, published in *Star* 1 (July 1832): [5].

[28]One complication was the necessity of feeding Indians that the government was settling to the west of Independence.

[29]For example, Book of Commandments, chap. 54, v. 40, dated June 1831; revelation of November 1831, published in *Star* 1 (October 1832): [3]; and a revelation of May 1831 published in *Star* 1 (November 1832): [7].

[30]As in most contemporary pioneer communities women were also

expected to work. This was defended in the following extract from a letter of the elders in Zion, published in July 1833: "It is said, that women go out to work; this is a fact, and not only women, but men too; for in the church of Christ, all that are able, have to work to fulfill the commandments of the Lord. . . . " *Star* 2 (July 1833): 110-11.

[31]Many writers have associated Mormonism with the Millerites and others who momentarily expected the second coming of Christ. The careful economic planning by officials in Kirtland and Zion indicates otherwise. Those who were planning to leave for Zion were advised to pay their debts, husband their property and savings carefully, secure improved breeds of cattle, sheep, and hogs to bring with them, garden seed, etc. "For the disciples to suppose that they can come to this land without ought to eat, or to drink, or to wear, or anything to purchase these necessaries with, is a vain thought. For them to suppose that the Lord will open the windows of heaven, and rain down angel's food for them by the way, when their whole journey lies through a fertile country, stored with the blessings of life from his own hand for them to subsist upon is also vain. . . .

"The disciples of Christ . . . should be wise and not take the way of the world, not build air-castles, but consider, that when they have been gathered to Zion, means will be needed to purchase their inheritances, and means will be needed to purchase food and raiment. . . .

"And notwithstanding the fulness of the earth is for the saints, they can never expect it unless they use the means put into their hands to obtain the same in the manner provided by our Lord." "The Elders Stationed in Zion to the Churches Abroad," pp. 110-11.

[32]*Autobiography of Parley Parker Pratt,* ed. Parley P. Pratt, Jr., 3rd ed. (Salt Lake City: Deseret Book Co., 1938), pp. 72, 93. Another participant, Newel Knight, mentioned the "cheerful hearts" of the people and said that they were "united, and peace and happiness abounded." "Newel Knight's Journal," in *Scraps of Biography* (Salt Lake City, 1883), pp. 72, 73, 75.

[33]Each steward was required, according to a revelation given December 4, 1831, to render an account of his stewardship to the bishop. *Star* 1 (December 1832): [5-6]. In line with instructions from Joseph Smith, a clerk was appointed to record all consecrations and inheritances, as well as "their manner of life, and their faith and works; and also . . . all the apostates, who apostatize after receiving their inheritance." Joseph Smith to W. W. Phelps, November 27, 1832, HC 1:298. This manuscript record, if it is in existence, cannot be located.

[34]See Appendix 1 for examples of deeds of consecration and stewardship. Those extant are located in the Edward Partridge papers, Church Archives.

[35]As Jonathan R.T. Hughes has pointed out to us, if the fee-holder

under the original wording of the revelation agreed, without consideration, to an arrangement barring his heirs, the court would probably not
have upheld the action. The church could not have held the property.
The document would seem to be an example of subinfeudation; i.e., the
fee-holder gives the rights of himself and his heirs to another who, with
his heirs, now has a superior property right in the estate of the original
fee-holder's heirs. Such an arrangement would have had doubtful le-
gality.

[36]One of the earliest anti-Mormon works described Mormon economic institutions as follows: "Their [the Mormon] common stock principles appear to be somewhat similar to those of the Shakers. Each one,
however, is allowed to 'manage his own affairs in his own way,' until he
arrives in Missouri. There the Bishop resides; he has supreme command
in all pecuniary matters, according to the revelations given by the
prophet. . . . He holds a deed of the lands, and the members receive a
writing from him, signifying, that they are to possess the land as their
own, so long as they are obedient to [Joseph] Smith's commandments."
E. D. Howe, *Mormonism Unvailed* (Painesville, Ohio, 1834), p. 129; and
"Letter VII" of Ezra Booth, ibid., p. 200. That church leaders were sensitive to the common-stock allegation is indicated by the frequent public
denials of its practice. For example, "I am well aware, that an opinion is
had abroad by many, that . . . the church is a common stock concern. . . .
As to giving and 'common stock' if any candid man or woman, will read
the book of *Doctrine and Covenants*, he or she may undeceive themselves."
W. W. Phelps to the editor, *Latter Day Saints' Messenger and Advocate* 2
(December 1835): 230. In the *Elders' Journal* 1 (July 1838): 43, Joseph
Smith unequivocally stated that the Mormons do not believe in having
all things in common; and in a lengthy letter to the church, written in
December 1838, while he was in Liberty Jail, Missouri, he devoted two
paragraphs to the charge that the Mormons believed in community of
wives and of property. HC 3:230-31.

[37]HC 1:341. The language of an April 1832 directive indicates that
Joseph Smith approved, at that time, of giving provisional property rights
to newcomers furnished with land by the church. According to this advice, widows were permitted to remain upon their husbands'
inheritances provided their late husbands had not died while in
transgression. *Star* 1 (January 1833): 6. The wording of this revelation
was later changed to read that in such cases widows might remain upon
the inheritance "according to the laws of the land," but not have fellowship in the church. See D&C 83:1-3.

[38]Joseph Smith, Jr., to Edward Partridge, May 2, 1833, as cited in O.
F. Whitney, "The Aaronic Priesthood," *Contributor* 6 (October 1884): 7.

[39]After this change in policy in April and May 1833, the earlier
revelations were edited to show clearly: (a) that a person's inheritance

belonged to him and his family regardless of his status in the church (see the present versions in D&C 42:37; 51:5; 83:3); and (b) that the purpose of the consecrations was to provide for the poor and the needy (see the present versions in D&C 42:30-31, et passim). The changes, of course, were believed to have been inspired. With reference to (b), Joseph Smith wrote Edward Partridge (May 2, 1833): "The consecrated property . . . is given . . . to purchase inheritances for the poor. . . . And it is your duty to see that whatsoever is given, is given legally; therefore it must be given for the consideration of the poor Saints, and in this way no man can take any advantage of you in law."

The first printing of the edited version was in a reprint of the July 1832 number of the *Star* issued at Kirtland, Ohio, in February 1835, by the *Latter Day Saints' Messenger and Advocate*. The first edition of the Doctrine and Covenants was issued at Kirtland later that year and reproduced the edited version verbatim. The editing was under the direction of a committee appointed in September 1834, consisting of Joseph Smith, Oliver Cowdery, Sidney Rigdon, and Frederick G. Williams, and their product was accepted as the word of the Lord. HC 2:243ff. It may be significant that W. W. Phelps, editor of the *Star* in Zion, was called to Kirtland before the revision of the revelations, and served as secretary of the committee making the revisions. HC 2:232.

[40]Statement of Oliver Cowdery in the August 1832 issue of the *Star* reprinted at Kirtland, March 1835. Italics in original.

[41]Orson Pratt, a leading church theologian and close associate of Joseph Smith during the Mississippi Valley phase of Mormonism, seems to have regarded this action of granting deeds to the holders of stewardships as an unavoidable concession to the property laws of "Babylon." Even after 1835, Pratt interpreted the Law of Consecration and Stewardship to mean that no steward would hold title to his property. Under the "perfect" law of the Lord, he wrote, "all the riches and wealth of Zion shall be common property." Orson Pratt, "The Equality and Oneness of the Saints," pp. 290-94, esp. 292.

[42]The Joseph Knight, Jr., deed, following the earlier form, is dated October 12, 1832. We assume that the altered form (Appendix 1) was printed between that date and July 1833, when persecution led to the destruction of the Mormon printing establishment. The altered form was first noticed by Mario DePillis and discussed in his "Mormon Communitarianism," pp. 203-4.

[43]Editorial in the *Star* 2 (June 1833): 100; also "The Elders Stationed in Zion to the Churches Abroad," pp. 110-11.

[44]"Nearly all the abstracts of title to land in the eastern part of Kansas City show [in 1936] the title to the land in the name of Edward Partridge, the presiding bishop of the Mormon Church . . . but I could not get possession of it, because, under the law, adverse possession for a

certain number of years gives one a title." Heber J. Grant, *Deseret News*, Church Section, August 22, 1936.

[45]"Laws for the Government of the Church"; Book of Commandments, chap. 51, v. 6; D&C 51:3. These revelations were dated March and May 1831.

[46]HC 1:364-65.

[47]Not to be confused with cooperative communities organized in Utah in 1874 under the name United Order.

[48]The United Firm was entrusted with the management of a steam sawmill, a tannery, a printing press, and various pieces of rural and urban real estate. Most of these enterprises were financial liabilities and continued to lose money until April 1834, when a revelation was announced distributing the property in the form of personal stewardships. D&C 104.

[49]Mercantile stores had been set up by those called to do so in Kirtland (Newel K. Whitney & Company) and in Jackson County (Gilbert, Whitney & Company) to serve as outlets for goods collected in the storehouse. Legally, these were private enterprises; practically, they were stewardships. The latter status was confirmed with the establishment of the United Order or Firm. The United Firm was to have a working monopoly of Mormon trade in Missouri and Geauga County, Ohio, but it seems not to have been absolute. Its primary purpose could not have been profit-making since Joseph Smith criticized one of the agents, Sidney Gilbert, for withholding credit from the poor, and admonished him that it was his duty "to assist all the poor brethren . . . as they must have assistance; and the Lord established him in Zion for that express purpose." HC 1:341.

[50]D&C 82.

[51]Brigham Young sermon, April 7, 1873, JD 16:11.

[52]A complete statement of the Missouri difficulties, from the Mormon point of view, can be found in Brigham H. Roberts, *A Comprehensive History of the Church of Jesus Christ of Latter-day Saints: Century I*, 1:314-69.

[53]William W. Phelps to Joseph Smith, December 15, 1833, HC 1:457.

[54]D&C 104.

[55]According to the revelation the treasurer was to honor the drafts of any member as long as he was in full fellowship with his brethren. The treasury somewhat undercut, or replaced, the bishop's storehouse.

[56]It is interesting to note that the Law of Consecration was observed by this group. According to one of the participants, "Every man gave into the treasury [of Zion's Camp] the amount of means he had for the journey except those that had families who were directed to provide for themselves inasmuch as they had means to do so." Joseph Holbrook Diary, 2 vols., typescript, 1:17-18, Church Archives. Another participant,

Milo Andrus, wrote in his autobiography: "On the 11th of May [1834], we joined the main camp west of Mansfield, and on the 12th the camp was organized, and the law of consecration was for the first time presented and we shelled out to the last cent, and our money went into a Commissary's hands and our supplies were brought by him." "Autobiography of Milo Andrus, 1779-1875," typescript, p. 4, Brigham Young University Library, Provo, Utah. See also Nancy Clement Williams, *After 100 Years* (Independence, Missouri: Zion's Printing & Publishing Co., 1951), p. 76, for mention of the activities of Frederick G. Williams, who was given charge of all the monies and properties of the group to distribute as needed.

[57]D&C 105. That no effort was made to observe the Law of Consecration and Stewardship in Kirtland from June 1834 until the departure of the Mormons from that place in 1837-38 is indicated by a study of the *Latter Day Saints' Messenger and Advocate* (Kirtland, 1834-37), and the *Elders' Journal* (Kirtland, Ohio, and Far West, Missouri, 1837-38), as well as HC, vols. 1 and 2, passim. Poor immigrants to Kirtland were variously assisted by voluntary charitable donations by their "home" church congregation, by wealthier Kirtland settlers, and by the central purchase of land by the church on behalf of the immigrants.

[58]The land used for the city of Far West was apparently purchased by the church out of consecrated funds. Building lots were sold, and the proceeds were to be devoted to the purchase of additional farming lands, for the erection of a temple, and for the public benefit of the church. See HC 2:524; also the *Elders' Journal* 1 (July 1838): 36-38.

[59]D&C 119:1-5; also the version in "History of Joseph Smith," *Latter-day Saints Millennial Star* 16 (1854): 183.

[60]"Eleventh General Epistle of the Presidency of the Church . . . ," *Millennial Star* 16 (1854): 427; also D&C 101:6; D&C 103:14.

[61]HC 3:47. It was agreed by those present that Joseph Smith and his two "counselors" retain certain properties "for their support," and that the remainder "be put into the hands of the Bishop or Bishops." Ibid.

[62]"Eleventh General Epistle," p. 427. The diary of at least one faithful churchman, Joseph Holbrook, indicates that he did not fully understand the revelation. In July 1838, he wrote: "I gave to the church ten acres of land being in Clinton County [Missouri] for paying the church debts, being the 23rd day of July 1838." Holbrook Diary, 1:21-22.

[63]Brigham Young sermon, June 3, 1855, JD 2:306-7.

[64]HC 3:63-64. After the fall harvest, the Western United Firm, in casting about for remunerative employment for its members, dispatched two individuals to the west to make estimates and present a bid on a government road contract south from Fort Leavenworth. Although their bid was only $14,000 for the grading and bridging of almost forty miles of road, their bid was not the lowest and was therefore not accepted.

Holbrook Diary, 1:22. See also the Conference Minutes and Record Book of Christ's Church of Latter-day Saints, also known as the "Far West Record," April 6, 1838, MS, Church Archives.

[65]See Fawn Brodie, *No Man Knows My History: The Life of Joseph Smith, the Mormon Prophet* (New York: Alfred A. Knopf, 1946), pp. 220-22. Mrs. Brodie incorrectly assumes additional revelations proclaiming the restoration of "the Lord's plan."

[66]Corrill, *A Brief History*, p. 46. See also the statement by George A. Smith in his sermon of May 7, 1874, JD 17:60.

[67]George A. Smith sermon, May 7, 1874.

[68]HC 4:93.

[69]HC 6:37-38.

[70]See "An Epistle of the Twelve Apostles to the Saints of the Last Days," December 13, 1841, HC 4:472-75. An examination of the diaries of several faithful church members living in Nauvoo and environs in the 1840s indicates that tithing payments were not as systematic and as regular as they came to be in pioneer Utah. For example, Joseph Holbrook made his first tithing settlement in October 1845. Holbrook Diary, 1:41.

[71]Joseph Smith, "Latter Day Saints," in I. Daniel Rupp, ed., *An Original History of the Religious Denominations Existing in the United States* (Philadelphia, 1844), pp. 404-10.

[72]In an "epistle" to the church written in 1854, Brigham Young and other church officials explained the failure of the Law of Consecration and Stewardship as follows: "There were many obstacles in the way why these requirements could not be carried out: the Church was in its infancy, and had to meet the ignorance, bigotry, and intolerance of a wicked and benighted world. The brethren themselves had not been able to throw off their own traditions; and in many instances, apostacy and persecution well nigh overwhelmed the people of God, and caused them to be driven from place to place, until they have finally found a resting place amid the valleys of these mountains." "Eleventh General Epistle," p. 427.

[73]Brigham Young sermon, October 8, 1860, *Millennial Star* 23 (1861): 49. Brigham Young added: "If you think you can keep the money from me, you will be mistaken, for I shall have what is necessary to carry on this work; and those who take a course to hedge up my way in business transactions, pertaining to carrying on this work, will go to the Devil."

[74]George A. Smith sermon, May 7, 1874.

[75]Orson Pratt, who was a church missionary in this early period, wrote that when the law was in force "the rich refused to gather because the law required them to consecrate all their property." *The Seer* 2 (July 1854): 291.

[76]Book of Commandments, chap. 58, verses 19-20, June 1831; D&C

104:18. That this threat would be effective only among religious worshipers may explain why religious groups have often been more successful than secular societies in overhauling economic institutions.

[77]Book of Commandments, chap. 58, v. 21, June 1831.

[78]J. Reuben Clark, Jr., *The United Order and the Law of Consecration as Set Out in the Revelations of the Lord* (Salt Lake City: Published by the Church, 1945), p. 29. For example, a passage in a revelation dated December 16, 1833, described the situation in Jackson County under the Order: "Behold, I say unto you, there were jarrings, and contentions, and envyings and strifes, and lustful and covetous desires among them; therefore by these things they polluted their inheritances." D&C 101:6. Another passage in the revelation of June 22, 1834: "But behold, they have not learned to be obedient to the things which I required at their hands, but are full of all manner of evil, and do not impart of their substance, as becometh Saints, to the poor and afflicted among them; and are not united according to the union required by the law of the celestial kingdom." D&C 105:3-4.

CHAPTER 3
Becoming one:
Informal cooperation
after 1844

[1]"History of Joseph Smith," *Millennial Star* 16 (1854): 730-31.

[2]Ibid., p. 732.

[3]Roberts, *Comprehensive History* 2:537.

[4]JH, September 13, 1845.

[5]Manuscript History of Brigham Young, 47 vols., 1:179, MS, Church Archives.

[6]John Taylor sermon, September 22, 1878, JD, 20:57.

[7]Perpetual Emigrating Fund Record Book, 1849-51, MS, Church Archives.

[8]James Linforth, ed., *Route from Liverpool to Great Salt Lake Valley* (London, 1855), p. 9.

[9]Rev. John Todd, *The Sunset Land; or the Great Pacific Slope* (Boston, 1870), p. 182.

[10]Linforth, ed., *Route from Liverpool*, pp. 15, 120.

[11]Gustive O. Larson, *Prelude to the Kingdom: Mormon Desert Conquest* (Francestown, N.H.: Marshall Jones Co., 1947), p. 234. Larson has concluded that of 85,220 immigrants who came to Utah from Europe between 1840 and 1887, as many as 70,000 were brought through the services of the PEF.

[12]Linforth, ed., *Route from Liverpool*, p. 12.

[13]Brigham Young sermon, September 16, 1855, JD 3:5.

[14]*The Year of Jubilee: A Full Report of the Proceedings of the Fiftieth Annual Conference of the Church of Jesus Christ of Latter-day Saints* (Salt Lake City, 1880), pp. 61-65, 106-9. The conference reports contain transcripts of sermons delivered during the semiannual Mormon Church conferences, held in early April and October each year. Publication of the reports began in 1880 and has continued, at first intermittently but since 1897 semiannually, to the present. They will hereafter be cited as *Conference Report.*

[15]Larson, *Prelude to the Kingdom*, p. 278; also Gustive O. Larson, "The Story of the Perpetual Emigration Fund," *Mississippi Valley Historical Review* 18 (1931-1932): 184-94.

[16]"History of Joseph Smith," *Millennial Star* 16 (1854): 231-32.

[17]JH, September 5, 1845.

[18]JH, May 10, 20, 31, 1846. A sympathetic account of these and other cooperative efforts of the Mormons will be found in Thomas L. Kane, *The Mormons, a Discourse Delivered before the Historical Society of Pennsylvania,*

March 26, 1850 (Philadelphia, 1850).

[19]JH, March 5, 6, 1848.

[20]Manti Ward Historical Record, vol. 1, 1850-54, minutes of church meeting, April 11, 1852, MS, Church Archives.

[21]Journal of Orson Pratt, quoted by Edward W. Tullidge, *History of Salt Lake City* (Salt Lake City, 1886), p. 41.

[22]Wilford Woodruff Diary, July 24, 1847, MS, Wilford Woodruff Collection, Church Archives.

[23]Howard Egan, *Pioneering the West, 1846 to 1878* (Salt Lake City, 1917), p. 129.

[24]Epistle of Brigham Young and the Twelve, JH, September 9, 1847.

[25]*Millennial Star* 10 (1848): 325-26.

[26]JH, May 22, 1848.

[27]Isaac C. Haight Journal, July 16, 1848, MS, Church Archives.

[28]JH, August 8, 1848; *Millennial Star* 11 (1849): 22.

[29]*The Autobiography of Parley Parker Pratt* (Salt Lake City, 1874), p. 406.

[30]First General Epistle, *Millennial Star* 11 (1849): 228-30.

[31]Correspondent of the New York *Tribune* writing from Salt Lake Valley, JH, July 8, 1849.

[32]John Taylor in *Millennial Star* 12 (October 1849): 86.

[33]Manuscript History of Jordan Stake, MS, Church Archives.

[34]Howard Stansbury, *An Expedition to the Valley of the Great Salt Lake* (Philadelphia, 1855), pp. 128-30.

[35]JH, July 19, 1853.

[36]JH, June 8, 1856.

[37]JH, February 5, 1852.

[38]*Acts, Resolutions and Memorials of the Territory of Utah* (Great Salt Lake City, 1852), p. 96.

[39]Minutes of the Salt Lake County Court, Book A, 1852-1857, June 25, 1852, State Archives, Salt Lake City.

[40]Ibid., September 4, 1854.

[41]George A. Smith letter cited in Feramorz Y. Fox, "The Mormon Land System: A Study of the Settlement and Utilization of Land Under the Direction of the Mormon Church" (Ph.D. diss., Northwestern University, 1932), p. 139.

[42]Sanpete Stake History, MS, Church Archives.

[43]George Thomas, *The Development of Institutions under Irrigation, with Special Reference to Early Utah Conditions* (New York: Macmillan, 1920), p. 45.

[44]Fredrick Haynes Newell, *Irrigation in the United States* (New York, 1902), p. 289.

[45]See especially Wells A. Hutchins, *Mutual Irrigation Companies in Utah* (Logan, Utah: Utah State Agricultural College, 1927); also Leonard J. Arrington and Dean May, "A Different Mode of Life: Irrigation and So-

ciety in Nineteenth-Century Utah," *Agricultural History*, 49 (January 1975): 3-20.

[46]JH, March 27, 1848.

[47]JH, June 25, 1856.

[48]*Deseret News*, November 2, 1854.

[49]William Hepworth Dixon, *New America*, 2 vols. (London, 1867), 1:252-53.

[50]Ibid., pp. 261-62.

[51]Brigham Young sermon, February 3, 1867, JD, 11:297.

[52]"Seventh General Epistle," *Millennial Star* 14 (1852): 323-24.

[53]JH, January 26, 1850. Those appointed to serve with Wells were Norton Jacobs, foreman of joiners and carpenters; Samuel Ensign, foreman of carpenters; Alderman Raleigh, foreman of masons; and Alonzo H. Raleigh, foreman of tithing hands.

[54]*Deseret News*, August 7, 1852.

[55]Heber C. Kimball to William Kimball, quoted in Tullidge, *History of Salt Lake City*, p. 114.

[56]Brigham Young sermon, March 5, 1860, JD 8:11-12.

[57]See Nels Anderson, *Desert Saints: The Mormon Frontier in Utah* (Chicago: University of Chicago Press, 1942), chap. 15, and Kimball Young, *Isn't One Wife Enough?* (New York: Henry Holt, 1954).

[58]A full account of nineteenth-century Mormon economic practices is presented in Leonard J. Arrington, *Great Basin Kingdom: An Economic History of the Latter-day Saints, 1830-1900* (Cambridge, Mass.: Harvard University Press, 1958).

CHAPTER 4
Property on the altar:
The consecration movement
of the 1850s

[1]Hamilton Gardner, "Communism Among the Mormons," *Quarterly Journal of Economics* 37 (November 1922): 157. See also Edward J. Allen, *The Second United Order Among the Mormons* (New York: Columbia University Press, 1936), p. 157, and Tullidge, *History of Salt Lake City,* p. 386.

[2]T.B.H. Stenhouse, *The Rocky Mountain Saints* (New York, 1873), pp. 501-2. The deed is also found in Phil Robinson, *Sinners and Saints* (Boston, 1883), p. 222. See also Roberts, *Comprehensive History* 5:489. Roberts, who seems to have been unaware of the extensive consecrations of 1855-1865, ascribed the deed to 1875 instead of 1857. The interested reader will find many references to consecration and unity in temporal affairs in the JD, 1853-1856.

[3]Book A of Deeds, p. 264, Pioneer Records, Salt Lake County Recorder's Office, Salt Lake City, Utah. Yet Woodruff's diary contains no reference to his deed of consecration on or near July 9.

[4]JD 2:259-66.

[5]Original minutes of the general conference of The Church of Jesus Christ of Latter-day Saints, April 1854, MS, Church Archives.

[6]Record of Bishops' Meetings, 1851-1862, MS, Church Archives.

[7]"Eleventh General Epistle," April 10, 1854, pp. 427-28.

[8]The reference is to a form provided for in an act approved January 18, 1855. See *Acts, Resolutions, and Memorials of the Territory of Utah* (Great Salt Lake City, 1855), chap. 73.

[9]*Deseret News,* October 31, 1896; Andrew Jenson, *Latter-day Saint Biographical Encyclopedia,* 4 vols. (Salt Lake City, 1901-1936), 3:156-59.

[10]Pratt, "The Equality and Oneness of the Saints," pp. 289-300.

[11]Brigham Young address, May 18, 1855, at Parowan, Utah, "Addresses, n.d., 1844-55," Brigham Young Collection, Church Archives.

[12]Parley P. Pratt sermon, March 27, 1853, JD 1:85-86.

[13]Amasa Lyman said: "Mormonism is worth everything. If you reject consecration and pay only tithing, you give only one-tenth for all." JH, December 20, 1855.

[14]Orson Pratt sermon, September 10, 1854, JD 2:104; also sermon of April 7, 1855, JD 2:259-66.

[15]Orson Hyde sermon, December 21, 1856, JD 4:214-15.

[16]Brigham Young sermon, September 16, 1855, JD 3:6.

[17]Lorenzo Snow, April 9, 1857, JD 5:64-65.

[18]Brigham Young sermon, August 17, 1856, JD 4:29.

[19]*Deseret News,* October 18, 1857.

CHAPTER 5
The uniting of means:
Cooperative mercantile
and manufacturing associations

[1]"Historical Address of George A. Smith," October 8 and 9, 1868, JD 13:122.

[2]*Deseret News,* May 26, 1869.

[3]*Millennial Star* 16 (1854): 753. George A. Smith lists twenty-two firms and individual merchants in 1854, with a combined capital of nearly a million dollars.

[4]Brigham Young sermon, March 28, 1858, JD 7:47.

[5]JH, July 4, 1860.

[6]JH, July 11, 1860. Those present at the meeting were Brigham Young, Heber C. Kimball, Daniel H. Wells, Abraham O. Smoot, Elias Smith, David Candland, William Staines, John L. Smith, Robert C. Campbell, Erastus Snow, John Taylor, Edwin D. Woolley, and Edward Hunter.

[7]Brigham Young sermon, October 6, 1860, JD 8:193.

[8]Heber C. Kimball, February 9, 1862, JD 9:375.

[9]Tullidge, *History of Salt Lake City,* p. 382.

[10]Brigham Young sermons, June 22 to 29, 1864, JD 10:335.

[11]Brigham Young sermon, December 11, 1864, JD 11:19.

[12]Brigham Young sermon, October 9, 1865, JD 11:139.

[13]*Deseret Evening News,* November 30, 1865.

[14]*Salt Lake City Daily Telegraph,* December 20, 1866.

[15]*Deseret News,* January 2, 1867.

[16]Ibid.

[17]"Summary of Instructions," June and July 1865, JD 11:114.

[18]Brigham Young sermon, April 8, 1867, JD 12:407 [32].

[19]Brigham Young sermon, May 26, 1967, JD 12:54.

[20]Hamilton Gardner, *History of Lehi* (Salt Lake City, 1913), p. 187.

[21]JH, April 10, 1869.

[22]Hamilton Gardner, "Cooperation Among the Mormons," *Quarterly Journal of Economics* 31 (May 1917): 478.

[23]"Historical Address," October 8 and 9, 1868, JD 13:124.

[24]Brigham Young sermon, October 8, 1868, JD 12:301.

[25]*Deseret News,* October 14, 1868.

[26]*Deseret News,* October 28, 1868; *Utah Magazine,* October 24, 1868.

[27]ZCMI Records, Book A, pp. 11, 14, MS, Church Archives.

[28]Ibid., p. 3.

[29]Ibid., p. 21.

³⁰The institution was not legally incorporated until after February 13, 1870, when the first general incorporation law was passed by the legislative assembly. Revised articles of association were then prepared and filed.

³¹See Appendix 3 for copy of the Constitutions and By-Laws.

³²ZCMI Records, Book A, p. 38.

³³Orson F. Whitney, *History of Utah,* 4 vols. (Salt Lake City, 1892-1904), 2:285-86.

³⁴Advertisement in *Deseret News,* April 21, 1869.

³⁵Albert E. Wilson, "Gemeinwirtschaft und Unternegmungsformen im Mormonomenstaat," *Jahrbuch für Gesetzgebung* 31 (1907): 80-139. Translation by Philip Flammer in possession of Leonard Arrington.

³⁶*Salt Lake Daily Telegraph,* October 13 to 19, 1868.

³⁷Address to Latter-day Saints, July 10, 1875, quoted in Gardner, "Cooperation Among the Mormons," p. 489.

³⁸Brigham Young sermon, April 6, 1869, JD 12:372.

³⁹Arden B. Olsen, "The History of Mormon Mercantile Cooperation in Utah" (Ph.D. diss., University of California, Berkeley, 1935), p. 146.

⁴⁰ZCMI Records, Book A, p. 57.

⁴¹Olsen, "Mormon Mercantile Cooperation," p. 146.

⁴²ZCMI Records, Book A, p. 35.

⁴³From remarks of April 6 and 8, 1869, reported in *Deseret News Weekly,* May 26 and June 16, 1869.

⁴⁴Arrington, *Great Basin Kingdom,* pp. 310-13.

⁴⁵*From Report of U.S. Treasury Department for 1890;* Part II, Commerce and Navigation, p. 862, cited in Olsen, "Mormon Mercantile Cooperation," pp. 170-90. The Banking Act, as amended in 1865, imposed taxes on certain circulated bank notes, hoping thereby to eliminate issues by state banks.

⁴⁶ZCMI Records, Book A, p. 31, November 13, 1868.

⁴⁷*Deseret News,* February 2, 1869.

⁴⁸See Appendix 4, where Olsen's list has been reproduced.

⁴⁹See Olsen, "Mormon Mercantile Cooperation," pp. 126-29.

⁵⁰Susa Amelia (Young) Gates and Leah D. Widtsoe, *The Life Story of Brigham Young* (New York: Macmillan, 1930), pp. 302-3.

⁵¹ZCMI Record Book B, p. 48, MS, Church Archives.

⁵²See statement of Lorenzo Snow in Chapter 6 on Brigham City.

⁵³*Tullidge's Quarterly Magazine* 3 (April 1884): 160-61.

⁵⁴Olsen, "Mormon Mercantile Cooperation," p. 118.

⁵⁵*Deseret Evening News,* November 14, 1868.

⁵⁶Cited by Olsen, in "Mormon Mercantile Cooperation in Utah," *The Journal of Marketing* 6 (October 1941): 136-42, from the *Deseret News,* April 13, 1870, and June 17, 1871. Subsequent references to Olsen, "Mormon Mercantile Cooperation," refer to Olsen's dissertation (see

footnote 39 above) and not to this published work.

[57]ZCMI Record Book B, pp. 20, 28.

[58]Quotes are from an Apostolic Letter of July 10, 1875, Church Archives, Salt Lake City. It will be recalled that the ZCMI charter limited membership to tithe payers. In the case of this institution, tithing was deducted at the source both from earnings and from wages and paid to the church until 1891, when attorney Franklin S. Richards, in answer to a letter from Superintendent T. G. Webber, returned an opinion that the practice was illegal.

[59]John Taylor, *An Epistle to the Presidents of Stakes, High Councils, Bishops, and other Authorities of the Church* (Salt Lake City, 1882), pp. 1-4.

[60]*ZCMI Advocate*, March 15, 1886, quoted in Dyer D. Lum, *Social Problems of Today; or The Mormon Question in its Economic Aspects* . . . (Port Jervis, N.Y., 1886), pp. 16-17.

[61]Olsen, "Mormon Mercantile Cooperation," p. 238. The eight stores were located at Cleveland, Coalville, Moroni, Orderville, Richmond, Spanish Fork, Santa Clara, and Emery, Utah. It is safe to surmise that most were in the hands of a small number of owners.

[62]ZCMI Records, Book B, pp. 2, 55.

[63]JH, October 8, 1878, and the words of Mormon Church president John Taylor as quoted in *Tullidge's Quarterly Magazine* 1 (April 1881): 396.

[64]*Deseret News*, March 21, 1889.

[65]See Joseph C. Felix, "The Development of Cooperative Enterprises in Cache Valley, 1865-1900" (Master's thesis, Brigham Young University, 1956).

[66]Leonard J. Arrington, "The Provo Woolen Mills: Utah's First Large Manufacturing Establishment," *Utah Historical Quarterly* 21 (1953), pp. 97-116.

[67]Ibid.; Arrington, *Great Basin Kingdom*, pp. 317, 319.

[68]Arrington, *Great Basin Kingdom*, pp. 315-16. Also Leonard J. Arrington, "Banking Enterprises in Utah, 1847-1880," *Business History Review* 29 (December 1955), pp. 312-34, esp. 323-26.

[69]Arrington, *Great Basin Kingdom*, pp. 309-10.

[70]George Q. Cannon sermon, April 6, 1869, JD 13: 95-103.

CHAPTER 6
*The Brigham City
Cooperative:
Steppingstone to the United Order*

The primary source material on the Brigham City cooperative and United Order, all in the Church Archives, includes: (a) Letters of Lorenzo Snow to Brigham Young, Bishop Henry Lunt, and Franklin D. Richards, as published in the *Deseret Evening News*, August 20, 1873; *Tullidge's Quarterly Magazine* 2 (January 1883): 400-7; and Eliza Roxey Snow Smith, *Biography and Family Record of Lorenzo Snow* . . . (Salt Lake City, 1884), pp. 291-96. (b) The Manuscript History of Box Elder Stake. (c) Scribbling Book of Brigham City, containing copies of letters by Lorenzo Snow. This manuscript was in the possession of the late LeRoi C. Snow at the time Leonard Arrington examined it (1948), though its present whereabouts is not known. (d) Minute books and account books of various Brigham City cooperative enterprises and the Brigham City United Order Minute Book.

Secondary source material includes "United Order of Northern Utah," in Kate Carter, ed., *Heart Throbs of the West* (12 vols., Salt Lake City: Daughters of Utah Pioneers, 1936-47), 1:53-56; Daughters of Utah Pioneers of Box Elder County, comps., *History of Box Elder County* (Brigham City, 1936); *Tullidge's Histories* . . ., 2 vols. (Salt Lake City, 1889), 2:289-304.

[1] Letter quoted by Thomas C. Romney in *The Life of Lorenzo Snow* (Salt Lake City: Sugarhouse Press, 1955), pp. 315-17. The original, in 1948, was in the files of LeRoi C. Snow.

[2] JH, October 7, 1853; also *Deseret News*, October 15, 1853. There were sixty families and 204 souls in the Box Elder settlement in 1854, most of whom were Welsh and Danish. All were very poor.

[3] Lorenzo Snow to Brigham Young, August 6, 1873, *Deseret Evening News*, August 20, 1873.

[4] Lorenzo Snow to Bishop Henry Lunt, October 1876, *Tullidge's Quarterly Magazine* 2 (January 1883): 401.

[5] Ibid., 401-2.

[6] Smith, *Biography of Lorenzo Snow*, p. 292.

[7] *Deseret Evening News*, July 24, 1872.

[8] Brigham City United Order Minutes, December 1, 1875.

[9] Manuscript History of Box Elder Stake, October 28, 1877; Snow to Lunt, October 1876; Snow to Young, August 6, 1873.

[10] The articles of incorporation are to be found among the records in the Box Elder County Courthouse, Brigham City, Utah. Of the 126 stock-

NOTES TO PAGES 114-117

holders, only 13 held more than 100 shares of stock (par value, $5 each). Lorenzo Snow was the largest stockholder, with 1,556 shares valued at $7,830. Samuel Smith, who possessed 1,000 shares valued at $5,000, was the second largest stockholder.

[11]Snow to Lunt, October 1876; Snow to Young, August 6, 1873; the machinery was purchased for $7,000 in greenbacks. D.U.P., *History of Box Elder County,* p. 105.

[12]Snow to Lunt, October 1876. Snow to Young, August 6, 1873.

[13]Information on the various departments can be obtained from Manuscript History of Box Elder Stake, July 12, 1872, October 28, 1877, April 28, 1878, and passim.

[14]Correspondent John R. Morgan, writing to the *Deseret News* under date of July 12, 1872, summarized the objectives of the system as follows: "A mercantile house was established, that for the time being it might serve the purpose of a paymaster, to enable other enterprises to be established; the tannery to avoid the importation of boots and shoes, and to produce a home market for hides; a shoe factory followed, to give employment to home operatives, and avoid the exportation of valley tan leather; a factory to use up the wool, and manufacture cloth for the people; a dairy to avoid the importation of cheese; a cooperative farm to supply the operatives in the various departments with flour."

[15]Edward L. Sloan, ed., *Gazeteer of Utah* (Salt Lake City, 1874), p. 55. In 1872 the capital stock totaled $75,000. Manuscript History of Box Elder Stake, January 4, 1872. In 1877 the secretary of the institution represented the total capital stock to be $191,000, with 585 shareholders. Some 340 hands were employed, and the income from the various departments was in excess of $260,000. Ibid., October 28, 1877.

[16]Snow to Lunt, October 1876; D.U.P., *History of Box Elder County,* p. 49. This "Indian Farm" became Washakie in Box Elder County and was administered by the LDS Church for the benefit of the Indians until recent years.

[17]*Deseret Evening News,* April 28, 1875.

[18]Smith, *Biography of Lorenzo Snow,* p. 294; Snow to Lunt, October 1876; D.U.P., *History of Box Elder County,* pp. 11-13, 286.

[19]Snow to Young, August 6, 1873. According to the local history, ecclesiastical authorities advised the people to give all their patronage to cooperative industries after 1869. D.U.P., *History of Box Elder County,* p. 118. A descendant of one of the men whose concern failed as the result of the cooperative told Feramorz Y. Fox that his grandfather formed a partnership with another prominent Brigham City citizen in the late 1860s for the purpose of establishing a haberdashery. The business was the only place in Brigham City where other than homespun material could be purchased, and it succeeded beyond the best hopes of its founders. This man and his partner were asked to join the association,

but they declined. Immediately, according to the story, the people of the city were instructed not to trade with them. When some townspeople persisted in trading with these men despite the orders of Church officials, members of the Church were allegedly placed at the door of the haberdashery to record the names of all persons who traded therein. This, despite the fact that members of the partnership were members of the church in good standing. As the result, the business is said to have soon failed and the men were forced to seek a livelihood elsewhere.

The Minutes of the General Council of the United Order of Box Elder County for July 20, 1880, contain the following: "It was moved and carried unanimously that the council disapprove, discountenance, and disfellowship all persons who would start an opposition store or who would assist to erect a building for that purpose."

[20]*Salt Lake Herald,* October 25, 1876.

[21]Manuscript History of Box Elder Stake, October 28, 1877. More than $950 was rendered by this department in 1877.

[22]D.U.P., *History of Box Elder County,* p. 110.

[23]L. F. Moench in the *Deseret News,* as cited in D.U.P., *History of Box Elder County,* p. 109n.

[24]Snow to Lunt, October 1876.

[25]Snow to Young, August 6, 1873.

[26]A photograph of a specimen is reproduced in Anderson, *Desert Saints,* p. 377. Merchandise scrip was "Good only to Stockholders and Employees of Brigham City."

[27]Snow to Lunt, October 1876. In 1873, according to Lorenzo Snow, the production of all the departments was about $60,000, and some $10,000 to $12,000 in cash was required to keep them in operation. This cash was supplied "in part by the profits of the store, the balance by sales of products. It is only to make up this balance," he wrote, "that we are required to seek a market for our manufactured products." Snow to Young, August 6, 1873.

[28]Martin Buber, in *Paths in Utopia,* intr. by Ephraim Fischoff, trans. R.F.C. Hull (Boston: Beacon, 1966), differentiated between full cooperation, or cooperation in producing as well as consuming, and cooperation in either producing or consuming alone—the latter two being much easier to achieve.

[29]Brigham Young sermon, April 21, 1878, JD 19:345.

[30]Minutes of the Meetings of the Board of Directors of the Brigham City Mercantile and Manufacturing Association, July 3, 1874.

[31]JH, June 28, 1874.

[32]*Deseret News,* August 31, 1875.

[33]*Millennial Star* 37 (1876): 695.

[34]Minutes of the United Order of Box Elder County, April 22, 1877.

[35]*Deseret News,* August 31, 1875.

[36]*Tullidge's Quarterly Magazine* 2 (January 1883): 400.

[37]"Successful Co-operation," *Salt Lake Herald*, October 25, 1876.

[38]*Millennial Star* 38 (1876): 694.

[39]John Taylor sermon, August 4, 1878, JD 20:44-45.

[40]The letter is found in the Scribbling Book of Brigham City.

[41]Brigham City United Order Minutes, July 20, 1880.

[42]Scribbling Book of Brigham City; Brigham City United Order Minutes, December 1, 1875, March 25, 1876. In 1875 the association distributed 500 bushels a month to its wage earners.

[43]Brigham City United Order Minutes, December 29, 1875; Scribbling Book of Brigham City, letter of 1873.

[44]Scribbling Book of Brigham City, letter in fall of 1873.

[45]Ibid.

[46]*Deseret Evening News*, March 7, 1872; January 2, June 26, and August 28, 1878.

[47]Smith, *Biography of Lorenzo Snow*, pp. 303-6.

[48]Ibid., pp. 314-15.

[49]Brigham City United Order Minutes, October 27, 1878.

[50]Scribbling Book of Brigham City.

[51]See Chapter 14 in this volume for a full discussion on this effort.

[52]Minutes of the Directors, March 13, 1880.

[53]Smith, *Biography of Lorenzo Snow*, pp. 308-9. As noted earlier, the Brigham City Mercantile and Manufacturing Association was established long before the United Order came into existence and continued for many years after the Order was a mere memory. The term "United Order" was never used until February 1874, and a branch of the Order was not established in Box Elder County until much later in that year. Lorenzo Snow and other directors of the co-op and the superintendents of departments became members of the United Order Council, so that it was of little moment in considering the affairs of the cooperative association whether those concerned met as the Council of the United Order or as a board of directors and department heads. Meeting as the United Order, though, brought the people of the community into conformity with the churchwide plan and the wishes of Brigham Young and gave the cooperative movement added strength through recognizing the sentiment that people had for the Order as the plan of the revered head of the church.

[54]Brigham City United Order Minutes, July 20, 1880.

[55]Minutes of the Directors, March 17 and November 18, 1880; March 21, 1882; January 2 and June 22, 1888; February 25, 1892; March 10, 1893; November 21, 1895.

CHAPTER 7
The United Order
of Enoch:
The order of heaven

[1]From a typescript of a July 10, 1875, report of ZCMI, in the possession of Leonard Arrington.

[2]Orson Pratt sermon, November 1, 1868, JD 12:320-23.

[3]Géorge Q. Cannon, October 8, 1872, JD 15:207-9.

[4]Brigham Young, April 7, 1869, *Deseret News,* June 2, 1869.

[5]For discussion of the impact in Utah of the panic of 1873, see Arrington, *Great Basin Kingdom,* pp. 323-24.

[6]St. George Stake Historical Record, November 10, 1870, MS, Church Archives.

[7]Ibid., March 28, 1871.

[8]Ibid., November 9, 1871.

[9]Ibid., November 3, 1872.

[10]Ibid., January 18, 1873.

[11]Ibid., June 10, 1874.

[12]George Q. Cannon sermon, October 8, 1872, JD 15:207-8.

[13]Brigham Young sermon, October 9, 1872, JD 15:158-167. Brigham Young states that he had a revelation at Winter Quarters showing the organization of the kingdom of God in a family capacity, but others could not see it. He would have put all he had into such a system in 1847 if others had been ready to receive it. Brigham Young sermon in Third Ward, *Deseret News,* June 21, 1874.

[14]Orson Pratt sermon, March 9, 1873, JD 15:354-59.

[15]Brigham Young sermon, April 7, 1873, JD 16:8-9.

[16]Lorenzo Snow sermon, October 7, 1873, JD 16:277.

[17]Brigham Young sermon, June 29, 1873, JD 6:122.

[18]See Appendix 5 for names of officers and for the articles of association.

[19]JH, May 31, 1874. See Appendix 5 for complete rules.

[20]Orson Pratt sermon, April 6, 1874, JD 17:24-36.

[21]Quoted in *Deseret News,* April 22, 1874, from *Beaver Enterprise.*

[22]Quoted in *Deseret News,* April 29, 1874, from *Beaver Enterprise.*

[23]*Salt Lake Daily Tribune,* March 7, 1874.

[24]*The Compiled Laws of the Territory of Utah* (Salt Lake City, 1876), chap. 4.

[25]JH, May 9, 1874; *Deseret News,* May 13, 1874.

[26]See reports of sermons in JD, vol. 17.

[27]Erastus Snow sermon, May 8, 1874, JD 17:76.

[28] A complete list of the personnel appears in Appendix 7.

[29] JH, May 31, 1874.

[30] JH, June 21, 1874.

[31] Frederick Kesler Journal, June 28, 1874, MS, Western Americana Collection, University of Utah Library, Salt Lake City, Utah.

[32] Brigham Young sermon, June 23, 1874, JD 18:248.

[33] Brigham Young sermon, August 9, 1874, JD 17:157-58.

[34] *Salt Lake Daily Tribune*, March 7, 1874; Davis Bitton and Gary L. Bunker, "Enoch's Advocate (1874): A Forgotten Anti-Mormon Periodical," paper presented at a Brigham Young University symposium on the "Mormon Role in the Settlement of the West," November 13 and 14, 1975, typescript in Church Archives.

[35] Kesler Journal.

[36] *Millennial Star* 36 (1874): 501, quoting from the *Ogden Junction*.

[37] JH, August 11 to 13, 1874.

[38] "Rules . . . of the United Order," broadside, Church Archives.

[39] Brigham Young sermon, August 9, 1874, JD 17:157.

[40] John Taylor sermon, October 9, 1874, JD 17:177-80.

[41] George Q. Cannon sermon, October 8, 1875, JD 18:104. See also chapter 11 on Kanab, where the wealthier citizens chose the more communal form of Order.

[42] John Taylor sermon, August 31, 1875, JD 18:80.

[43] See Chapter 9 on Sevier Stake United Order.

[44] *Salt Lake Daily Tribune*, May 5, 1862.

[45] Articles filed in the Salt Lake County Clerk's Office.

[46] Corporation file, Salt Lake County Clerk's Office.

[47] *Gazeteer of Utah and Salt Lake City Directory*, comp. E. L. Sloan (1874), p. 314; corporation file, Salt Lake County Clerk's Office.

[48] *Salt Lake Daily Tribune*, May 5, 1874.

[49] St. George Stake Manuscript History, July 31 to September 5, 1875, MS, Church Archives. Joseph L. Townsend, in a personal interview with Feramorz Young Fox, October 14, 1940, said he was engaged to construct at Payson a baptismal font on the creek where, after being baptized himself, he assisted in baptizing all.

[50] Edward J. Allen, *The Second United Order Among the Mormons* (New York: Columbia University Press, 1936), p. 98.

CHAPTER 8
St. George:
Oneness
in heart and hand

Primary sources in the Church Archives include James G. Bleak's "Annals of the Southern Utah Mission"; Manuscript History of St. George Stake; St. George Stake Historical Record; "The United Order Book," in the office of the County Recorder of Washington County, Utah, which contains the articles of incorporation of the United Orders of St. George, Washington, and St. George First Ward.

[1]JH, February 28, 1874.

[2]George Q. Cannon sermon, October 8, 1872, JD 15:207.

[3]St. George Stake Manuscript History, January 16, 1873, MS, Church Archives.

[4]Ibid., January 16 and 26 and February 16, 1873.

[5]Ibid., January 2, 1874.

[6]Ibid., January 26, 1874.

[7]Angus M. Woodbury, "The Mormon United Order in Utah," p. 6, paper dated 1954, Church Archives.

[8]St. George Stake Manuscript History, February 14, 1874.

[9]Ibid., February 15, 1874.

[10]Ibid., March 26, 1874.

[11]Ibid., April 11, 1874.

[12]The letter of inquiry is in the St. George Stake Historical Record, Book B, 1873-1877, August 2, 1874, MS, Church Archives. The reply is in the same source under date of September 6, 1874.

[13]St. George Stake Historical Record, Book B, September 14, 1874.

[14]St. George Stake Manuscript History, November 9, 1874.

[15]St. George Stake Financial United Order Accounts, Church Archives.

[16]St. George Stake Manuscript History, January 10, 1875.

[17]Woodbury, "The Mormon United Order," p. 15.

[18]St. George Stake Manuscript History, March 26, 1874.

[19]Notation on slip found in St. George Stake, Financial, United Order Stockholders' Fund Ledger, Church Archives.

[20]*Millennial Star* 36 (May 12, 1874): 299.

[21]Brigham Young sermon, October 9, 1872, JD 15:227.

[22]George Q. Cannon sermon, October 8, 1874, JD 17:237-38. Cannon underestimated·the number. There were 17 men and 79 persons in all.

[23]St. George Stake Manuscript History, February 16, 1875.

[24]Ibid., January 9, 1877.

[25]*Deseret News*, August 22, 1877.

[26]St. George Stake Historical Record, Book B, September 6, 1874.

[27]St. George Stake Manuscript History, September 13 and 14, 1874.

[28]Ibid., September 20, 1874.

[29]Ibid., September 1875.

[30]Ibid., December 18, 1875.

[31]*Deseret News*, February 13, 1877.

[32]St. George Stake Manuscript History, May 12, 1876.

[33]Sevier Stake, Miscellaneous, United Order Record Book, July 16, 1877, MS, Church Archives.

[34]*Deseret News*, June 27, 1877; JH, July 20, 1877. The full text of the agreements is given in Appendix 6.

[35]St. George Stake, United Order Stockholders' Fund Ledger.

[36]St. George Stake Manuscript History, September 15, 1877.

[37]Ibid., October 7, 1877.

[38]Ibid., December 31, 1877.

[39]Ibid., June 9, 1878.

CHAPTER 9
Richfield:
Combatting the feeling
of "mine"

[1]Sevier Stake Historical Record, December 7, 1873, MS, Church Archives.

[2]Saint George Stake Manuscript History, April 5, 1874.

[3]Sevier Stake Historical Record, March 14, 1874.

[4]*Deseret News,* July 24, 1875.

[5]Sevier Stake United Order Record Book, June 22, 1874, MS, Church Archives. This book of more than 500 pages is the principal source from which our study of the Richfield United Order has been drawn. It contains, along with other items of United Order business, minutes of the meetings of the board of directors of the United Order of Richfield held every few days from April 1874 through March 1878. It has not been felt necessary to cite the exact location of everything drawn from the book for use in the present account, especially in cases where a particular incident is chosen only because it is typical of many detailed throughout the record. The reader can assume that any account for which a specific footnote is not given is from this source.

[6]Ibid., January 13 and February 13, 1875.

[7]Ibid., November 9, 1874. This reference contains only the articles of incorporation. Young's schedule of property and those of others who entered the order were apparently attached to the articles of incorporation at the time Feramorz Fox did his original study in the 1930s, but they have been lost or misplaced since that time. The figures given by Fox have been rounded and rearranged for clarity.

[8]Ibid., in order of use in the text: April 18, 1874; September 4 and 29, October 23, and December 4, 1875; May 18 and June 3, 1876.

[9]Sevier Stake Manuscript History, October 1875, MS, Church Archives.

[10]Sevier Stake, United Order Record Book, January 29, 1875.

[11]Ibid., January 18 and February 27, 1875.

[12]Ibid., April 10 and 17, 1875.

[13]Ibid., December 2, 1876.

[14]Ibid., August 27, 1877.

[15]Ibid., October 14 and November 12, 1874; February 23 and 26, August 28, and September 16, 1875; February 5 and 9, April 12, August 12, and November 7, 1876; February 20, 1877.

[16]Ibid., November 11-14, 1876.

[17]Brigham Young to W. H. Seegmiller and A. K. Thurber, October 13, 1875, in St. George Stake Manuscript History.

[18]Sevier Stake United Order Record Book, July 1-10, 1876.

[19]Ibid., August 1, 1876, and subsequent entries.

[20]Ibid., October 3, 1876.

[21]St. George Stake Manuscript History, January 22, 1877.

[22]*Deseret News,* June 10, 1877.

[23]Sevier Stake United Order Record Book, July 16, 1877.

[24]Ibid., April 19, 1874.

[25]Ibid., September 7, 1874.

[26]Ibid., August 27, 1877.

CHAPTER 10
The proliferation of United Orders:
Utah Valley, Cache Valley,
Bear Lake Valley, City Orders

[1]See Brigham Young sermon, October 9, 1872, JD 15:220-29; also Brigham Young sermon, August 31, 1873, JD 16:169-71.

[2]Brigham Young to D. H. Wells, et. al., telegram of March 11, 1874, Brigham Young Telegrams, MS, Church Archives. Punctuation supplied.

[3]See 1776 accounts by Escalante and Miera in Herbert E. Bolton, *Pageant in the Wilderness; The Story of the Escalante Expedition to the Interior Basin, 1776* (Salt Lake City: Utah State Historical Society, 1950), pp. 184-85, 245.

[4]*Deseret Evening News*, March 31, 1874. A former mayor of Salt Lake City, Smoot had settled in Provo early in 1868 and was immediately appointed "Bishop of Provo City and President of the High Council." There were several wards already established in Provo at the time, but his jurisdiction was apparently regional, analogous to that of the present-day stake president. In 1877 when the Utah Stake was organized Smoot was made stake president.

[5]Statistics are from the 1870 U.S. manuscript census, schedules of population and agricultural data, Church Archives.

[6]Pleasant Grove, Board of Directors of the United Order Minutes, April 27, 1874, MS, Church Archives.

[7]Ibid., May 5, 14, 17, and 31, 1874.

[8]Ibid., June 14, 1874, and March 3, 1875.

[9]The number 130 is a count of the names of individuals who had active accounts in the United Order books in 1876. The percentage is computed from 1870 population data, which, of course, had grown by 1876.

[10]Pleasant Grove United Order Minutes, September 18, 1874, May 7, and June 7, 1876.

[11]Ibid., December 27, 1875, January 6, 1876, and subsequent entries. The site of the mine was not mentioned.

[12]Ibid., June 7 and March 10, 1876.

[13]Spanish Fork United Order Minute Book, May 2, 1874, MS, Church Archives.

[14]Ibid., June 14, 1874.

[15]Population is based on the 1870 U.S. manuscript census. Order accounts are found in Spanish Fork United Order Account Books, MS, Church Archives.

[16]Spanish Fork United Order Minute Book, March 22, 1875.

¹⁷Ibid., June 2, 1877; Spanish Fork United Order Account Books.

¹⁸The Order assets were $38,148, and the community wealth four years earlier was $31,375. Land values are not included in either figure, as the Order did not own a significant amount of real estate. See the 1870 U.S. manuscript census, agricultural; Pleasant Grove United Order Minutes, March 9, 1876.

¹⁹See the 1870 U.S. manuscript census, agricultural.

²⁰Joel E. Ricks, "First Settlements" and "Expansion of Settlement," and Leonard J. Arrington, "Railroad Building and Cooperatives, 1869-1879," in Joel E. Ricks, ed., *The History of a Valley* (Logan, Utah: Cache Valley Centennial Committee, 1956); 1870 and 1880 U.S. manuscript census. Intercensal populations are estimated on a straight-line basis, a procedure that for small populations introduces little error.

²¹Leonard J. Arrington, *Charles C. Rich: Mormon General and Western Frontiersman* (Provo, Utah: Brigham Young University Press, 1974), pp. 247-71; 1870 and 1880 U.S. manuscript census.

²²Brigham Young sermon, JD 16:169-71.

²³Russell R. Rich, *Land of the Sky-Blue Water: A History of L.D.S. Settlement of the Bear Lake Valley* (Provo, Utah: Brigham Young University Press, 1963), pp. 121-24.

²⁴Arrington, "Railroad Building and Cooperatives," pp. 200-1.

²⁵*Deseret News,* June 8, 1874; August 18, 1875; August 1, 1877; *History of Idaho Territory* (San Francisco, 1884), p. 223.

²⁶*Deseret News,* August 1, 1877; February 24, 1879; Jesse R.S. Budge, "Early Days in Bear Lake Valley—The 'Paris Co-op,' " *Utah Humanities Review* 2 (January 1948): 78-79.

²⁷*Deseret News,* February 24, 1879.

²⁸*History of Idaho Territory,* p. 222.

²⁹Charles C. Rich was among those who attributed the decline of the United Order to the coming of the railroad. See Arrington, *Charles C. Rich,* pp. 280-81.

³⁰Rich, *Land of Sky-Blue Water,* pp. 126-27. The most extensive recent study of the Paris cooperatives is by Dean L. May, "Mormon Cooperatives in Paris, Idaho, 1869-1896," *Idaho Yesterdays* 9 (Summer, 1975): 20-30.

³¹See the list in Appendix 8, prepared by Feramorz Y. Fox, of United Orders founded with dates of founding and initially elected officers. Paradoxically, the one city ward for which no record exists of an Order having been founded was the Eighteenth Ward—to which Brigham Young and family belonged.

³²Officers of the group are listed in Appendix 7.

³³United Order Number One Minutes, August 4, 1875, MS, Church Archives.

³⁴Ibid., August 19, 1875. A partial schedule of Brigham Young's

properties was presented and read in the meeting as well.

[35]Ibid., August 31, 1875.

[36]The section on the Logan United Order is from Leonard Arrington's chapter in Ricks, ed., *History of a Valley*, pp. 198-99.

CHAPTER 11
Kanab:
Many men,
many minds

[1]Adonis Findley Robinson, ed., *History of Kane County* (Salt Lake City: Daughters of Utah Pioneers, 1970), pp. 2-5.

[2]Ibid., pp. 6-7.

[3]Ibid., pp. 20-21.

[4]William Thomas Stewart Journal, pp. 1-4, 6, photocopy of holograph, Church Archives. Also U.S. Bureau of the Census, microfilm of 1870 and 1880 manuscript census for Kanab, Kane County, Utah (hereafter cited as manuscript census).

[5]Levi Stewart to Brigham Young, received May 2, 1874, MS, Brigham Young Incoming Correspondence; manuscript census, Kanab, 1870; Robinson, *History of Kane County*, p. 21.

[6]James Lovett Bunting Diary, April 28, 1870, typescript, Church Archives.

[7]Ibid., December 2, 1870. "Kanab" is an anglicized form of the Piute word for "willows." The creek reportedly was given its name because a dense growth of willows at one time lined its banks. See Robinson, *History of Kane County*, p. 1.

[8]Bunting Diary, September 8 and December 18, 1870.

[9]Ibid., January 28, 1871. The arrival of this group and the circumstances leading to their choice of the Kanab region as a site for settling is not recorded. Something of their significance can be inferred from the fact that in 1880 18 percent of the married adult population of Kanab had been born in the South or the border states. By contrast New England was the birthplace of 11 percent of the adult married population, England 17 percent, the American Midwest 17 percent, and Utah 32 percent.

[10]On July 17, 1873, Bishop Stewart counseled returning Arizona Mission members to settle in the Kanab area, offering the advice in a manner that suggests that it came from the central church authorities. See William H. Solomon Diary, July 17, 1873, typescript, Church Archives.

[11]Data compiled by the authors from 1870 manuscript census for Kanab. Because the composition of Levi Stewart's company is relatively well documented, those who cannot be identified as members of the Stewart group are assumed to be in Hamblin's group, except for two single teamsters, one of which has been arbitrarily assigned to each group.

[12]Data compiled by the authors from 1874 Kanab United Order Census in Kanab Stake United Order Minutes 1874-1880, pp. 63-71, MS, Church Archives. According to one account, two men in the community did not join the United Order. Since there is no certain means of determining who they might have been, they and their families (presuming they had families) were probably not counted in the census and do not enter into the present statistical summaries. J. R. Young, Levi Stewart to Brigham Young, June 23, 1874, Brigham Young Telegrams. These data, as do all data in this study, include Pahreah and Johnson as part of the Kanab community.

[13]Andrew S. Gibbons, his wife, Rizpah Knight, and their families were from the Muddy Mission. St. Thomas Ward, Muddy Mission, Historical Record and Record of Members 1865-1870, MS, Church Archives.

[14]U.S. Geographical and Geological Survey, *Map of the Territory of Utah,* 1878, shows the main travel routes in the Kanab area. See also Robinson, ed., *History of Kane County,* pp. 99-101.

[15]Kanab Ward Historical Record, Book A, 1870-1881, MS, Church Archives. Bishop W.D. Johnson, Jr., compiled this record in 1881 from various sources, not all of which have survived. This entry was from the diary of M.F. Farnsworth, September 11-13, 1870 (pp. 6-7 of the Johnson compilation).

[16]Kanab Ward Historical Record, March 18, 1871, pp. 9-10. Stewart was not, however, a member of the board of directors; Edward Pugh, J. G. Brown, and Philander Brown served in that office.

[17]Bunting Diary, February 13 and September 7, 1871; February 10, 1872. Also Kanab Agricultural Association Minutes, 1873-1876, MS, Church Archives.

[18]Bunting Diary, April 19 and October 5, 1873.

[19]Stewart Journal, p. 8.

[20]Telegrams, March 4, 6, 17, and 18, 1874, Brigham Young Telegrams.

[21]John R. Young, *Memoirs* (Salt Lake City, 1920), pp. 152-53 et passim. See also Jenson, *LDS Biographical Encyclopedia* 2:274-76.

[22]Stewart and John R. Young to Brigham Young, June 23, 1874, Brigham Young Telegrams.

[23]Kanab Stake Historical Record, 1877-1914; March 12 and 18, April 9 and 12, and May 23, 1874.

[24]A. F. McDonald to Brigham Young, July 13, 1874, Brigham Young Telegrams.

[25]JH, May 31, 1874.

[26]Levi Stewart to Brigham Young, July 9, 1874, MS, Brigham Young Incoming Correspondence, Church Archives.

[27]Bunting Diary, July 6, 1874.

[28]Ibid., July 19, 1874.

[29]Solomon Diary, August 18, 1875.

[30]John R. Young to Brigham Young, August 19, 1847, MS, Brigham Young Family Correspondence, Church Archives.

[31]Kanab Stake United Order Minutes, September 7, 12, and 14, 1874.

[32]Ibid., September 16, 1874; the minutes of the meeting in which Young was re-elected are undated, but succeed directly after minutes of September 15 in the minute book.

[33]Bunting Diary, November 8, 1874.

[34]Solomon Diary, undated retrospective entry in version of typescript at the Marriott Library, University of Utah, Salt Lake City.

[35]Kanab Stake United Order Minutes, pp. 112-16. The pages are here cited rather than customary dates because the clerk has confused the dating of the meeting. The clerk's description falls after his entry of December 23 and before his entry of December 24. He described it in the minutes only as a meeting held as appointed by J. R. Young on December 12. Bunting's diary entry of December 13 and the minutes of the J. R. Young United Order make it certain that the meeting was held on that day and that the clerk, possibly copying from notes he had taken at the meeting, wrote it into his journal in the wrong chronological sequence.

[36]See James Lewis, et al., "To the Presidency at St. George," December 17, 1874, in the Kanab United Order Minute Book, pp. 82-83, MS, Church Archives.

[37]Kanab Agricultural Association Minutes, January 8 and February 6, 1875.

[38]Kanab United Order Minute Book, January 4, February 9, March 20, and May 29, 1875.

[39]Kanab Ward Home Teachers' Report Minutes, 1872-1881, February 7, 1875, MS, Church Archives.

[40]Stewart Journal, p. 8; also P. T. Reilly, "Kanab United Order: The President's Nephew and the Bishop," Utah Historical Quarterly 42 (Spring 1974): 144-64.

[41]Solomon Diary, undated retrospective entry in version of typescript at Marriott Library.

[42]Kanab United Order Minute Book, December 17, 1874.

[43]John R. Young to Brigham Young, February 7, 1875, MS, Brigham Young Family Correspondence.

[44]John H. Standifird Journal, January 5, 1875, photocopy of typescript, Church Archives.

[45]John R. Young to Brigham Young, March 1, 1875, MS, Brigham Young Family Correspondence.

[46]J. R. Young to Brigham Young, March 23, 1875, MS, Brigham Young Family Correspondence.

[47]See minutes of meetings in the Kanab United Order Minutes Book for the dates indicated.

[48]The relationship between the various leaders was important, as Reilly has suggested in his "Kanab United Order." We feel, however, that a more satisfying grasp of United Order problems in Kanab can be gained through attempting to build a broader historical context of community structure and interrelationships upon which the Order was imposed. Our study was virtually completed before the appearance of Reilly's piece in the *Utah Historical Quarterly*.

[49]The 1875 population of Kanab has been estimated by assuming an arithmetic, straight-line growth between the 1874 United Order Census and the 1880 U.S. Census, a procedure which for so small a population and so short a period would introduce little error. The J. R. Young Order population has been reconstructed from 1870 and 1880 census data, the Kanab United Order Minute Book listing of heads of household members (see December 17, 1874, entry) and from "family group sheets" (family reconstitution data sheets) in the Genealogical Society Archives of The Church of Jesus Christ of Latter-day Saints, Salt Lake City, Utah.

Only sixteen heads of families signed the letter sent to Brigham Young on December 17, 1874, announcing that an insurgent United Order group had been started. Others joined the group later. The total of twenty-three represents all who can be determined from the minutes either joined the Order or were clearly working under Order auspices, and hence are presumed to have joined the Order. They included Nathan Adams, Brigham Young Baird, William M. Black, Joseph G. Brown, James S. Bunting, Abel A. DeWitt, Thomas F. Dobson, Allen Frost, Andrew S. Gibbons, Mary A. Hamblin, Ira Hatch, Z. K. Judd, James Lewis, James H. Lewis, James A. Little, Jehiel McConnell, Charles H. Oliphant, Thomas Robertson, Charles M. Tyler, George Watson, Lorenzo Watson, Jared Young, and John R. Young. All of these persons had families except Jared Young; some of them several families.

[50]Diary of L. John Nuttall, April 20, 1877, typescript, Church Archives.

[51]Information on individuals in the Young Order has been gathered from a variety of sources, especially Robinson, *History of Kane County*, pp. 1-24; U.S. manuscript census records, 1870 and 1880; the Kanab United Order Minute Book; diaries of Bunting and Frost; Jenson, *L.D.S. Biographical Encyclopedia*; Derrel Wesley Judd, "Zadock Knapp Judd— Soldier, Colonizer, Missionary to the Lamanites" (M.A. thesis, Brigham Young University, 1968); Young, *Memoirs*; and family group sheets in the LDS Genealogical Society Archives.

[52]Henry S. Shryock, Jacob S. Siegel and Associates, *The Methods and Materials of Demography*, 2nd ed. rev., 2 vols. (Washington: U.S. Government Printing Office, 1973), 1:192. The table in this source on "Sex Ra-

tios by Region and Residence, for the United States: 1960" was adapted from *U.S. Census of Population: 1960*, vol. 1, *Characteristics of the Population, Part 1, United States Summary, 1964,* table 58.

[53]Modern age-dependency ratios range from 51.4 in Sweden (51.4 dependents for every 100 workers) to 104.1 in Syria, a nation whose population structure closely resembles that of Utah during the United Order period. Shryock and Siegel, *Materials of Demography* 1:235, Table 8-25. The data represents the Young Order in 1875, the whole community in 1874, and the territory in 1880. In a population as small as Kanab, the year-to-year differences were not great (Kanab was adding about thirty persons per year to its population at the time). Differences between Kanab and the territory in sex ratio, age-dependency ratio, and median age are almost precisely the same when the 1880 census figures for village and territory are compared as in our comparison here of 1874 village and 1880 territorial data.

[54]Reilly, "Kanab United Order," p. 150.

[55]Kanab United Order Minute Book, pp. 48-54. Because two male heads of household in the Young Order were not in the tax lists, they were not counted in computing the mean. Mary A. Hamblin did not appear either but was counted in the computation because it seemed possible that she, a widow, was omitted because she had little or no wealth to report or was not taxed by county and territory. If all names are counted (including the three not found in the tax evaluation lists), a mean of $778.70 emerges; if none of those missing in the tax lists are counted, the mean is $895.50. The median varies from $400.00 to $447.50, according to which figure for N (23, 21, or 20) is used.

[56]Bunting Diary, November 8, 1874.

[57]JD 4:209; 12:120; 24:116; 25:111-12; 26:14-15, 219-21. Partly in consequence of such preachments, Mormon fertility has continued into the twentieth century to be significantly higher than national norms. See Brian L. Pitcher, et. al., "Residency Differentials in Mormon Fertility," *Population Studies,* 28 (March 1974): 43-51.

[58]Kanab Stake United Order Minutes, December 13, 1874, p. 115.

[59]Kanab Ward Home Teachers' Report Minutes, February 7 and May 19, 1875.

[60]McConnell to Brigham Young, June 23, 1875, MS, Brigham Young Incoming Correspondence.

[61]Brigham Young to Jehiel McConnell, July 7, 1875, Brigham Young Letterbooks, MS, Church Archives.

[62]Brigham Young to Levi Stewart, John P. Young, and L. J. Nuttall, August 30, 1875, Brigham Young Letterbooks.

[63]Bunting Diary, September 5, 1875; Kanab United Order Minute Book, September 17, 1875.

[64]Phrenological report of Henry Clegg, March 8, 1867, L. J. Nuttall

Papers, MS, Church Archives.

[65]Kanab United Order Minute Book, January 3 and 6, 1874; September 17, 1875, to January 3, 1876.

[66]Kanab Stake United Order Minutes. See the minutes for meetings of the first few months of 1876, esp. February 9, 1876.

[67]Pencilled, undated notations on a loose scrap of paper in the Kanab United Order Book.

[68]Brigham Young to L. John Nuttall, October 15, 1875, Brigham Young Letterbooks. The same letter was sent to several other bishops.

[69]Kanab Stake United Order Minutes, September 15, 1876; Allen Frost Diary, September 15 and 16, 1874, typescript, Church Archives.

[70]Frost Diary, March 1, 1876.

[71]Ibid., December 10, 1876.

[72]Kanab Stake United Order Minutes, December 18, 1876.

[73]Ibid., December 19 and 20, 1876.

[74]Ibid., January 1, 1877.

[75]John Nuttall to Brigham Young, March 19, 1877, MS, Brigham Young Incoming Correspondence.

[76]Kanab Stake United Order Minutes, June 8, September 15, and November 17, 1877.

[77]Kanab Ward Historical Record, Book A, April 18, 1877.

[78]Ibid., August 7, 1877.

[79]Ibid., December 8 and 9, 1877. For references to Johnson's contribution as teacher in Kanab see Robinson, *History of Kane County*, pp. 41, 223-24.

[80]Ibid., June 15, 1878.

[81]John Oakley to Brigham Young, January 16, 1877, MS, Brigham Young Incoming Correspondence.

CHAPTER 12
Orderville: A little family

Sources of information about the Orderville United Order include Orderville United Order Books of Account, in possession of LeGrande Heaton, Orderville, Utah, in 1935; also Orderville Ward Historical Record, Book A; Willard Carroll, Record Book; Emma Carroll Seegmiller Higbee, "A Study of the United Order of Orderville," and Francis K. Porter [History of the Orderville United Order, 1873-1910], pp. 49-50, all in Church Archives. Earlier works have cited this last source "Orderville Ward Historical Record, Book A." The book is a manuscript history of the United Order, written by one of its clerks, Francis K. Porter. Porter had access to books of original entry that he designated "historical record, books A, B, C or D," and has copied excerpts from these into his history. We have been unable to locate extant copies of all of these records. The record book containing Porter's history was later used for keeping minutes of various meetings of church groups in Orderville until 1910. Because of the varied nature of its contents, which are in no clear chronological order, page designations are used for citation rather than dates. Porter was an active member of the Order from its beginnings and served as clerk during much of the period. His record therefore has been quite properly treated by most students as an original source. Hereafter cited as Porter, History of Orderville.

[1]Charles Nordhoff, *The Communistic Societies of the United States* (1875; reprinted., New York: Hillary House Publishers, Ltd., 1961), p. 407.

[2]Porter, History of Orderville.

[3]Ibid., p. 48.

[4]Ibid., p. 50.

[5]The Order was incorporated for a period of twenty-five years in July 1875, with a maximum capitalization of $100,000, consisting of 10,000 shares at ten dollars each. While each donor was given book credit for capital stock in the corporation according to the value of his contribution, it was formally agreed that such stock did not entitle the owner to dividends or to any share of the corporation assets. The original document, "Articles of Incorporation," is among the James G. Bleak manuscripts in the Huntington Library and Art Gallery, San Marino, California. See also *Deseret News*, October 1, 1875.

[6]E. M. Webb, in the Orderville Ward Manuscript History, 1878, MS, Church Archives.

[7]Young, *Memoirs*, p. 225; Porter to Bleak, December 14, 1903, Bleak MS.

[8]Phil Robinson, *Sinners and Saints* (London, 1883), pp. 231-32.

[9]When apostle Lorenzo Snow, later president of the church, served an eleven-month term in the Utah penitentiary in 1886-87 for the practice of plural marriage, he jokingly remarked that he was living in the United Order for the first time in his life. Prison society, he said, was a first-class United Order. All prisoners wore the same clothes, ate the same food, lived in rooms of the same house, lived the same abstemious life, and were subject to an over-all discipline. JH, March 13, 1887, pp. 4-5; April 8, 1887, p. 8; May 17, 1887, p. 4.

[10]In 1879 the group decided to eat all together, but in family units. To accommodate all, there was a first and a second serving.

[11]See "Partial List of Products and Manufacturers of U.O.O. for 1879" and "History of the Broading Department," Bleak MS.

[12]Mark A. Pendleton, "The Orderville United Order of Zion," *Utah Historical Quarterly* 7 (1939): 154. The Order planted and maintained five acres of grain for the Indians.

[13]A complete account of the production of the community in 1879 and 1880 is among the Bleak MSS.

[14]In 1879 the tannery produced 702 pairs of shoes and 15 pairs of boots. Some 674 pairs of shoes were repaired in the same year. "Partial List of . . . Manufacturers . . . for 1879."

[15]The machinery consisted of one set of cards, 1 spinning jack, 4 looms, 1 yarn twister, 1 blanket loom, and a duster, all run by water power. Two of the looms were operated by men who had lost a leg.

[16]See "The Journal of Priddy Meeks," *Utah Historical Quarterly* 10 (1942): 145-223.

[17]One officer, Samuel Claridge, wrote a "United Order Song," which was sung at many of their religious and social gatherings. The words are reproduced in Emma Carroll Seegmiller, "Personal Memories of the United Order of Orderville, Utah," *Utah Historical Quarterly* 7 (1939): 191-92.

[18]See financial statements of the Orderville United Order for the years 1879-1885, Bleak MS.

[19]*Deseret News*, January 13, 1877.

[20]Young to Howard O. Spencer, January 17, 1877, as reproduced in Orderville Ward Manuscript History, 1877.

[21]Kate B. Carter, comp., *Heart Throbs of the West*, 12 vols. (Salt Lake City: Daughters of Utah Pioneers, 1936-1951), 4:28; "History of the Boarding Department" and "History of the Cloth Manufacturing Department," Bleak MS.

[22]Cited in Carter, comp., *Heart Throbs* 4:28.

[23]An example of the waiver of surplus credits was that signed by Francis L. Porter cancelling credits earned by Porter and his family in previous years. On January 1, 1880, Porter had a surplus labor credit to his account of $331.70. He signed the following: "I accept of the above,

my account with Orderville United Order to date as correct, and have this day for the sum of Three Dollars Lawful money of the United States to me in hand paid the receipt of which is hereby acknowledged, Bargained, sold, and Transfered to Said Orderville United Order, Three hundred and Eleven dollars and Seventy cents, the amount that was standing to my credit in the above account. This I have done of my own free will and accord, In witness whereof I hereby set my hand the date above given. Francis L. Porter." Porter, History of Orderville, p. 67.

[24]Pendleton, "Orderville United Order," pp. 154-55.

[25]According to the various sources available, the Order operated, at one time or other, the following departments: blacksmith and wagon repair, boarding house, board of appraisers, board of sisters (women's labor), cabinet and carpentry shop, canal, commissary, coopering, cotton farm, farming (at least ten different farms, each with a foreman), freighting, garden, grist mill, hennery (poultry), home improvement, knitting, livestock and dairy, midwifery, millinery, miscellaneous or special, public works, sawmill, schools, sheep, shoe shop, soap and broom, stock-feeding, store, tailoring, tannery, telegraph, tin shop, woolen cloth manufacturing.

[26]Cited in Joel E. Ricks, "Forms and Methods of Early Settlement in Utah and the Surrounding Region, 1847-77" (Ph.D. diss., University of Chicago, 1930), pp. 152-54. Paragraphing supplied.

[27]For a copy of a letter written by a person desiring to join the community, together with the reply of the president of the Order, see Seegmiller, "Personal Memories," pp. 168-69.

[28]The "Rules and Regulations to be observed and subscribed to by all the members of the United Order of Orderville that have arrived at the years of accountability" are found in the Orderville Ward Manuscript History, 1878.

[29]Samuel Claridge Autobiography, MS, pp. 35-36. This MS is in the possession of Dr. S. George Ellsworth, Logan, Utah. According to the Samuel Claridge Diary, also in Dr. Ellsworth's possession, the interview with President Taylor took place July 4, 1878.

[30]As cited in Seegmiller, "Personal Memories," p. 173. The same author wrote that a university professor asked one of the Orderville oldtimers, "How did you get the lazy ones to work?" The reply was calculated to put the professor on the defense: "How sir, do you get your lazy students to study?" Emma Seegmiller Higbee, "History of the United Order of Orderville," MS, p. 89, Brigham Young University Library.

[31]F. L. Porter, "Historical Items of the O. U. O.," Bleak MS. The resolution was dated April 16, 1878.

[32]While all Orderville histories give the 1880 flood as the immediate reason for the cessation of communal eating, some diaries indicate that

consideration had been given as early as January 1879 to a proposal to discontinue the practice. For example, L. John Nuttall, Diary of L. John Nuttall, January 26, 1879, MS, Brigham Young University Library.

[33]Erastus Snow, April 19, 1877, as reported in *Deseret News*, May 9, 1877.

[34]JH, June 10, 1883.

[35]Allen, *Second United Order Among the Mormons*, p. 113; Woodbury, "The Mormon United Order," pp. 27-28; and "Esplin," W.P.A. MS, Library of Congress. See also the remarks of Erastus Snow, as recorded by the secretary in the minutes of the case Hoyt v. Ingle, as tried before the Kanab Stake high council in March 1883, Bleak MS. Also see Porter to Bleak, December 9, 1904, Bleak MS. According to the Order secretary, Francis L. Porter, Snow's remarks "caused many of the people of the Order to shed tears of sorrow . . . they felt that to turn everything they possessed into the United Order . . . and offering themselves wholly to the service of the Lord in Temporal as well as in Spiritual things, and be of one heart and mind in being directed by the Priesthood from the Highest Calling in the Church to the lowest under their direction, was more than other cooperative institutions in the land. . . . They felt that the property was the Lord's. . . . That dividends belonged to the Lord for the benefit of all the people of the Order and not for Individual gain. And that the rich and poor should be equal in all things. . . . If one individual had more intelligence than another that is his reward, not that he should go well dressed and fed while the one with less intelligence should go ragged and hungry." Porter to Bleak, August 9, 1904, Bleak MS.

[36]Thomas Robertson to Reddick Allred, August 18, 1883, Orderville Ward Manuscript History, 1883.

[37]Porter to Bleak, February 24, 1904, Bleak MS. Porter gives August 1884 as the date for this change, but other sources indicate the date used. Also see Seegmiller, "Personal Memories," p. 172.

[38]Porter to Bleak, June 13, 1904, Bleak MS.

[39]Cited in Seegmiller, "Personal Memories," pp. 170-71.

[40]"Order Money" consisted of locally made paper bills and metal coins, usually referred to as "commissary tickets" and "milk tickets." These orders, issued by the Order secretary, entitled the bearer to obtain goods from a department. They were a form of bookkeeping as well as a convenience. Such tickets were sometimes traded to persons outside the Order.

[41]L. John Nuttall records in his diary a visit to Orderville in September 1883 in which he discussed the problems of the Order and served as arbitrator in certain disputes involving persons withdrawing from the Order. Diary of L. John Nuttall, September 10, 11, 12, and 13, 1883. The settlement, which is detailed in the Orderville Ward Manu-

script History, entailed a not inconsiderable disentanglement of the Order properties. For example, Howard Spencer, in withdrawing, was permitted to take the following: "Mt. Carmel farm (57 $\frac{1}{2}$ acres) with house and corrals, etc., $250; Hop Gulch and Maxwell ranches for $125; 50 sheep for $112.50; 150 bushels of wheat for $180; 100 bushels of potatoes for $60; 25 bushels of corn for $28; tools to the amount of $50, 30 gallons of molasses at Mocassin for $30, 5 tons of hay for $75, and all the hay at Elk Farm at $10 per ton, on the Blacksmith Shop $25, Elk Farm for $900, 10 yearlings for $180; amount transferred to Lucy and Nellie Spencer [plural wives] ($200 each) $400; cash $50, horse $75, amount to be paid his book account since July 1 [1883], and the articles he has credited for and has the use of himself." Orderville Ward Manuscript History, 1883.

[42]John R. Young, who organized the Mt. Carmel United Order and represented Orderville as a missionary, wrote that he thought the death of Brigham Young in 1877 took away the guiding spirit of the United Order and thus doomed such experiments as the Orderville U.O. to gradual extinction. He wrote: "President Brigham Young was the pilot, the guiding star. When he died the master mind was gone. The visible leader, who said, 'Unless you are one in temporal things, how can you be one in spiritual things?' and 'The way the world does business is a sin, the strong build themselves up by putting the weak ones down.' That was the voice of the Good Shepherd to that people, and when that voice was hushed in death, the light was gone—and the community dissolved. It needs the Leadership of the Priesthood to establish the United Order." Young, *Memoirs*, pp. 225-27.

[43]Diary of L. John Nuttall, April 28, 1884. Punctuation supplied.

[44]As cited in Pendleton, "Orderville United Order," pp. 157-58.

[45]Seegmiller, "Personal Memories," p. 173. Leonard Arrington has been told by a number of people that Latter-day Saints in other communities of southern Utah envied and feared the growing power and affluence of the Orderville U.O. and were quick to magnify its weaknesses and defects. One of the reasons for the lack of enthusiasm of church leaders for the Orderville experiment may have stemmed from the flow of complaints from inhabitants in surrounding towns claiming that the Orderville U. O. was swallowing them up. Apparently, President John Taylor was told several times that if there was any property to be sold in the vicinity of Orderville, nobody but the Order could buy it. See also Emma Seegmiller Higbee, "History of the United Order of Orderville," p. 89.

[46]"Final Settlement of the Order: Given by Edwin Dilworth Woolley to his daughter, Elizabeth, in 1917," in Carter, comp., *Heart Throbs* 4:47-48. The final settlement is also described at some length in Porter to Bleak, February 24, 1904.

[47]The repaired dining hall remained the property of the community (or church) and was converted into a social hall.

[48]A report of the celebration sponsored by the Orderville United Order Memorial Association is found in the *Deseret News,* August 4, 1900. At the time the Order expired there were fifty stockholders holding stock valued at $4,880.

[49]Willard Carroll in *Deseret News,* August 31, 1885.

[50]*Deseret News,* March 4 and 28, 1892.

[51]Henry Fowler in Carter, comp., *Heart Throbs* 1:59.

[52]Francis A. Webb, as cited in Higbee, "History of the United Order of Orderville," p. 88.

[53]See Thomas C. Romney, *The Mormon Colonies in Mexico* (Salt Lake City: Deseret Book Company, 1938), pp. 106-8.

CHAPTER 13
Extending the borders of Zion:
Arizona's Little Colorado settlements;
Bunkerville, Nevada; and Cave Valley, Mexico

[1]Orson Pratt sermon, JD 16:7.

[2]Charles S. Peterson discusses the significance of the meetings between Young and Kane in *Take Up Your Mission: Mormon Colonizing Along the Little Colorado River 1870-1900* (Tucson: University of Arizona Press, 1973), pp. 5-6. Peterson's is the most complete account of the Arizona United Orders. The authors have benefitted much from his wise suggestions and interpretations.

[3]Peterson, *Take Up Your Mission*, p. 12; quoted from Andrew Amundson, "Journal of a Mission to the San Francisko Mountains, Commenced March 26th, 1873," May 28, 1873, MS, Church Archives.

[4]Peterson, *Take Up Your Mission*, p. 94; quoted from Brigham Young to Lot Smith, et al., January 10, 1877, Lot Smith Papers, University of Arizona.

[5]References to the broader mission of the Arizona colonizing effort occur frequently in Minutes of the Little Colorado Stake Conferences, photocopy of MS, Church Archives. See especially February 28 and November 29, 1879, and February 29, 1880.

[6]*Millennial Star* 35 (1873): 534.

[7]A useful account of the settling is in James H. McClintock, *Mormon Settlement in Arizona* (Phoenix, 1921), pp. 130-47. Also of use has been the large body of material on Arizona settlement collected by George S. Tanner and placed in the Church Archives. See, in addition, Kenneth E. Porter, "Little Colorado River Settlements: Brigham City, Joseph City, Obed, and Sunset" (M.A. thesis, Arizona State University, 1956). Also Adele B. Westover and J. Morris Richards, *Unflinching Courage* (privately published, ca. 1967).

[8]*Deseret News,* May 24, 1876.

[9]Ibid., October 30, 1878.

[10]Ibid., June 18, 1879.

[11]Sunset United Order, account books and minute books, MS, Church Archives. See also the more extensive account in Peterson, *Take Up Your Mission,* pp. 118-22.

[12]Joseph City, Arizona, United Order Minute Book, April 4, 1878, MS, Church Archives.

[13]Joseph City, United Order Minute Book, November 7, 1882.

[14]Edward Bunker Autobiography, pp. 26-29, MS, Church Archives.

[15]Santa Clara Ward Manuscript History, 1873-1875, MS, Church Ar-

chives; Bunkerville Ward Manuscript History, 1877, MS, Church Archives; William Edward Bunker, "Biography of," in *The Bunker Family History,* ed., Josephine B. Walker, vol. 1 (Delta, Utah: Privately Published, 1957), p. 114.

[16]Juanita Brooks, "The History of Bunkerville," typescript, Church Archives. Also Juanita Brooks, "The Water's In," *Harpers Monthly Magazine,* May 1941, pp. 608-13; Bunker Autobiography, pp. 29-30.

[17]William Elias Abbott, "The Story of My Life," typescript in Church Archives, p. 18; Brooks, "History of Bunkerville," pp. 3-4; St. George Stake Historical Record, Book B, 1873-1877, December 31, 1877, MS, Church Archives.

[18]Brooks, "History of Bunkerville," p. 5; James Lang Bunker, "Autobiography," in *The Bunker Family History,* pp. 121-23.

[19]St. George Stake Historical Record, Book C, 1878-1885, August 5, 1879.

[20]These by-laws are typed into the Bunkerville Ward Manuscript History, 1879, from an unidentified source. It is presumed to be a product of the 1879 reorganization because of its positioning in the manuscript history and because of its stress upon stewardship, known from other sources to be a major aspect of that reorganization.

[21]St. George Stake Historical Record, Book C, 1878-1885, October 1880.

[22]Myron Abbott Diary, September 26 to October 4, 1880, microfilm of typescript in the Library of Congress Collection of Mormon Diaries, Church Archives.

[23]St. George Stake Historical Record, Book C, October 1880.

[24]Myron Abbott Diary, November 21 and 22, 1880, passim; February 1, 2, and 4, and April 10, 1881.

[25]Myron Abbott Diary, after entry of July 16, 1882.

[26]Juarez Stake History, MS, Church Archives.

[27]Details were obtained by personal interview with Thomas M. Carroll.

CHAPTER 14
Zion's Central Board of Trade
and the decline
of the United Order

[1]John Taylor sermon, April 19, 1874, JD 17:48.

[2]Ibid., pp. 47-48.

[3]Ibid., p. 49.

[4]Scribbling Book of Brigham City, MS, in possession of Leroi C. Snow in 1948.

[5]John Taylor sermon, October 7, 1877, JD 19:120.

[6]George Q. Cannon sermon, April 6, 1878, JD 20:83-84.

[7]John Taylor sermon, September 21, 1878, JD 21:54.

[8]John Taylor sermon, March 2, 1879, JD 20:165.

[9]JH, September 5, 1878.

[10]*Deseret News,* April 10, 1872.

[11]Cache Valley Historical Record, Book A, February 1, 1879, MS, Church Archives.

[12]*Deseret News,* June 17, 1878.

[13]JH, October 6, 1878.

[14]JH, October 8, 1878.

[15]Ibid.

[16]*Deseret News,* April 20, 1881.

[17]JH, October 8, 1878.

[18]Ibid.

[19]*Salt Lake Herald,* October 19, 1878.

[20]JH, June 15, 1879.

[21]Moses Thatcher's voice became even more authoritative when he became a member of the Council of the Twelve Apostles, April 7, 1879.

[22]*Deseret News,* February 11, 1879.

[23]*Tullidge's Quarterly* 1 (1881): 420.

[24]Vernon A. Mund, *Open Markets: An Essential of Free Enterprise* (New York: Harper, 1948), p. 119.

[25]*Deseret News,* April 20, 1881.

[26]See the interpretation in *Tullidge's Quarterly* 1 (1881): 420.

[27]See Leonard J. Arrington, "Iron Manufacturing in Southern Utah in the Early 1880's: The Iron Manufacturing Company of Utah," *Bulletin of the Business Historical Society,* 25 (1951): 149-68, where full bibliographic reference is given.

[28]See Leonard J. Arrington, *Beet Sugar in the West: A History of the Utah-Idaho Sugar Company, 1891-1966* (Seattle and London: University of Washington Press, 1966.)

[29]*Logan Leader,* June 2, 1882.

[30]*Salt Lake Herald,* September 28, 1884; *Deseret News,* April 7, 1884.

[31]*Deseret News,* July 16, 1879, and October 23, 1880; JH, May 25, 1880.

[32]*Deseret News,* April 1, 7, and 8, 1882; *Salt Lake Herald,* July 1, 1882; JH, June 18, 1880.

[33]*Deseret News,* August 2, 1897; *Logan Leader,* September 10, 1880.

[34]*Deseret News,* October 10, 1883.

[35]Ibid., July 14, 1894.

[36]*Deseret News Weekly,* June 20, 1896; *Deseret News,* August 2, 1897.

[37]JH, January 27, 1898. At a meeting of Mormon Church authorities President Cannon was advised to accept an invitation to meet with the president of the Salt Lake Chamber of Commerce for the purpose of encouraging cooperation between Mormon and non-Mormon businessmen.

[38]John Taylor, *An Epistle to the Presidents of Stakes, High Councils, Bishops and Other Authorities of the Church* (Salt Lake City, Utah, 1882).

CHAPTER 15
Taking care of their own:
The Mormon welfare system,
1936-1975

[1]See Leonard J. Arrington and Thomas G. Alexander, *A Dependent Commonwealth: Utah's Economy from Statehood to the Great Depression*, ed. Dean May (Provo, Utah: Brigham Young University Press, 1974).

[2]Lester V. Chandler, *America's Greatest Depression* (New York: Harper & Row, 1970), pp. 53-66.

[3]D&C 88:224.

[4]Caroline Bird, *The Invisible Scar* (New York: David McKay Co., 1966), p. 61.

[5]Book of Mormon, Alma 34:32.

[6]*Deseret News*, August 7, 1931.

[7]*Conference Report*, October 7, 8, and 9, 1932.

[8]Paul C. Child to Spencer W. Kimball, June 12, 1971, typescript, Church Archives.

[9]Quoted by Leonard J. Arrington, "Harold B. Lee," in *Presidents of the Church* by Preston Nibley (Salt Lake City: Deseret Book Co., 1974), p. 444.

[10]*Deseret News*, Church Section, August 17, 1937.

[11]*Deseret News*, January 4, 1935.

[12]Ibid., October 23, 1935.

[13]J. Reuben Clark, Jr., *Church Welfare Plan: A Discussion*, a talk given June 20, 1939 (Salt Lake City, [1939]), p. 8.

[14]*Conference Report*, October 1936, p. 3.

[15]Leonard J. Arrington and Wayne Hinton, "Origin of the Welfare Plan of The Church of Jesus Christ of Latter-day Saints," *BYU Studies* 2 (Winter 1964): 78.

[16]*Conference Report*, October 5, 1941, pp. 112-13.

[17]Ibid., October 1936, passim.

[18]Ibid., April 6, 1941, pp. 120-21.

[19]Ibid., October 3, 1936, p. 59.

[20]Ibid., October 4, 1936, p. 114.

[21]"The Church Welfare Plan," *Improvement Era* 41 (June 1938): 352-54; also *Deseret News*, April 7, 1936.

[22]*What Is the "Mormon" Security Program?* (Independence, Mo.: Zions Printing & Publishing Co., [1938]), pp. 9-10.

[23]LDS Church Welfare Committee, *Handbook of Instructions* [Salt Lake City]: Published by the Church, [1940]), p. 62.

[24]*Deseret News*, April 27 and June 1, 1937.

[25]Harold B. Lee, "Church Security: Retrospect, Introspect, Prospect," *Improvement Era* 40 (April 1937): 206.

[26]*Deseret News,* June 9, 1936.

[27]Marc A. Rose, "The Mormons March Off Relief," *Reader's Digest,* June 1937, pp. 43-44. See also "Tithes and Security," *Time,* August 1, 1938, p. 26.

[28]Frank H. Jonas, "Utah: Sagebrush Democracy," in Thomas C. Donnelly, ed., *Rocky Mountain Politics* (Albuquerque: University of New Mexico Press, 1940), p. 48.

[29]*Conference Report,* April 1936, p. 3.

[30]Ibid., April 1937, pp. 3-4; Albert E. Bowen, *The Church Welfare Plan* (Salt Lake City: Published by the Church, 1946), pp. 20-21.

[31]Clark, *Church Welfare Plan: A Discussion,* p. 19; *Deseret News,* April 22, 1937.

[32]In an address to regional church officials in May 1936, Elder Melvin J. Ballard stated that the church was "deeply concerned to help the government and we are not criticizing or fighting the government." The objectives of the church, he said, were to care adequately for those who were already on church relief and to be in a position to care for those on government relief when the heavy appropriations for relief ceased. The church plan should be a blessing to the government, he added, for the latter is striving to find a practical way to stop its vast expenditures on relief. *Deseret News,* May 9, 1936.

[33]Dixon Wecter, *The Age of the Great Depression* (New York: Macmillan, 1948), p. 212.

[34]Marriner Eccles, *Beckoning Frontiers* (New York: Alfred A. Knopf, 1951), pp. 120-21.

[35]"Welfare Progress," *Improvement Era* 43 (May 1940): 273.

[36]*Deseret News,* Church Section, August 17, 1940.

[37]*Conference Report,* October 3, 1942, pp. 55-59. Clark's theme has been reiterated at regular intervals by subsequent church leaders. Apostle Marion G. Romney quoted extensively from Clark in 1966 when he explained to members that reestablishment of the United Order must await the "redemption of Zion" (reestablishment of Mormon hegemony in Jackson County, Missouri). In the meantime, he advised, "we . . . should live strictly by the principles of the United Order insofar as they are embodied in present church practices, such as the fast offering, tithing, and the welfare activities." In *Conference Report,* April 9, 1966, pp. 95-101.

[38]Annual Report, Welfare Plan, Church of Jesus Christ of Latter-day Saints, 1946, pp. 258-59.

[39]Ibid., 1971, pp. 7-9, 14.

[40]See for example, the judgment of DePillis in "Mormon Communitarianism," p. 288.

[41]Book of Mormon, Mosiah 4:16-19.

CHAPTER 16
Reflections on
the Mormon United Order
movement

[1]Printed in Mary Audentia Smith Anderson, *Ancestry and Posterity of Joseph Smith and Emma Hale* (Independence, Mo.: Herald Publishing House, 1929), pp. 62-65.

[2]The setting is described in Gordon C. Wood, *The Creation of the American Republic* (Chapel Hill: University of North Carolina Press, 1969); also Fred Somkin, *Unquiet Eagle: Memory and Desire in the Idea of American Freedom, 1815-1860* (Ithaca, New York: Cornell University Press, 1967).

[3]An excellent concise review of the social setting of the Smith family history is in Marvin Hill, "Quest for Refuge: An Hypothesis as to the Social Origins and Nature of the Mormon Political Kingdom," *Journal of Mormon History* 2 (1975): 3-20. Also the classic study of Whitney R. Cross, *The Burned-over District* (Ithaca: Cornell University Press, 1950), and Richard L. Anderson, *Joseph Smith's New England Heritage: Influence of Grandfathers Solomon Mack and Asael Smith* (Salt Lake City: Deseret Book Co., 1971).

D&C 38:27.

[5]The scripture in the Old Testament prophecy of Micah 4:12 is a favorite among Mormons and is interpreted as having direct reference to their own role in setting up Christ's reign on earth.

[6]Marion G. Romney, conference address printed in *Improvement Era* 69 (June 1966): 535-37.

[7]Reminders of the Latter-day Saint heritage of cooperation appear frequently in church literature. See, for example, articles in the *Church News*, August 28, 1971, p. 11; April 10, 1971, p. 2; and January 25, 1974, p. 18; and in the *New Era* 1 (April 1971): 19-33. A recent musical play, set in the village of Orderville, Utah, deals sensitively and skillfully with the problems of religious communal life. It has been widely produced for Mormon audiences. See Carol Lynn Pearson and Lex de Azevedo, *The Order Is Love* (Provo, Utah: Trilogy Arts, 1973).

Index